F R A M E W O R K S

Purchasing

Fourth Edition

Kenneth Lysons
MA, MEd, PhD, FInstPS

THE
CHARTERED INSTITUTE OF
PURCHASING & SUPPLY

PEARSON EDUCATION LIMITED
Edinburgh Gate, Harlow
Essex CM20 2JE, England
and Associated Companies throughout the world

Visit us on the World Wide Web at:
http://www.pearsoneduc.com

Fourth edition published in Great Britain 1996, reprinted 1999

© Pearson Professional Limited 1996

ISBN 0 273 63422 4

British Library Cataloguing in Publication Data
A CIP catalogue record for this book can be obtained from the British Library.

10 9 8 7 6 5 4 3

Printed and bound in Great Britain by Bell and Bain Ltd, Glasgow

The Publishers' policy is to use paper manufactured from sustainable forests.

CONTENTS

PREFACE

The first edition of this book appeared in 1981. Advantage has been taken of the publisher's request for a new fourth edition to substantially rewrite and re-arrange the book and include much new material. There are completely new chapters on Purchasing Strategy, Human Resources in the Supply Chain, Contrasting Approaches to Supply and Support Tools while all the former chapters have been updated.

The present book covers the new syllabuses of the Chartered Institute of Purchasing and Supply in respect of the Foundation Stage subject *'Introduction to Purchasing and Supply Management'* and the Professional Stage (Core Subjects) of *Purchasing and Supply Chain Management I : Strategy* and *Purchasing and Supply Chain Management II : Tactics and Operations* (except for the syllabus sections on Storing Supplies and Transporting Goods). It also largely covers the specialist options in *Purchasing*.

The book is not, however, only a textbook. The writer hopes that it may also be useful as a source of reference to purchasing practitioners.

As stated in the original Preface, the modern emphasis is on integrated study and in writing the book the author has drawn on many disciplines that contribute to a sound knowledge of purchasing practice and techniques. These include accountancy, costing, economics, information technology, ethics, human resources management, law, operational research, marketing, negotiation and psychology. No one book can deal with all that these diverse disciplines can offer to purchasing personnel. The writer hopes, however, that the bibliographies at the end of each chapter will suggest sources of further reading. The range of disciplines referred to above also indicates that any purchasing specialist wishing to appropriate the title of 'professional' must be a well-rounded person with a knowledge of the many fields which contribute to efficient procurement.

Note: a reference in the text such as (see 8:**6**) refers to numbered section 6 of Chapter 8; a reference such as (see **12** below) refers to numbered section 12 of that particular chapter.

ACKNOWLEDGEMENTS

The writer is indebted to many organisations and people. Industrial and commercial organisations include BICC, the British Standards Institution for permission to reproduce material in Chapter 5, the Ford Motor Co, Marks and Spencer for help with Chapter 10, Rolls Royce, The Society of British Aerospace Companies and Tarmac.

Every writer is indebted to libraries and I would put on record the courteous assistance I have received from the staff of the British Library, the Department of Trade and Industry Library, the Institute of Management Foundation, the Institute of Personnel and Development, the Pictor Library of the City of Liverpool, the Prescot Branch of the Library Service of the Metropolitan Borough of Knowsley, the St Helens College and the Universities of Liverpool and Manchester.

The Chartered Institute of Purchasing and Supply kindly gave permission to use questions from papers set at recent examination.

It is impossible to mention by name all who have contributed to this book but I would specially mention Ken Burnett, Information Officer of the Chartered Institute of Purchasing and Supply, who was unfailingly courteous and never failed to come up with the answers and John Cushion of Pitman who saw the book through from its rewriting to its completion. I also am grateful to Roger Banks, of the Ellis Williams Partnership, Pam Beckley of HMSO, Carol Cannon of the Public Sector Procurement Division of HM Treasury, Stephen Cannon, Gary Cheeseman a1d Alan Prescott of BICC, Eric Evans, a former colleague, Maurice Elms of ICL, Howard Jones of Rolls Royce, Gerald Morris of British Electro-technical and Allied Manufacturing Association, Michael Quayle, Drs S New and S Young of UMIST, Dr P Niruwenhuis of Cardiff Business School, John Stevens, Professor John Smith of the Ford Motor Co and Steve Young of A T Kearney.

Finally, I would again put on record the help given by my loyal friend and assistant Jeanne Ashton. The book has been expertly text processed by Glennis Bate who has patiently coped with the author's handwriting and changes in the text.

> *To Jeffrey Kenneth Lysons*
> *Beth Charlotte and Wesley Nathan Jones*

1

WHAT IS PURCHASING?

1. DEFINITION

Organisational purchasing may be defined as: that function responsible for obtaining by purchase, lease or other legal means, equipment, materials, supplies and services required by an undertaking for use in production. In this definition, the term production is used in the economic sense of creating utilities, i.e. goods and services that satisfy wants. It is not, therefore, confined to manufacturing output but also applies to servicing, distributing, etc. organisations.

2. THE PURCHASING ENVIRONMENT

The above definition owes much to the excellent analysis of Marrian [1] who defines organisational buyers as 'those buyers of goods and services for the specific purpose of industrial or agricultural production or for use in the operation or conduct of a plant, business, institution, profession or service'. Organisational buyers are, therefore, those who buy on behalf of an organisation rather than for individual or family use of consumption. Within this broad group of organisational buyers, it is possible to make further distinctions as between industrial, institutional and intermediate buyers. These are defined by Marrian as:

(a) 'Industrial buyers are those buying goods and services in some tangibly productive and commercially significant purpose, e.g. manufacturers, primary (extractive) producers, agricultural, forestry, fishery and horticultural producers.'

(b) 'Institutional buyers are those buying goods and services for institutional (in the sense of providing a service which is often intangible) and not necessarily commercially significant purposes: e.g. schools, hospitals, armed forces, central and local government, professions, hotels.'

(c) 'Intermediate buyers are those buying goods and services for resale or for facilitating the resale of other goods, in the industrial or ultimate consumer markets, e.g. distributors, dealers, wholesalers, retailers, service trades.'

These distinctions are important since 'The different objectives for which schools, hotels and manufacturing firms are established will dictate in broad, general terms their purchasing needs and behaviour. Organisations performing similar activities to achieve like objectives will tend towards a similarity in buying behaviour.'

While this book will be of use to all three categories of organisational buyers, it is for industrial and institutional buyers that it is primarily written.

3. THE EVOLUTION OF PURCHASING

Purchasing represents a stage in the evolution of civilised human relationships since it substitutes trading for conquest, plunder and confiscation for the procurement of a desired object. It is a very ancient activity. Harold Ward, an American researcher, reports that a cuneiform clay tablet excavated at El-Rash Shamra, dated about 2800 BC, carries an inscription which roughly translated reads: 'HST is to deliver 50 jars of fragrant smooth oil each fifteen days after [a starting date] and during the reign of AS. In return he will be paid 600 small weight in grain. This order will continue indefinitely until the purchaser or his son removes his consent.'

Despite its long history, however, it is only in the latter half of the present century that the importance of efficient purchasing has been widely recognised. There are still organisations in which purchasing is generally regarded as a routine clerical function or a service function concerned mainly with spending. Three important developments have, however, enhanced the status of purchasing in both private and public sector organisations. These factors are (1) the contribution of purchasing to profitability and added value, (2) the evolution of professional purchasing, (3) the recognition of the strategic importance of purchasing.

4. PURCHASING, PROFITABILITY AND ADDED VALUE

Managements started to give increased importance to purchasing when they recognised its potential contribution to profitability through cost cutting. The greatest scope for saving lies in the areas of greatest expenditure. For most organisations the areas of greatest expenditure are purchasing and payments to personnel. As a result of technology labour costs are tending to reduce substantially. Conversely, manufacturing organisations may find it cheaper to buy assemblies and components from specialised suppliers that were formerly made in-house. These tendencies are shown by Figs 1.1 and 1.2 which relate to the expenditures of a manufacturing company known to the writer for years 1979 and 1994 respectively.

The greatest scope for saving lies in the area of bought-out items, which in 1994 had superseded labour as the area of greatest expenditure. It follows therefore that

- Assuming other variables remain constant every pound saved on purchasing is a pound of profit.

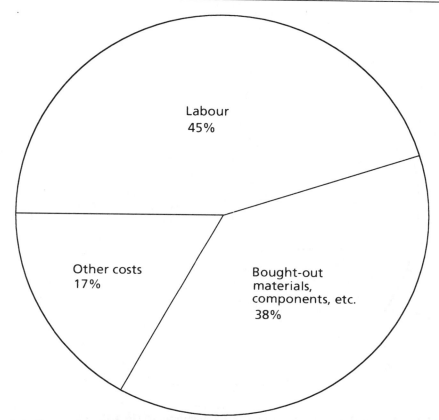

Fig 1.1 Costs of manufacturing company 1979

- For many reasons, e.g. increased defects or poorer deliveries, a pound off the purchase price does not necessarily represent a pound of profit.
- When purchases form a high proportion of total costs a modest saving on bought-out items will result in a similar contribution to profits as a substantial increase in sales. As shown below, a 4 per cent reduction in purchase costs makes the same contribution to profits as a 20 per cent expansion of turnover.

		SALES	
Then	*Now*	*Increase*	*Extra Profit*
£	£	%	£
100,000	120,000	20	2000 (assuming 10% on turnover)
		PURCHASES	
50,000	48,000	−4	2000
		(i.e. a saving)	

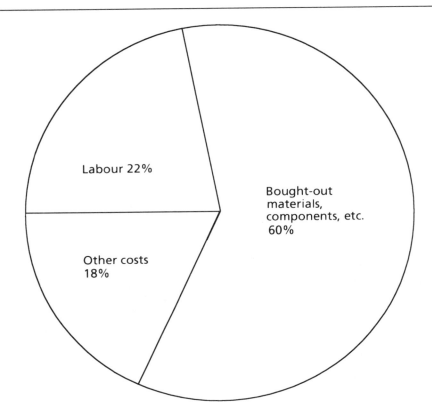

Fig 1.2 Costs of the manufacturing company shown in Fig 1 1994

Since the proportion of expenditure on purchases items varies widely, it follows that the contribution of purchasing to profitability varies between organisations. The profit contribution may be low, for example, in the pharmaceutical industry where the ingredients of a patent medicine can be insignificant compared with the costs of marketing the product.

Conversely it will be significant in the motor vehicle industry where the proportion of material costs to total factory costs will be high.

Purchasing as a factor in profitability is likely to be critical where:

(i) Bought-out items form a high proportion of total expenditure.
(ii) Short-run prices fluctuate.
(iii) Judgements relating to innovation and fashion are involved.
(iv) Markets for the finished product are highly competitive.

Purchasing will be less critical, though still important, where:

(i) Bought-out items form a small proportion of total expenditure.
(ii) Prices are relatively stable.
(iii) There is an absence of innovation in operations.

The term 'profitability' has, however, a wider meaning than 'pecuniary gain or buying more cheaply' and can be extended to cover anything that is beneficial or advantageous to an enterprise. This wider perspective is provided by the concept of *value chain analysis* developed by M E Porter [2] in which procurement is viewed as a support activity which contributes to the competitive advantage of a business unit by *adding value*. A value chain may be defined as 'a linear map of the way in which value is added through a process from raw materials to finished, delivered product (including continuing service after delivery)' [3].

Porter's approach may be summarised as follows:

(i) Within an industry many business units produce products or services that are similar if not identical to those of their competitors.

(ii) A business unit can obtain a competitive advantage over its rivals in two basic ways: *cost leadership* and *differentiation*. *Cost leadership* means that the business unit has a significant cost advantage over the competitors. *Differentiation* implies that the product or service offers something unmatched by its competitors that it values more than a lower price.

(iii) The activities of a business unit can be classified into five *primary* and four *support* activities each of which can contribute to the competitive advantage of the business. These constitute the value chain (see Table 1.1).

(iv) Each activity within a value chain provides inputs which after processing constitute added value to the output, which the ultimate customer receives in the form of a product or service or as the aggregate of values at the end of the value chain.

(v) Each primary support activity has therefore the opportunity to contribute to the competitive advantage of the business unit by enabling it to produce, market and deliver products or services which meet or surpass the value expectations of buyers in comparison with those resulting from other value chains.

(vi) The procurement activity which interacts or 'links' both with the other eight internal activities and also with the external environment, e.g. supplier, has tremendous potential to contribute to the competitiveness of the business unit. This contribution is not limited to reducing the cost of purchased materials but may include:

(a) Ensuring that, since the supply environment is the critical element in determining added value in the products of many enterprises, strategic decisions relating to supply are based on the best available information relating to:

(i) Potential shortages and surpluses of materials and consequent prices of sensitive commodities.

(ii) Currency implications of overseas trading.

(iii) Comparative power positions of buyers, suppliers and competitors.

(iv) Impact of new materials.

(v) Technological developments in the supply market.

(b) Advising on the likely consequences for sourcing and supply of strategic decisions relating to such issues as:

Table 1.1 Activities in the value chain

Primary	Support
Those involved in the physical movement of raw materials and finished products, production of goods and services, marketing sales and subsequent services to outputs of the business unit.	Those that provide support to both the primary activities *and each other*.

Primary

Those involved in the physical movement of raw materials and finished products, production of goods and services, marketing sales and subsequent services to outputs of the business unit.

(1) *Inbound Logistics* – receiving, storing, materials handling, warehousing, inventory control, vehicle scheduling, returns to suppliers.

(2) *Operations* – transferring inputs into final product form (e.g. machining, packaging, assembly, equipment maintenance, testing, printing and facility operations.

(3) *Outbound Logistics* – distributing the finished product (e.g. finished goods warehousing, material handling, delivery vehicle operation, order processing and scheduling.

(4) *Marketing and Sales* – inducing and facilitating buyers to purchase the product, e.g. advertising, sales force, quoting, channel selection, channel relations, pricing.

(5) *Service* – maintaining or enhancing value of product after sale, installation, repair, training, parts supply and product adjustment.

Support

Those that provide support to both the primary activities *and each other*.

(6) *Procurement* – purchasing of raw materials, supplies and other consumable items as well as assets.

(7) *Technology Development* – know how, procedures and technological inputs needed in every value chain activity.

(8) *Human Resource Management* – selection; promotion and placement; appraisal; rewards; management development; and labour/employee relations.

(9) *Firm Infrastructure* – general management, planning, finance, accounting, level, government affairs and quality management.

(i) Vertical or horizontal integration.

(ii) Purchasing segments of external product capacity.

(iii) Assisting and developing new suppliers.

(iv) Global purchasing.

(v) Make or buy decisions.

(vi) Buying policies and 'futures' trading if applicable.

(c) Identification of critical materials/components for detailed study with reference to:

   (i) Ensuring security of supply.

   (ii) Identifying alternative materials/components or suppliers.

(iii) Value analysis.

(d) Recognising the responsibilities of purchasing as a link in the supply chain with reference to:

(i) Sharing insights, knowledge and expertise with other supply chain functions.

(ii) Providing goods/services required by internal supply chain customers in the appropriate quantities and qualities and at the required time and place.

(iii) Reviewing designs and specifications from the standpoints of cost, quality, availability etc.

(iv) Total Quality Management.

(e) Promoting profitable purchasing by researching possible supply sources:

(i) Evaluating the performance of existing suppliers.

(ii) Discovering and appraising potential new suppliers.

(iii) Investigating the advantages/disadvantages of sourcing abroad.

(f) Building long-term collaborative relationships with suppliers. Strategic sourcing is quite simply the process of creating value-adding supply relationships to provide competitive advantage [4]. Purchasing can contribute to such competitive advantage by:

(i) Single sourcing

(ii) Supplier involvement in design

(iii) Supplier development

(iv) Supplier motivation through positive reinforcement and feedback.

(g) Negotiation of added value in respect of purchased items while recognising that the lowest price does not always mean the lowest cost. Such added value may be obtained by such means as:

(i) Knowing what might be paid, allowing for a fair profit, as distinct from the prices quoted.

(ii) Initiating joint exercises with designers and end users to reduce costs by modifying components, or substituting materials without detriment to price and quality.

(iii) Investigating the scope for standardisation and simplification.

(iv) Determining the right quality for a particular application.

(v) Evaluating 'value in use' factors, e.g. reliability and maintenance factors.

(vi) Purchasing assemblies rather than components.

(vii) Buying the experience of suppliers.

(viii) Negotiating benefits not directly indicated in the price, e.g. the willingness of the supplier to hold stocks until required by the purchaser.

(h) Enhancing the working capital of the enterprise. Working capital is the surplus of current assets (such as stocks of materials and components, debtors, bank and cash balances) over current liabilities (such as trade creditors or bank overdrafts). Three ways in which the amount of working capital required may be decreased are:

(i) Minimising the time in which stocks of bought-out items are held through JIT.
(ii) Turning redundant stocks into cash.
(iii) Negotiating extended payment times for purchases.

(i) Improving the administrative procedures of the purchasing function by:
(i) Controlling and, where possible, reducing the expenditure on the purchasing cost centre.
(ii) Installing appropriate technology, e.g. EDI, electronic mail, facsimile, to reduce paperwork and increase the speed of communication to and from suppliers, thus reducing lead times and expediting information flow.

(j) Increasing the competence of purchasing staff through training, development and empowerment particularly with respect to:
(i) Changing their concept of purchasing to profit generation rather than cost cutting.
(ii) Providing a vision that spans the entire value chain beginning with the purchased material and ending with the customer.
(iii) Thinking strategically as well as operationally.

(k) Enhancing the standing of the enterprise by consistently striving to achieve a reputation for fair dealing and adherence to high ethical principles.

5. PURCHASING AND PROFESSIONALISM

Under this heading it is useful to consider the concept of professionalism and the evolution of purchasing as a quasi-profession.

(a) The concept of professionalism. An analysis by Millerson [5] lists the following essential features of a profession;

(i) a profession involves a skill based on theoretical knowledge;
(ii) the skill requires training and education;
(iii) the professional must demonstrate competence by passing a test;
(iv) integrity is maintained by adherence to a code of conduct;
(v) the service is for the public good;
(vi) the profession is organised.

The same writer offers the following definition of a profession:

A type of higher-grade non-manual occupation with both subjectively and objectively recognised occupational status, possessing a well defined area of study or concern and providing a definite service after advanced training and education.

(b) The evolution of professionalism in purchasing. The development of purchasing as a quasi-profession is evidenced by:

(i) The establishment of institutions concerned with promoting the concept of

professional purchasing. Such institutions include the Chartered Institute of Purchasing and Supply (CIPS) in Great Britain and the National Association of Purchasing Management (NAPA) in the USA. Currently (1995) 41 national purchasing associations are affiliated to the International Federation of Purchasing and Materials Management.

(ii) The identification of a body of specialised purchasing knowledge and techniques. Specialised knowledge is derived from a number of contributory disciplines including accounting, costing, economics, electronic data processing, ethics, law, operational research, marketing, management and psychology. Techniques related directly or indirectly to purchasing include variety reduction, value analysis, learning curve analysis, supply analysis, the processes and procedures of negotiation and sophisticated developments such as materials requirements planning made possible by computerisation.

The dissemination of such knowledge and techniques has been assessed by:

- the growth of undergraduate and postgraduate courses with a purchasing content
- the establishment of 'chairs' of purchasing at some universities
- increased interest in research into aspects of purchasing
- the publication in many countries of textbooks and specialist journals relating to purchasing. The latter include *Purchasing and Supply Management* (UK), *European Purchasing Management* and *The International Journal of Purchasing and Materials Management*.

(iii) The formulation by the purchasing institutions of standards of academic and practical experience which members are required to possess.

Although purchasing is not fully professionalised since unlike architecture, dentistry, law and medicine, the practice of purchasing is not restricted to those registered with a statutorily recognised regulatory body such as the British Medical Association, the status of purchasing in Britain was enhanced when in 1992 the Institute of Purchasing and Supply was granted a Royal Charter.

(iv) A number of professional purchasing institutions including the CIPS and the NAPA have published codes of conduct or ethics with which members are expected to comply (see Appendices 1 and 2).

6. THE STRATEGIC IMPORTANCE OF PURCHASING

The strategic importance of procurement in the value chain has been referred to in **4** above and is considered in greater detail in Chapter 3. The importance of involving purchasing in strategic decisions intended to strengthen the competitive advantage of a business unit has been enhanced by such factors as

(i) The change in many industries from a relatively stable to a dynamic environment which is a key factor in determining the added value of products.

(ii) Intensified competition associated with the globalisation of manufacturing has emphasised the importance of quality not only in relation to design but also the materials, parts and components that comprise the product.

(iii) The contribution of procurement to supply chain strategy and management which, as shown later, has many parallels with the value chain concept.

As Monczka and Trent [6] observe, a consequence of such factors is that the role of the supplier is shifting from simply providing operational support to the buying firm to becoming a critical source contributing to the firm's performance objectives. The role of purchasing is also shifting from being a passive function to one that supports the strategic objectives of the firm.

Pearson and Gritzmacher [7] point out that in many undertakings the strategic contributions that purchasing can make to the design, development, manufacture and marketing of products that will enable the company to compete more effectively both nationally and internationally is evidenced by:

(i) The commitment by top management of resources to the purchasing function including the employment of professional purchasing staff with a consequent expansion of purchasing's decision making authority.

(ii) More interaction with other functions including marketing, finance and production.

(iii) A shift in focus from cost cutting to profit generating.

(iv) An increased concern for product quality and greater emphasis on research and negotiations leading to more co-operative relationships with suppliers.

7. THE STATUS OF PURCHASING WITHIN THE ORGANISATION

Status may be defined as the position or standing of a person, group or function within an organisation or, more commonly, as the evaluation of that person, group or function on a scale of relative esteem. Within a particular undertaking purchasing may be accorded a high or relatively low status. This will depend on the contribution to competitive advantage and also on other factors considered in 5–6 above. The status of purchasing within the organisation is important for at least three reasons:

- The status accorded by top management to the purchasing function influences the esteem in which the function is held at lower organisation levels.
- The status accorded to the purchasing function affects the status of groups and individuals within that function.
- Status has a motivational factor. If the needs for status, esteem and self-actualisation are not met, then performance may be adversely affected and staff turnover may increase.

(a) Where purchasing has a high status:

(i) It will have strong support from top management in its efforts to negotiate economically and effectively.

(ii) There will be equality of standing between purchasing and other departments such as design, finance, etc.

(iii) Considerable freedom of action will be given to purchasing staff.

(iv) Purchasing will be consulted in the critical stages of product development with regard to the preparation of specifications and the price, quality and availability of materials.

(v) The contribution of purchasing to organisational profitability and effectiveness will be regularly evaluated.

(vi) The professionalism, expertise and morale of purchasing staff will be high.

(b) Where purchasing has a relatively low status:

(i) Buyers may seek to gain status and authority by rule-book procedures, e.g. insisting that all contracts with suppliers are through the purchasing department, and other strategies as indicated in Chapter 2. The tendency for purchasing to be bypassed is an indication that the function is held in low esteem.

(ii) Purchasing will not be consulted regarding the preparation of specifications, sources of supply or the procurement of capital goods and equipment.

(iii) The buyer may not have a knowledge of the use to which his purchases are to be put, thus preventing him from buying economically from alternative sources or ensuring that quality specifications are related to the requirements of the product.

(iv) Buyers will tend to 'do what they are told' by design and production departments.

(v) The ability of the buyer to provide a high level of efficiency and job performance may be impaired by the failure of ordering departments to requisition early or rationalise quantities.

(vi) The professionalism, expertise and morale of purchasing will tend to be low.

(c) Indicators of purchasing's status.

The status of the purchasing function within a particular organisation is indicated by structural and influential factors. *Structural* factors include:

(i) What is the job title of the executive in charge of purchasing?

(ii) To whom, and at what level, does the executive in charge of purchasing report?

(iii) What salary does the chief purchasing executive receive?

(iv) Of what committees is the chief purchasing executive a member?

(v) How many staff are directly involved in purchasing and the associated functions for which it is responsible?

Influential factors include:

(i) What recognition is given to the purchasing function by top management?

(ii) What is the total annual spend for which the purchasing function is responsible?

(iii) How crucial is efficient purchasing to the success and profitability of the undertaking?

(iv) What financial limits are placed on the various grades of purchasing staff to commit the undertaking without reference to higher authority?

(v) What is the influence of purchasing in organisational buying decisions as perceived by persons external to the enterprise, e.g. sales persons, and internal staff, e.g. end users, of purchases.

(vi) What is the influence of purchasing as a member of the buying centre? (The concept of 'buying centre' is referred to within Chapters 10, 11 and 14.)

8. PURCHASING OBJECTIVES

Purchasing objectives may be both general and specific.

(a) The 'classic' definition of the overall purchasing task is:

*To obtain materials of the right **quality** in the right **quantity** from the right **source** delivered to the right **place** at the right **time** at the right **price**.*

This definition is somewhat simplistic for the following reasons:

(i) The term 'right' is situational: each company will define 'right' differently.

(ii) What is 'right' will change as the overall purchasing context and environment changes.

(iii) The above rights must be consistent with corporate goals and objectives from which functional goals and objectives are derived.

(iv) In practice some rights are irreconcilable, e.g. it may be possible to obtain the right quality but not at the right price – 'the best suppliers are often the busiest but also the dearest'.

Purchasing objectives have therefore to be balanced according to the overall corporate strategy and requirements at a given time .

An alternative definition of the key purpose for the Purchasing and Supply Chain, devised for the UK Purchasing and Supply Lead Body for National Vocational Qualifications by the University of Ulster, is: 'To provide the interface between customer and supplier in order to plan, obtain, store and distribute as necessary, supplies of materials, goods and services [m, g, s] to enable the organisation to satisfy its external and internal customers'.

The major functions supporting the above key function are identified as:

(1) Contribute to the formulation, communication and implementation of policies, strategies and plans.
(2) Contribute to the establishment and improvement of purchasing and supply systems.
(3) Create and maintain a database of purchasing and supply information.
(4) Establish and improve sources of supply.
(5) Acquire supplies.
(6) Provide goods and materials to internal and external customers through storage, movement, distribution and transport.
(7) Monitor and control the purchasing, supply, storage and distribution and transport chain.

(8) Contribute to effective working.

An expanded statement of purchasing objectives for a manufacturing organisation would be along the following lines:

To enhance the profitability and survival of the undertaking by promoting its competitive advantage in such ways as:

(i) The provision of intelligence regarding economic, legislative, political, technological and other factors that may influence the cost and availability of supplies.

(ii) Researching, evaluating and advising on suppliers able to meet the value requirements of the undertaking with respect to quantity, quality, delivery at the lowest overall total cost.

(iii) Co-operating with the design, production and marketing departments on such matters as preparation of quality specifications, make-or-buy decisions, subcontracting standardisations and value analysis.

(iv) Monitoring the performance of vendors with regard to quality, overall cost and reliability of delivery in respect of materials, components, etc. supplied to the undertaking.

(v) Advising as required on all aspects of inward logistics, including receiving, inventory control, security or stocks, and surplus disposal.

(vi) Ensuring that the administration of the procurement function is provided efficiently through such means as the employment of professional purchasing staff, reduction of paperwork and utilisation of technology.

(vii) Building up supplier relationships by such means as fair dealing, sharing expertise, provision of co-operation and assistance and prompt payment.

(viii) Reviewing purchasing policies, procedures and staff development so that the above objectives can be most effectively achieved.

(b) Purchasing and corporate objectives Examples of how functional purchasing and supply objectives are derived from overall business objectives are given in Table 1.2.

(c) Specific objectives. There is a danger that long-term general objectives such as those listed above may remain vague statements of intent unless they are translated into *strategies* as indicated in 3:1. Similarly, short-term objectives need to be identified and translated into *tactics*. Specific objectives may be derived from general objectives by 'closing down' the latter to a point where an achievable end has been defined. A way of 'closing down' is to ask the question, 'how?', repeating this for successive statements until a systematic approach and plan for action is evolved. Specific objectives should relate to a defined period of time and, where possible, be quantified. The subsequent performance or attainment by the purchasing function and individuals within that function can then be measured against the original objective distinguishing between factors relating to attainment or non-attainment for which the function and designated staff can or cannot be held responsible. Some ways of setting specific objectives for purchasing include:

Table 1.2 Purchasing and corporate objectives

Business objectives	Purchasing and supply objectives
A statement of the position the firm is aiming for in its markets, including market share	The objective of providing the quantity and quality of supplies required by the market share and market positioning objectives
A key objective of, say, moving out of speciality markets and entering volume markets	A key objective of developing new, larger, suppliers and materials flow systems more geared to larger numbers of fewer parts while keeping total inventory volume low
A key objective to build new businesses which will generate positive cash flow as well as reasonable profits	Contribute to cashflow improvement through lower average inventory and by negotiating smaller delivery lots and/or longer payment terms
A plan to develop some specific new products or services	A plan to develop appropriate suppliers
An overall production/capacity plan, including an overall policy on make or buy	A plan to develop systems which integrate capacity planning and or purchase planning, together with the policy on make or buy
A plan to introduce a cost reduction programme	A plan to introduce supplies standardisation and supplier reduction programmes
A financial plan, setting out in broad terms how the proposed capital expenditure is to be financed; together with an outline timescale and an order in which the objectives need to be achieved	A financial plan, setting out broadly the profit contribution expected from purchasing and supply, together with the time in which it should be achieved and the priorities of the objectives.

Source: DTI, Building a Purchasing Strategy, HMSO, 1991.

(i) Purchasing budgets. These will show the purchased material and components requirements for a given volume of output, determined by the reconciliation of the sales and production budgets in terms of order quantities and order value for the budget period.

(ii) Standard material costs. These relate to specific items and are based on the standard specification and quantity of each material and component to be purchased. Among the material variances that can be investigated are material cost and material price. These variances are discussed in Chapter 12.*

(iii) Setting targets for specific areas of activity e.g. 'to reduce material costs or inventory for the next financial year by x per cent'.

Table 1.3   A comparison of changes in traditional and current concepts of purchasing roles (1995)

Concept	Traditional	Current
(a) Organisational		
(i) Decision making	Limited to operational short-term tactical decisions	Involvement in strategic long-term decisions
(ii) Perceived contribution to profitability	Cost cutting through negotiation of lower prices, better discounts, improved payment terms etc.	Adding value as part of the value chain
(iii) Organisational structure	Emphasis on centralisation to obtain economies of scale	Movement to decentralisation to be near to potential problems
(iv) Internal relationships	Purchasing as a discrete functional department guarding its information and expertise from other functional discrete departments. Subordinate to design and production	Purchasing as an integrated activity sharing its information and expertise with other links in the supply chain, especially design, production and marketing
(v) Status	Low as a routine clerical order processing function	High, especially where the function can demonstrate professionalism with respect to expertise and service
(b) Suppliers		
(vi) Relationships	Supplier perceived as an adversary to be kept at arms length	Supplier as a partner with a mutual interest in achieving cost reduction and quality improvements
(vii) Negotiations	Win-lose	Win-win
(viii) Supplier base	Wide, on the basis that availability of multiple sources will ensure reliability of supplies	Narrow, with emphasis on single sourcing on which reliability of supplies derives from efficient supplier logistics

Continued overleaf

Table 1.3 *(continued)*

Concept	Traditional	Current
(ix) Supplier location	Local/National	Global (although for some purposes, e.g. JIT, reasonable proximity to the purchaser reduces lead times and increases certainty of delivery)
(x) Duration of relationship	Short-term	Long-term
(c) Operational factors		
(xi) Response to environment	Reactive	Proactive
(xii) Major tasks/activities	Placing orders, expediting, dealing with quality and payment problems	Supplier investigation, co-operation and management. Value related activities such as value and price analysis, cost reduction etc
(xiii) Major emphasis	Commercial	Commercial with the addition of technical/ logistical factors
(xiv) Communication with suppliers	Written/typed orders and other documentation. Much paperwork	Electronic mail, EDI, direct mail links, bar coding. Movement towards the elimination, so far as possible of orders and other documentation. Greatly reduced paperwork
(xv) Inventory	High importance atttached to inventory management and control	Where appropriate with production line manufacturing JIT will reduce the importance and time spent on inventory management and control

9. PURCHASING AND CHANGE

Some of the most important changes in the role and scope of the purchasing function since 1970 are summarised in Table 1.3. The factors identified are of course general *trends* and may not apply within a particular industry or organisation.

References

[1] Marrian J. *Marketing Characteristics of Industrial Goods and Buyers* in Wilson (Ed), *The Marketing of Industrial Products*. Hutchinson, 1965, p 11.

[2] M E Porter. *Competitive Advantage: Creating and sustaining superior performance*. Free Press, 1985.

[3] Lamming Richard. *Beyond Partnership: Strategies for innovation and lean supply*. Prentice Hall, 1993, Chap. 4, p 90.

[4] Speakman R E , Kamauff J W and Salmond D J. *At last purchasing is becoming strategic. Long Range Planning*. Vol 27, No 2, 1994, p 76–84.

[5] Millerson Geoffrey: *The Qualifying Associations*. Routledge and Kegan Paul, 1964, p 4.

[6] Monczka Robert H and Trent Robert J: *International Journal of Physical Distribution and Logistics Management*. Vol 21, No 5, 1991 pp 4–12.

[7] Pearson John N and Gritzmacher Karen J: *Integrating purchasing into strategic management. Long Range Planning*. Vol 23, pp 91–99.

Progress test 1

1. Define the term 'organisational purchasing'.

2. Show how a small saving in purchasing can have the same effect on profitability as a substantial increase in turnover.

3. Under what circumstances will the contribution of purchasing to profitability be high?

4. What is a 'value chain'?

5. Outline Porter's concept of procurement as a support activity which contributes to the competitive advantage of a business by adding value.

6. What, according to Porter, are the primary and secondary activities that constitute the value chain?

7. How, apart from reducing the cost of purchased materials, can procurement contribute to the competitiveness of a business?

8. What is a 'profession'?

9. What factors have contributed to the 'professionalism' of purchasing?

10. What factors have enhanced the strategic importance of the purchasing function?

11. List some indicators of the status of purchasing in a particular organisation.

12. Explain the statement that 'purchasing objectives may be both general and specific'.

13. Give examples of some differences between traditional and current concepts of purchasing roles.

14. Set out in detail the arguments which you would use to convince a sceptical chief executive that purchasing is more than a routine clerical activity dealing with the processing of purchase orders.

(CIPS. *Introduction to Purchasing and Supply Management* (1992))

15. Sir Graham Day – a former Rover Group Chairman – is on record as saying 'We live or die by the purchasing function'. Explain what you feel he meant by this statement, and discuss the influences which have brought about the enhanced status of purchasing and supply, of which this is an example.

(CIPS. *Introduction to Purchasing and Supply Management* (1994))

2

PURCHASING STRATEGY

Table 1.1 (Chapter 1) sets out the relationship between corporate and purchasing and supply objectives. When corporate and functional objectives have been set the next step is to determine strategies. Any discussion of purchasing strategy, however, must be preceded by an understanding of what strategy is, the levels at which it operates and how strategy is formulated.

1. DEFINITIONS OF STRATEGY

There are many such definitions including

(i) Strategy is 'the organisation's preselected means or approach to achieving its goals or objectives, while coping with current and future external conditions' [1].
(ii) Strategy can be defined as

- a plan – some sort of consciously intended course of action
- a pattern which emerges over time
- a position which provides for competitive advantage
- a perspective – an abstraction which exists in the minds of people [2].

(iii) Strategic management is concerned with policy decisions affecting the entire organisation; the overall objective being to position the organisation to deal effectively with its environment [3].

2. LEVELS OF STRATEGY

Strategies are formulated, implemented and evaluated at four organisational levels: institutional, corporate, business and functional.

(a) Institutional strategy involves making decisions and commitments that define the human and social standards by which the organisation operates. It asks the strategic question 'what kind of reputation, character or personality do we wish this enterprise to have?'. Institutional strategy has therefore strong ethical implications.

(b) Corporate strategy involves making decisions that set and guide resource allocations for the total enterprise. It asks the strategic question 'what business or businesses should we be in?' Corporate strategy is concerned with decisions relating to the three 'alternative' grand strategies, i.e.

(1) *Growth* – when an organisation seeks to expand its relative market share by such strategies as:

- Market development: finding new markets for existing products.
- Product development: creating new products by research.
- Horizontal integration: combining two or more broadly similar businesses to reduce competition or obtain economies of scale.
- Vertical integration: acquiring suppliers or distributors to offset uncertainties in product supply or product distribution.
- Joint ventures: expansion through partnerships in the other organisations to share expertise, costs and resources.

(2) *Stability* – aimed at achieving a steady but slow performance improvement.
(3) *Retrenchment* – aimed at reversing a decline in performance by such strategies as:

- Harvesting: maximising short-term profits and cash flow while minimising investment in a product line.
- Turnaround: attempting to restructure operations to restore earlier performance levels.
- Divestiture: selling off one or more units to raise cash or concentrate on 'core' activities.
- Liquidation.

(c) Business strategy is the strategy for a single division or strategic business unit (SBU) that operates with some autonomy within a larger organisation. In a single business organisation institutional and corporate strategy will also be the business strategy. Business strategy involves making decisions concerned with the achievement of competitive advantage by making the best use of the distinctive competences of the enterprise and integrating the various functional areas of the business. It seeks to answer the strategic question 'How are we going to compete in this particular business area?' Two well known approaches to sell strategic planning are:

(1) The *competitive strategy* of Michael Porter [4]. This identifies three strategies that can be used to give a SBU a 'competitive advantage'. These strategies are:

- *Cost leadership:* pursuing operating efficiencies so that an organisation is the low-cost producer in its industry.
- *Differentiation:* attempting to develop products that are regarded industrywide as unique.
- *Focus:* concentration on a specific market segment.

(2) The *adaptive strategy* of Miles and Snow [5] based on the premise that an organisation should formulate strategies that will allow each of its SBUs to adapt to its unique environmental challenges. Four major strategies are identified:

- *Defender.* This emphasises output of reliable products for steady customers and is appropriate for very stable environments.
- *Prospector.* This emphasises a continuous search for new market opportunities and innovation and is appropriate for dynamic environments with untapped opportunities.
- *Analyser.* This emphasises stability while responding selectively to opportunities for innovation and is appropriate for moderately stable environments.
- *Reactor.* This is really no strategy. Reactors respond to competitive pressures by crisis management.

(d) Functional and operational strategy involves making decisions that guide activities with a specific functional or operational area, e.g. finance, marketing, production, purchasing, research and development. It asks the strategic question 'How can we best apply functional knowledge, skill and competence to serve the needs for the SBU or organisation?'

3. STRATEGIC MANAGEMENT AND PLANNING

An alternative definition to those given in **1** above is that strategic management is concerned with

'the formulation, implementation and evaluation of strategies designed to achieve the objectives of an enterprise and functions within that enterprise'.

The strategic planning process. Mintzberg [6] states that strategy formulation can:

(i) be created *entrepreneurially* by a visionary strategic leader who recognises the environmental opportunities and threats facing an organisation;
(ii) emerge *incrementally* as managers, through the organisation, adapt corporate and functional strategies to meet environmental changes;
(iii) be *planned* rationally and systematically.

Strategic planning can be defined as:

The process aimed at achieving an enterprise's mission and objectives by reconciling its resources with opportunities and threats in the business environment [7].

The strategic planning process is shown in Fig 2.1.

4. PURCHASING STRATEGY

Kraljic [8] states that 'A company's need for supply strategy depends on two factors:

(1)	**ENVIRONMENTAL SCANNING OF**	

EXTERNAL ENVIRONMENT
to ascertain *opportunities* and *threats*
outside the organisation not usually within
short term control of top management

INTERNAL ENVIRONMENT
to ascertain *strengths* and *weaknesses*
within the organisation not usually within
the short term control of top management

(2) **STRATEGY FORMULATION**

MISSION STATEMENT
(Defines organisational mission and purpose in a written statement which is
the basis for functional/operational mission statements)

OBJECTIVES
(End results of the planned activities required to enable the organisation to
fulfil its mission and the basis of functional/operational objectives)

DETERMINATION OF STRATEGIC DECISIONS
(Deciding which of the possible alternative strategic plans will best enable
the organisation to achieve its mission and objectives at corporate, business
and functional/operational levels. The plan adopted will be that which will
maximise competitive advantage and minimise competitive disadvantage)

(3) **STRATEGIC IMPLEMENTATION**
(Sometimes termed operational planning. This is the process by which
corporate/business strategies are expressed in functional/operational
mission statements and objectives are implemented through:)

ORGANISATIONAL STRUCTURES
(Structure is the means by which the organisation seeks to achieve its
strategic objectives and implement strategies and strategic changes)

RESOURCE ALLOCATION
(Resources may be financial, physical, human and technological. Resources
are mainly allocated through *budgets* and controlled or affected by *policies*.)

POLICIES
(Broad guidelines that link strategy formulation at all levels with the
implementation. Policies are implemented through procedures.)

PROCEDURES
(Sometimes called standard operation procedures (SOP) are a system of
sequential steps or techniques describing how a task or job is done.)

(4) **STRATEGIC EVALUATION AND CONTROL**
(The process of comparing actual performance with desired results to enable
managers at all levels to take corrective action and solve problems)

FEEDBACK
(For evaluation and control to be effective managers must obtain prompt
and unbiased feedback from their subordinates at each stage of the above
process)

Fig 2.1 The strategic planning process

(i) The strategic importance of purchasing in terms of the value added by the product line, the percentage of materials in total costs and so on.

(ii) The complexity of the supply market gauged by supply scarcity, pace of technology and/or materials substitution, entry barriers, logistics cost or complexity and monopoly or oligopoly condition.

Kraljic claims that:

'By assessing the company's situation in terms of these two variables, top management and senior purchasing executives can determine the type of supply strategy the company needs both to exploit its purchasing power vis-a-vis important suppliers and reduce its risks to an acceptable minimum.'

The application to purchasing of the four stages of the strategic planning process: environmental scanning, strategy formulation, implementation and evaluation, can now be considered.

5. ENVIRONMENTAL SCANNING

Speakeman [9] has identified two major components in environmental analysis: environmental monitoring and determination of strategic impacts.

(a) Environmental monitoring: this involves three stages:

(i) Searching the environment for signals that may portend significant changes, e.g.

- monetary trends
- inflation
- strikes
- shortages
- technological breakthroughs
- industry overcapacity

(ii) Identification of commodities/materials which may be threatened or benefit from environmental changes. These include so-called 'sensitive' commodities (see 10:**10**) .

(iii) Evaluation of the possible consequences to the organisation of changes in supply conditions arising from such environmental changes and the probability of such changes occurring.

(b) Determination of the strategic impact of a given supply item on (1) profit and (2) supply risk. Kraljic [10] states that the *profit impact* of a given supply item can be defined in terms of:

volume purchased
percentage of total purchase cost
impact on product quality or business growth.

Supply risk is assessed in terms of:

availability
number of suppliers

Table 2.1 Classifying purchasing materials requirements

Procurement focus	Main tasks	Required information	Decision level
Strategic items (high profit impact, high supply risk)	Accurate demand forecasting Detailed market research Development of long-term supply relationships Make-or-buy decisions Contract staggering Risk analysis Contingency planning Logistics, inventory, and vendor control	Highly detailed market data Long-term supply and demand trend information Good competitive intelligence Industry cost curves	Top level (e.g. vice president purchasing)
Bottleneck items (low profit impact, high supply risk)	Volume insurance (at cost premium if necessary) Control of vendors Security or inventories Backup plans	Medium term supply demand forecasts Very good market data Inventory costs Maintenance plans	Higher level (e.g. department heads)
Leverage items (high profit impact, low supply risk)	Exploitation of full purchasing power Vendor selection Product substitution Targeted pricing strategies Negotiations Contract/spot purchasing mix Order volume optimisation	Good market data Short to medium term demand planning Accurate vendor data Price/transport rate forecasts	Medium level (e.g. chief buyer)
Noncritical items (low profit impact, low supply risk)	Product standardisation Order volume monitoring/ optimisation Efficient processing Inventory optimisation	Good market overview Short-term demand forecast Economic order quantity inventory levels	Lower level (e.g. buyers)

competitive demand
make or buy opportunities
storage risks
substitution opportunities.

Kraljic points out that on the basis of the above profit and supply risk criteria all purchase items can be assigned to one of the four categories shown in Table 2.1.

An evaluation of such impacts can enable managers at the appropriate level to prioritise what materials and allied supply considerations require immediate attention.

(c) Other approaches to environmental scanning

(1) *PEST (political, economic, social and technology analysis)* . This has been extended by Hussey [11] to incorporate legal, ecological and demographic classifications. All such factors are interdependent and in practice the pattern of inter-relationships may be difficult to interpret. PEST factors input into SWOT analysis.

(2) *SWOT (strengths, weaknesses, opportunities and threats analysis)* . This approach assesses *internal* strengths and weaknesses *in relation to* its *external* opportunities and threats. By definition at corporate, business and functional levels an effective strategy will take advantage of the organisation's strengths and weaknesses while endeavouring to minimise or overcome its weaknesses and threats.

Potential strategies can be identified by showing internal and external appraisals in a cruciform chart. Fig 2.2 shows such a chart in respect of a purchasing situation.

In this example it might be possible to identify that the company is in some danger due to the reliance of a major product on a highly sensitive material obtainable from a limited supply source. Strategies might be to examine alternative materials or, on a grand strategy, to seek security of supplies through vertical integration.

STRENGTHS	WEAKNESSES
• Purchasing power • Purchasing probity and goodwill	• Highly 'sensitive' imported strategic materials
THREATS	OPPORTUNITIES
• Competition for materials from competitors • Monopolistic position of suppliers	• Alternative materials • Possibility of vertical integration with suppliers

Fig 2.2 SWOT analysis and purchasing

Evans [12] suggests that as a variation on SWOT analysis it is more useful to determine the strategic *issues* facing purchasing in the future, e.g.

- difficulty in recruiting purchasing staff of the right calibre
- suppliers going out of business
- increasing use of technology
- patents, leading to monopoly supply sources
- exchange rate fluctuations.

For each issue relevant strengths and weaknesses can be identified, e.g.

Issue	*Strengths*	*Weaknesses*
Make or buy	Appropriate machinery Skilled workforce On pure cost basis can make more cheaply if part of manufacturing capacity is dedicated to this purpose	Capacity for manufacture already below requirements Buying effectively expands the manufacturing resources of enterprise Time required for changeover Added value greater by making

(3) *Life cycle analysis.* This is based on the concept that all products in their original, unmodified form, have a final life span as shown in Fig 2.3.

The product life cycle, or Gopertz curve, plots the actual or potential sales of a new product over time and shows the stages of development, growth, maturity, decline and eventual withdrawal. Important aspects of product life cycles are

(i) Their length – from development to withdrawal. This may be short with products subject to rapid technological advances.

(ii) Their shape – not all products have the same shape to their curve. So-called 'high learning', 'low learning', 'fashion' and 'fad' products have different curves reflecting different marketing strategies.

(iii) The product – this can vary dependent on whether the product life cycle applies to a *class*, i.e. the entire product category or industry; *form*, i.e. variations within the class; or a *brand*.

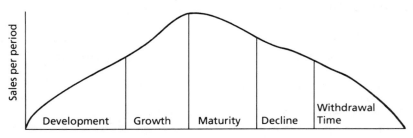

Fig 2.3 Product life cycle

The concept of the product life cycle helps a marketing manager to recognise that a product may need continual changes to prevent sales decline and formulate a marketing strategy to stimulate sales. This strategy may also have implications for purchasing strategy such as how far in advance to place orders, what materials or components are likely to change, etc.

(4) *Scenario planning* consists of developing a conceptual forecast of the future based on given assumptions. Thus by starting with different assumptions many different future scenarios can be presented. The assumptions can be based on the examination of trends relating to economic, political and social factors that may affect corporate objectives and supply and demand forecasts. Planning therefore involves deciding which scenario is most likely to occur and devising appropriate strategies. An example is examining the effect on price changes of sensitive commodities resulting from the scenarios of 'glut' or shortage factors.

(5) *Portfolio analysis.* This approach seeks to answer the question 'In what businesses should we compete?' and is therefore applicable to the planning of corporate strategy.

The basic concept is that an organisation should be seen as a portfolio of businesses or products with each business/product having a strategy appropriate to its capabilities and competitive needs.

The growth share matrix developed by the Boston Consulting Group [13], together with a later matrix [14] which developed the original approach, is typical of a number of planning models developed by consultants to assist managers to understand the competitive position of their overall portfolio of businesses/products.

The original BCG matrix analysed businesses or products according to market growth and market share into:

- *Stars* – high-share/high-growth businesses/products
- *Cash Cows* – high-share/low-growth businesses/products
- *Question Marks* – low-share/high-growth businesses/products
- *Dogs* – low-share/low-growth businesses/products

The resultant matrix and recommended strategies are shown in Fig 2.4.

The alternative BCG matrix enriches the above approach by adding broader descriptions of industry structure as shown in Fig 2.5.

To use the matrix it is necessary to assess judgementally:

(*i*) Whether there are few or many ways of achieving competitive advantage. This depends largely on the capabilities of differentiation within the industry.
(*ii*) Whether the extent and sustainability of the advantage is small or large.

The results of portfolio analysis can have significant implications for purchasing strategies and policies. Thus expenditure on supplies will be substantially higher for products identified as Stars or Cash Cows.

(6) *System modelling* in which computer-based models are developed to simulate key aspects of a function, e.g. purchasing and its environment. Purchasing staff then proceed through a number of 'what if?' situations to determine the

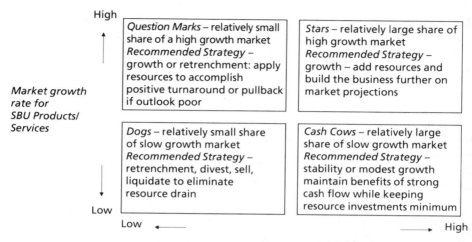

Fig 2.4 A portfolio model for alternative strategies within the original BCG matrix

consequences of a particular strategy. Likely consequences can thus be evaluated before the strategy is implemented.

(7) *Strategic issue management* (SIM). This involves the identification of one or a few key issues that are perceived as crucial to the function in achieving its performance objectives and evaluating the impact of such issues and their potential consequences both positive and negative for the function. An example

Size of competitive advantage

	Small	Large
Many	FRAGMENTED *Generic Strategy:* Many ways to compete. Look at relative strengths and unique competencies	SPECIALISATION *Generic Strategy:* Either niche in a segment of the market or cover the entire market with differentiated products
Few	STALEMATE *Generic Strategy:* Survive, reduce costs, maximise productivity	VOLUME *Generic Strategy:* Lowest cost position Sales leadership

Ways to compete

Fig 2.5 The alternative BCG matrix

would be the loss of a preferred supplier or an unacceptable rise in prices. Awareness of potential environmental changes allows purchasing a longer time in which to formulate alternative strategies.

(8) *Delphi method*. This is a subjective approach to forecasting based on a systematic approach to reaching agreement among a group of forecasters. The forecasters do not initially communicate with each other but receive reports on each others opinions. The various reports are then adjusted until opinion is reached.

(d) Porter's Five Forces Model. All the above approaches to environmental scanning tend to focus either on opportunities and threats within the general environment or on the strengths and weaknesses of the particular organisation. Porter's concept of *value chain analysis* to which reference was made in 1:4 focuses on the position of an SBU *within the industry to which it belongs*. As shown by Fig 2.6 Porter identifies five competitive forces that determine the intensity of competition in an industry and the total value of profits or value generated in that particular industry.

Each of the five forces in Porter's analysis can be broken down into their constituent elements. As Mintzberg [15] points out:

'The collective strength of the forces may be painfully apparent to all the antagonists but to cope with them the strategist must delve below the surface and analyse the sources of each. For example what makes the market vulnerable to entry? What determines the bargaining power of suppliers?'

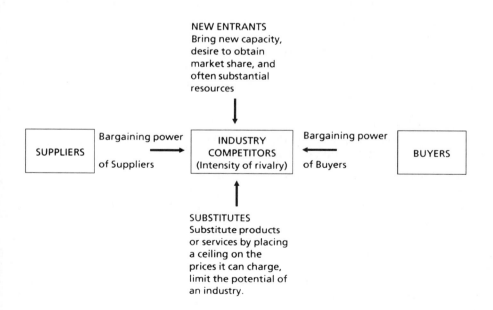

Fig 2.6 Porter's five forces model of industrial attractiveness
(adapted from M E Porter, *Competitive Advantage* 1985)

Analysis of each of the underlying services provides the groundwork for a strategic agenda of action. Mintzberg [16] points out that they:

- highlight the critical strengths and weaknesses of the company
- animate the positioning of the company in its industry
- clarify the areas where strategic changes may yield the greatest payoff
- highlight the places where industry trends promise to hold the greatest significance as either threats or opportunities

(1) *New entrants* [17]. The seriousness of the threat of entry depends on the barriers present and the likely reaction of existing competitors. *Barriers to entry* derive from six main sources:

- Economies of scale, e.g. high initial investment in production, research, marketing
- Product differentiation, e.g. brand identification requires heavy advertising to overcome loyalty
- Capital requirements, e.g. the need to invest large capital resources
- Cost advantages independent of size, e.g. patents, 'know-how', access to best material resources
- Access to distribution channels, e.g. the more existing competitors have these tied up the tougher entry to the industry will be
- Government policy, e.g. licence requirements and limits on access to raw materials.

Reaction of existing competitors can take such forms as:

- Resources to meet the threats posed by new entrants, e.g. financial strength, productive capacity, power to influence distributors and customers
- Price cutting to keep market share or because of excess capacity industry wide
- Slow industry growth probably causing the financial performance of all competitors to decline

(2) *Industry competitors.* 'Jockeying for position' among existing competitors uses such tactics as price competition, product introduction, comparative advertising. Factors relating to rivalry include:

- Equality in size and power of competitors
- Slow industry growth precipitating fights for market shares
- High fixed costs or perishable products with the temptation to cut prices if demand slackens
- High exit costs
- Demand characteristics.

(3) *Substitute products.* The more attractive the price-performance trade-off offered by substitute products, the firmer the lid placed on the industry's profit potential.

(4&5) *Suppliers and Buyers.* Suppliers can exert bargaining power by:

(i) raising prices

(ii) reducing the quality of purchased goods and services

Customers also can

(i) force down prices

(ii) demand higher quality or more service

(iii) play competitors off against each other

all at the expense of industry profits.

Porter states [18] that a *supplier* group is powerful if:

(i) It is dominated by few companies and is more concentrated than the industry it sells to.

(ii) Its product is unique or at least differentiated, or if it has built up switching costs. Switching costs are fixed costs buyers face in changing suppliers. These arise because, among other things, a buyer's product specifications tie it to particular suppliers, or it has invested heavily in specialised ancillary equipment, or in learning how to operate a supplier's equipment (as in computer software), or its production lines are connected to the supplier's manufacturing facilities (as in some manufacture of beverage containers) .

(iii) It is not obliged to contend with other products for sale to the industry. For instance, the competition between the steel companies and the aluminium companies to sell to the can industry checks the power of each supplier.

(iv) It poses a credible threat of integrating forward into the industry's business. This provides a check against the industry's ability to improve the terms on which it purchases.

(v) The industry is not an important customer of the supplier group. If the industry is an important customer, supplier's fortunes will be closely tied to the industry, and they will want to protect the industry through reasonable pricing and assistance in activities like R and D and lobbying.

A *buyer* group is powerful if:

(i) It is concentrated on purchases in large volumes. Large volume buyers are particularly potent forces if heavy fixed costs characterise the industry, which raises the stakes to keep capacity filled.

(ii) The products it purchases from the industry are standard or undifferentiated. The buyers are sure that they can always find alternative suppliers, and may play one off against another.

(iii) The products it purchases from the industry form a component of its product and represent a significant fraction of its cost. The buyers are likely to shop for a favourable price and purchase selectively. Where the product sold by the industry in question is a small fraction of buyers costs, buyers are usually much less price sensitive.

(iv) It earns low profile, which creates great incentive to lower its purchasing costs. Highly profitable buyers, however, are generally less price sensitive (where, of course, the price does not represent a large fraction of these costs).

(v) The industry's product is unimportant to the quality of the buyers' products or services. Where the quality of the buyers' products is very much affected by

the industry's products, buyers are generally less price sensitive. Industries in which this situation obtains include oil field equipment, where a malfunction can lead to large losses, and enclosures for electronic medical and test instruments where the quality of the enclosure can influence the user's impression about the quality of the equipment inside.

(vi) The industry's product does not save the buyer money. Where the industry's product or service can pay for itself many times over, the buyer is rarely price sensitive; rather, he is interested in quality. This is true in services like investment banking and public accounting, where errors in judgement can be costly and embarrassing.

(vii) The buyers pose a credible threat of integrating backward to make the industry's product . . . sometimes an industry engenders a threat to buyers that its members may integrate forward.

Hax and Majlief [19] suggest that Porter's terminology 'bargaining power of suppliers and buyers' implies a threat imposed on the industry by an excessive use of power on the part of these two agents which the SBU will have to neutralise. The approach of partnership sourcing, however, emphasises the importance of treating suppliers not as rivals or adversaries but as the depositories of a long-lasting friendly relationship and an extension of the organisation itself.

6. STRATEGY FORMULATION

(As shown by Fig 2.1.) Strategy formulation at corporate, business and functional levels relates to:

The preparation of a mission statement
The deriving of objectives
The determination of strategic decisions.

Each of these stages is considered from a purchasing perspective:

(a) The preparation of a mission statement. At all levels, a good mission statement helps in strategy formulation by providing a sense of purpose that maintains the focus of strategic plans.

At the functional level a mission statement should indicate:

(i) The overall aim of the function
(ii) How the aim will be achieved
(iii) The basis of internal and external relationships
(iv) The link with corporate strategies

These four points are exemplified in Fig 2.7 [20].

(b) Deriving objectives. As shown in Fig 2.1 objectives can be corporate/business or functional. Typical purchasing objectives and the relationship between corporate/business and purchasing supply objectives are given in 1:**7a–c**.

> **The MISSION of the purchasing function in BICC Cables Limited is ...**
>
> | Overall Aim | to create sustainable competitive | How the aim will |
> |---|---|---|
> | | advantage for the company by managing | be achieved |
> | | the purchase of all | |
> | Basis of internal | materials, plans and services, achieving | |
> | and external | best overall value whilst satisfying | |
> | relationships | internal customers' needs and managing | |
> | | the company's relationship with the | Link with |
> | | supply market in ways consistent with | corporate strategy |
> | | BICC Codes, corporate strategies and | |
> | | business practices | |

Fig 2.7

(c) Determination of strategic decisions. Earlier in this chapter three levels of strategy decision making are identified: corporate, business and functional. For the single business corporate and business strategies become synonymous. Corporate, business and functional strategies represent different levels of strategic decision making or formulation within an organisation.

Corporate/business level strategy decisions will, however, guide subsequent decisions on functional or operational strategy. Some distinctions between procurement strategy at the corporate and functional/operational levels are shown in Table 2.2.

Any attempt to detail the full range of corporate and functional strategies would be lengthy. In any case such strategies vary between organisations.

7. STRATEGY IMPLEMENTATION

The principal distinctions between strategy formulation and strategy implementation are shown in Table 2.3.

Strategy implementation as shown in Fig 2.1 relates to
Organisational structures
Resource allocation
Policies and
Procedures.

(a) Organisational structures. Organisation structure provides the manager and staff of a function with information regarding their place in the organisation, their upwards, downward and lateral relationships, and tasks and responsibilities. Purchasing organisation is considered in Chapter 3.

(b) Resource allocation. In most organisations the financial, physical, human and technological resources allocated to a function will be reduced to

Table 2.2 Procurement strategy at corporate and functional levels

Corporate/Business Level	Functional/Operational Level
Formulated at higher levels in the hierarchy	Taken at lower levels in the hierarchy
Emphasise purchasing effectiveness	Emphasise purchasing efficiency
Based on widespread environmental scanning. Some of this information will be communicated upwards from functional level	Based on information from a more limited environmental scanning. Some information obtained from suppliers etc. may be communicated upwards
Corporate strategy must be communicated downwards	Integrated with corporate strategies so far as these are communicated and understood
Focused on issues impacting on future long-term procurement requirements and problems	Focused on issues impacting on current tactical procurement requirements and problems
Typical strategies relate to:	
'Grand' strategies relating to procurement, e.g. forward or backward integration. Reciprocal buying	Operational issues within the 'grand' strategies, e.g. servicing of supplies
Organisational structure and the position of purchasing within the structure	Organisation of staff with purchasing responsibilities, their recruitment, training and development
Allocation of resources to procurement	Strategies to ensure that financial human and other resources are most effectively used to obtain the greatest competitive advantage
Ethical aspects of procurement derive from the institutional strategy	Strategies and policies to ensure that procurement conforms to such policies
Decisions relating to large scale capital expenditure	Decisions relating to revenue expenditure

quantitative terms and expressed in budgets or financial statements of the resources required to achieve a set of finite objectives or implement a formulated strategy. Budgets and purchasing budgets are referred to in Chapter 12.

(c) Policies are instruments for strategy implementation. They may be defined as *a body of principles, express or implied, laid down to direct an enterprise towards its objectives and guide executives in decision making.* Policy may be a collective noun and corporate or business policy can be sub-divided into functional and operational (e.g. marketing, purchasing, personnel) policies.

Like strategies, policies may be considered at three levels:

Table 2.3 Contrasts between strategy formulation and implementation [21]

Strategy formulation	Strategy implementation
(i) The positioning of forces before the action	Management of forces during the action
(ii) Focuses on effectiveness	Focuses on efficiency
(iii) Is primarily an intellectual process	Is primarily an operational process
(iv) Requires good initiative and analytical skills	Requires special motivation and leadership skills
(v) Requires co-ordination among a few individuals	Requires co-ordination among many persons

(i) Corporate policies reflect the mission of the undertaking and can serve as guidelines in evaluating strategies.
(ii) Functional policies relate to the activities of major business units
(iii) Operating policies are concerned with day-to-day decision making.

It is useful to consider the advantages of policy and purchasing policies.

(1) *The advantages of policy.* At corporate, functional and operational levels policies have the following advantages:

(i) Corporate policies provide guidelines to executives in formulating functional and operating strategies.
(ii) Policies provide authority based on principle and / or precedent for a given course of action.
(iii) They provide a basis for management control, allow co-ordination across organisational units and reduce the time managers spend in making decisions.
(iv) They promote management by exception by providing guidelines for routine action; a new decision is only required in respect of exceptional circumstances.
(v) Policies lead to uniformity of procedures and consistency in thought and action.

(2) *Purchasing policies.* These include:

(i) Policies relating to *supply relationships,* e.g.

'Our policy is to be selective about the types of relationships we establish with suppliers, but in all cases to treat them with professional respect and to hold our dealing with them as confidential to the parties concerned.'

'We should aim to actively promote an image rather than let one form by default. We wish to be seen as fair, tough, totally professional and demonstrably operating according to the highest standards of business practice.'

(ii) Internal policies, e.g.

'Our policy is to support internal suppliers to the fullest extent and to develop product and service quality to the same high standards as those available in the external market. Employees may not use the Company's name or purchase leverage to obtain materials or services at preferential rates for their personal use, or for use by other parties in whom the 'buyer' has an interest.'

(iii) Sourcing policies, e.g.

'Only those suppliers who satisfy the requirements of the Company's supplier appraisal process and are able to meet their contractual obligations to the company in full should be used. Buyers should actively source from the world market where practical, taking into account corporate guidelines and statutory regulations.'

Purchasing policies may be varied to meet an exceptional situation, e.g. a breakdown in supplies, but this should only be done on the authority of the executive with ultimate responsibility for purchasing.

(d) Procedures are the formal arrangements through which policies are implemented. A cluster of related procedures each consisting of a number of operations which together provide information or guidance to managers and staff relating to an activity is termed a *system*. Basic purchasing procedure is referred to in Chapter 4.

8. STRATEGY EVALUATION AND CONTROL

Evaluation differs from control.

(a) Evaluation takes place when a strategy has been formulated and after the strategy has been put into effect. After a strategy has been formulated it should, before implementation, be checked against such criteria as:

(i) Consistency: any mutually inconsistent goals and policies should be harmonised.

(ii) Consonance: the strategy must be a realistic adaptive response to the external environment and anticipated changes within it at the time of formulation.

(iii) Advantage: the strategy must aim at the creation and maintenance of a competitive advantage in the selected area of activity, e.g. procurement of supplies and services.

(iv) Feasibility: the strategy must neither over tax available resources nor create unsolvable sub-problems.

Evaluation should also be undertaken at regular intervals to ascertain whether the current strategy is still appropriate to changed environmental conditions and what changes or modifications are required to meet consequential opportunities and threats.

(b) Control is the process of checking that actual performance conforms to that planned. Controlling comprises four basic steps:

(i) Establishing performance standards
(ii) Measuring individual, organisational and functional/operational performance
(iii) Comparing actual to planned performance standards
(iv) Taking appropriate corrective action.

Appraisal of the performance of purchasing personnel is dealt with in Chapter 6. Performance measurement as applied to the purchasing function is considered in Chapter 14.

9. STRATEGIC OPTIONS

Johnson and Scholes [22] state that in measuring strategic options it is important to distinguish between three inter-related aspects of any strategy:

(a) The **generic strategy** to be pursued, i.e. the basis on which the organisation will compete or sustain excellence, namely:

- *Cost leadership* through
    cost structure
    product experience
    special skills, systems and
    technologies
- *Differentiation* which is recognised and valued by consumers/users, e.g.
    product life
    reliability
    convenience
    economy
    after-sales service
    esteem value, etc.
- *Focus* – a combination of cost leadership and differentiation directed at a
    particular target, e.g.
    a national/international market
    a niche strategy directed at a very small part of the market secure from
    large organisations

(b) Alternative directions in which the organisation may choose to develop, e.g.
    Do nothing
    Withdrawal
    Consolidation
    Market penetration
    Market development
    Diversification
      related
      unrelated

Table 2.4 Typical aspects of purchasing strategies, tactics or contributions to corporate development strategies

Aspect of strategic development	Typical purchasing strategies/tactics contributions
Generic Strategy Cost leadership	Lower purchase costs through consolidation of purchases, single servicing, global procurement. Reduction in costs of purchasing systems and administration. Value for money spent. Logistical contributions to competitive advantage. Buying of sub-assemblies in lieu of components etc.
Differentiation	Involvement of suppliers in product design and development, value analysis, total quality management, alternative materials. Stimulation of technological developments in one supplier market etc.
Focus	Location of specialist suppliers, make or buy decisions for specialist components, subcontracting, outsourcing etc.
Alternative Directions Do nothing	–
Withdrawal	Running down/disposal of inventory. Negotiation of contract cancellations etc.
Consolidation	Moving to standard/generic materials/compents to increase potential use. Negotiation of limited period contracts etc.
Market penetration	Provision of information regarding competitors, price volatility, unused capacity in the supplier market. Negotiation of contracts with options for increased supply or stocking of inventory and suppliers etc.
Product development	Liaison with design and production. Partnership sourcing; supplier appraisal. Negotiation re ownership of jigs and tools for bought out items. Timing of supply deliveries. MRPII. Value engineering etc.
Market development	Liaison with marketing. Partnership sourcing specifying packaging and shipping instructions. Identification of vital points in the supply/value chain
Diversification	Supply considerations, e.g. effect on set-up costs and production runs. Purchasing quantity considerations. Promotion of interchangeability of materials and components etc.
Alternative Methods Internal development	Organisational aspects of purchasing. Recruitment or development of purchasing staff. Integration of purchasing into materials management or logistics.
Acquisition	Corporate level issues relating to: (i) Backward integration – activities concerned with securing inputs, e.g. raw materials by acquisition of supplies (ii) Forward integration – activities concerned with securing outputs, e.g. acquisition of distribution channels, transport undertakings etc. (iii) Horizontal integration – activities complementary to those currently undertaken, e.g. consortia, franchising, licensing or agency agreements

(c) **Alternative methods** by which any direction of development may be advanced, e.g.

Internal development
Acquisition
Joint development

Typical purchasing strategies/tactics or contributions for each of the above three aspects of strategic development are shown in Table 2.4.

References

[1] Digman LA (1990). *Strategic Management – Concepts, Decisions, Cases.* Irwin.
[2] Mintzberg, Quinn and James (1988). *The Strategy Process: Concepts, Contexts and Cases.* Prentice Hall.
[3] Gunnigle and Moore (1994). *Linking business strategy and human resource management: issues and implications. Personnel Review.* Vol 23, No 1, pp 63–83.
[4] Michael E Porter (1980). *Competitive Strategy: Techniques for Analysing Industries and Competitors.* New York. MacMillan.
[5] Raymond E Miles and Charles C Snow (1978). *Organisational Strategy Structure and Process.* McGraw Hill.
[6] Mintzberg H. *Strategy making in three modes. California Management Review,* Vol 16 (2). Winter 1973.
[7] Smit and Cronje (Ed). *Management Principles.* Jula and Co, South Africa, 1993. Chap 5, p 107.
[8] Kraljic Peter. *Purchasing must become supply management. Harvard Business Review.* Sept–October 1983, p 110.
[9] Speakeman R E. *A strategic approach to procurement planning. Journal of Purchasing and Supplies Management.* Winter 1981, pp 2–7.
[10] Kraljic Peter. *Purchasing must become supply management. Harvard Business Review.* Sept-October 1983, p 110.
[11] Hussey D E. *Corporate Planning: Theory and Practice.* Second Edition. Pergamon, 1984.
[12] Evans E. *Strategic planning in purchasing. Purchasing and Supply Management.* May 1994, p 36.
[13] See Hedley B. *Strategy and the business portfolio. Long Range Planning.* February 1977, pp 9–15.
[14] Adapted from Hofer C. *Strategy Formulation: Analytical Concepts.* West Publishing Co. 1978, p 34.
[15] Mintzberg H and Quinn J B. *The Strategy Process.* Second Edition. Prentice Hall, 1991, Chapter 4, p 63.
[16] Mintzberg H and Quinn J B. *The Strategy Process.* Second Edition. Prentice Hall, 1991, Chapter 4, p 63.
[17] The analysis of the five forces in Porter's analysis of competitive advantage above is based on Porter M E. *How competitive forces shape strategy. Harvard Business Review.* March/April 1979, pp 137–145.
[18] The analysis of the five forces in Porter's analysis of competitive advantage above is based on Porter M E. *How competitive forces shape strategy. Harvard Business Review.* March/April 1979, pp 137–145.
[19] Hax A C and Majlief N S. *The Strategy Concept and Process.* Prentice Hall, 1991, Chap 5, pp 43–44.

[20] Courtesy of BICC Ltd.

[21] Adapted from David F R. *Concepts of Strategic Management*. Third Edition. Maxwell MacMillan, 1991, Chap 7, p 253.

[22] Johnson G and Scholes K. *Exploring Corporate Strategy, Text and Cases*. Prentice Hall, 1989, Ch 6, pp 147–169.

Progress test 2

1. Define the term 'strategy'.

2. What are the four 'levels of strategy?'

3. What are the four stages of the 'strategic planning process?

4. What are the two factors on which a company's supply strategy depends?

5. Distinguish between 'environmental monitoring' and 'determination of strategic impact'.

6. What are the four categories into which purchase items can be assigned from the standpoints of profit and risk?

7. What are PEST and SWOT?

8. What other approaches can be used in relation to environmental scanning?

9. Describe Porter's Five Forces Model.

10. What factors influence the strength of a supplier group?

11. What factors influence the strength of a buyer group?

12. What should a functional mission statement indicate?

13. In what ways does procurement strategy differ at the corporate and functional levels?

14. Distinguish between strategy formulation and implementation.

15. Define the term 'policy'.

16. What are the advantages of policies?

17. Define the term 'procedures'.

18. Distinguish between the terms 'evaluation' and 'control'.

The CIPS Professional Stage paper – *Purchasing and Supply Management 1 – Planning, Policy and Organisation* – comprises two sections: Section A (compulsory) consists of three tasks based on a mini-case study and carries a maximum of 50 marks; Section B comprises 5 questions of which candidates are required to answer 2.

For 1993 and 1994 the following tasks based on the mini-case study were set for Section A.

(1) *(a)* Produce a SWOT analysis for World Enterprises. (10 marks)
    (b) What other strategic tools of analysis would you use in identifying and addressing the problems facing WE? (10 marks)
    (c) Suggest a mission statement for WE and those strategies which could be adopted to implement it. (15 marks)
    (d) What role could a pro-active purchasing and supply activity play in improving the financial position of WE? (15 marks)

    May 1993

(2) *(a)* Prepare a general SWOT analysis and, using this information, formulate a 'strategic mission statement' for HF. (20 marks)
    (b) Assuming you have been given the post of strategic planner, evaluate three strategic forecasting techniques that could be used. (10 marks)
    (c) Discuss how the purchasing and supply function could assist in the strategic requirements of closer links with major suppliers and developments in the field of EDI. (20 marks)

    November 1993

(3) *(a)* Using appropriate tools of strategic analysis, identify the current position facing European Products (EP). (25 marks)
    (b) After completing your review, suggest a mission statement for European Products. (10 marks)
    (c) What role could a centralised purchasing and supply activity play in the future development of the organisation? (15 marks)

    May 1994

(4) *(a)* Using strategic tools of analysis, identify the major problems facing the organisation. (20 marks)
    (b) Produce a mission statement. (5 marks)
    (c) What alternative strategies are open to Baldwin Industries? (15 marks)
    (d) What contribution could a more developed purchasing function make to the organisation? (10 marks)

    November 1994

(5) You have recently joined the board of a newly formed manufacturing company as the purchasing director, and one of your first tasks is to formulate purchasing policies for the company.
    (a) Discuss the main topic areas which you would include in the purchasing policy manual.
    (b) Explain the advantages to the organisation of having well defined purchasing policies.

    (IPS, *Purchasing and Supply Management* (1986).)

(6) The relationship between buyer and supplier is of considerable strategic importance. Explain why this has become more apparent in recent years, and discuss the implications of this with respect fo purchasing policy.

    (IPS, *Purchasing Planning, Policy and Organisation* (1990).)

3

PURCHASING ORGANISATION

1. WHAT IS ORGANISATION STRUCTURE?

Hay and Williamson [1] point out that the internal design of an organisation comprises such elements as:

- the definition and allocation of specific tasks – 'who does what?'
- the group of similar tasks into functional departments, e.g. purchasing
- the creation of systems that facilitate the co-ordination of activities between and within departments
- the allocation of responsibility within a department – e.g. along hierarchical lines
- the distribution of formal authority across the organisation.

The structure of the organisation as a whole and of functions within the organisation is determined by strategy. Thus, as Chandler states [2], structure follows strategy, or more precisely, a strategy of diversity forces a decentralised structure.

2. FACTORS INFLUENCING PURCHASING ORGANISATION

There is a significant distinction between the purchasing *function* and the purchasing *department*. The former is a basic function common to all types of enterprise. The latter is an organisational unit of an undertaking, the duties of which vary according to the nature of the business, its historical development and management orientation. This diversity of purpose activity and strategy is reflected in a corresponding diversity of organisation structure which is as it should be since the organisation structure should suit the undertaking and not vice-versa. A number of factors have, however, influenced both the organisation of purchasing and its place within the particular enterprise. These include:

- The need for integrated decision making relating to supply chain activities
- The importance of cross-functional co-ordination and communication on supply issues
- The expansion of purchasing and supply management responsibilities that have traditionally been carried out by other functional areas, e.g. transport inwards, stores and inventory

- Technological developments, e.g. the impact of computers and integration through databases and EDI make it easier to share information and response to changes in demand, supply, etc.
- Lean supply approaches, emphasising fewer suppliers, JIT and the emphasis on the reduction of the total system cost and not just the cost of purchased components, e.g. the elimination of non-value adding transactions, minimum paper flow and over specialisation
- Human relations approaches such as the concept of empowerment with the delayering of organisational structures.

Recent developments, however, have enabled three broad approaches to purchasing organisation to be identified:

- Purchasing as a discrete function
- Purchasing as a function within a wider materials management function
- Purchasing as a function within a wider logistics management system.

The first part of this chapter will consider purchasing as a discrete function from the standpoints of:

Departmentation
Centralisation and decentralisation
Co-ordination of purchasing
Purchasing within the management structure
The internal organisation of purchasing departments
Purchasing and its functional contacts
Purchasing and inter-departmental conflict.

In the second and third parts of this chapter, consideration will be given to the modern integrative approaches of:

Materials management
Logistics management

3. CENTRALISATION OF PURCHASING

There are several approaches to the centralisation of purchasing. These include:

- The use of supply consortia
- Joint contracting
- Departmentation within the organisation

Supply consortia and joint purchasing which are of increasing importance within local authority purchasing have the strengths and weaknesses shown in Fig 3.1 [3].

4. CENTRALISATION AS DEPARTMENTALISATION

Cammish and Keough [4] trace the development of purchasing within an organisation through four stages:

Strengths	Weaknesses
Consortium	
(i) Bulk purchasing gives strong negotiation position over wide range of goods	(i) Cannot insist upon compliance by individual LAs
(ii) Can economically develop wide ranging product expertise	(ii) It may be more difficult to agree standard specifications
(iii) Costs are clearly identified	(iii) Lines of communication between user, buyer and supplier are longer
	(iv) Significant areas of spend are not covered
Joint contracting	
(i) Reduced costs of contracting	(i) Covers contract negotiating and maintenance only
(ii) Strong negotiating position for limited range of items	(ii) Depends on agreement between authorities
(iii) Can provide product expertise which would otherwise be too expensive	(iii) Applies to a limited range of commodities only

Fig 3.1 Strengths and weaknesses of consortium and joint contracting by local authorities

1 Purchasing as a service function for manufacturing: the primary task being to find appropriate suppliers and ensure that the plant does not run out of raw materials and supplied components. At this stage purchasing may be carried out by the entrepreneur as was the case with William Morris (later Lord Nuffield), who initially did his own negotiations for the supply of car engines from the USA. As the business evolves, however, purchasing typically reports to a production or plant manager.

2 Purchasing as a means of reducing unit cost: At this stage a higher type of purchasing manager is recruited who can negotiate credibly with suppliers for lower prices and improved quality and delivery. Maintaining the low unit cost stance requires some independence from user functions like manufacturing with the result that purchasing, while reporting to a senior executive, has a full degree of autonomy at lower organisational levels.

3 Co-ordinated purchasing: led by a strong central purchasing department to implement uniform buying policies and systems, the emphasis being on cross-unit co-ordination and compliance with nationally negotiated contracts. This stage may lead to purchasing bureaucracy and lack of responsiveness.

4 Strategic purchasing: i.e. world class purchasing. At this stage the emphasis is on cross-functional problem solving with the objective of reducing total system cost and not just the unit cost of purchased components. These cross-functional efforts often include key suppliers as joint problem solvers and a move from confrontational to partnership sourcing.

At all stages except (1) however, there are many advantages of departmentalisation. These include:

(a) Economics of scale. Centralised purchasing enables an undertaking to use its bargaining power or 'leverage' to the best effect since:

(i) Consolidation of quantities can take place resulting in quantity discounts or rebates.

(ii) Suppliers dealing with a central purchasing department have the incentive of competing for the whole or a substantial proportion of the undertaking's requirements.

(iii) Cheaper prices may result since the fixed overheads of the supplier can be spread over longer production runs.

(iv) Specialist purchasing staff can be employed for each of the major categories of purchase.

(v) Specialist ancillary staff may be feasible within the purchasing office, e.g. an expert on import procedures where substantial purchases are made abroad.

(vi) Lower administrative costs apply, e.g. it is cheaper to place and process one order for £10,000 than ten each of £1,000.

(vii) The use of computers to facilitate the collection, summarising and analysing of data which can improve purchasing efficiency. Efficient data processing systems cannot be designed on a piecemeal basis.

(b) Co-ordination of activity

(i) Uniform policies can be adopted, e.g.
single sourcing
partnership sourcing

(ii) Uniform purchasing procedures can be followed.

(iii) Competitive buying between departments within the organisation is eliminated.

(iv) Standardisation is facilitated by the use of company-wide specifications.

(v) The determination of order quantities and delivery dates is facilitated.

(vi) Back-up services, especially stock control and progressing, can be co-ordinated.

(vii) Staff training and development can be undertaken on a systematic basis.

(viii) Purchasing research into sources, qualities and supplier performance is facilitated.

(ix) Suppliers find it more convenient to approach one central purchasing department than a number of individuals or plants.

(c) Control of activity

(i) The purchasing department may become either a separate cost centre, i.e. a location within the organisation in relation to which costs may be ascertained, or a profit centre, i.e. a unit of the organisation which is responsible for revenues and profits as well as expenditures. This matter is dealt with in Chapter 14.

(ii) Budgetary control may be applied both to the purchasing department and to the total expenditure on supplies.

(iii) Uniformity of purchase prices obtained by centralised purchasing assists standard costing.

(iv) Inventories can be controlled, reducing obsolescence and loss of interest on capital locked up in excessive stocks.

(v) Approaches such as Just-in-Time and MRP II can be implemented.

(vi) Purchasing department performance can be monitored by setting objectives and comparing actual results with predetermined standards.

(d) The disadvantages of departmentalisation, all of which have implications for purchasing, include [5]:

(i) Co-ordination among related functional areas is more difficult, hence the move to materials management and logistics approaches.

(ii) Departmentalisation can foster a parochial emphasis on functional object-ives with a minimum appreciation of or concern for overall organisational goals.

(iii) Employee identification with a specialist group or function can make it difficult to implement change.

(iv) Training of managers with broad perspectives and wide understanding of business may be inhibited.

(v) Interdepartmental rivalry and conflict may be encouraged.

(vi) Where buyers lack technical knowledge time is often saved if design or user departments deal directly with suppliers.

(vii) User departments will resort to informal procedures if formal purchasing procedures are too slow, unreliable or otherwise unsatisfactory.

The best ways of meeting these objectives are for purchasing to take the initiative in setting up consultative procedures through which users can express their views and preferences and to offer such a standard of service to production and other functions that the need to circumvent purchasing does not arise.

5. CENTRALISATION AND DECENTRALISATION IN GROUP UNDERTAKINGS

When an undertaking is located on a single site, purchasing will normally take place in one centralised office. Where the undertaking's activities are spread over many plants, the question arises as to where purchasing should be located. There are three possibilities:

(i) Purchasing may be completely centralised at the head office or a particular plant.

(ii) Purchasing may be completely decentralised, i.e. each plant will undertake its own purchasing.

(iii) A combination of centralisation and decentralisation may apply.

Purchasing will tend to be *completely centralised* where the items required at each plant are largely homogeneous. An example would be a confectionery company with a large number of plants, each using large quantities of flour, sugar, etc. In this case, orders would be placed centrally and deliveries made against the contract as required by the local plants.

Purchasing may be *completely decentralised* where the group is a conglomerate consisting of a number of plants each producing widely dissimilar products. In this case, purchasing is done at plant level since the materials and components used are specific to that location. Complete decentralisation is supported by such arguments as:

- Since the efficiency of purchasing influences profitability, the manager of each plant should have control over the expenditure incurred on materials for his plant
- Centralised purchasing proliferates paperwork and leads to delays
- Some plants are so large that the economies of scale referred to earlier are already present and there is an optimum after which *diseconomies* of scale set in.

One relevant objection to complete decentralisation is that the competition between plants may lead to a loss of group purpose.

In most group undertakings there is a compromise, some purchasing activities being undertaken centrally and others at plant level. It is, therefore, necessary to determine:

- What functions shall be undertaken centrally?
- What functions shall be decentralised?
- How shall co-ordination between central and plant level purchasing be achieved?

In each case the answers will depend on the undertaking but the following arrangements are typical:

(a) Centralised functions

(i) Determination of major purchasing strategies and policies, e.g. organisation, single sourcing, reciprocal purchasing

(ii) Preparation of standard specifications for the whole undertaking

(iii) Negotiation of bulk contracts for homogeneous items used by a number of plants

(iv) Purchase of stationery and office equipment and computerised systems

(v) Purchasing research into market conditions, suppliers, etc.

(vi) Rationalisation of the share of orders to be received by suppliers. This will apply particularly when the purchasing undertaking controls a large section of the available orders or, for social reasons, needs to spread its purchasing power fairly among a number of dependent suppliers.

(vii) Control of group inventory

(viii) Staff training and development.

(b) Decentralised functions

(i) Small order items

(ii) Items used only by that plant

(iii) Emergency purchases, i.e. where local initiative may avoid an interruption of production

(iv) Local buying to save transport costs

(v) Local purchasing undertaken for social reasons, i.e. plant is part of the community in which it is situated and can by the exercise of the purchasing power contribute to the prosperity of the locality.

(vi) Staff purchases

Currently the shift is towards *decentralisation* due to:

(i) The need for purchasing decisions to be made as closely as possible to the problems to be solved.

(ii) General trends towards independent profit centres with decentralised responsibility. The view is sometimes expressed that if purchasing costs account for more than half of the total costs, then each profit centre should be given the right to make its own decisions regarding purchasing and suppliers.

(iii) Normally decentralisation facilitates closer relationships with suppliers.

(iv) The trend away from functional specialisation towards integrated problem solving.

6. CO-ORDINATION OF PURCHASING

Prior to the development of electronic communication such as EDI the main disadvantages of centralised buying in group undertakings resulted from long lines of communication and lack of knowledge of local needs and problems. Electronic communication makes possible improved co-ordination between central purchasing and users or other associated functions by enabling each to provide the other with relevant real time information. Apart from electronic communication by fax or EDI co-ordination may be achieved through:

- Purchasing and stores manuals containing directives on policies and procedures including the limitations placed on the authority of plant buyers
- Returns and memoranda
- Regular meetings between centralised and plant level purchasing staff
- Training courses emphasising group policies and procedures
- Systems approaches as reflected in the development of materials and logistics management.

7. PURCHASING WITHIN THE MANAGEMENT HIERARCHY

The place of purchasing in the management hierarchy differs from one undertaking to another. It may be:

- a top or senior management function
- a middle management function
- a routine clerical procedure.

(a) Purchasing as a top management function. The term 'top management' may include in addition to the board and its officers the few very senior appointments at the head of the major divisions of operation and service specialisation. The inclusion of these 'divisional heads' in the compass of top management – whether they are directors or not – is justified by the roles allotted to them in the very character of their appointment: they are each the chief source of management knowledge and decisions over a particular field of special attention and accordingly also the chief source of and contribution to strategy formulation and policy for that specialisation.

Mintzberg [6] identifies ten different but highly interrelated roles that a typical top-level manager performs. These roles, likely to be performed by a Purchasing Director, are separated into three basic categories: *inter-personal roles* (figurehead, leader, liaison), *informational roles* (monitor, disseminator, spokesperson) and *decisional roles* (entrepreneur, disturbance handler, resource allocator, negotiator). Sometimes such roles conflict, e.g. monitoring the performance of suppliers may conflict with disturbance handling.

Fig 3.2 shows the senior management of a medium-sized engineering company.

(b) Purchasing as a middle-management function. In traditional organisation structures there may be two or three levels of authority between purchasing and top or senior management. These levels may be reduced as a result of:

(i) The concept of *empowerment.* Empowerment refers to a set of motivational techniques designed to improve employee performance through increased levels of employee participation and self-determination. The consequences of empowerment include flatter organisations and leaner workforces.
(ii) The influence of technology enabling more rapid communication between strategic and operational purchasing levels.

Where purchasing is regarded as a middle management function the purchasing executive may report to one of the following:

(i) The production manager or controller since these are respectively responsible for the use or planning the usage of materials
(ii) A logistics or materials manager or executive

Fig 3.2 Senior management structure (large-sized engineering company)

(iii) The financial director on the basis that the purchasing officer is spending money and finance is responsible for the control of funds. This often applies in central and local government, hospitals, etc. In practice control is exercised through spending limits and budget procedures.

(iv) The commercial manager or company secretary.

(c) Purchasing as a routine clerical function. This will be the case in very small businesses or undertakings where the range of purchases is small and standardised. It may also apply in group purchasing or large purchasing departments where purchasing policy and negotiations are determined centrally so that there is little scope for the exercise of initiative or authority at the operational level. This may adversely affect the motivation of the purchasing staff who feel that they cannot aspire to responsibilities beyond those of routine order clerks. It is this lack of motivation that the concept of empowerment aims to counteract.

Where purchasing is routine, those responsible for the activity may report direct to the owner, works manager, accountant or office manager who will often decide what, when and how much to purchase and the source of supply.

(d) What determines the level at which purchasing operates? The place of purchasing in the management hierarchy depends on many factors, in addition to those mentioned in 1:7–8 and the contributions to strategies discussed in Chapter 2. These include:

(i) The proportion of expenditure on outsourcing to total expenditure. As stated earlier (1:4) the scope for greatest savings lies in the areas of greatest expenditure.

(ii) The perceived contribution of the purchasing system to competitive advantage.

(iii) The role of purchasing in building up partnership relationships with suppliers.

(iv) The contribution of purchasing to increasing profits through efficient control and reduction of inventory through JIT, where applicable, depending on sound supplier selection to ensure reliability in respect of quality, delivery and quantities.

(v) The perceived expert contribution of purchasing in relation to specific purchases, e.g. the purchase of high-cost fixed assets involving high-risk decisions.

(vi) Where purchasing operates under conditions of uncertainty, as in the purchase of sensitive commodities subject to considerable price volatility.

(vii) Where the organisation needs to adapt rapidly to external change, requiring what Burns and Stalker (*The Management of Innovation*) identified as organic systems which, *inter alia*, emphasise the contributive nature of special knowledge and experience to the common task of the concern.

(viii) The overall nature of purchasing decisions. H A Simon distinguished between programmed and non-programmed decisions:

(1) *Programmed decisions are* 'repetitive and routine to the extent that a definite procedure has been worked out for handling them so that they don't have to be treated as *de novo* each time they occur.'

(2) *Non-programmed decisions* are 'novel, unstructured, consequential, and involve questions of strategy consisting of major policies and plans.'

An example of a non-programmed decision in purchasing occurs where the executive concerned has to decide when, where and how much to buy in the case of a sensitive commodity such as copper, where prices may fluctuate considerably. Here the buyer will have to possess not only a highly specialised knowledge of copper and the markets where dealings take place, but also the ability to evaluate economic and political factors influencing present and future prices. Simon further points out:

(1) Programmed and non-programmed decisions are not really distinct types 'but a whole continuum with highly programmed decisions at one end of that continuum and highly unprogrammed decisions at the other end'.

(2) Different techniques are used for handling non-programmed and programmed decisions.

Non-programmed decisions, which, of decreasing complexity, may be undertaken from top management downwards, are often arrived at by simulation approaches where the object is to find acceptable (not necessarily the best) solutions. Programmed decisions lend themselves to approaches based on the application of operational research and data processing.

8. THE INTERNAL ORGANISATION OF PURCHASING DEPARTMENTS

Two important considerations are the division of responsibility for buying operations and the organisation of support services. As the scale of purchasing is extended the work of the department may be subdivided between several buyers each responsible for a particular area of procurement as shown in Fig 3.3.

In designing departmental structures, it should be remembered that the greater the number of levels, e.g. purchasing director/manager, senior buyers, assistant buyers, the smaller will be the amount of delegated authority exercised by junior staff with the consequent de-motivation referred to in 7c above.

Among the bases on which purchasing may be subdivided are:

- by major groups of purchased items
- by the products for which purchased items are to be used, e.g. conveyors, cranes, buildings in an engineering company
- by stage of manufacture, e.g. raw materials, partly finished components, finished components
- by plant location, e.g. plant buyers in Sheffield, Middlesbrough and Stoke
- by customer, e.g. where an undertaking has a few major customers such as government departments

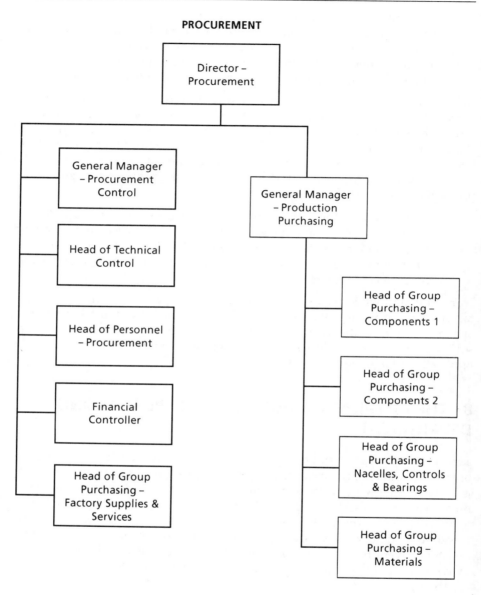

PROCUREMENT

Fig 3.3

Supporting services can be organised on a *vertical* or *horizontal* basis. In the vertical system, supporting services such as stock control, progressing and work processing are completely covered in each section and form a vertical line as in Fig 3.4. In the horizontal system services are distinct functions as shown in Fig 3.5.

The advantages of one system are largely the disadvantages of the other.

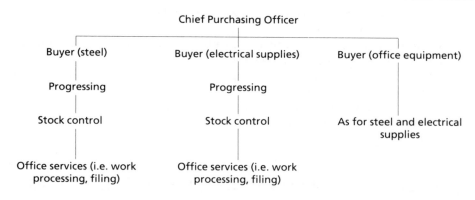

Fig 3.4 Supporting services (vertical structure)

(a) Advantages of a horizontal system

(i) Staff concentrate on a specific activity, such as stock control, in which they become specialist.

(ii) A specialised function such as stock control or progressing will be better able to assess the needs of the organisation as a whole and to adjudicate between pressure from different buyers.

(iii) Easier staff training programme.

(iv) Preparation of departmental statistical and other statements, e.g. disposal of scrap, is facilitated when such activities are the responsibility of a specialised section.

(v) Possibly increased job satisfaction for support staff since they report directly to the chief purchasing officer and not to a buyer.

(b) Disadvantages of a horizontal system

(i) Support staff attached to a particular section of buying will have a better knowledge of the work of that section.

(ii) Communication may be slower since a buyer requiring information on the

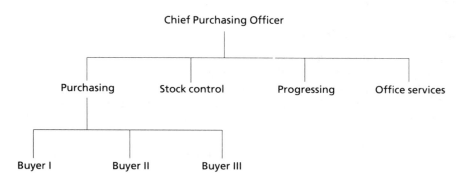

Fig 3.5 Supporting services (horizontal structure)

progress of an order has to refer the matter to another section head instead of someone in his own section.

(iii) Staff in an integrated section obtain a better grasp of how their function relates to the work of the whole section.

(iv) Irritation may be caused to suppliers when they deal with different sections for purchasing, progressing, etc.

(v) People employed in supporting activities, e.g. progressing, may have less opportunity of becoming buyers than if they were attached to a vertically integrated section.

9. PURCHASING AND ITS FUNCTIONAL RELATIONSHIPS

The systems approach to management. Many of the concepts of 'general systems theory' derive from the work of a German biologist, Ludwig von Bertalanffy, who defined a system as 'an organised or complex whole'. The word 'system' is now in common use, and we thus speak of computer and transport systems. Both cars and the human body are complex systems, each with a number of subsystems. Thus, cars have cooling, steering and suspension subsystems and the human body circulatory, nervous and respiratory subsystems. Similarly the departments of an organisation, e.g. design, production, marketing, finance, etc., can be considered as subsystems.

Systems theory distinguishes between *closed* and *open* systems. A *closed* system is isolated from and independent of its environment. An *open* system, such as a business organisation, is in constant interaction with its environment, receiving inputs such as labour, finance and materials, and through a series of activities transforms them into outputs such as information, services and products, as in Fig 3.6.

A system is healthy or 'in balance' when all the subsystems work together to achieve the corporate objectives of the organisation. Purchasing, as a subsystem, probably works most closely with the design and production departments. It also has close contacts with marketing and finance. Some areas in which consultation and co-operation may take place between purchasing and these four functions are listed below.

(a) Purchasing and design

(i) Preparation of specifications for purchased materials and components

(ii) Quality assurance or 'defect prevention'

(iii) Value engineering and value analysis

(iv) Information to design departments regarding availability of materials, suppliers and costs

Input	$\longrightarrow$	Transformation process	$\longrightarrow$	Output

Fig 3.6

(*v*) Agreement of alternatives when specified materials are not available

(*vi*) Issues arising from the increasing importance of buying rather than making, i.e. reduction of vertical integration

(*vii*) Importance of buying complete systems rather than individual components

(*viii*) Evaluation of cheaper alternative materials

(*ix*) Building co-makership/designership relationships

(*x*) Creation of a library of books, catalogues, journals and specifications for joint use by the design and purchasing departments.

(b) Purchasing and production of 'user' departments

(*i*) Preparation of material schedules showing how much is required, when and at what location

(*ii*) Negotiation of delivery schedules to meet Just-in-Time requirements

(*iii*) Ensuring that delivery schedules are maintained

(*iv*) Control of inventory to meet production requirements

(*v*) Disposal of scrap and obsolete items

(*vi*) Quality control or defect detection and correction

(*vii*) Approval of 'first-off' samples

(*viii*) Make or buy decisions

(*ix*) Sub-contracting decisions

(*x*) Supplier development

(*xi*) General involvement in such techniques and systems as Optimised Production Technology, Computer Integrated Technology and MRP and MRP II (see Chapters 7 and 8).

This functional approach in which purchasing works independently of other departments and setting its own objectives and rules, i.e. selecting the lowest price supplier and using multiple supply sources, may not coincide with the objectives of other functions. What purchasing perceives as the right quality, quantity, source, place and time might not be the case when viewed from the standpoints of design, production, finance or marketing.

In any event, materials management and logistics approaches (see later in this chapter) stress the need to build bridges across departmental divides. Such approaches aim to provide better co-ordination of functions through synchronous management of all the elements of the supply chain.

(c) Purchasing and marketing

(*i*) Provision of sales forecasts on which purchasing can base its forward planning of materials, components, etc

(*ii*) Ensuring that, by efficient buying, purchasing contributes to the maintenance of competitive prices

(*iii*) Obtaining materials on time to enable marketing and production to meet promised delivery dates

(*iv*) Exchange of information regarding customers and suppliers

(*v*) Marketing implications of partnership sourcing

(*vi*) Liaison with respect to reciprocal trading

(d) Purchasing and finance

(*i*) Budget preparation, since the 'limiting factor' for sales and production budgets is sometimes the availability of materials
(*ii*) Providing information in which standard material costs can be computed, and notifying variances
(*iii*) Ensuring that all other costing information relative to materials is accurate
(*iv*) Preparation of cost data for use in negotiation with suppliers
(*v*) Forward buying of goods and currencies
(*vi*) Certifying invoices for payment
(*vii*) Certifying progress payments
(*viii*) Agreeing price adjustments
(*ix*) Negotiating guarantee and warranty claims
(*x*) Reduction of administrative costs per purchase transaction by reduction or elimination of paperwork, e.g. dispensing with purchase order forms
(*xi*) Stocktaking, i.e. estimating the value of inventory for use in preparing the annual account
(*xii*) Advising on insurance in respect of inventory.

10. ORGANISATIONAL CONFLICT

Organisational conflict arises where there is a divergence of interests between individuals (interpersonal conflict) or groups (intergroup conflict) .

Intergroup conflict between purchasing and other departments has two characteristics:

- It is normally unorganised and expressed through negative actions such as withholding information or co-operation.
- It is usually lateral with other functional departments of approximately the same standing within the organisational hierarchy, e.g. production and quality control, finance.

Interfunctional conflict involving purchasing may arise from any of the following:

(*i*) Competition between purchasing and other functions involving the allocation of scarce resources, e.g. budget conflicts.
(*ii*) Role conflict arising from differing perspectives of organisational behaviour. For example, the purchasing department may assume that its role is to buy at the right price, time, quality, etc. which may entail buying from sources different to those prescribed by production, which assumes that its role includes the prerogative of specifying supply sources with purchasing only providing a servicing function. This can be an example of role ambiguity.
(*iii*) Differences between the objectives and priorities of purchasing and other functions, e.g. engineers are primarily concerned with quality and reliability and place less emphasis on such purchasing objectives as price and delivery.
(*iv*) Pressure from competing non-purchasing functions to adjudicate between them, e.g. where marketing seeks to reduce price at the expense of

quality. This adjudication expectancy arises from the centrality of the purchasing manager in the buying communication network.

(v) Pressure from other functions for purchasing to deviate from standard policy and procedures to meet their needs, e.g. rush orders, or favouring a particular supplier.

(vi) Conflict arising from attempts to extend the authority and status of the purchasing function, as Strauss observes [7]:

'The ambitious agent feels that placing orders and expediting deliveries are but the bare bones of his responsibilities. He looks upon his most important function as that of keeping management posted about market developments, new materials, new sources of supply, price trends and so forth. And to make this information more useful he asks to be consulted before the requisition is drawn up . . . He feels that his technical knowledge of the market should be accorded recognition equal to the technical knowledge of the engineer and accountant.'

Strauss has also identified six headings under which the techniques developed by purchasing for dealing with other departments may be summarised:

(1) *Rule-oriented tactics,* e.g. working to the book such as requiring all requests to purchase to be in writing.

(2) *Rule-evading tactics,* e.g. going through the motions of complying with requests to obtain urgent delivery but with no expectation that the demands will be satisfied.

(3) *Personal-political tactics,* e.g. the buyer projects an aura of friendship and exchanges favours.

(4) *Educational tactics,* e.g. direct and indirect persuasion designed to encourage members of other functions to think in purchasing terms and appreciate purchasing problems.

(5) *Organisational-interactional tactics,* e.g. seeking to have production planning confer with purchasing regarding the possibility of quick delivery before issuing a requisition.

(6) *Organisational change tactics,* e.g. where the buyer gradually attempts to evolve changes in organisation procedures such as placing other functions such as transport, stores and production planning in a combined materials management department.

In practice the purchasing department may use all the above tactics, adapting the tactic used to the particular problem. The concept of internal quality chains (see Chapter 7) should however ensure that such tactics are now regarded as outmoded.

Conflict within organisations is both inevitable and desirable, since it is both a cause and a consequence of change. Mary Parker Follett [8], an American writer on management, identified three methods of dealing with conflict:

(1) *Domination,* in which the stronger or more influential manager or function

wins by exploiting power. This approach only results in the perpetuation of grievances.

(2) *Compromise*, in which both sides give ground to secure a short-term resolution to the conflict. This approach rarely produces a satisfactory solution, since each contestant gives up something when neither wishes to give up anything.

(3) *Integration*, which Follett advocates, involves moving from conflicting ideas and attitudes to the discovery of common objectives, power *with* rather than power *over* people, joint responsibility and multiple leadership. This can only be achieved through:

- encouraging open communication
- providing facilities for continued consultation and negotiation, e.g. through the appointment of a representative of purchasing on appropriate committees concerned with design, budgeting and production, and through informal contacts between the executives responsible for these functions.

Other approaches to the resolution of inter-departmental conflict and the promotion of co-ordination include:

(a) **Task forces,** i.e. the creation of a temporary group of workers or managers to work on a project or solve a problem, e.g. the preparation of a procedure manual or the preparation of purchase or contract specification.

(b) **Team building** refers to an organised effort to improve the effectiveness of a selected group of managers/staff. Team building can be compared to the functioning of professional football teams based on the assumption that it is not sufficient to rest on past accomplishments but to strive for enhanced team effort based on such values as openness, listening, support, trust and risk taking.
  Team building involves concern for:

(i) The work itself including related processes, products, services, policies and objectives.
(ii) The 'team' itself and its functioning involving such factors as group needs, feedback and leadership style.

Team building can, however, only survive and be successful if the proper structure, commitment and resources are in place. Typical purchasing applications include participation in design teams, value analysis teams, supplier appraisal teams and quality circles.
  With partnership sourcing the 'team' may include representatives of suppliers.

(c) **Matrix structures.** These were first developed by the USA aerospace industry to meet demands that each government contract should be controlled by a single contract manager through whom all instructions and requests for information could be channelled. For general direction, team members report to the project leader. For technical expertise, however, they look to their functional

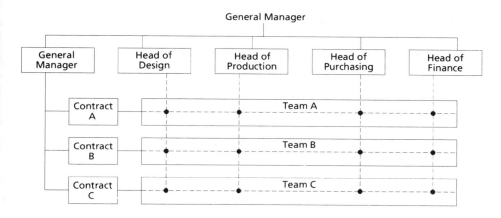

Fig 3.7 Typical matrix organisation structure

head. Attachment to a team is for the duration of the project. The matrix is simply constructed by overlaying a set of hierarchical connections over a first but at right angles as shown in Fig 3.7.

In practice matrix structures introduce the possibility of conflicts of command particularly where authority intersects. The authority of project managers often amounts to little more than persuasiveness. The major advantages and disadvantages of matrix structures are set out in Table 3.1.

Grinnel and Apple [9] state that matrix structures should be considered only in the following situations:

- when complex, short run products are an organisation's principal products, e.g. aerospace, construction contracts
- when a complicated product design calls for both innovation and timely completion

Table 3.1 Some major advantages and disadvantages of matrix structures

Advantages	Disadvantages
• Establishes one person as the focal point for all matters relating to the project	• Unity of command is lost (team members report to more than one head)
• Makes it possible to respond to needs of several projects simultaneously	• Authority and responsibilities of managers may overlap causing conflicts and gaps in effort across units and in respect of priorities
• Makes maximum use of a limited pool of functional specialists	
• Ensures that functional expertise is equally available to all projects	• Places a premium on teamwork
	• Slows down decision making
• Provides excellent training for running a diversified organisation	• It is difficult to explain to team members

- where a number of separate skills are needed in designing, building and testing a product – skills that need continual updating and development
- when a rapidly changing market calls for significant changes in products, perhaps even between their design and delivery.

(d) Networks. Purchasing managers, like other executives, fulfil their responsibilities through both internal and external relationships. Internal relationships include vertical relationships with a variety of supervisors and subordinates and lateral relationships with peers. They also include external relationships with suppliers of goods and services. Along with the marketing manager the head of purchasing is arguably the widest known person external to the organisation. The ability to develop, maintain and work well within networks is increasingly seen as an important aspect of purchasing management. Fig 3.8 depicts the complexity of the interpersonal networks maintained by purchasing managers.

(e) Supply chain management. This is defined by Cooper and Ellran [10] as 'an integrative philosophy to manage the total flow of a distribution channel from the supplier to the ultimate user'. The same writers state that supply chain management can be likened to a well balanced and practised relay team in which the entire team is co-ordinated to win the race. The supply chains may be 'primary' or 'support'. The former relate to those concerned with supplies to be used as a manufacture or re-sale to external customers, the latter to supplies bought for internal use. Approaches such as materials and logistics management aim to reduce interdepartmental conflict and promote interdepartmental co-ordination.

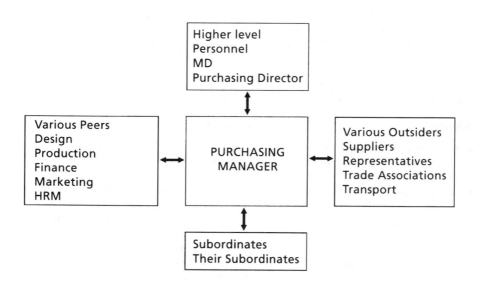

Fig 3.8 Vertical and lateral relationships of a purchasing manager's interpersonal networks

11. MATERIALS MANAGEMENT

(a) Introduction. A close analogy exists between materials management (MM) and marketing. With the latter the aim is to co-ordinate effectively a number of related activities, i.e. market research, product research, sales analysis, forecasting, promotion and selling, under one executive. MM seeks a similar co-ordination of activities relating to materials. The essence of the MM approach is shown by Dean S Ammer in Fig 3.9, where (a) and (b) represent the pre-MM and MM approaches respectively.

(b) Definitions

(i) 'Materials management is concerned with the flow of materials to and from the manufacturing departments.' (Dean S Ammer) [11].

(ii) Materials management is a co-ordinating function responsible for the planning and controlling of materials flow. Its objectives are as follows:
- *Maximise the use of the firm's resources*
- *Provide the required level of customer service.* (Arnold J R T) [12].

(iii) 'Materials management is the total of all those tasks, functions, activities and routines which concern the transfer of external materials and services into the organisation and the administration of the same until they are consumed or used in the process of production, operations or sale.' (Institute of Purchasing and Supply (GB).)

(a)

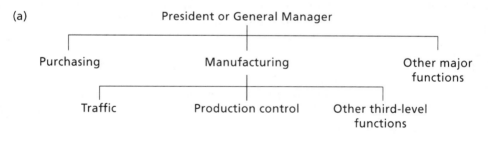

(b)

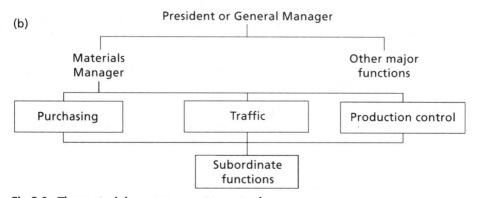

Fig 3.9 The materials management approach
(Source: Ammer D, 'Materials management as a profit centre'. *Harvard Business Review* (Jan–Feb 1969))

(iv) 'The management process which integrates the flow of supplies into, through and out of an organisation to achieve a level of service which ensures that the right materials are available at the right place at the right time, of the right quantity and quality and at the right cost. It includes the functions of procurement, materials handling and storage, production and inventory control, packaging, transport and associated information systems and their application throughout the supply, manufacturing, service and distribution sectors.' (The Institute of Materials Management (GB).)

(c) Activities assigned to materials management. The above definitions confirm Ammer's statement that there is no general agreement about precisely what activities are embraced in materials management [11]. He restricts the activity as extending to 'the point where manufacturing converts it [material] into a product', although he later concedes that the materials manager may also provide warehousing, traffic and transportation services for manufacturing and purchasing. The IPS definition also includes services. The Institute of Materials Management includes 'finished products' and 'distribution sectors' and very closely approaches the concept of logistics management (see below).

Some aspects of MM that may be included under one or other of the five principal stages of the materials 'flow' are:

Materials flow	**Typical activities**
Planning	Preparation of materials budgets, product research and development, value engineering and analysis, standardisation of specifications.
Procurement	Determining order quantities, processing of works and stores requisitions, issue of enquiries, evaluation of quotations, supplier appraisal, negotiation, placing of contracts, progressing of deliveries, certifying payments, vendor rating.
Storage	Stores location, layout and equipment, mechanical handling, stores classification, coding and cataloguing, receipt of purchased items, inspection, storage or return, protection of stores, issue to production, provision of cost data, stock records, disposal of obsolete, surplus or scrap material.
Production control	Forward ordering arrangements for materials, preparation of production schedules and sequences, issue of orders to production, emergency action to meet material shortages, make or buy decisions, quality and reliability feedback and adjustment of supplies flow to production line or sales trends.
Distribution	Warehousing, packaging, external transportation.

Some factors influencing the activities assigned to MM include the following:

(i) Purchasing is normally the 'key' activity.

(ii) Production planning and control may be assigned to MM or manufacturing. The former tends to apply when production is material oriented, e.g. in an assembly factory; the latter when production is machine/process oriented.

(iii) Receiving inspection is sometimes excluded from MM on the grounds that inspection should provide an independent check on purchasing efficiency.

(d) Appraising materials management. In general, the MM approach is especially applicable when:

- material costs make up a large part of total costs
- purchasing is regarded as a profit-oriented rather than a service function.

The advantages claimed for MM include the following:

(i) Improved co-ordination of related functions and a reduction in conflict between activities which, if departmentalised, might have differing objectives.

(ii) The MM approach facilitates the introduction of data processing and operational research techniques which improve decision-making, co-ordination and control. 'The growth of materials administration as a development of the systems approach to company control runs parallel with the increase in computer-oriented thinking in a large part of industry' (Ericsson).

(iii) Materials management encourages the co-ordination of materials 'flow' from the supplier to the plant once within the plant.

(iv) Reduction in costs of purchased items, inventory, materials handling, transportation, clerical procedures and staff.

(v) Improved supplier relations.

(vi) Improved customer service due to smoother scheduling of requirements and purchases.

(vii) Improved morale, especially for smaller subfunctions which recognise more clearly their contribution to the effectiveness of the organisation.

Some possible disadvantages are as follows:

(i) MM may be unsuitable for some undertakings, e.g. industries which process basic raw materials such as sugar where material prices are subject to frequent fluctuation and material quality is crucial.

(ii) Co-ordination between activities such as purchasing and production can be achieved through other co-ordinating mechanisms, e.g. committees or liaison personnel such as purchase liaison engineers. In any event the emphasis of modern management is on participation and consultation rather than autocratic relationships.

(iii) Materials managers having a sound grasp of all the diverse activities involved are difficult to recruit.

12. LOGISTICS MANAGEMENT

(a) Definitions

(i) 'The process of strategically managing the acquisition, movement and storage of materials, parts and finished inventory (and the related information flows) through the organisation and its marketing channels in such a way that current and future profitability is maximised through the cost-effective fulfilment of orders.' (Gattorna) [13]

(ii) 'Logistics is the total management of the key operational functions in the supply chain – procurement, production and distribution. Procurement includes purchasing and product development. The production function includes manufacturing and assembling, while the distribution function involves warehousing, inventory, transport and delivery.' (Knight Wendling) [14]

(iii) Logistics systems consist of the integration of procurement, transportation, inventory management and warehouse activities to provide the most cost-effective means of meeting internal and external customer requirements [15].

(iv) The process of managing both the movement and storage of goods and materials from the source to the point of ultimate consumption and the associated information flow [16].

(v) The time-related positioning of resources [17].

(b) The logistics concept. Logistics, from the French verb *lager* (to lodge or quarter), was initially a military term referring to the techniques of moving and quartering armies (i.e. quartermaster's work). Later, the expression was widened to mean the organisation of supplies.

Some definitions of both materials management (MM) and logistics management (LM) make it difficult to distinguish the activities that may be assigned to each field. It is, however, useful to differentiate between MM and physical distribution management (PDM). The former refers to the input phase of moving bought-out items such as raw materials and components from suppliers to production; the latter relates to the output phase of moving finished goods from the factory through the appropriate channels of distribution to the ultimate consumer. Figure 3.10 shows that activities such as storage, inventory control and transportation are common to both the input (MM) and output (PDM) phases and that logistics management subsumes both.

It has been stated that the perspective of the logistician is 'what flows can be made to flow faster'. From this standpoint, the logistician studies the costs incurred, beginning with the initial input factor, spanning the production process and terminating when the customer pays for the product or service received. The longer the time at each stage of the supply chain, the higher the costs incurred by the enterprise. A reduction in the time at any stage will provide an opportunity of cost reduction which can, in turn, lead to a reduction in price. This can be explained by the cost value curve shown in Fig 3.11.

(1) The lowest cost value is at the procurement stage when supplies are purchased.

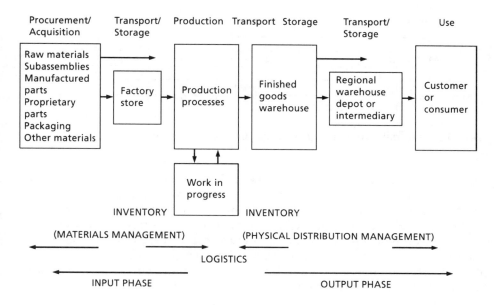

Fig 3.10 Scope of logistics management
(adapted from Gattorna J, Strategic issues in logistics, *Focus on Physical Distribution and Logistics Management* (Oct–Nov 1986))

(2) During transportation of supplies, value remains low because little capital is invested until raw material and components enter production; the only costs incurred refer to acquisition and holding costs (see 8:**6**).

(3) The curve becomes steeper as raw materials and components are gradually incorporated into the final product. This is because of accumulated manufacturing costs and increasing interest costs that reflect the value of the capital invested.

(4) The curve becomes flatter at the end of the production process because no more manufacturing costs apply. At this stage the invested capital is at its highest value and the cost of stocking finished goods instead of selling them involves higher opportunity costs than holding the initial supplies. This shows why the logistician is, if anything, more concerned with PDM than MM, since the potential for cost reduction is the highest at this point of the total supply chain. Cost reduction by speeding flows of materials, work in progress and finished

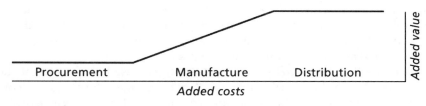

Fig 3.11 The added value aspect of logistics

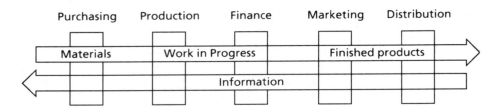

Fig 3.12 Material, product and information flows across an organisation

products is not the only concern of the logistician. Logistics management involves two flows. The first, as stated above, is the flow of materials and work in progress across the organisation to the ultimate customer. The second, as shown in Fig 3.12, is a reverse flow of information in the form of orders or other indicators on which future demand forecasts can be based. Such forecasts, as Gattorna states, can in turn 'trigger replenishment orders which produce inventories at distribution centres. These orders influence production schedules which, in turn, help determine the timing and quantities with which raw materials are procured.'

Logistics management should be regarded as a total system rather than a function. Essentially it is a way of thinking about, planning and synchronising related activities. Figure 3.12 also shows how logistics management crosses conventional functions.

(c) Some important logistics concepts

(1) *Total systems management*, emphasising a total rather than a limited departmental viewpoint. Total systems management has been facilitated by the availability of information technology.

(2) *Trade-offs*. A trade-off is where an increased cost in one area is more than offset by a cost reduction in another, so that the whole system benefits. This may give rise to interdepartmental conflicts due to different objectives. Thus, purchasing may advocate bulk purchases of materials to secure larger supplier discounts. This policy might be opposed by finance because of money tied up in working capital and by inventory because of the increased cost of warehousing. The conflict should be settled on the basis of which policy yields the greater trade-off. Similarly, purchasing may have to consider whether the security of supply consequent on having a number of suppliers is offset by the economies resulting from lower ordering costs and larger production runs obtained from single-source buying. Thus, the effects of trade-offs may be assessed by their impacts on total systems cost and sales revenue.

Thus, higher inventory costs may result from increased stocks, yet quicker delivery may increase total sales revenue. Obtaining the information to computer trade-offs requires the breaking down of functional barriers which protect departmental 'territory' and discourage information sharing.

(3) *Co-operative planning.* This can work forwards to customers and backwards to suppliers. The change from product- to customer-oriented supply chains, and thus faster supply responses, can provide customers with alternatives such as make to stock, make to order and finish to order. Conversely, from the inward supply side, effective co-operative planning may relate to zero defects, on-time delivery, shared products and information exchanges relating to such matters as shared specifications, design support, multi-year commitments, technology exchange. Overall, both supply and customer can benefit from reduced costs of inventory, capacity, order-handling and administration. This utilises, as appropriate, manufacturing and scheduling techniques including:

Manufacturing
    Computer Aided Design (CAD)
    Computer Integrated Manufacture (CIM)
    Flexible Manufacturing Systems (FMS)
    Materials Requirements Planning (MRP)
    Manufacturing Resources Planning (MRP II)
    Optimised Production Technology (OPT)
    Strategic Lead Time Management (STM)

Production
    Just-in-Time (JIT)
    Materials Requirements Planning (MRP)
    Manufacturing Resources Planning (MRP II)

(d) Logistics management objectives. The whole purpose of logistics is to provide 'availability'. Everyone will be familiar with the old cliché, 'the right product in the right place at the right time'. If one adds 'at the least cost' then that is precisely the objective of logistics management.

Apart from reduced costs and increased availability, logistics management seeks to:

(i) reduce conflict and promote co-operation and co-ordination between subsystems concerned with material and information flows, based on the recognition that their activities are interrelated and interdependent

(ii) reduce the time spent at every stage of the chain from procurement to delivery to the customer, i.e. lead time, production time, transportation time

(iii) add value at every step of the logistics 'pipeline'

(iv) ensure the highest possible level of customer service and satisfaction by achieving the right combination of product availability and dependability

(v) control and, where possible, reduce inventory of materials, work in progress and finished goods to provide stock levels at which the costs of stockholding are balanced by production requirements and customer service

(vi) encourage a commitment to quality improvement so that both bought-out supplies and the products in which they are incorporated are right first time, every time.

13. THE CONTRIBUTION OF PURCHASING TO MM AND LM

Developments such as MM and LM can both change and enhance the role of
purchasing. MM and LM will tend to lead to more buying out rather than the
making of components and will thus both increase the value of purchases and
enhance the importance of quality and reliability of supplies. It is for this reason
that the education and training of purchasing personnel is incomplete without
a knowledge of MM and LM.

Purchasing can contribute to MM and LM by:

(i) linking the external supply network with production, transportation and
marketing

(ii) providing suppliers with accurate forecasts of requirements, lead times
and delivery quantities

(iii) appraising potential vendors from the standpoint of their capacity and
capability to provide

  quality

  delivery at specified times and in required quantities (JIT)

  proximity to purchase

  technical and commercial co-operation

  competitive prices

  financial stability

  modern plant and technology

  communication, e.g. electronic data exchange

  transportation

(iv) evaluating the performance of selected vendors

(v) reducing the number of suppliers and developing co-makership and
long-term stable relationships with those retained

(vi) reducing inventory by negotiating required lead times and the application
of MRP I, MRP II and JIT approaches

(vii) securing the maximum possible reductions in material and ancillary costs
through the implementation of value analysis, value engineering and quality
circle techniques

(viii) negotiating, where appropriate, the best possible arrangements and
terms in respect of transportation and distribution.

References

[1] Hay M and Williamson P. *The Strategy Handbook.* Blackwell, 1991, pp 194–195.
[2] Quoted in Mintzberg H and Quinn J B. *The Strategy Process.* Prentice Hall, 1991, Ch. 6,
p 311.
[3] Audit Commission. *Improving Supply Management in Local Authorities.* HMSO 1987,
p 14.
[4] Cammish and Keough. *A strategic role for purchasing.* McKinsey Quarterly No 3, 1991,
pp 22–39.
[5] See Price J L. *The impact of departmentalisation on inter-occupational co-operation. Human
Organisation* 27, 1968, pp 362–368.

[6] Mintzberg H. *The Nature of Managerial Work.* Harper and Row, 1973, pp 54–99.

[7] See Strauss, G. (1962) . *Tactics of lateral relationships: the purchasing agent. Administrative Science Quarterly*, 7(2) pp 161–186.

[8] Follet, M P. *Constructive Conflict* in Metcalf and Urwick *Dynamic Administration.* Pitman, 1963, pp 30–49.

[9] Grinnel S K and Apple H P. *When two bosses are better than one. Machine Design.* Jan 9 1975, p 86.

[10] Cooper M C and Ellram L M (1993) . *Characteristics of supply chain management and the implications of purchasing and logistics strategy. International Journal of Logistics Management.* Vol 4, No 2, pp 13–24.

[11] Ammer D S. *Materials management as a profit centre. Harvard Business Review.* Jan–Feb 1969.

[12] Arnold J R T. *Introduction to Materials Management.* Prentice Hall, 1991, Chap 1, p 4.

[13] Gattorna J. *Effective Logistics Management.* MBC University Press, 1994.

[14] Knight Wendling. *Logistics Report.* 1988 (published for private circulation).

[15] Burgh J G. *Cost and Management Accounting.* West Publishing, 1994, Chap 13, p 607.

[16] Compton H K and Jessop D. *Dictionary of Purchasing and Supply Management.* Pitman, 1995, p 111.

[17] Institute of Logistics (UK): publicity pamphlet 1995.

Progress test 3

1. What are the main elements of 'organisation structure?

2. What are some of the factors which influence purchasing organisation?

3. There are several approaches to the centralisation of purchasing'. Name three such approaches.

4. The development of purchasing within an organisation can be traced through four stages. Name the four stages.

5. In what ways can centralised purchasing enable an undertaking to use its bargaining power or 'leverage'?

6. What are some of the disadvantages of departmentalisation?

7. In group undertakings purchasing is undertaken both centrally and at plant level. Indicate some purchasing activities that may properly be carried out at each level.

8. State some of the ways in which co-ordination between central purchasing and users or other functions may be achieved.

9. What are the ten senior management roles identified by Mintzberg?

10. What factors may influence the level at which purchasing operates within an undertaking?

11. What are the advantages of (i) horizontal and (ii) vertically organised purchasing departments?

12. List some of the matters regarding which the purchasing executive might liaise with (a) finance and (b) marketing?

13. Why might conflict arise between purchasing and other functions?

14. What are some advantages and disadvantages of matrix structures?

15. Define the term Materials Management.

16. What activities might be assigned to Materials Management?

17. Define Logistics Management.

18. What, in the context of logistics management, are 'trade-offs'?

19. List the objectives of logistics management.

20. What are some of the contributions that purchasing can make to MM and LM?

21. Theoretically it can be argued that the concept of materials management is logical and sound, but in practice it can create many problems and consequently some of the benefits claimed for it are questionable. Discuss this statement.

    (IPS. *Purchasing and Supply Management* (1988))

22. Using a specific department as an example, explain the importance to an organisation as a whole of sound co-operative relationships between that department and the supply function.

    (IPS. *Introduction to Purchasing and Supply* (1988))

23. Examine the costs and benefits inherent in the operation of a totally integrated, predominantly automated logistics system of a distribution centre used by a large retail food chain.

    (IPS. *Logistics* (1991))

24. Explain how efficient logistics management can help a manufacturing company achieve it corporate goals.

    (IPS. *Logistics* (1990))

25. If purchasing and supply is to develop in the long term, it must improve the quality and level of its interface with other functional areas. Examine the ways in which purchasing and supply might achieve such an objective.

    (IPS. *Planning, Policy and Organisation* (1991))

26. It is often said that 'strategy determines structure'. Explain the meaning of this statement in the organisation of purchasing and supply activities.

(IPS. *Planning, Policy and Organisation* (1993))

27. The quality of the interface that the purchasing activity has within an organisation is an important indication of its effectiveness. Explain how the purchasing activity can improve such interfaces and the likely benefits.

(IPS. *Planning, Policy and Organisation* (1993))

4

PURCHASING PROCEDURES, DOCUMENTATION AND RECORDS

1. INTRODUCTION

In Fig 2.1 it is stated that procedures are a system of sequential steps or techniques describing how a task or job is done. Rules are extensions of procedures and are directives relating to specific activities which sometimes specify penalties for their breach.

Procedures are also the formal arrangements through which policies linking strategy formulation at all levels are implemented. A cluster of related procedures each consisting of a number of operations which together provide information enabling staff to execute or managers to control an activity is termed a *system*.

2. BASIC PURCHASING PROCEDURE

Apart from pre-purchase activities such as participation in design and budget decisions, all purchasing falls into three main phases.

(a) The notification phase. Notification of the need to purchase is usually in the form of either:

    (i) a requisition issued by the stores or stock control, or
    (ii) a bill of materials issued by the drawing office or control departments.

(b) The ordering phase. On receipt of the requisition or bill of materials the buyer responsible will check them for accuracy, conformity to any standard specifications and with purchase records to ensure whether the items have been previously purchased and, if so, in what quantities and the sources of supply.

If the item is standard and has been previously purchased from a satisfactory supplier at an acceptable price, a repeat order may be issued.

If, however, the item is not standard and has not been ordered before, or for some reason a change of supplier is required, the following additional steps will be involved:

(i) Enquiries will be sent to possible suppliers accompanied by additional documents, e.g. drawings, specifications, etc. which will enable them to quote.
(ii) Quotations will be received in response to the enquiries and compared with respect to price, quality, delivery, tool costs, etc. and terms of business.
(iii) When quantities are substantial and quality and/or delivery of great importance, further negotiation with suppliers including an evaluation of their capacity to undertake the order may be required.
(iv) A purchase order will be issued to the vendor whose quotation, amended where necessary by subsequent negotiation, is most acceptable. A copy of the order will be retained in the purchasing department. (Sometimes two copies are retained for filing alphabetically and numerically.) Further copies of the order may be provided for:

(1) department originating requisition
(2) progress section
(3) stores
(4) production control
(5) computer section
(6) accounts
(7) inspection.

(v) An order acknowledgement should be required from the vendor. On receipt the acknowledgement should be examined to ensure that the order has been accepted on the terms and conditions agreed and filed.

(c) The post-ordering phase

(i) It may be necessary to progress the order to ensure that delivery dates are met or to expedite delivery of overdue orders.
(ii) An *advice note* notifying that the goods have been despatched or are ready for collection will be issued by the supplier. Copies of the advice note may be sent to relevant departments, e.g. progress and stores.
(iii) On receipt, the goods will be checked for quantity by the stores. Where matters of quality or specification are involved they will be examined by the inspection department. If satisfactory, a *goods received note* will be completed and copies sent to the purchasing department. If not satisfactory, the purchasing department will be notified so that the complaint can be taken up with the supplier.
(iv) An *invoice* for the value of the goods will be received from the supplier. This will be compared with the purchase order and goods received note. Usually prices will be checked by the purchasing department, paying special attention to the legitimacy of any variations from the quoted price. If satisfactory, the invoice will be passed to the accounts department for payment.
(v) On completion the order will be transferred to a 'completed orders file'.

3. PURCHASING DOCUMENTATION

For the reasons indicated in 5:3, very few organisations of any size now utilise manual purchasing systems. A knowledge of basic documentation is, however, still required, firstly to understand the purposes of documents and, secondly, where appropriate, their legal significance.

(a) Basic documents. With both manual and computerised purchasing systems, the basic documents used in purchasing are:

(i) Purchase requisitions or bills of materials
(ii) Enquiry forms
(iii) Purchase orders
(iv) In addition, special forms may be used to confirm cancellations or amendments to orders, or for such purposes as analysis of quotations, vendor appraisal, etc.

(b) Purchase requisitions

(1) *Purpose*
- to notify the purchasing department that a need exists
- to specify what is required to meet the need
- to authorise procurement
- to provide evidence as to what was requisitioned, when and by whom.

(2) *Number of copies.* Normally two copies are sufficient, one for transmission to purchasing and one for retention by the issuing department.

(3) *Entries.* The information entered on the form will usually include:
- the title, i.e. 'Purchasing Requisition', at the head of the form
- a formal instruction to the purchasing department, e.g. 'Please order . . .'
- requisition number
- date prepared
- quantity of goods required
- description of goods required
- suggested supplier
- stores identification
- date by which goods are required
- location to which goods are to be delivered
- special instructions (if any)
- account or code number against which the requisitioned items are to be charged
- 'requisitioned by'
- 'authorised by'
- space for order number to be inserted.

(c) Bill of materials or parts list

(1) *Purpose.* These serve the same purposes as a purchase requisition in

engineering undertakings when materials and components are bought specifically for each order or contract received.

(2) *Number of copies.* A parts list is either attached to the drawing or printed on the drawing. Engineering buyers check each part against the drawing and indicate in the order number column whether it is to be provided from stock or 'bought out'. In the latter case the purchase order number will be entered before the drawing is passed to production control where the appropriate number of drawings will be marked up in accordance with the marked-up list received from purchasing, for issue to the manufacturing departments when bought-out items have been received.

(3) *Entries* The information provided will include:

- drawing reference
- 'number of' each part reference
- description of each part
- remarks column
- order number or stock column.

(d) Enquiry forms

(1) *Purpose.* To obtain information from possible suppliers relating to price, quality, delivery and terms of business for bought-out items.

(2) *Number of copies.* One copy will be kept for reference in the purchasing department. Two copies, one for retention the other for return, will be sent to each prospective supplier who is asked to quote. The number of vendors approached will depend on the importance of the order but a minimum of three is usual. The enquiry should be accompanied by drawings, specifications and the buyer's terms and conditions of purchase.

(3) *Entries.* The information entered on the form will usually include:

- the title, i.e. 'Purchase Enquiry', at the head of the form
- name, address, telephone number, etc. of the purchaser
- a formal request to the vendor, e.g. 'Please quote best price and earliest delivery . . .'
- name and address of vendor
- date
- purchaser's reference
- quantity required
- short descriptions of items required
- delivery date required
- place of delivery
- space for vendor to indicate price
- space for vendor to indicate payment terms
- space for vendor to indicate delivery
- signature of person preparing quotation
- requisition reference
- order number reference (for use if quotation is accepted).

(e) Purchase order forms

(1) *Purpose.* To communicate to the supplier particulars of the purchaser's requirements, the price and delivery applicable and the conditions on which the order is placed. A purchaser's order becomes a legal contract:

- when it constitutes an acceptance by the buyer of a formal quotation submitted by the vendor
- when it is accepted unconditionally by the vendor if it is submitted without a prior quotation to the buyer.

(2) *Number of copies.* One copy will be sent to the supplier (two where the order incorporates an acknowledgement for the supplier to return). The number of copies made for internal use varies. In addition to those retained in the purchasing department, copies may also be sent to other departments as indicated in **2(b)** (iv).

(3) *Entries.* The information entered on the form will usually include:

- the title, i.e. 'Purchase Order', at the head of the form
- name, address, telephone number, etc. of the purchaser
- order number
- a formal instruction to the vendor, e.g. 'Please supply'
- name and address of the vendor
- supplier's reference
- purchaser's reference
- name and telephone extension of buyer to contact in respect of queries
- quantity(ies) of item(s) to be supplied
- description(s) of item(s) to be supplied
- reference to any drawings, specifications, terms and conditions of purchase
- purchase price(s)
- terms of payment
- delivery date
- VAT reference number
- delivery address (if different from that at head of form)
- any special instructions for packaging or transportation
- requisition number
- signature of person authorised to issue the order

In addition the purchase order form may include:

- acknowledgement for return by supplier
- terms and conditions of purchase on reverse of form.

Purchase order forms vary widely in format and attempts at standardisation so far have been unsuccessful. A format is recommended by the BSI but it is doubtful if one form in actual use conforms to this layout. Nevertheless, students should be aware of this standard (BS 1808), as shown in Fig 4.1.

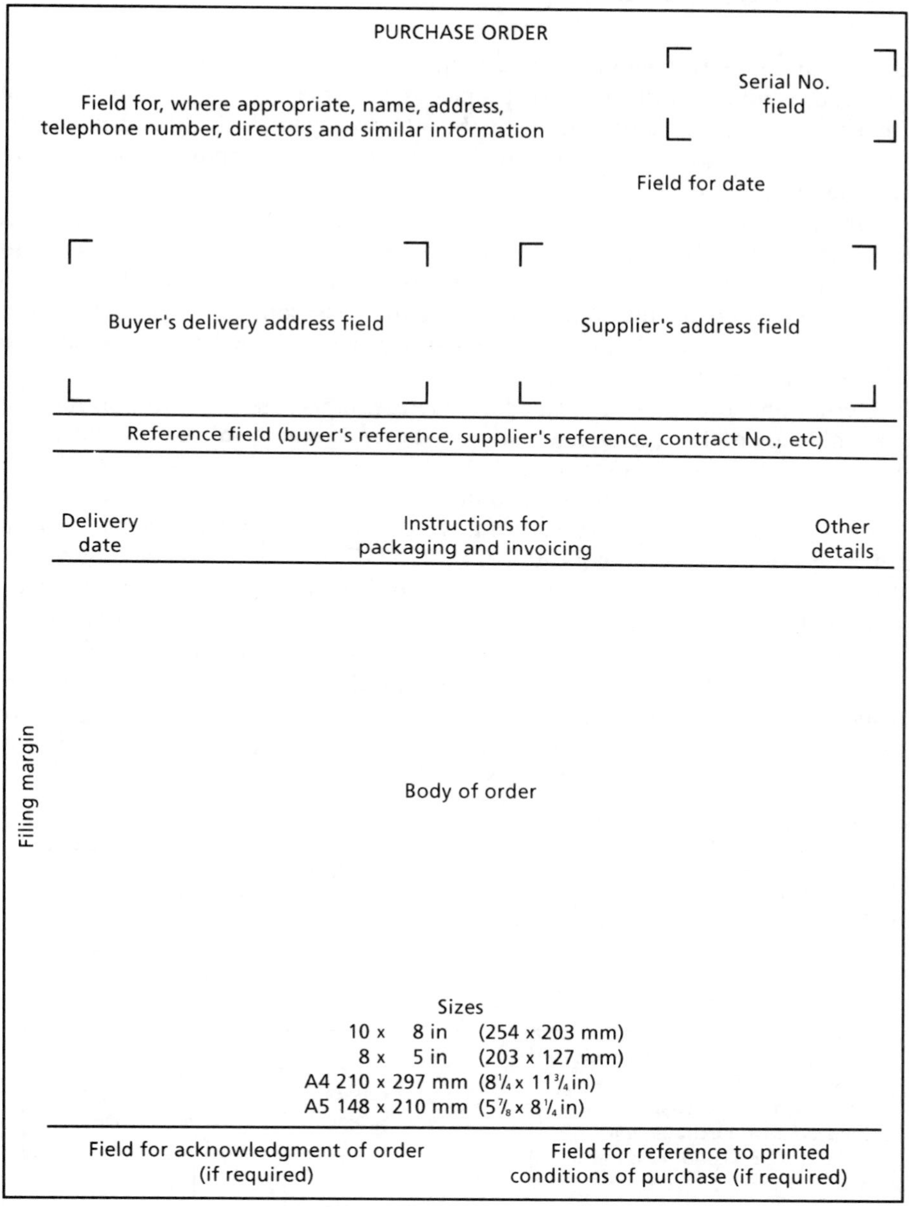

PURCHASE ORDER

Serial No.
field

Field for, where appropriate, name, address,
telephone number, directors and similar information

Field for date

Buyer's delivery address field

Supplier's address field

Reference field (buyer's reference, supplier's reference, contract No., etc)

| Delivery date | Instructions for packaging and invoicing | Other details |

Filing margin

Body of order

Sizes
10 x 8 in (254 x 203 mm)
8 x 5 in (203 x 127 mm)
A4 210 x 297 mm (8$\frac{1}{4}$ x 11$\frac{3}{4}$ in)
A5 148 x 210 mm (5$\frac{7}{8}$ x 8$\frac{1}{4}$ in)

| Field for acknowledgment of order (if required) | Field for reference to printed conditions of purchase (if required) |

Fig 4.1 British Standard purchase order (BS 1808)

4. 'THE BATTLE OF THE FORMS'

One of the essential elements of a valid contract (i.e. a contract that can be enforced) is an unconditional acceptance by the offeree (i.e. the party to whom the offer is made) of an offer made by the other party known as the offerer. If the acceptance seeks to vary the terms of the offer in any way there is a counter-offer and the original offer lapses.

Thus, in the case of *Hyde* v. *Wrench* (1840), Wrench (W) offered to sell a farm to Hyde (H) for £1000. H replied offering £950 which W refused and without informing H of his intention sold the farm elsewhere. Hyde later wrote accepting the original price of £1000 and, on finding the farm sold, sued W for breach of contract. The court held that the counter-offer of £950 rejected the original offer which could only be revived by W.

Quotations, order forms and acknowledgements often contain, on their reverse side, or make reference to, standard conditions of sale or purchase. The situation that can arise is shown in Fig 4.2.

The term 'battle of forms' was coined by Lord Denning in the case of *Butler Machine To Co Ltd* v. *Ex-Cell-O Corporation (England) Ltd* (1979) which arose from differing sets of standard conditions. Butler M T, the sellers, made a quotation offering to sell a machine tool to Ex-Cell-O, the buyers, for £75,000. The offer was stated to be subject to terms and conditions which 'shall prevail over any terms and conditions in the Buyer's order'. These included a price variation clause for the goods to be charged at the price ruling on the date of delivery. The buyers ordered the machine, their order being subject to terms and conditions materially different from those of the sellers and containing no price variation clause. At

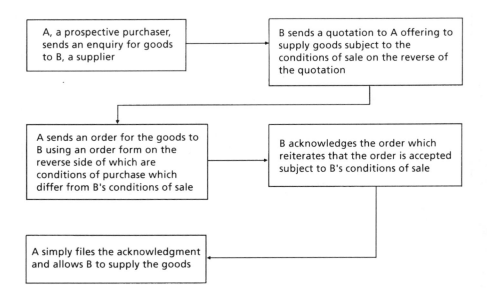

Fig 4.2 In the event of a dispute between A and B which conditions prevail?

the foot of the buyers' order was a tear-off acknowledgement of receipt of the order stating: 'We accept your order on the Terms and Conditions stated thereon'. The acknowledgement was completed by the sellers and returned to the buyers with a letter stating that the buyers' order was being entered in accordance with the seller's quotation.

On delivery the sellers claimed a price increase of £2892 which the buyers refused to pay. The sellers brought an action claiming that the variation clause entitled them to increase their price. Although the buyers contended that the contract had been concluded on their terms and was therefore a fixed price contract the Judge found for the sellers on the grounds that the contract had been concluded on the basis that the sellers' terms were to prevail since price variation was stipulated in the opening offer and this applied to subsequent negotiations.

This verdict was, however, reversed on appeal on the grounds that the sellers, by completing and returning the buyers' acknowledgement slip, had accepted the counter-offer on the buyers' terms and could not therefore claim to increase the price under the price variation clause contained in their offer. The sellers' letter referring to the quotation was irrelevant since it referred only to the price and identity of the machine and did not incorporate the sellers' terms into the contract.

The case is important since it emphasises that whether the buyers' or sellers' terms and conditions apply depends on the facts of the case. As Lord Denning stated:

> In most cases when there is battle of forms there is a contract as soon as the last of the forms is sent and received without any objection being taken to it. . . . The difficulty is to decide which form or part of which form is a term or condition of the contract. In some cases the battle is won by the man who fires the last shot. He is the man who puts forward the latest terms and conditions and if they are not objected to by the other party, he may be taken to have agreed to them. In some cases the battle is won by the man who gets his blow in first. . . . There are yet other cases where the battle depends on the shots fired by both sides. . . . The terms and conditions of both parties are to be construed together.

Thus in the situation shown in Fig 4.2 it would be the seller's terms and conditions that would probably prevail.

It is advisable for buyers to include a clause in their conditions of purchase stating that liability will only be accepted for orders placed subject to the terms and conditions stated on their order forms which the seller accepts by signing and returning an acknowledgement form referring to those conditions within a stipulated time, e.g. 14 days.

5. PURCHASING RECORDS

Purchasing records are concerned with the storage of information. With manual systems this information will be entered on card indexes or filed in appropriate systems. Computerisation using master files or databases not only enables vast amounts of information to be stored but also obviates duplication and ensures the efficient retrieval of data. It would be impracticable to reproduce rulings or purchase records in this book. Apart from files of requisitions, purchase orders and other original documents, purchase records may include:

- supplier index giving details of addresses, telephone, staff and items supplied
- supplier rating giving details of supplier performance relating to price, quality, delivery, etc
- supplier visits giving details of visits paid to suppliers to inspect their facilities
- record of items purchased giving details of standard descriptions of bought-out items and particulars of suppliers and the orders placed
- price trends of 'sensitive' commodities – graphs of the trend of prices
- records of material issued to subcontractors
- jigs, tools and patterns owned by the purchaser whether in the possession of suppliers or otherwise
- contract records, i.e. contracts for the supply of materials or components over a specified period of time and quantities called off against them
- order registers providing a record of all orders placed each day to:
   (i) facilitate reference to orders placed and filed alphabetically, numerically or by project
   (ii) provide information regarding the number of orders placed during a given period
   (iii) facilitate checking actual against budgeted purchasing expenditure.

6. SIMPLIFYING PROCEDURES

For manual procedures this can be done in several ways including the simultaneous preparation of forms, combining forms and simplified procedures for small, low value or routine orders.

(a) **Simultaneous preparation of forms.** This usually involves the use of a unit set consisting of a pad of two or more forms which can be completed simultaneously in one writing, e.g. copies of a requisition for forwarding to purchasing and retention for record purposes by the originator. Word processing has virtually eliminated the production of multiple copies by typewriter. 'Writing', in this context, can be manual by ball-point pen or any form of text-processing.

(b) **Combining or eliminating forms.** Some examples include:

- *Travelling requisitions.* These, used for repetitive purchases, are kept in the stores or department responsible for issuing the requisition. As shown by Fig 4.3 the requisition, printed on thick card for durability, gives details of what is required and provides a history of orders placed for the item. Frequently the prices column is omitted. When stocks need replenishing the left-hand columns are completed and the requisition sent to the purchasing department where the columns relating to the items

TRAVELLING REQUISITION

Stock No ....   Title ....   Card No ....

Specification ....   Max Stock ....

Supplier   (1) ....   Order Point ....

               (2) ....   Min Stock ....

               (3) ....

Data	Stock	Quantity Required	Date Required	Approved by	Date received by Purchasing	Order No.	Supplier	Quantity Ordered	Price each	Delivery	Remarks

Fig 4.3 Travelling requisition form

purchased are filled in and the card returned to the stores. Considerable writing is thus obviated and inaccuracies in transcript eliminated.

- Combined requisition/enquiry forms
- Combined requisition/purchase order forms
- Combined purchase order/acknowledgement forms
- Combined purchase order/goods received noted.

(c) Simplified procedures for small value orders. Foryszewski [1] states that research in the UK and US has shown that for major corporations 60% of the volume of purchasing and accounts payables transactions (generally £500 or less, but the threshold varies) often represents only 5% of the total value of purchase expenditure. It therefore follows that 60% of administrative effort is directed at only 5% of spend. Estimates of processing costs vary but estimates of £30-£75 per transaction are not uncommon. Low-value orders therefore both increase costs and hamper both purchasing and accounting productivity. A low-cost, by-pass system is required to efficiently handle low-value purchases. Some methods are:

(i) Telephone orders. The requirements are telephoned to the supplier who is provided with an order number against which the goods can be invoiced but no order is sent.

(ii) Credit cards, e.g. Access, Amex, Barclaycard, Visa Purchasing, etc. Employees who would normally initiate purchase requisitions are provided with a Purchasing Card to procure goods and services from suppliers up to a designated limit. Suppliers request authorisation to proceed which is transmitted for approval to the purchasing organisation's bank. After authorisation the supplier delivers the goods and receives payment from the bank. The accounts department of the purchasing organisation pays against the monthly cardholder statement subject to prior verification of transactions by the purchasing manager. Special procedures are required in respect of VAT charges and recovery.

(iii) Petty cash purchases. Items obtained directly from local suppliers on presentation of an authorised requisition and paid for at once from petty-cash. The main problem is that of controlling the number and size of purchases. This can be done by providing the purchasing department with a petty cash imprest out of which such purchases are made.

(iv) Standing orders. These are placed for small, regularly required items, e.g. food, newspapers; the supplier contracts to deliver until the order is countermanded and submits an invoice at monthly intervals.

(v) Blanket orders. All orders for a range of items, e.g. electrical fittings or stationery, are placed with one supplier for a period of twelve months. A special discount is often negotiated and quantities may or may not be specified. Required items are called off by user departments usually by the purchasing department against the blanket order.

(vi) Stockless buying. This is virtually the same as the blanket order system but the supplier agrees to maintain stocks of specified items.

(vii) Blank-cheque orders. A system devised in the USA in which a cheque form with a specified liability limit is incorporated into the order form. On forwarding the goods, the supplier fills in the cheque which he deposits in his own bank. The need for invoicing and forwarding of payment is thus avoided.

(viii) Self-billing. This usually utilises EDI. Pugsley [2] for example reports that when the Rover Group which trades electronically receives goods from a supplier, it checks that the goods were ordered and then simply pays. The supplier does not need to raise an invoice. Self-billing therefore means that both customer and supplier can make savings.

7. PURCHASING MANUALS

(a) Purchasing manual. Essentially this is a medium for communicating information regarding purchasing policies, procedures, instructions and regulations.

(i) Policies: may be general or consequential. *General* policies state in broad terms the objectives and responsibilities of the purchasing function. *Consequential* policies state, in expanded form, how general policies are applied in specific activities and situations, e.g. the selection of suppliers.

(ii) Procedures: prescribe the sequence of actions by which policies are implemented, e.g. the receipt of bought-out goods.

(iii) Instructions: give detailed knowledge or guidance to those responsible for carrying out the policies or procedures, e.g. the number of copies of a purchase order required and their distribution.

(iv) Regulations: detailed rules regarding the conduct of purchasing and ancillary staff in the various situations arising in the course of their duties, e.g. concerning the receipt of gifts from suppliers.

When drafting a purchasing manual it is useful to keep these distinctions clearly in mind.

(b) Advantages. The advantages claimed for purchasing manuals include the following:

(i) Writing helps precision and clarity.

(ii) The preparation of a manual provides an opportunity for consultation between purchasing and other departments, to look critically at existing policies and procedures and, where necessary, to change them.

(iii) Procedures are prescribed in respect of activities undertaken or controlled by purchasing, thus promoting consistency and reducing the need for detailed supervision of routine tasks.

(iv) A manual is a useful aid in training and guiding staff.

(v) A manual can help the annual audit.

(vi) A manual co-ordinates policies and procedures and helps to ensure uniformity and continuity of purchasing principles and practice. It also provides a point of reference against which such principles and practice can be evaluated.

(vii) A manual may help to enhance the status of purchasing by showing that top management attaches importance to the procurement function.

(viii) Computerisation, which needs detailed and well-documented systems, has given further impetus to the preparation of purchasing manuals.

(c) Disadvantages. The disadvantages urged against manuals are as follows:

(i) Manuals are costly to prepare.

(ii) Manuals tend to foster red tape and bureaucracy and stifle initiative.

(iii) Manuals must be continually updated to show changes in procedures and policy.

(d) Format. A manual should be:

(i) Normally of A4 size

(ii) Loose-leaf, to permit the issue of sections to separate parts of the organisation and insertion of amendments

(iii) Simply written and illustrated by relevant flowcharts, etc.

(iv) Well produced, easily handled, durable and clearly printed.

The main factors to be considered when deciding on the format are:

- durability of content
- ease of storage
- ease of reference
- legibility
- portability
- ease of updating by user
- ease of updating by author
- compactness
- cost.

(e) Contents. A purchasing manual may consist of three main sections dealing respectively with organisation, policy and procedures.

(i) Organisation
- Charts showing the place of purchasing within the undertaking and how it is organised both centrally and locally
- Job descriptions for all posts within the purchasing function including, where applicable, limitations of authority to commit the undertaking
- Administrative information for staff, e.g. absences, hours of work, travelling expenses, etc.

(ii) Policy
- Statements of policy setting out the objectives, responsibilities and authority of the purchasing function
- Statements, which can be expanded, of general principle relating to price, quality, etc.
- Terms and conditions of purchase
- Relationships with suppliers, especially regarding gifts, entertainment, etc.
- Supplier selection
- Employee purchases
- Reports to management.

(iii) Procedures
- Descriptions, accompanied by flowcharts, of procedures relating to requisitioning, ordering, expediting, receiving, inspecting, storing and payment for goods
- Procedures relating to the rejection and return of goods
- Procedures in respect of the disposal of scrap and obsolete or surplus items
- Illustrations of all documents used in connection with purchasing and ancillary activities, with instructions for their use and circulation
- Reference to purchase records and their maintenance.

(f) Distribution. Complete copies of the manual should be sent to:

(i) the board of directors or similar body
(ii) the chief executive of the undertaking

(iii) heads of departments with whom purchasing has functional contacts
(iv) members of the purchasing staff both centrally and locally.

Sections of the manual may be sent to:

(v) activities or functions controlled by purchasing, e.g. stores
(vi) other functions within the organisation, e.g. marketing, production etc.
(vii) suppliers.

References

[1] Foryszewski Stefan. *Visa offers a solution to low value purchasing. Purchasing and Supply Management.* Feb 1995, pp 26–27.
[2] Pugsley W. *EDI implementation – who is in the driving seat? Purchasing and Supply Management.* May 1994, pp 22–23.

Progress test 4

1. List the main steps involved in purchasing procedure from the receipt of a requisition to the payment of the supplier's invoice.

2. List the main information that you would expect to find on (a) a purchase requisition, and (b) a purchase order.

3. What is meant by the 'Battle of the Forms'?

4. What records do you suggest should be maintained by the purchasing department?

5. State three ways in which purchasing procedures may be simplified.

6. State three advantages and three disadvantages of purchasing manuals.

7. Draft a 'table of contents' for a typical purchasing manual.

8. Explain what is meant by 'The Battle of the Forms' and, using examples to illustrate your meaning, identify the techniques which may be used to avoid the associated problems.
(IPS. *Introduction to Purchasing and Supply Management* (1991).)

9. Write short notes on each of the following purchasing and supply documents, showing their typical content, purpose and importance:
   (a) Purchase Order
   (b) Purchase Enquiry
   (c) Stores Requisition
   (d) Goods Received Note.
   (CIPS. *Introduction to Purchasing and Supply Management* (1992).)

10. You have been asked to produce a purchasing procedures manual. Explain how you would achieve this objective, the scope of the manual, and those with whom you would consult.

   (CIPS. *Purchasing and Supply Management 1 Planning Policy and Organisation* (1993).)

11. Explain the activities which take place at each stage of the Purchasing Cycle and assess the importance of each in contributing to the effectiveness of supplies management.

   (CIPS. *Introduction to Purchasing and Supply Management* (1993).)

12. Copies of purchase orders are often routed or computer access provided to other departments within an organisation. Using individual departments as examples, explain fully the purpose of this procedure and the benefits which it creates.

   (CIPS. *Introduction to Purchasing and Supply Management* (1993).)

5

PURCHASING AND IT

1. INTRODUCTION

The need for effective purchasing systems derives from:

(a) An environment requiring enterprises to demonstrate
- speed
- innovation
- cost competitiveness
- quality.

(b) The importance to business competitiveness of strategies based on cost, product differentiation and customer focus.

(c) The concept of *lean supply* defined by Lamming [1] as:

> *The state of business in which there is dynamic competition and collaboration of equals in the supply chain, aimed at adding value at minimum total cost, while maximising end customer service and product quality.*

The above factors highlight the importance of Management Information Systems (MIS) as a support to decision making at the operational, tactical and strategic control levels within an organisation.

2. MANAGEMENT INFORMATION SYSTEMS

An MIS is defined by Lucy [2] as:

> *A system to convert data from internal and external sources into information and to communicate that information, in an appropriate form, to managers at all levels in all functions to enable them to make timely and effective decisions for planning, directing and controlling the activities for which they are responsible.*

Some key terms in the above definition are:

(1) *System* – see 3:**9**.

(2) *Data* are raw facts, figures, opinions and predictions from which information is drawn, e.g. figures relating to materials requisitioned, prices paid and items delivered.

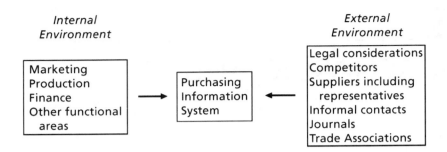

Fig 5.1 Some contributions to a purchasing MIS

(3) *Information* is processed data relevant to a manager in making decisions, e.g. a rising trend in defective components received from supplier x.

(4) *Internal and external sources.* As shown in Fig 5.1 purchasing managers obtain information from other internal functional areas and integrate this with that from the external environment to create a purchasing information system.

(5) *'To managers at all levels'.* Fig 5.2 shows that the information requirements of an organisation, activity or function differ according to the hierarchical level at which it is needed.

At the *operational level* information is provided through a transaction processing and reporting system that processes transactions as they occur to update internal records and provide documents and reports. Information at this level will be scheduled, detailed, frequent, largely historic and narrowly focused.

At the *tactical* level managers receive information collected from transaction processing systems or operational staff and also from internal and external sources. This information will be utilised for planning and control activities and,

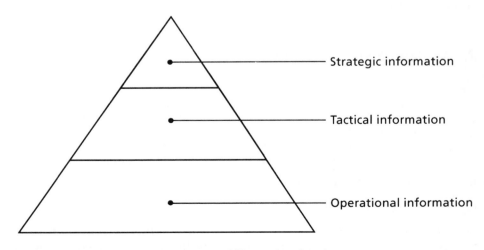

Fig 5.2 Information requirements at different levels

where appropriate, transmitted in summarised form to top management to support strategic planning.

At the *strategic* level information from internal and external sources is required to enable top management to appraise organisational strengths, weaknesses, opportunities and threats. Information at this level will be unscheduled, summarised, infrequent, forward looking and wide ranging.

(6) *'To make timely and efficient decisions'*. The function of MIS is to assist decision making.

At the *operational level* information in association with policies, procedures and rules is usually applied to *programmed* or routine decision making (see 3:**7d**(viii)).

The *tactical* level highlights decision support (DSS) and group decision support systems (GDSS). The former enables the individual manager to make *non-programmed*, non-routine tactical decisions related to short duration, adaptive action–interaction realignments used to accomplish limited goals.

At the *strategic level* information is used to make *non-programmed*, non-routine strategic decisions related to adaptations towards longer-term, more broadly conceived ends.

3. THE DISADVANTAGES OF MANUAL SYSTEMS

Especially in relation to transaction processing and reporting, some data processing may still be done manually. Applied to purchasing, however, manual systems of obtaining, processing, storing and retrieving information have been largely superseded by information technology (IT) for the following reasons:

(*i*) As Killen and Kamauff point out [3]:

'In many organisations administrative paperwork often serves merely to document a chain of events or to provide a logistical paper trail. Leading edge purchasing organisations need to transform this administrative function into a value-added process by reducing, eliminating or combining steps whenever possible.'

(*ii*) Manual systems tend to result in multiple copies of the same document being circulated to and retained by different people.

(*iii*) Considerable effort is devoted to the maintenance of information on purchase record files.

(*iv*) A number of purchase order and ancillary files are maintained in different locations all of which must be kept up to date.

(*v*) In multi-plant companies there may be a lack of cross-flow of information between plants regarding suppliers of common items thus preventing:

- consolidation of orders
- centralised purchasing
- recognition of potential spends with suppliers which could well result in negotiated group discounts
- partnership sourcing.

(vi) Inadequate group stock information so that further purchases are made when surplus stocks at locations other than the user plant could be utilised.
(vii) The volume of information relating to suppliers makes it impracticable to analyse, report and act upon data relating to
- supplier performance
- inventory
- standardisation, especially specifications, quality and nomenclature.

(viii) Although feasible, applications such as material requirements planning (MRP) and optimised production technology (OPT) would be impracticable if only manual systems were available.

It should be remembered, however, that most forms and reports, now computerised, were, at some time, manually processed and produced.

4. INFORMATION TECHNOLOGY (IT)

This is defined [4] as:

The acquisition, processing, storage and dissemination of vocal, pictorial, textual and numeric information by a microelectronics-based combination of computing and telecommunications.

The major components of IT are therefore:
- computers
- telecommunications.

5. WHAT IS A COMPUTER?

A computer may be defined as:

Any device which is capable of automatically accepting data, applying a sequence of processes to the data and supplying the results of these processes [5].

The elements of a computer can be divided into hardware and software.

(a) Hardware. Hardware is the physical equipment of a computer, i.e. the components we can see and touch. As shown by Fig 5.3 computer hardware comprises:

(1) A *central processing unit* (CPU) comprising
- A *memory* (or central memory) which is divided into bits (the smallest units of storage), bytes (8 bits to store a character) and words (usually 2 or 4 bytes).
- A *control unit* which ensures that program instructions are executed.
- An *arithmetical/logical unit* which does the arithmetic and logical operations.

(2) The main kinds of memory are:
- RAM (random access memory) which programmers can write to and read from.

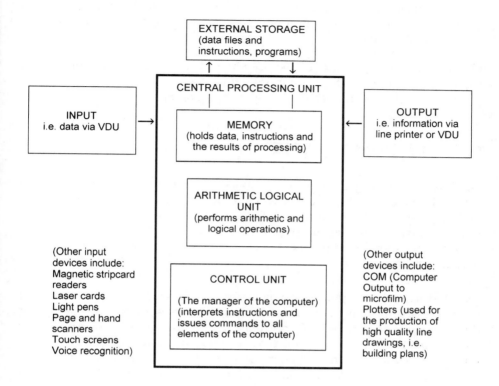

Fig 5.3 The hardware components of a computer

- ROM (read only memory) which can only be read.

(3) The *peripherals*. These include the input and output devices and the external store.

An example of an *input device* is a Visual Display Unit (VDU) comprising a keyboard (for typing) and a screen (for displaying what is typed).

An example of an *output device* is a line printer which prints out information on paper (hard copy) a line at a time. A VDU screen can also be used as an output device when it is used to display computer information where hard copy is not essential.

An *external store* provides secondary storage to supplement the computer's primary storage, memory.

When the peripheral units are not directly linked to the CPU they are said to be 'off line'. Conversely the term 'on line' is applied when peripherals are connected to and under the control of the CPU.

(b) Software. This comprises the programs which turn the computer into an effective tool. Software may be either:

(1) *Applications programs,* i.e. written to solve the problems of end-users, e.g. stock and production control programs, purchasing programs, computer aided design programs, or

(2) *Systems programs* which enable users to use computer facilities efficiently, e.g. the creation of files for storing programs and data or making additions or deletions to files; sorting, searching and merging of files.

6. TYPES OF PROCESSING

(a) Batch processing. As the name implies this involves accumulating transactions into batches of suitable size before processing commences. Batch processing is applicable when a run of data requires to be processed at given intervals but an immediate result is not required. Examples of batch processing would be the month-end payment of supplier's invoices or a weekly listing of overdue orders.

(b) On-line real-time processing. This is used when the computer is required to be accessed for immediate use. When data is processed quickly enough for the outcome of operations to be controlled, the computer is said to be operating in real time. In on-line processing, for example, particulars of a purchase order can be entered through the keyboard of a computer and displayed on a VDU. The computer can then interrogate its files to validate the order and notify immediately any errors detected. On-line processing assists buyers, therefore, by giving immediate access to purchasing data, e.g. supplier particulars, delivery prices and lead times, and provides an efficient means of administering the whole purchasing cycle from the placement of the purchase order, expediting, monitoring of performance and payment of the supplier.

Real-time and batch processing can be carried out on the same computer, the former, for example, being undertaken in the day and the latter at night-time, thus providing maximum utilisation. Methods of processing are determined by requirements rather than technology and exist to complement rather than compete with each other.

(c) Microcomputers. These include personal computers (PCs), portable micros and laptop computers. Microcomputers emphasise user power. Purchasing together with other functional staff now have much greater flexibility in accessing computer support than was the case when computers were managed by a central computer department. Because microcomputers can function either as terminals forming part of the output of the mainframe computer or independently in their own right, users have the best of both worlds. The user department can either access the vast information provided by the mainframe (where available) or work from micro software programs such as word processing, inventory control or spreadsheets independently of the mainframe.

7. COMPUTER SYSTEMS

These are broadly of three kinds
Specific applications
Integrated systems
Databases

(a) **Specific applications.** Early computers tended to be applied piecemeal in the limited context of a single information sub-system, e.g. payroll or inventory control. With the development of microcomputers, the system has come full circle and there is sufficient software to enable a microcomputer to reliably perform most office functions such as accounting, purchasing, stock control etc.

(b) **Integrated systems.** These have developed from the recognition of the interdependence of functions and that an item of data may have many applications. In a computerised system for the administration of production management and ancillary activities or CAPM, purchasing, as shown in Fig 5.4, is related to other areas including forecasting, production scheduling, inventory management and cost and quality planning and control. This integration is achieved through a LAN (Local Area Network) which is a collection of computers and peripherals connected by cables and usually confined to one building or site. The term LAN is frequently applied to a number of linked PCs often controlled by a more powerful computer. A LAN has a number of advantages over a collection of stand-alone microcomputers including:

- shared resources, i.e. disk storage, printers and possibly a mini or mainframe computer
- shared information held on disk and accessible to all users
- shared software
- ability to communicate with other network users – a facility that is advantageous when computers are distributed round a large building.

(c) **Database systems.** These are management information systems based on a centrally located data file which stores all the data supporting the operations of the organisation. A database is the ultimate development in integration since each item of data to be used throughout the organisation is stored once only. The overlap that can occur when data processing applications are developed separately by different functions is thus avoided. This approach will, it is claimed, eliminate discrepancies, save storage space and organise data so that it can be utilised by all applications in the organisation, thereby improving planning, execution and control.

(d) **OMAC.** The OMAC (On-line Manufacturing and Control) Production Management system, part of the ICL Computer Integrated Manufacturing (CIM) product, is a typical system incorporating elements of all the above three approaches. The OMAC Production Management System comprises twelve

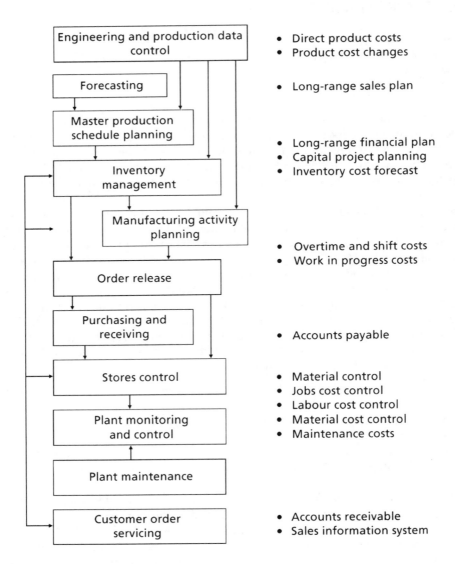

Fig 5.4 The interdependence of function
(courtesy of IBM Ltd)

modules only one of which, the Manufacturing Database (MDB), is mandatory. The *Manufacturing Database* maintains details of all parts, structures, components, operations and work centres, company, site and currency details. All this information is fed into the OMAC system just once and is then available to all authorised users whenever they need it. Each of the remaining eleven modules corresponds to a major management function. The modules, which can be operated singly, in groups or as a totally integrated system, comprise the following:

- *Stock Control* (STC) provides a comprehensive management inventory system.
- *Work-in-Progress Control* (WIP) provides facilities for monitoring the flow and progress of manufacturing orders through the factory.
- *Just-in-Time* (JIT) monitors manufacturing where work is continuous.
- *Purchasing* (PUR) provides facilities to maintain accurate information about requisitions and orders, making this information available to purchasing management, materials and stores personnel.
- *OMAC Expert* (ECP) enables the expert knowledge of material controllers to be applied to the output from Material Requirements Planning to Categorise MRP actions.
- *Capacity Requirements Planning* (CRP) provides an advance picture of the potential load by work centre resulting from firm, proposed or tentative manufacturing orders.
- *Materials Requirements Planning* (MRP) determines what parts are needed, made or bought out, how many and when.
- *Cost Establishment* (CES) automatically calculates standard and current costs of products based upon the cost of component parts and operational costs incurred.
- *Cost Monitoring* (CMN) provides for the valuation of stock assets in a business and for the detailed monitoring of costs actually incurred compared with the costs expected.
- *Master Manufacturing Schedule* (MMS) enables the user to generate and tune a master manufacturing schedule from a customer delivery schedule by rough cut capacity planning techniques.
- *Lot Traceability* (TRC) allocates a unique lot identifier to each batch, archives data compactly and provides for subsequent retrieval and analysis.

8. COMPUTER OPERATION

(a) Input. Data for processing will first be collected from a source document, e.g. a purchase requisition or goods received note. Source data will need to be recorded on a suitable medium and fed into the computer via an input device. With on-line data the entry may be entered directly into the computer.

(b) Storage

(1) *The main store.* The main store is the connection between the control unit and all other devices comprising the computer. The main store holds the program instructions and data being processed as well as processed data (information) awaiting transfer to output devices.

(2) *The external store.* This complements the main store and uses tape or magnetic disk storage. Disks are increasingly replacing tapes since they provide significant improvements in both storage capacity and speed of access to information. On-line processing usually requires disk storage as this is the only method of

obtaining data from the external store with sufficient speed for real-time response. The external store is used for the off-line storage of programs and master files.

(3) *Files.* *Master files* contain data relating to a particular set of records such as suppliers and inventory. These files contain both permanent data, e.g. a part number and its description, and data which, by its nature, will change each time a transaction occurs, e.g. the changing stock balance of that part after receipts or issues. Master files are used for reference purposes and therefore have to be maintained accurately and efficiently so as to provide current data. This is done by means of *transaction files* made up from the various transactions created by the source documents. Transaction files are also used to summarise or analyse the records contained therein, e.g. the number of purchase orders issued in a particular month. Typical master files used in supplies work would be:

(i) Part number master file containing a record for every material part number used on every piece of equipment manufactured by the undertaking. Each of these records could also contain master data for that specific part number, i.e. description, exact type of equipment, lead-time requirement, stock level, ordering policy, total purchase requisitions, total purchase orders.

(ii) Supplier master file containing a record for each supplier. Each record could contain information such as the supplier's name and address, telephone number, details of the last delivery made, prices and discounts applicable to a particular supplier, orders not acknowledged and particulars relative to a supplier's performance, e.g. over-due deliveries, rejects, etc.

(iii) Purchase master file containing a record for every part number purchased. Each record containing details of the most recent quotations received from suppliers and a record of the most recent purchases of the item.

The three processes applicable to master files are those of interrogating, updating and amending. Interrogating or referencing the master file has been termed the *raison d'etre* of master file records. An example of interrogation is the ascertainment of the last price paid for a purchased item. Updating means bringing a master record up to date, e.g. changing prices for bought-out items. Amending is the insertion of new and the deletion of obsolete records, e.g. a component no longer purchased. As indicated earlier, with a database these master files would be inapplicable.

(c) Control. The control unit is the nerve centre of the computer and, because of its co-ordinating and controlling activity, has been compared with the conductor of an orchestra or the supervisor of an office. The functions of the control unit are to receive and interpret data and program instructions from the main store and issue commands to all parts of the computer configuration.

(d) Computer processing. The commands given by the control unit will be obeyed and any arithmetical operations carried out on the data by the arithmetic-logical unit. This unit is also used to modify the program by amending the instructions held in the main store.

(e) Output. The results of the data processing operation are assembled in the main store in readiness for output to a visual display unit, line printer or other output device.

9. A TYPICAL COMPUTERISED PURCHASING APPLICATION

A hypothetical example of the application of a real-time/batch system to purchases and stores is as follows:

(a) Configuration (hardware)

> *(i) Data processing control* – CPU, disk storage, line printer, control console
> *(ii) Purchasing department* – VDUs (numbers will be decided by the systems analyst in conjunction with the end-users), hard copy of VDU screens, purchase order sets, goods received notes
> *(iii) Stock control* – VDUs (numbers determined as above), printer for hard copy
> *(iv) Goods inward* – VDUs (as above)
> *(v) Accounts* – VDUs (as above).

(b) Software. Programs will be provided and loaded into the CPU.

(c) Files. Two files, i.e. a purchase order master file and a stock master file, will be created from the manual records. Thereafter new entries will be made via the computer system.

> *(i) Purchase order master file.* This will contain data relating to all outstanding purchase orders, i.e. order number, supplier, part number, description, quantity ordered, quantity outstanding, delivery schedule, delivery promises, last goods received note, last supplier's advice, price per stock unit.
> *(ii) Stock file.* This will contain data relating to stock, i.e. part number, description, current stock level, stock unit, reorder level, reorder quantity, last goods received note number, last issue docket number, ABC classification.

(d) Operating information. Files may be accessed at any time during the day, information being current to within five seconds. Information on the VDU screen may be printed on a terminal printer for working copies. Information input to the computer is by fixed format; the screen will explain what is to be entered and where. Information that is immediately available includes the following:

> *(i)* value of forward commitments by date
> *(ii)* value of business placed on any supplier
> *(iii)* outstanding orders on any supplier
> *(iv)* overdue orders from any supplier with promised delivery dates
> *(v)* details of any outstanding order by order number
> *(vi)* details of any outstanding orders by part number
> *(vii)* stock level of any part code

(*viii*) value of inventory

(*ix*) list of any parts currently below reorder levels.

(e) Operating procedure

(*i*) Manufacturing generates demand for part from stock control.

(*ii*) Stock control interrogates computer by VDU.

(*iii*) Computer scans stock file and reports stock level on VDU.

(*iv*) Stock control instructs stores to issue part to manufacturing.

(*v*) Stores issue part to manufacturing; stores issue note is passed to stock control.

(*vi*) Stock control enters stores issue note into VDU.

(*vii*) Computer accepts data, locates appropriate stock record, deducts issued quantity from stock balance, posts new stock balance and latest stores issue note number. Checks new stock balance against minimum stock level. If stock level is satisfactory no action is taken. If the stock level is below the minimum, computer searches purchase order file for outstanding orders (if any) and promised delivery dates. This information will be printed on line printer.

(*viii*) Stock control analyses print of stock situation and, as appropriate, instructs purchasing to chase outstanding order, or reschedules outstanding order to issue new requisition to purchasing. The information will be conveyed to purchasing on hard copy generated by the computer in step (*vii*).

(*ix*) Purchasing receives and analyses requisition and proceeds to issue enquiries, analyse quotations and place the purchase order.

(*x*) Order details are entered into the computer.

(*xi*) Computer receives data, prints supplier's copy of order on printer, adds order to purchase order file, calculates commitment, advises stock control by line printer of order placed and anticipated delivery date.

(*xii*) Supplier acknowledges order; details entered into computer by purchasing.

(*xiii*) Computer compares acknowledgement with purchase order, records date and number, advises purchasing by line printer of any discrepancy between order and acknowledgement.

(*xiv*) Seven days before due delivery date, computer generates instruction on line printer to purchasing so that order can be expedited.

(*xv*) Expediter follows up delivery with supplier. Details of confirmation of existing or details of new delivery date are keyed into the computer.

(*xvi*) Computer compares new delivery promise with that originally stated on the purchase order and advises stock control of any change. If necessary step (*xiv*) is repeated.

(*xvii*) Goods are delivered by supplier.

(*xviii*) Goods inwards department interrogates computer to confirm delivery date. Delivery details are punched into the computer.

(*xix*) Computer locates purchase order, subtracts delivered quantity, updates delivery schedule, deletes existing goods received note and supplier's invoice numbers, and inserts new goods received note and supplier advice numbers. Computer prints hard copy of goods received note on printer, calculates value

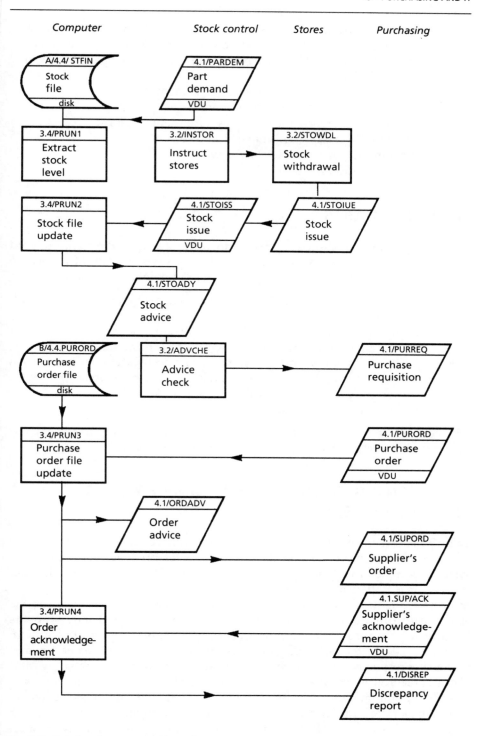

Fig 5.5 Purchasing system flowchart

of goods, deducts from commitment; adds delivered quantity to stock balance on stock file, and adds value of goods to stock value. If the purchase order is complete it is transferred to an orders completed file; if still open it is returned to current order file.

(xx) Supplier sends invoice to accounts department.

(xxi) Accounts interrogates computer by VDU.

(xxii) Computer searches files, locates order and indicates to accounts department on VDU that goods have been received.

(xxiii) Accounts department pays invoice.

(xxiv) End of operation.

10. FLOWCHARTS

These are prepared to show the flow of documents around the computer and the processing involved. A flowchart relating to steps *(i)*–*(xiii)* of the above operating procedure is shown in Fig 5.5. Important points are as follows:

- The top of the flowchart gives the name of each function concerned with the system
- The left-hand side of the chart shows inputs into the system.
- The right-hand side of the chart shows outputs from the system.
- Appropriate symbols (otherwise known as designations or flags), each with a reference code, are used in the relevant column to depict processes.
- Each symbol gives a brief description.
- Lines and arrows are used to connect symbols.

(The convention for reading flowcharts is to read first from top to bottom and then from left to right. The contraflow is indicated by arrows.)

11. ESSENTIAL FEATURES OF A COMPUTERISED SUPPLIES SYSTEM

Table 5.1 shows the replies of 71 respondents to a survey reported in *Purchasing and Supply Management,* April 1992, regarding the features commonly sought in systems designed to support purchasing functions. These responses, modified in their presentation, are used by permission.

From the table it is clear that most organisations have similar views on the essential features that any system must provide. Thus 77 per cent of respondents identify purchase order generation as an essential feature of any effective system; 74 per cent see the recording of goods received as essential, and 65 per cent and 64 per cent respectively regard recording of stock issues and stockholdings and supplier records as essential. Conversely, only just over a third of respondents consider the automatic generation of enquiry and tender documents as essential.

The generation of purchase orders, continuous monitoring of stock and recording of issues are all dependent on the level of business activity in an organisation. It is therefore, essential that any system installed in support of the

Table 5.1

Ranking as Essential	Feature	Essential	Important	Helpful	Not Necessary	Total Respondents*
1	Purchase order generation	51	11	3	1	67
2	Goods received recording	49	12	5	0	66
3	Supplier records	46	19	5	1	71
4	Stock recording	41	9	9	6	65
5	Issue recording	40	8	6	7	61
6	Coding/classification	39	17	4	4	64
7	Purchase order status monitoring	38	15	8	1	62
8	Price records	37	20	6	3	66
9	Purchase management information	36	19	7	0	62
10	Receipt/invoice matching	35	12	16	2	65
11	On-line stock enquiry	32	14	6	9	61
12	Supplier evaluation	23	27	12	2	64
13	Enquiry/tender production	23	27	15	7	62
14	Parts catalogue	22	19	15	17	73
15	Supplier rating	22	25	13	6	66
16	Contract planning and monitoring	22	12	18	9	61
17	Reorder calculation	21	15	18	9	73
18	Purchase price variation analysis	21	17	19	8	65
19	Multi-currency pricing	19	12	17	12	60
20	Demand forecasting	18	14	15	13	60
21	Tender evaluation	10	22	25	9	66
22	Quality inspection recording	9	22	18	12	61
23	Quality inspection analysis	6	21	15	18	60
24	Staff performance monitoring	3	16	22	19	60

* *Note:* Responses do not total 71 because some respondents use two or more systems concurrently and not all respondents marked all categories.

supplies function should be capable of interfacing with the main organisational information systems.

12. SOME COMPUTER ADVANCES AFFECTING THE PURCHASING AND SUPPLY FUNCTION

(a) Bar coding [6]. With increasing computerisation plain language descriptions of products and services need to be replaced by *codes* that are usable in all trade and industry sectors worldwide. The EAN (international article numbering system) was established in 1977 and provides a unique and unambiguous numbering system that enables an item to be identified anywhere in the world. These numbers are represented by bar codes, a pattern of wide and narrow black bands and alternating white spaces that a computer reads with the aid of an optical scanner or wand. The code can be printed directly on the item or on the attached label.

Although there is a choice of four bar code numbers, i.e. EAN 8, EAN 13, ITF 15 and EAN 128 used for small items, consumer and traded unit and container codes, the standard article number has 13 digits and is therefore EAN 13. For administrative purposes EAN 13 comprises the following three parts:

Company Prefix Number	Item Reference	Check Digit
5012345	67890	0

(i) The *company prefix number* is unique and allocated to the company manufacturing or distributing the products. Numbers that begin with 50 have been allocated by the Article Numbering Association (ANA) which promotes EAN in the UK.

(ii) The *item reference* is allocated by the company to the products or services it wishes to identify.

(iii) The *check digit* is calculated from the first twelve and is used to ensure, by the use of the item reference, that the complete number is unique to the product or service being numbered.

The benefits through the supply chain for the manufacturer, distributor, wholesaler and retailer are summarised by the ANA as:

(i) Fast and accurate data capture at every point in the supply chain including goods received, warehousing, packing, despatch and point of sale.

(ii) Better, more timely management information.

(iii) Less stockholding and less waste.

(iv) Greater responsiveness to trade customers and to consumers.

(v) The ability to automate warehousing.

(vi) Better control over distribution and storage.

(vii) Fewer errors in the recognition of goods.

(viii) Improved company to company communications throughout the supply chain.

(ix) One standard for use with all trading partners and therefore no conflicting demands.

(b) Spreadsheets. A spreadsheet is a powerful computer program that can be used to design and develop anything from a simple costing sheet for a new product to a large and complicated financial model of a new business. An example of a spreadsheet 'matrix' or 'grid' (often referred to as a 'worksheet') is shown in Fig 5.6. Although larger spreadsheets are available, a typical program will display about 250 rows and 60 columns. Each row and column is identified by its row number and column letter. The lines drawn to define the rows and columns form 'cells' or 'locations'. Using as many or as few of the rows and columns as are required for the particular application, one of three types of information is entered into a cell by means of the computer keyboard:

(i) *Text,* such as column or row headings, notes or descriptions. Text columns are ignored when calculations are performed.

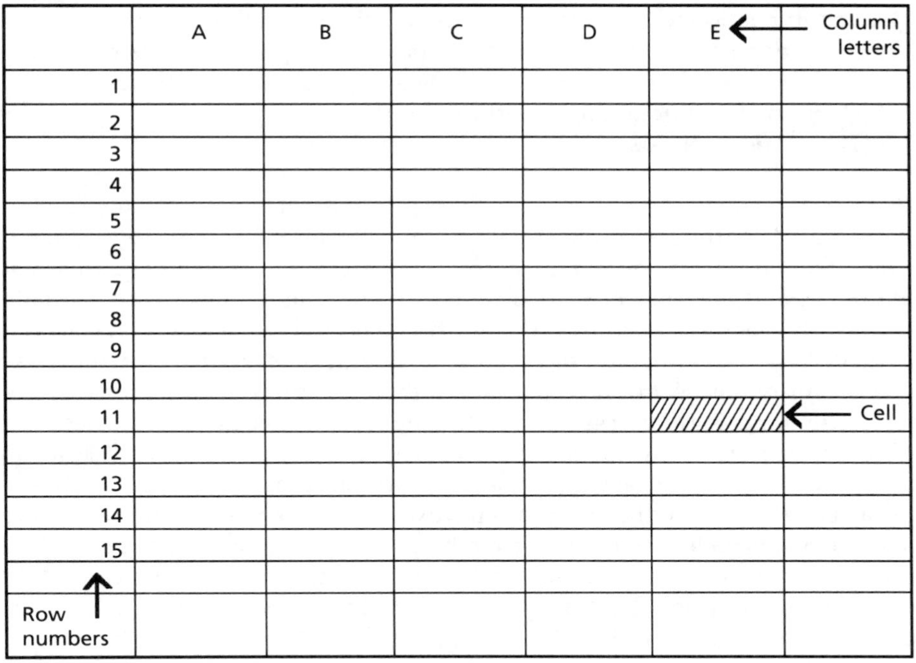

	A	B	C	D	E	Column letters
1						
2						
3						
4						
5						
6						
7						
8						
9						
10						
11					/////////	Cell
12						
13						
14						
15						
Row numbers ↑						

Fig 5.6 A spreadsheet matrix

(ii) *Numbers*, which can be specified as whole numbers, decimals, straight numbers or currency.

(iii) *Formulae* expressing the relationship between numbers.

The only difference between using a spreadsheet program on a microcomputer and working out problems with a calculator, pen and paper is the amount of effort required to carry out repeated computations. Once the worksheet has been set up on the program, different ideas or models involving changes to the figures can be easily and quickly evaluated.

The list of potential spreadsheet models applicable to purchasing is limited only by the creativity of the individual user. Important purchasing and stores routines facilitated by the use of spreadsheets include:

(1) Project evaluations, such as the centralisation of the supplies function.
(2) Bill of materials evaluation.
(3) Materials requirements planning.
(4) Phasing of projects to meet total cash flow criteria.
(5) Capacity planning for production and logistics.
(6) Evaluation of the effects of changes in sales volume and phasing on stocks, stockholding costs and customer service levels.
(7) Inventory management, e.g. EOQ models and extensions, ABC analysis and stocktaking evaluations.

(8) Supplier comparisons when a range of volume-related price bands apply and in relation to quantity discounts and expected failure rates.

(9) Collection and analysis of data for departmental performance operation.

(10) Evaluation of alternative stockholding and purchasing strategies.

(11) Departmental budgeting, reporting and variance analysis.

(12) Time series analysis of data for forecasting purposes.

(c) Expert systems. These are computer programs that provide for solving problems in a particular application area by drawing inferences from a knowledge base acquired by human expertise. With an expert system the user sits at a terminal and answers questions posed by the computer which eventually reaches a diagnosis or decision and informs the user how that decision has been reached. Expert systems are often used to design other systems or diagnose manufacturing faults. Lorin [7] states that there are numerous, significant opportunities for using expert systems technology to improve the effectiveness and efficiency of purchasing management decisions and instances the following: supplier evaluation and selection; materials price forecasts; and the purchase of major capital assets. In the latter case the expert system would consider a wide range of factors including final cost, method of financing, purchase, installation process, effects on labour and the workplace, impact on quality of products, fit with existing technology, training required for operation, and effects on productivity to mention a few.

(d) Decision support systems. These systems are designed to enable an individual (DSS) or a group (GDSS) to make a decision by summarising all relevant available information whether held in the organisation's database or externally, e.g. interest rates, currency changes. Such systems often incorporate electronic spreadsheets and graphics to provide clear representation of available data in forms such as line or pie-charts. One form of GDSS allows participants in decision making to be in different locations. This association of GDSS with teleconferencing can significantly reduce management travelling costs. Decision support systems are particularly applicable to purchasing and supplies problems relating to the analysis of risk and the outcomes of varying scenarios.

13. SOME ADVANTAGES OF COMPUTERISED PURCHASING

Purchasing is, of course, only a special application of the general benefits that computerisation may bring to any function. These include the ability to store and retrieve a great quantity of data, process such data rapidly with a high degree of accuracy, eliminate much routine effort and use exception techniques which save time by notifying these variations from plans or standards which require management action. Specifically, some of the benefits to purchasing and supplies from an integrated computer system include the following:

(i) Reduction of routine clerical activity by the automatic preparation of documents, e.g. purchase requisitions, orders, acknowledgement forms, progress letters, etc.

(ii) Formalising of procedures and achieving a streamlining that might not otherwise be contemplated.

(iii) Provision of accurate and up-to-date information essential for routine purchasing, e.g. forward material requirements, supplier data, outstanding and overdue orders.

(iv) Reduction of staff and consequent costs.

(v) A computer can easily cope with fluctuations in workload.

(vi) Reduction, as a result of combining *(i)*, *(ii)* and *(iii)*, of the time required to process orders.

(vii) Rapid calculation of order quantities, consolidation of orders, EOQs (economic order quantities) and variations in price from standards and budgets with price increases related to material and labour indices.

(viii) Ultimately, savings due to improved stores recording and inventory control, e.g. stock/order information and analysis, ABC classifications, stock reports and minimising of inventory.

(ix) Rapid provision of reports at prescribed intervals, e.g. daily, weekly, monthly, etc., enabling more informed decision-making to be undertaken. Here the possibilities are almost infinite but may include:

- value of orders placed in period
- value of orders to any one supplier
- list of suppliers in order of spend
- orders for which no acknowledgement has been received
- value of forward commitments
- current expenditure/commitment against appropriate budgets
- updated expenditure against each capital project
- orders overdue
- stock of each item on hand and on order
- excess stocks
- slow moving and dead stocks
- current/average value of stock
- vendor rating reports
- stock movements statement
- supplier's invoices received.

(x) As a result of *(i)*–*(vi)* the purchasing officer can devote the time saved to such activities as:

- preparing for negotiations which will be based on more and better information
- sourcing suppliers
- studying market trends
- measuring the performance of the department
- enhancement of the purchasing department's standing and reputation to service and reliability throughout the organisation.

With manual systems the routine aspects of purchasing take up a disproportionate amount of time leading to the exclusion of the more significant aspects of purchasing activities. The reduction of routine clerical work may also provide job enlargement with consequent higher job satisfaction for purchasing staff although the number of staff consequent on the implementation of computerised procedures may be considerably less. Finally the introduction of a new system into a working situation often has the effect of a change agent in that it provides management with an opportunity to review all purchasing and supply functions and procedures.

14. TELECOMMUNICATIONS

Essentially telecommunications are concerned with the transmission of information over distances by such means as electrical signals along a conductor, light signals along optical fibres or by radio waves.

As stated in **7(b)** above, LANS link computers in the same office. Wide area networks (WANS) using the public telephone system or other forms of telecommunications facilitate the electronic exchange of information between organisations. Since the privatisation of UK telecommunication services, network operators such as International Network Services (INS), IBM(UK) and AT and T Instel are able to lease communication facilities from the telecommunications authority, e.g. BT or Mercury, add some kind of extra value or service and resell the network capacity to users. The network together with the associated service is known as a value-added network or VAN. It is the added value that distinguishes a VAN from a normal network, i.e. a LAN or a WAN. An important VAN application is electronic data interchange (EDI).

15. ELECTRONIC DATA INTERCHANGE (EDI)

EDI has been defined [8] as:

The technique based on agreed standards, which enables computers in different organisations to successfully send business or information transactions from one to the other.

In the above definition:

(a) Business transactions include orders, invoices, delivery advices and payment instructions. Information transactions convey details about a person or organisation for administrative purposes, e.g. price lists, production facilities etc.

(b) Standards. The transmission of commercial messages between organisations by EDI requires that transmitters should know what information to send and in what order. Conversely the receiving computer must know what the transaction comprises and how to process the information. Examples of messages are quotation requests, quotations, orders acknowledgements, order amendments, acknowledgement of amendments, delivery notes, delivery discrepancy advices, and invoices. Similarly the process of instructing a bank to make payments can involve messages relating to payment instructions with remittance details, payment instruction acknowledgements, credit advices and credit acknowledgements. Such messages can be broken down into:

(1) *Syntax.* This provides the conventions of the message, e.g. in written English, a sentence ends with a full stop. Syntax is therefore similar to the function of grammar in a language. The correctness of the message to be sent is checked by a *message translator* which also adds the syntax.

(2) *Segments.* These are the blocks of information from which messages are built. Each segment contains elements of information termed *data elements.* Thus, in a purchase order the segment is the name and address of the purchaser or supplier. This segment is broken down into such data elements as organisation name, address line 1, address line 2, address line 3, post code, country.

(3) *Standardised codes,* required to represent each data element. Data elements and codes will be described in a *directory* for the message standard. By the use of such standards which are national or international, organisations can trade electronically.

Early message standards were developed by groups or communities of organisations, e.g. automotive, banking, construction, electronic enterprises which had an interest in trading together. Thus automotive manufacturers in ten European countries, i.e. Ford, General Motors, Saab, Renault, Fiat, Austin Rover, Citroen and suppliers Lucas, Perkins, Bosch, CKN, SKF and BCS set up ODETTE (Organisation for Data Exchange by Tele-Transmission in Europe) as a collaborative agreement for common messages and protocols [9]. In the USA, ANSIX12 is the trading standard. In 1985, however, the United Nations recognised the importance of having standards which would support trade worldwide and created the UK/EDIFACT standard (EDI for Administration, Commerce and Transport). This international standard has been ratified as international standard ISO9735.

Additionally there are a number of codes relating to specific industry groups or communities. These include ANA (retail and distribution), EDICON (construction), EDIFICE (electronics), and EDISHIP (international shipping).

(c) The advantages of EDI

(*i*) The replacement of the paper documents, i.e. purchase orders, acknowledgements, invoices, etc. used by buyers and sellers in commercial transactions, by standard electronic messages conveyed between computers often without the need for human intervention.

One of the best examples of EDI is EPOS (Electronic Point of Sale) at the supermarket. When a product is purchased, the check-out operator scans a bar code on its label which automatically registers the price on the cash till. That same signal also triggers a computer process which re-orders the item from the manufacturer, sets off a production cycle, arranges invoicing, payment and transportation of the new order. EDI effectively puts the product back on the shelf with no paperwork and a minimum of human involvement [10].

(*ii*) Cost savings due to reduced postage, stationery and associated clerical

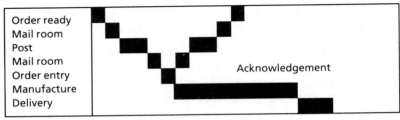

11 days to acknowledge
16 days to delivery

Fig 5.7   Reducing lead times pre EDI

operations. (Approximately 15 per cent of logistics expenses result from order processing, administrative and related costs.)

(iii) Cost savings through the avoidance of data re-entry and the error-free transmission of documents avoiding mistakes through re-keying.

(iv) Reduction in lead times through buyers and suppliers working together in a 'real time' environment. Armstrong and Jackson [11] provide the real life example in Figs 5.7 and 5.8 of pre and post EDI lead times in which the latter shows a reduction of 8 days to acknowledge and 5 days to deliver the order.

Reducing leadtimes pre EDI:
- Day 1:   Order prepared by buyer, printed.
- Day 2:   Authorised; enveloped; processed by mail room.
- Day 3:   In postal system.
- Day 5:   Processed by recipient's mail room; sits on desk.
- Day 6:   Information keyed onto recipient's order processing system; acknowledgement prepared.
- Day 7:   Manufacturing process begins (7 days); acknowledgement into mail room.
- Day 8:   Acknowledgement into postal system.
- Day 10:   Acknowledgement received by originator's mail room.
- Day 11:   Acknowledgement processed.
- Day 14:   Manufacturing complete.
- Day 16:   Delivery completed.

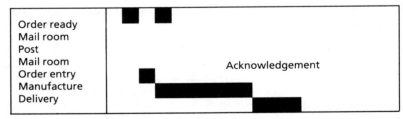

3 days to acknowledge
11 days to delivery

Fig 5.8   Reducing lead times post EDI

Typically in a post-EDI environment this same process would involve the following:

- Day 1:   Order prepared and authorised electronically; posted into EDI service.
- Day 2:   Order taken from EDI service by recipient and put straight into order processing system; acknowledgement created automatically and sent to EDI service.
- Day 3:   Manufacturing process begins (7 days); acknowledgement received by originator and processed automatically.
- Day 9:   Manufacturing complete.
- Day 11: Delivery complete.

(v) Reduction in the cost of inventory and release of working capital.

(vi) Promotion of such strategies as JIT as a consequence of (iv) and (v).

(vii) Better customer service.

(viii) Facilitation of global purchasing through international standards, e.g. EDIFACT which is compatible with most equipment in most countries. In 1970 Sitpro (The Simplification of International Trade Procedures Board) was established ' to guide, stimulate and assist the rationalisation of international trade procedures and the documentation and information flows associated with them'. Sitpro works with the BSI in connection with EDI standards.

(ix) Facilitation of invoice payment by the computer to computer transfer of money which eliminates the need for the preparation and posting of cheques.

(x) The integration of functions particularly marketing, purchasing production and finance.

(xi) EDI tends to promote long-term buyer-supplier relationships and increases mutual trust.

Other applications of EDI include transmission of information relating to engineering specifications, requests for quotations, engineering drawings and forecasts and schedules relating to blanket orders.

(d) Some potential problems in implementing EDI. Killen and Kamauff [12] point out that before adopting EDI an organisation should:

(i) Ensure that exchanging information electronically supports the overall organisational strategy.

(ii) Consider the cost and ramifications of EDI standard tools and techniques including implementation, software maintenance, manpower and participant training and how to promote systems and applications integration.

(iii) Consider the organisational and process changes involved.

In relation to (ii) Normal [13] states that the more data that is being processed and reprocessed the more room there is to save time and money. Potential EDI users should therefore calculate the cost per transaction. If it is cheaper to fax or manually perform the task the buyer probably lacks the volume to invest in EDI. Monczka and Carter [14] instance the following indicators of a reasonable opportunity for the application of EDI in the purchasing environment:

(i) A high volume of paperwork transaction documents

(ii) Numerous suppliers

(iii) A long internal administration lead time associated with the purchasing cycle

(iv) A desire for personnel reductions, new hire avoidance, or both

(v) A need to increase the professionalism of purchasing personnel.

For references to CAD, CAM and CAE see 7:**5**.

16. ELECTRONIC MAIL

This is a general term for the process by which letters, orders or other documents are sent by a computer along telephone lines to appear on a VDU at their destination. By this system the process of sending documents and receiving replies can take minutes rather than days. Facsimile machines (fax) resemble long-distance photocopiers. Written materials or diagrams can quickly be transmitted by fax to destinations which may be thousands of miles distant.

17. THE IMPACT OF IT ON PURCHASING AND SUPPLIES

Information technology is an important factor in breaking down the concept of purchasing as a discrete function and emphasising the wider, more integrative materials management and logistics approaches in which the interrelationship of marketing, production, purchasing and transportation is recognised. It is also an important factor in relation to improving the competitive advantage provided by the purchasing function in an organisation. Developments such as MRP and JIT, which require on-line data transmission between suppliers and customers for the automatic replenishment of stocks, also highlight the importance of EDI in supplies operations.

The trend in electronic office technology is also towards the integration or 'convergence' of office equipment, processes and procedures relating to communication, computer information storage and retrieval, reprographics and mailing. Such developments require purchasing staff to have an awareness of the possibilities if they are to be involved in the planning of IT systems and able to take full advantage of the benefits such systems can provide. The need to develop staff with the ability to purchase effectively within a computerised environment without becoming subservient to it has important implications for purchasing education and training.

References

[1] Lamming R. *Beyond Partnership – Strategies for Innovation and Lean Supply.* Prentice Hall, 1993, Chap 9, p 239.

[2] Lucy T. *Management Information Systems.* DP Publications, 1987, p2.

[3] Killen K H and Kamauff J W. *Managing purchasing. National Association of Purchasing Management (USA)*. 1995, Chap 2, pp 17 and 18.

[4] Longley D and Shain M. *Dictionary of Information Technology*. Macmillan, 1982, p 165.

[5] Chandor A. *The Penguin Dictionary of Computers*. Penguin Books, 1986, p 88.

[6] The writer is indebted to the ANA publication *Product Numbering* for this information.

[7] Lorin R C. *Expert systems in purchasing: applications and development. International Journal of Purchasing and Supply Management*. Fall 1992, pp 23–24.

[8] Blacker K. *The Basics of Electronic Data Interchange*. Edistone Books, 1994, Chap 1, p 5.

[9] Lee Alan, *UK sets the pace towards paperless trading. Purchasing and Supply Management*. Feb 1988, pp 25–26.

[10] John Sanders, quoted by Tyler G in *Is paperless trading finally a reality. Purchasing and Supply Management*. Dec 1991, p 26–29.

[11] Armstrong V and Jackson D. *Electronic Data Interchange. A Guide for Purchasing and Supply*. CIPS, 1991, pp 15–16.

[12] Killen K H and Kamauff. *Managing Purchasing*. Irwin (USA), 1995, Chap 4, p 60.

[13] Norman G. *Is it time for EDI? Logistics Supplement to Purchasing and Supply Management*. June 1994, p 20.

[14] Monczka and Carter. *Implementing Electronic Data Interchange. Journal of Purchasing and Materials Management*. Summer 1988, pp 2–9.

Progress test 5

1. Define 'lean supply'.

2. Define the term 'Management Information System'.

3. State four disadvantages of manually operated purchasing systems.

4. Define the term 'Information Technology'.

5. Distinguish between 'hardware' and 'software'.

6. What is the difference between 'batch' and 'on-line, real time processing'?

7. Explain 'specific applications', integrated systems, and database systems.

8. Describe a typical application of a real time/batch system in purchasing.

9. What are the advantages to manufacturers, distributors, wholesalers and retailers of bar coding?

10. Give examples of ways in which spreadsheets are applicable to purchasing.

11. What is an 'expert system'? State some possible applications to purchasing.

12. Describe six advantages of computerised purchasing.

13. Define EDI.

14. What are the elements of an EDI standard? What is EDIFACT?

15. What are some advantages of EDI?

16. What are key indicators of the suitability of EDI?

17. The installation of a computer in an organisation must be considered very carefully. Outline the organisational problems which must be overcome, and the advantages of the computer to the purchasing and supply function.

(CIPS. *Introduction to Purchasing and Supply* (1987))

18. Electronic Data Interchange (EDI) represents an increasingly significant element in many logistics information processes.
(a) Define EDI, and show the stages in its development up to the current time. Illustrate your answer with practical examples.
(b) Explain the primary objectives behind a firm's use of EDI and examine the major effects of EDI and the firm's inventory control and distribution strategies.

(CIPS. *Logistics* (1990))

19. Discuss the benefits and problems which the introduction of information technology brings to the purchasing and supply function.

(CIPS. *Introduction to Purchasing and Supply* (1990))

20. Examine the applications to which information technology may be put in the context of modern supplies management by drawing attention to the ways in which such techniques will contribute to the overall effectiveness of the function.

(CIPS. *Introduction to Purchasing and Supply Management* (May 1992))

21. It has been said that modern communications systems and information technology have 'revolutionised' modern purchasing and supply management. Critically evaluate this statement, using specific examples to illustrate your answer.

(CIPS. *Introduction to Purchasing and Supply Management* (1994))

6

HUMAN RESOURCES IN THE SUPPLY CHAIN

1. INTRODUCTION

Human Resources Management (HRM) may be defined as *responsibility for an organisation's productive use of and constructive dealings with its employees* [1].

As shown in Chapter 1, HRM like procurement is regarded by Porter as a support activity. The use of the term HRM rather than 'personnel' reflects that, in the same way procurement is regarded as an added value rather than a cost cutting activity, so those who work for an organisation (the human resources of an enterprise may not be confined to its employees) when managed from a strategic perspective are considered as a source of competitive advantage to the enterprise concerned. A comparison by Guest [2] of stereotypes of personnel and HRM is given in Table 6.1.

Purchasing managers need to have an awareness of HRM because if human resources are really regarded as critical for business success, they, along with other functional managers, have responsibility for the effective delivery of HRM policies, conducting team briefings, performance appraisal, interviews, target setting, encouraging employee commitment, managing performance-related pay and similar activities.

Many writers extend the scope of HRM to include organisational behaviour covering such subjects as motivation, inter personal and group behaviours, attitudes, job satisfaction, leadership communication and organisational change. It is not possible to deal adequately with these areas within the constraints of this book. There are however four 'generic' HRM functions that are performed within all organisations, i.e. recruitment and selection, appraisal, reward, and training and development. Along with human resource planning and job analysis, the above four activities are considered from the standpoint of the purchasing function.

2. HUMAN RESOURCE PLANNING

This may be defined as an information and decision-making process designed to ensure that enough competent people with appropriate skills are available to perform jobs where and when they will be needed. For purchasing, as for all

Table 6.1 Stereotypes of personnel management and human resources management

	Personnel management	HRM
Time and planning perspective	Short-term, reactive, ad-hoc, marginal	Long-term, proactive, strategic, integrated
Psychological contract	Compliance	Commitment
Control systems	External controls	Self-control
Employee relations	Pluralist, collective, low trust	Unitavist, individual, high trust
Preferred structures/systems	Bureaucratic, mechanistic, centralised, formal defined roles	Organic, devolved, flexible roles
Roles	Specialist/professional	Largely integrated into line management
Evaluation criteria	Cost minimisation	Maximum utilisation (human asset accounting)

other staff, human resource planning will depend on both external and internal factors.

External factors will depend on:

(i) Whether the organisation operates under conditions of certainty or uncertainty – the more uncertain the environment, the more frequently human resource plans will need to be updated.

(ii) World trade prospects.

(iii) The organisation's competitive position within the industry.

(iv) External changes in technology, equipment and work methods.

(v) Age trends in the general population.

(vi) Education/skill requirements and their availability.

Internal factors will include a human resources audit including consideration of such factors as:

(i) Ages of the present staff.

(ii) Likely losses through retirement, leaving, etc.

(iii) Labour turnover for each grade of staff employed.

(iv) Anticipated promotions and transfers.

(v) Skills analysis, regularly updated, in respect of each employee.

(vi) Effects of human resources requirements due to the introduction of technology, organisational replanting, etc.

(vii) Temporary losses through illness, pregnancy, training absence, etc.

Other internal factors include budget allocations for personnel and training. Analysis of such factors will enable human resource plans to be formulated relating to the positions to be filled in the short, medium and long term; analysis of education and skills likely to be required; and career plans for existing staff with accompanying training and development plans.

3. JOB ANALYSIS

This may be defined as *'the examination of the facts about a certain job to determine its essential component factors and the qualities required by the employee to perform it satisfactorily'*. The elements of job analysis with definitions are shown below:

- *Job description.* The recording under an appropriate job title of the tasks and responsibilities involved in a job (job content). See **4b** below.
- *Job specification.* A specialised job description emphasising personal requirements designed to assist in the selection of employees (job requirements). See **4c** below.
- *Job evaluation.* The process of analysing and assessing jobs to ascertain their relative worth, using the assessments as a basis for a balanced wage structure (job worth).
- *Job classification.* The process by which jobs similar in content, remuneration and status are classified into designated groups (job grading).

4. RECRUITMENT AND SELECTION

This entails deciding whether and how to recruit staff, the preparation of job descriptions and specifications and the attraction and selection of candidates.

(a) Whether and how to recruit. Plumbley [3] has identified the following questions that should be asked before embarking on the recruitment process:

(*i*) What is the purpose of the job? Is it necessary? Is it fulfilling the purpose?

(*ii*) Could it be combined with another job or jobs or could tasks be allocated to make better use of other people in the department?

(*iii*) Can we learn any lessons from the record of the last job incumbent?

(*iv*) Could the vacancy be used as a temporary training position or to accommodate an employee redundant elsewhere, to provide easier work for an employee approaching retirement or in failing health, or as an opportunity to promote someone?

(*v*) Are we certain that no existing employee would be suitable? Could we afford to train someone?

(*vi*) Is the required type of person easier to recruit locally? Are there aspects of the job analysis (hours of work) or of the person specification which could be adjusted to attract a wider choice of candidates?

To the above we must add

(*vii*) Might it be more advantageous to appoint someone on a short-term consultancy basis?

(b) Job descriptions. A job description defining the overall purpose or role of his or her job and the main tasks to be carried out should be prepared for each member of the purchasing function. A typical job description will have the following headings:

(i) Job title

(ii) Responsible to – the person or function to whom the job holder reports.

(iii) Responsible for – a listing of the principal duties and responsibilities of the job.

(iv) Resources controlled.

(v) Special responsibilities – tasks emphasised as requiring particular attention.

(vi) Limitations on authority – particularly with regard to the amount the job holder may spend without reference to higher authority.

(vii) Functional contacts – relationship between purchasing and other functions as part of the supply chain.

(viii) Committees – organisational meetings which the job holder is expected to attend as an ex-officio member.

1. Job titles. An analysis by salary and sector of the vacancies advertised in *Purchasing and Supply Management* over the 12 months December 1993–November 1994 provides interesting information relating to job titles. Of the posts advertised 105 and 31 were in the private and public sectors respectively. These were categorised according to the highest level of remuneration offered into: £25,000 and under; over £25,000; salary not stated or negotiable. This analysis is shown in Table 6.2. The 136 vacancies were advertised under 53 different job titles as shown in Tables 6.3 and 6.4.

From the above a number of facts can be ascertained

(i) For both private and public sector organisations the most prevalent functional job title was 'Purchasing Manager' (21%). The second most used title 'Buyer' (19%) was more popular in the private sector.

(ii) Some job titles are related to pay. The titles 'Buyer', 'Senior Buyer', 'Purchasing Professional' and 'Controller' are more prevalent in posts with a salary ceiling of £25,000 or under. Clearly job titles including such designations as 'Head', 'Director' and 'Manager' are higher paid posts. For some appointments, however, a grandiloquent title does not always indicate high pay. Vacancies advertised as 'Company Buyer' and 'Materials Manager' were advertised with salaries of under £25,000.

Table 6.2 Analysis by highest level of salary specified and sector of 136 advertised purchasing vacancies 1993–1994

	£25,000 or under	Over £25,000	Not stated/ Negotiable	Total
Private Sector	43	21	41	105
Public Sector	17	13	1	31
	60	34	42	136

Table 6.3 **Analysis by job title of 105 private sector purchasing vacancies 1993–1994**

	Title	£25,000 or under	Over £25,000	Not Stated/ Negotiable	Total
1	Assistant Purchasing Manager	1			1
2	Buyer	9		7	16
3	Buyer (Communications)	1			1
4	Buyer (Company)	1			1
5	Buyer (Engineering)			1	1
6	Buyer (Engineer Contract Purchasing)			1	1
7	Buyer (Hotel Services)	1			1
8	Buyer (Ingredients)			1	1
9	Buyer (Project)		1		1
10	Buyer (Vehicles)	1			1
11	Commercial Contracts Negotiator	1		1	2
12	Contracts Manager	2		1	3
13	Contracts Officer	1		1	2
14	Contracts and Services Manager	1			1
15	Group Purchasing Manager		1		1
16	Head of Purchasing		1		1
17	Head of Procurement		1		1
18	Logistics Analysis Manager	1			1
19	Logistics Manager		1		1
20	Materials Manager	1	4	1	6
21	Parts Logistics Manager		1		1
22	Planning Manager		1		1
23	Procurement Engineer			1	1
24	Procurement Manager			3	3
25	Procurement Specialist	1	1		2
26	Product Stream Manager	1			1
27	Purchaser	1			1
28	Purchasing Agent	1			1
29	Purchasing Controller	1			1
30	Purchasing Executive			1	1
31	Purchasing Manager	1	5	13	19
32	Purchasing Professional	6	1	3	10
33	Senior Buyer	8	1	1	10
34	Senior Development Buyer	1			1
35	Supplies Manager			1	1
36	Supplies Development Manager		1		1
37	Supplies Manager			1	1
38	Senior Development Officer	1			1
39	Servicing Director			1	1
40	Vendor Audit Engineer			1	1
41	Vendor Manager			1	1
		43	21	41	105

Table 6.4 Analysis by job title of 31 public sector purchasing vacancies 1993–1994

	Title	£25,000 or under	Over £25,000	Not Stated/ Negotiable	Total
42	Assistant County Supplies Officer	1			1
43	Assistant Purchasing Officer	1			1
*	Buyer	1		1	2
44	Contracts Controller		1		1
*	Contracts Manager	1			1
*	Contracts Officer	1			1
*	Head of Procurement		1		1
45	Head of Supplies		1		1
46	Procurement Group Director		1		1
*	Procurement Manager		2		2
47	Principal Officer		1		1
48	Purchasing Administrator	1			1
*	Purchasing Manager	7	3		10
49	Purchasing Officer	2	1		3
50	Purchasing and Stores Officer	1			1
51	Purchasing Supplies Manager		1		1
52	Supplies Customer Service Manager	1			1
53	Strategic Purchasing Manager		1		1
		17	13	1	31

*Already used under private sector

(iii) Some advertisements for private sector appointments related to non-industrial enterprises, e.g. 'Head of Book Purchasing', 'Hotel Services Buyer'.
(iv) Some job titles in the private sector emphasised a supply chain approach, e.g. 'Logistics Analysis Manager', 'Logistics Manager', 'Materials Manager', 'Parts Logistics Manager'.

2. Examples of job descriptions. Examples of job descriptions relating to the posts of Assistant Director/Manager of Production Purchasing and Buyer in manufacturing organisations are given below [4].

TITLE: Assistant Director/Manager of Production Purchasing

Reports to: Director of Purchasing

Basic Function:
Plan, organise, and co-ordinate all Production Purchasing activities in support of the division's manufacturing and sales goals and objectives. This position will perform various assigned tasks and fill in for the Director of Purchasing as directed. Recommend objectives and initiate appropriate actions for his/her area of responsibility to meet the department goals.

Dimension:
Responsible for annual Spend of approximately £200 million.

Supervises four buyers, one senior buyer, one tooling expediter, and one quality assurance engineer assigned to Purchasing.

Nature and Scope:
This position reports to the Director of Purchasing and has overall responsibility for the purchase of all raw material and components that become a part of the finished product. The position requires a high degree of maturity, being conscientious and ethical to ensure control and the proper responsible expenditure of company funds. The person must keep constantly up-to-date about economic conditions and/or business situations as they affect the materials we use. This knowledge is necessary to make informed decisions to adequately meet changing conditions. The individual must be resourceful and protect the company's interests by understanding what needs to be done and taking the required action to protect production.

The position will interact at all levels of management both inside the company and outside in supplier company organisations. The individual will work closely with Product and Manufacturing Engineering, Sales, Finance, Production Planning, Quality Assurance, and cost improvement committees.

This position analyses, reviews, and finalises buyer sourcing decisions, conducts major negotiations including planning and development of strategy and tactics to reach objectives, and negotiates long-term contracts as appropriate. The individual is responsible for meeting the cost avoidance and reduction objectives of the Production Purchasing Department.

A significant responsibility is to plan, organise, and administer subordinate development. The individual is to provide guidance to employees relative to their dealings with suppliers and persons from other departments within the company. Develop and promote team work relationships between Production Purchasing and the rest of the organisation.

This position requires travel to supplier facilities to build relationships, review operations, expedite parts, troubleshoot, and help evaluate total management and manufacturing capabilities to increase the number of certified suppliers. The individual will approve all subordinate travel requests and approve travel expense reports for authorised business trips.

The position will assist the buyers in developing and updating commodity strategies, both long and short term, to assure supply base development in support of the company's production schedules and forecasts.

To be successful in this position, the person must have proven management abilities, a sound business understanding, articulate with good verbal and written communication skills, proven organisation and planning skills, experience in buying, experience in successful negotiations, thorough knowledge of the supply base, good interpersonal skills, ability to read drawings, good mathematical aptitude and have a knowledge of quality assurance philosophies, practices, and techniques.

Principal Accountabilities:
Performance will be measured by the individual's ability to:

1. Direct and co-ordinate the activities of the Production Purchasing Department personnel.

2. Operate within budget and meet the cost avoidance and reduction objectives as established by the company. (A means to this end is to actively convert action plans into production reality.)

3. Timely and satisfactorily execute the assignments and directives of the Purchasing Director.

4. Professionally resolve problems (both internal and external) in a fair and ethical manner while protecting the long-term interests of the company.

5. Support the production efforts of the company with parts, tooling, and necessary equipments.

TITLE: Buyer 1

General Statement
Performs, under relatively close direction, the administration of long-term agreements, and purchases items at the lowest price consistent with desired quality to meet specified requirement date.
Participates in negotiations with suppliers.
Requires considerable level of supervision.

Reports to: Procurement Manager

Duties and Responsibilities:

1. Receives and reviews each requisition for completeness, selects reliable sources, requests bids as necessary, evaluates quotation and makes final supplier selection.

2. Assures all requirements and special terms and conditions are met.

3. Provides complete and accurate status reports on requests.

4. Participates in negotiations with suppliers.

5. Approves supplier invoice exceptions for payment by the Accounting Department in accordance with governing procedures and instructions.

6. Co-ordinates and makes the necessary arrangement for processing discrepant supplied items and material and makes the proper disposition on rejected items. Issues replacement purchase orders as required on returned items and materials.

7. Performs liaison activities with appropriate purchasing and/or production control personnel in plant sites other than his or her own.

8. May monitor, analyse, and administer daily decisions in support of the formal MRP actions.

9. May maintain and monitor inventory levels on all assigned parts; recommend write-off of excess or obsolete inventory.

10. May be responsible for all Item Master and basic data information on assigned parts.

11. May initiate corrective actions to ensure that assigned piece part delivery schedules and/or reservations are in agreement.

The above statements are intended to describe the general nature and level of work being performed by people assigned to this job. They are not intended to be an exhaustive list of all responsibilities, duties, and skills required of the incumbent in this position.

Expected Qualifications for Position:

Education: Bachelors Degree

Experience: 0–2 years purchasing related experience.

(c) **Job specification.** These are often termed person specifications. The person specification is the development of the job description and deals with the qualities required by somebody ideally suited to do the job. The preparation of a person specification requires:

(i) a thorough knowledge of the job
(ii) a systematic approach
(iii) a readiness on the part of those preparing the specification to challenge their own preoccupations and, in the light of the job description, to see if these are justified.

A number of check lists for use in compiling a person specification have been devised. The best known and most widely used of these are the Seven Point Plan of Alec Rodger [5] and the Five Fold Grading System of J Munro Fraser [6].

1. The Seven Point Plan by Alec Rodger. This draws attention to seven aspects of the individual:

Physique:	health, strength, appearance, voice and other physical attributes
Attainments:	general education, job training and job experience
General intelligence:	capacity for complex mental work, general reasoning ability
Special aptitudes:	predisposition to acquire certain types of skill
Interests	inclination towards intellectual, social, practical, constructive or physically active leisure pursuits
Disposition:	steadiness and reliability, degree of acceptability to and influence over others, self-reliance
Circumstances:	mobility, age, domicile

2. The Five Fold Grading System of J Munro Fraser. This selects the following:

Impact on others:	relations with colleagues, customers and other contacts
Qualifications:	education, training and job experience
Brains:	innate abilities, quickness of apprehension

Motivation:	drive and initiative, personal standards and self composed goals
Adjustment:	ability to cope with stress and pressure, deviation from routine and general upsets

When drawing up job specifications and advertisements it is important to observe the following:

(i) Specify essential knowledge and skills that the job holder must possess, e.g. ability to read engineering drawings, knowledge of languages, previous experience with MRP systems.

(ii) Do not overstate requirements. Setting unrealistically high levels of qualification and experience increases the difficulty of attracting candidates.

(iii) Avoid anything that can be construed as discriminatory, e.g. references to age, sex, colour or nationality.

(d) Sources of applicants. Once the content of a purchasing job, the ideal characteristics of the job holder and the reward package relating to the job have been determined recruitment can begin. Sources and methods of attracting applicants for vacancies include:

(i) Advertising – which should be in the right media, e.g. quality papers, appropriate journals, e.g. *Purchasing and Supply Management,* and of the right format.

(ii) Department of Employment facilities.

(iii) The educational sector, i.e. university appointment boards, career offices.

(iv) Professional organisations, e.g. the Chartered Institute of Purchasing and Supply.

(v) Consultants, especially those specialising in the recruitment and selection of purchasing staff.

(vi) Internal advertisement.

All applicants should be required to complete an application form that enables information about candidates to be obtained in a standardised format.

(e) Selection procedures. The preliminary stage of selection involves sifting through the applications received and preparing a shortlist of candidates for interview. Roe and Greuter [7] state that it is important that selection procedures fulfil four main functions:

(i) Information gathering: This involves generating information about the organisation, the job, career paths, employment conditions on the one hand, and, on the other, about candidates, including their experience, qualifications and personal characteristics.

(ii) Prediction: Using information on past and present candidate characteristics as a basis for making predictions about candidates' future behaviour.

(iii) Decision making: Using the predictions about candidates' future behaviour as a basis for making decisions about whom to accept or reject.

(iv) Information supply: Providing information, on the one hand about the

organisation, the job and employment conditions to candidates, and, on the other providing information about the result of the selection process to the various parties involved – line manager, personnel specialist etc.

Anderson [8] has stated that other considerations that will shape the design of selection procedures include:

(v) The availability of managerial and specialist skills: Selection procedures must be developed in a way that can be implemented by available managers and specialist staff (e.g. purchasing and supply specialists).

(vi) Cost/benefit factors: The quality and soundness of selection procedures must be balanced against the cases involved.

(f) Interviews. Selection will be on the basis of an interview. Interviews may be carried out on an individual or group basis. The purposes of an interview are:

(i) To provide the applicant with information about the employee and the job.

(ii) To enable the prospective employee to provide the employer with information additional to that given on the application form and enable the employer to assess the suitability of the prospective employee.

(iii) To let the applicant feel that his/her application has been courteously, seriously and fairly considered.

Interviews have been criticised on the grounds of being unreliable, involved and subjective. Torrington and Hall [9] state that the most perceptive criticism is contained in the work of Webster (1964) who on the basis of extensive research concluded:

(i) Interviewers decide to accept or reject a candidate within the first three or four minutes of the interview and then spend the remainder of their time seeking evidence to confirm that their first impression is right.

(ii) Interviews seldom alter the tentative opinion formed by the interviewer based on the application form and appearance of the candidate.

(iii) Interviewers place more weight on evidence that is unfavourable than on evidence that is favourable.

(iv) When interviewers have made up their minds very early on in the interview, their behaviour betrays their decision to the candidate.

To improve the validity of the selection process interviews may be supplemented by some form of testing, including medical examinations, attainment tests, psychological tests, i.e. intelligence and personality tests, and the observation of candidates in group situations including group tasks, leaderless discussions and simulated business problems.

5. PERFORMANCE APPRAISAL

(a) Definition: *Assessment of the quality of a person's work and job.* Such assessment may be made by:

(i) The employee's immediate superior – this is the most common method.
(ii) The superior's superior.
(iii) Peers.
(iv) Subordinates.
(v) An assessment centre.
(vi) The appraisal, i.e. self appraisal.

(b) The purposes of appraisal: These differ according to organisational and individual perspectives.

From the *organisational* perspective appraisals may help to determine:

- individual objectives
- the extent to which individual objectives have been attained
- employees with promotion potential
- employees who might be transferred to other work
- individual training and development needs
- what an individual actually does, i.e. a comparison of job descriptions with what is done
- career succession and human resource planning
- salary increases.

From the *individual* perspective appraisal should be seen as:

- a career development exercise
- an opportunity to clarify what the organisation expects and how far the job holder is fulfilling those expectations
- an opportunity to discuss career aspirations and how far these can be met by the organisation
- a chance to constructively discuss problems relating to the job.

Sometimes purposes and perspectives conflict. Some writers advocate that performance appraisals and pay reviews should be kept separate.

(c) Objections to appraisals: Appraisals have been criticised on the grounds that they:

(i) are time consuming
(ii) generate paperwork
(iii) do not provide any information not already obtained by daily contact and observation
(iv) can be confrontational and a source of conflict
(v) put the appraiser in the conflicting roles of judge and helper
(vi) may cause the appraiser to 'fudge' comments to avoid the embarrassment inherent in criticising subordinates.

(d) Performance management. Torrington and Hall [10] suggest that 'the best and most effective use is made of the appraisal process by tying it into the larger and more complete system of performance management' which links individual objectives with organisational and functional strategic objectives. Applied to purchasing the system would be as shown in Fig 6.1. In this system

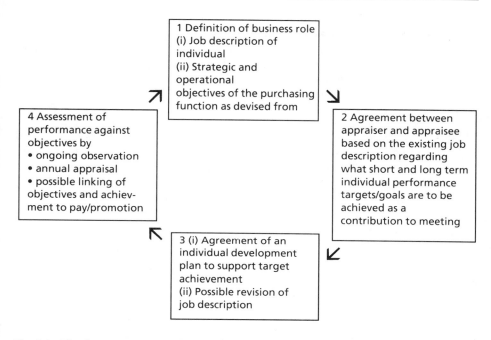

Fig 6.1 The four stages of a representative performance management system

(i) The objectives set are in terms of results to be achieved which are designed to challenge the individual to perform to his/her potential.

(ii) The development plan agreed between the appraiser and appraisee emphasises the importance of managerial support and coaching.

(iii) To avoid potential conflict between the openness and development approach aimed at improving job performance and the link with pay, performance and pay reviews are usually separated in time.

(e) Other approaches to appraisal. Other appraisal approaches include:

- Descriptive approaches, i.e. asking the appraiser to provide an unstructured narrative report on the job performances of appraisees.
- Checklists, i.e. a list of key results areas or of behaviour traits on which the appraiser is asked to comment.
- Ratings, i.e. in which the appraisee is scored alphabetically or numerically against the checklist.

Stevens [11] for example, provides an example of a detailed rating scale related to buyer performance under three main headings:

Personal traits, aptitudes and abilities
Basic purchasing knowledge and skills
Relationships with people.

Examples under each heading are:

(1) *Personal traits, aptitudes and abilities*

(2) *Letter writing*

Points

The buyer writes intelligently, concisely and expresses himself well. His grammar and composition are adequate to obtain a clear understanding by his correspondents. In this respect the buyer is:

Excellent	Good	Fair	Poor
10–9	8–6	5–3	2–1

Other ratings under this heading are: (1) memory, (3) telephone techniques, (4) personal appearance, (5) availability, (6) flexibility, (7) grasps situations, (8) aptitude, (9) persuasion, (10) ethics, (11) independence, (12) follows directions and instructions, (13) weighs problems, (14) accepts criticism, (15) organises work, (16) realises other's problems, (17) attitude, (18) punctuality.

(2) *Basic purchasing knowledge and skills*

(21) Delay of salesmen

Points

The buyer keeps to a minimum the length of time salesmen wait to see him. He informs them if there is to be any delay. In this respect he is:

Excellent	Good	Fair	Poor
6	5–4	3–2	1

Other ratings under this heading are: (19) adjustments, (20) materials standards, (22) summary sheets, (23) savings, (24) competition, (25) interviews, (26) delivery, (27) familiarity with items, (28) analysing requisitions, (29) discrepancies, (30) records, (31) order preparations, (32) paperwork, (33) new ideas and new products, (34) stock reductions .

(3) *Relationships with people*

(37) Other departments

Points

The buyer knows and has the respect of personnel in other departments. He is consulted by them on procurement problems and is co-operative and helpful. In this respect the buyer is:

Excellent	Good	Fair	Poor
25–22	21–13	12–4	3–1

Other ratings under this heading are: (35) supplier's personnel, (36) meetings, (38) own department, (39) supervisor.

The total points obtained for each factor are graded as follows:

Excellent	Good	Fair	Poor
648–588	549–359	320–133	94–41

In this scheme by limiting the choice to four categories the tendency for appraisees to pick the middle one when there are an odd number from which to choose is avoided. Although it may be objected that the use of numbers tends to give a falsely scientific and precise air to what is essentially an objective process this approach can provide a pay-linked formula and help to provide an analysis of overall performance standards.

6. TRAINING AND DEVELOPMENT

(a) Training may be defined as:

A planned process to modify attitudes, knowledge or skill behaviour through learning experience to achieve effective performance in an activity or range of activities. Its purpose in the work situation is to develop the abilities of the individual and to satisfy the current and future human resource needs of the organisation.

Training is closely associated with *education* and *development* which may be respectively defined as:

Education – activities which aim at developing the knowledge, skills, moral values and understanding required in all aspects of life, rather than the knowledge and skill relating only to a limited field of activity.

Development – the growth or realisation of a person's ability through conscious and unconscious learning.

(b) Training needs can be identified by a job training analysis. Job training analysis is 'the process of identifying the purpose of the job and its component parts and the specifying of what must be learnt for there to be effective work performance'.

A job analysis will reveal the 'training gap', which is the difference between a person's existing knowledge, skills and experience and the knowledge, skills and experience required for a specific job. Training needs can be considered both from organisational and individual standpoints.

At the organisational level the ascertainment of training needs involves asking such questions as:

- What knowledge and skills are required now and in the future?
- What is the shortfall between the capabilities of the staff at present and what is likely to be required of them in the future?
- How much staff training is required to get to the position we wish to reach?

At the individual level the ascertainment of training needs involves asking such questions as:

- What is your present job?
- How effectively can you do it at present?
- What are your future job aspirations:
- What training, if any, do you require to:
    - (i) Do the job as effectively as possible?
    - (ii) Cope with job changes?
    - (iii) Provide you with confidence and job satisfaction?
    - (iv) Enable you to meet your long-term aims?

(c) Training and development for purchasing and supply. This may be carried out 'in-house' or 'externally'.

In-house training is carried out within the employing organisation, but not necessarily at the workplace or in one location. In-house training may be carried out by:

(i) Working under the supervision of an experienced colleague or 'mentor'.

(ii) Job rotation, i.e. undertaking a variety of purchasing tasks on a planned basis, e.g. six months in progressing, six months in quality management, etc.

(iii) Understudying, i.e. undertaking the responsibilities of senior staff during their absence through holidays or sickness. Every employee should, in fact, be encouraged to be both a learner and a teacher:

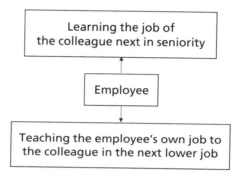

(iv) External courses. These are normally on a part-time or block release basis. Staff who have not obtained the qualifications of the Chartered Institute of Purchasing and Supply should be encouraged to do so.

External courses are those conducted by outside trainers at locations other than the employer's premises, e.g. courses provided by colleges, higher education colleges, universities, training organisations and training consultants. Training facilities also include such developments as open and distance learning.

Training methods appropriate to purchasing staff (other than those mentioned) include case studies, watching computerised learning packages, discussions, in-tray exercises, job rotation, lectures, management games, programmed learning, role playing, secondment to other organisations, videos and films.

(d) National Vocational Qualifications. The National Council for Vocational Qualifications (NCVQ) was set up by the British Government in 1986 to:

(i) 'Hallmark' qualifications which meet the needs of employment – National Vocational Qualifications (NVQs)

(ii) Locate them within a new structure so that everyone can use and understand the NVQ Framework. (In Scotland, the same remit was given to the Scottish Vocational Education Council (SCOTVEC) where the new qualifications are called Scottish Vocational Qualifications (SVQs). NVQs and SVQs are, however, in most respects identical.) In Northern Ireland a Vocational Qualifications Unit has been established to liaise with the NCVQ.

The terms NVQ Framework, Competence, Assessment and Standards need to be understood for the nature of NVQs to be comprehended.

(1) The NVQ Framework. The NVQ Framework is based on a functional analysis of work roles and occupational competences rather than tasks and provides the initial organising structure for a national system of broad, competence-based qualifications. The usefulness of the NVQ Framework, however, is not confined to the UK. The national framework together with the appropriate standards for each level also have applications to a number of employment functions including

- Job descriptions
- Job grading
- Job evaluation
- Selection and career development
- Education and training.

Currently the NVQ Framework comprises five levels. Definitions of each level and their applications to the purchasing and supply function are shown in Table 6.5.

(2) Competence in the NVQ context is defined as [12]

being able to perform whole work roles	(perform – not just know about – whole work roles rather than just specific skills and tasks)
to the standards expected in employment	(not just 'training' standards or standards divorced from industrial reality)
in real working environments	(i.e. with all the associated pressures and variations of real work)

(3) Assessment is defined by the NCVQ [13] as *the process of collecting evidence and making judgements on whether or not performance criteria have been met.* As a general rule, assessment of performance in normal work (by observation, work products, documents, contracts, etc.) against the performance criteria specified in the units of competence required for a NVQ at a given level offers the most natural form of evidence. Where performance evidence alone does not permit reliable inference that a candidate possesses the necessary knowledge and understanding – or competence – this must be separately assessed, e.g. by oral questioning, written answers, multiple choice tests, etc.

(4) Standards. Standards of competence are determined and endorsed by a lead body which comprises representatives of employers, working with employees (including trade unions) and their education and training advisers. The Purchasing and Supply Lead Body is responsible for standards of competence relating to the purchasing, materials management, contracts management and logistics part of the supply chain.

The structure of NVQs at Levels 2, 3 and 4 is (1995) under review but the titles of units and the units currently specified at each level are shown in Table 6.6. To

Table 6.5 NVQ framework levels

Level	Competence	Responsibility	Application to Purchasing and Supply
1	Range of varied work activities, most of which may be routine and predictable.	Usually under supervision	Stores/warehousing operative
2	Significant range of varied activities performed in a variety of contexts. Some activities are complex and non-routine. Collaboration with others may be a requirement.	Some individual responsibility or autonomy.	Stores/warehousing operative
3	Broad range of complex technical or professional activities performed in a variety of contexts, most of which are complex and non-routine.	Considerable responsibility and autonomy. Control or guidance of others often required.	Purchaser (Junior Buyer). Stores/Warehouse Supervisor.
4	Broad range of complex or professional work activities performed in a variety of contexts.	Substantial degree of personal responsibility and autonomy. Allocation of resources often required.	Purchaser (Senior Buyer). Stores/Warehouse Manager
5	Competence which involves the application of a significant range of fundamental principles and complex techniques across a wide and often unpredictable variety of contexts.	Personal accountability and autonomy feature strongly, and often significant responsibility for the work of others and for the allocation of substantial resources.	Purchasing Manager, Controller, Materials Manager, etc.

Table 6.6   Titles of units and units specified for Levels 1–4 NVQs in Purchasing and Supply (1995)

Unit no	Unit title	NVQ Level		
		2	3	4
001	Contributing to the health and saftey of the working environment	•	•	•
002	Creating and maintaining appropriate professional relationships with other people	•	•	•
003	Contributing to the installation and improvement of purchasing related systems	•		
004	Establishing and operating database of purchasing/stores information	•		
005	Communication to maintain supplier performance	•		
006	Acquiring specified supplies	•		
007	Progressing the delivery of supplies	•		
008	Contributing to the maintenance of systems for security and confidentiality	•	•	•
009	Data transmission	•		
010	Contributing to organisational strategy		•	•
011	Determining supplier performance and continuity of supply		•	
012	Contributing to the establishment and evaluation of current and future requirements for supply		•	
013	Maintaining the effectiveness of purchasing operations		•	
014	Selecting supplier for specified supplies		•	•
015	Contracting for supply		•	•
016	Contributing to the establishment and improvement of purchasing related systems		•	
017	Establishing and maintaining database of purchasing/stores information		•	
018	Negotiating improvements in supplier performance		•	
019	Determining conditions in the market for supplies			•
020	Determining potential suppliers through vendor evaluation			•
021	Optimising the supplier base			•
022	Entering into strategic sourcing arrangement			•
023	Contributing to the establishment and integration of purchasing related systems			•
024	Establishing and maintaining database of purchasing/stores and management information			•
025	Obtaining improvements in supplier performance			•
026	Establishing and evaluating current and future requirements for supply			•
027	Developing the effectiveness of purchasing operations			•

• denotes compulsory for this level

obtain a full NVQ candidates must achieve all the units of competence indicated at each level. A Certificate of Unit Credit is issued to candidates who achieve one or more units.

7. PURCHASING AND PAY

(a) The basics of pay. A distinction needs to be made between:

(i) Pay, i.e. the actual salary payable less tax and other agreed deductions
(ii) The 'total remuneration package' including such fringe benefits as:
  - insurance – life, private medical and permanent disability insurance
  - house purchase – bridging loans to assist with house purchase at little or no interest
  - company cars
  - loans, normally interest free to such purposes as car purchase or home improvements
  - employee share schemes – allowing agreed categories of staff to purchase company shares on advantageous schemes
  - assistance with school fees
  - payment of professional fees
  - discount on purchases of company products.

Payscales usually involve some form of job grading. Job grading can be related to job specifications so that the grade and pay attached to a job can take into account such factors as:

(i) length and variety of experience
(ii) general and vocational education
(iii) the scope of the job's responsibility
(iv) the scope and type of supervision exercised or received by the job holder
(v) the consequences of mistakes by the job holder
(vi) the physical, mental and social demands of the job
(vii) working conditions or job hazards.

The basic principle of a graded salary structure is that job holders advance within the salary grade for the job as they improve their performance or by securing promotion to a higher grade.

Apart from grading, salaries or remuneration packages may be based on such factors as:

(i) The actual or potential value of an individual's contribution and performance to the undertaking
(ii) Market rates as affected by supply and demand, general movements in pay levels and particular areas of market pressure
(iii) Salary relativities as between jobs within the organisation depending on the values attached to different jobs
(iv) The influence of trade unions on pay increases and differentials.

(b) Sources of information regarding purchasing pay. These include:

(i) Informal enquiries from other companies and employers' organisations.

(ii) Job advertisements, remembering that the advertisement is not always indicative of the job requirements and the salary quoted may not always be the salary paid.

(iii) The Department of Employment.

(iv) Professional associations.

(v) Published salary surveys. These are usually only available some time after they have been conducted. Such surveys include:

The Purcon Index [14] is a specialised survey of the salaries and total remuneration package of Purchasing and Supplies staff throughout Britain and is updated in March and September of each year. Purchasing costs are divided into six job levels under nine industry classifications and in eight regional locations. The six job levels are:

- *Job Level 1:* Assistant Buyer/Purchasing Officer, responsible for an annual spend of up to £2m, a stock level of up to £200k and no staff.
- *Job Level 2:* Buyer/Purchasing Officer, responsible for an annual spend of £2m to £5m, a stock level of £200k to £700k and up to 2 staff.
- *Job Level 3:* Senior/Chief Buyer, responsible for an annual spend of £5m to £15m, a stock level of £700k to £2m and 3 to 6 staff.
- *Job Level 4:* Chief Buyer/Purchasing Manager, responsible for an annual spend of £15m to £25m, a stock level of £2m to £4m and 7 to 15 staff.
- *Job Level 5:* Purchasing/Materials Manager, responsible for an annual spend of £25m to £50m, a stock level of £4m to £10m and 15 to 30 staff.
- *Job Level 6:* Purchasing/Supplies/Materials Manager/Director, responsible for an annual spend of over £50m, a stock level of over £10m and over 30 staff.

The Index provides data on average, median and upper and lower quartile total earnings for each job level in six age ranges (i.e. 20–25, 26–30, 31–35, 36–40, 41–50, 50+) both for the whole sample surveyed and those who are qualified. 'Qualified' in this context includes 'those who have a Degree or Higher National Certificate/Diploma, and/or are members of the Chartered Institute of Purchasing and Supply or British Production and Inventory Control Society.' Additional information relates to bonus earnings by job level and industry and the percentage frequency of company cars by job level, industry and location.

Other important salary surveys include those published by Remuneration Economics [15] and Reward [16].

Remuneration Economics publishes the *National Management Survey* which gives average, median and lower and upper quartile earnings by sales turnover, number of employees, industry groups, region and age groups for nine levels of management responsibility ranging from Senior Staff to Chief Executive.

Reward publishes the *Management Salary Survey* providing broadly similar information for several ranks, the lowest of which is Senior Clerical and Technician covering tasks in the office or a senior clerical nature such as Buying Assistant which require experience and a limited degree of initiative.

8. REWARD SYSTEMS, MOTIVATION AND COMMUNICATION

These topics are of relevance to any function and can only be discussed in a general way leaving the reader to work out their application to purchasing. Since they are also inter-related it is convenient to discuss them in the order, motivation, reward systems and communication.

Motivation in this context refers to the forces within an individual that account for the level, direction and persistence of effort expended at work.

(a) Theories of motivation. It is inappropriate in a specialist book to discuss these in detail. Full explanations are given in the many books concerned with Organisational Behaviour. Sufficient to state that theories of motivation fall into two classes:

> *(i) Content theories* explain human behaviour in terms of specific human needs or deficiencies that an individual feels some need to eliminate. The theories associated with the names of Maslow, Alderfer, McClelland and Herzberg are 'content' orientated.
>
> *(ii) Process theories* endeavour to provide an understanding of the cognitive processes that take place in the minds of individuals and act to influence their behaviour. The 'Equity' and 'Expectancy' theories associated respectively with the names of Adams and Vroom are examples.

(b) General statements regarding motivation

> *(i)* Motivation is a complex process because people have different needs.
> *(ii)* Motivation is linked to leadership because leaders should know what motivates a particular subordinate.
> *(iii)* Basic needs are related to the satisfaction of physiological, security and social needs. Until such needs are satisfied, so called 'higher order needs' for esteem and self actualisation do not normally operate.
> *(iv)* Money is an important motivator since it provides the means to satisfy a number of needs. Herzberg, however, points out that while lack of money can cause dissatisfaction, its provision does not give lasting satisfaction. Where reward systems are not seen to be fair and equitable money can demotivate.
> *(v)* Motivation at work can be extrinsic, i.e. what is done for employees by employers in order to motivate them, i.e. rewards and punishments, or intrinsic, i.e. the self-generated factors that influence people to effort, e.g. self actualisation, responsibility, achievement, recognition, the work itself.
> *(vi)* Performance = (Ability × Motivation)

Two important concept associated with motivation are commitment and empowerment.

(1) Commitment. This has been defined by Martin and Nicholls [17] as 'giving all of yourself while at work'. These writers state that the term entails such things as:

- using all of one's time constructively
- not neglecting details

- making that extra effort
- getting it right first time
- accepting change
- willingness to try something new
- making suggestions
- co-operating with others
- developing one's talents/abilities
- not abusing trust
- being proud of one's abilities
- seeking constant improvement
- enjoying one's job
- giving loyal support where needed.

Martin and Nicholls [18] postulate that creating commitment has three major pillars.

Pillar 1 A sense of belonging to the organisation derived from:
- *Informing people* by e.g.
  team briefing
  open disclosure
  simple language and examples
- *Involving people* by e.g.
  single status conditions
  consultation
  outings, visits and jamborees.
- *Sharing success with people* by e.g.
  share option schemes
  productivity gain sharing
  local lump-sum bonuses.

Pillar 2 A sense of excitement in the job derived from:
- *Creating pride* by e.g.
  responsibility for quality
  direct identification with output
  comparison with competitors
- *Creating trust* by e.g.
  abolition of piecework
  peer-group control
  removal of demarcation
- *Creating accountability for results* by e.g.
  pushing decision making down the line
  challenging assignments
  quality circles

Pillar 3 Creating accountability for results derived from:
- *Exerting authority* by e.g.
  no abdication to shop stewards
  willingness to discipline
  maintenance of standards and objectives

- *Showing dedication* by e.g.
  reduction of management overheads
  seeking productivity through people
  attention to commitment
- *Displaying competence* by e.g.
  establishing mission and objectives
  new management initiatives
  professional standards

(2) *Empowerment.* This is a term applied to a number of management approaches aimed at the reduction of employee powerlessness through the satisfaction of worker needs for esteem, self actualisation, participation and enhanced personal effectiveness.

Alpander [19] in a review of empowerment strategies related to employee needs in three countries, Australia, Germany and Japan, has stated that the common link seen as empowering in all three cases exhibits one of more of the following elements:

- Setting inspirational goals – managers envisage a desired state and show subordinates how to get there; by so doing they establish the basic component of the inspirational process.
- Providing or showing employees how to obtain resources and means to reach their goals.
- Reducing or removing constraints or showing employees how to do so.
- Expressing confidence in subordinates accompanied by high performance expectations.
- Modifying managerial styles, organisational policies and procedures to enable and empower subordinates to translate intention into action.
- Fostering opportunities to participate in decision making.
- Providing autonomy from bureaucratic constraints.

An empowering manager is therefore one who makes tasks intrinsically satisfying to the individual, not only by fostering in them feelings of self efficiency but also by eliminating conditions that create feelings of powerlessness. Empowerment is, to some extent, synonymous with enabling. The benefits claimed for empowerment include:

(i) Enhanced individual responsibility with a consequential motivation to reduce mistakes and improve quality.

(ii) Enlarged opportunities for employees to demonstrate creativity and innovation.

(iii) Improved processes and products through harnessing the skill and knowledge of the workforce.

(iv) Improved customer service by empowering employees nearest to the customer to make rapid decisions.

(v) Reduced labour turnover and absenteeism deriving from employee loyalty and involvement.

(vi) Increased productivity deriving from employee responsibility for work outcomes.

(vii) Emphasis on a team approach based on co-operation and a breakdown of interdepartmental conflict and barriers.

(viii) Fewer organisational levels.

(ix) Enhanced employee commitment deriving from a sense of belonging to the organisation, sense of excitement in the job and confidence in the management.

(x) Reduction in quality control procedures and personnel.

(xi) Increased competitiveness.

(xii) Improved labour relationships.

Eccles [20], however, takes a sceptical view of the practical application of empowerment and points out that its basic techniques derive from suggestion schemes, job enrichment and worker participation approaches which have been available but underused for years. He also claims that in larger (Western) organisations, higher involvement occurs, when at all, only at the professional and managerial levels. Outside professional partnerships empowerment does not extend to strategic power sharing. Eccles concludes

> 'The best new thing about empowerment is itself; the word empowerment which is so positive that it has enabled managers to embrace old, well known, more productive, ways of managing which have previously languished.'

(c) Reward systems. Armstrong [21] points out that the concept of reward management is replacing the essentially static techniques of salary administration because of the need to design remuneration structures which fit the corporate culture and can operate flexibly in the face of rapid change. Aspects of purchasing remuneration have been touched on earlier in this chapter in the section on 'Purchasing and Pay'. Rewards, however, include incentives, which may be financial or non-financial, performance pay and fringe benefits. Some types of performance pay systems are shown in Table 6.7.

In the table:

- *Individual output systems* link pay to relatively tangible and quantifiable measures of output performance, the unit of production or time saved

Table 6.7 Types of performance-based pay systems [22]

Type of Performance	Unit of Performance	
	Individual	*Collective*
Output	Piecework Commission Individual Bonus Individual performance-related pay	Measured daywork Team bonus Profit sharing Gain sharing
Input	Skill based pay Merit pay	Employee share Ownership schemes

with piecework, or sales achieved, with commission. It is also distinguished from *merit pay*, the major individual input scheme, which bases pay upon behavioural traits such as flexibility, co-operation or punctuality or *skill-based pay* which rewards employees for certain physical or mental capacities or capabilities they bring to the job.

- Collective output schemes rely upon a geared relationship between pay and performance of the collective whether this be the work of the group, plant or company, i.e. a stipulated level of performance expressed in terms of profit, sales, savings or added value leads automatically to a pay outturn. In contrast to most individual schemes those based on collective outputs do not require employee appraisal or the extensive use of managerial discretion and judgement.
- *Employee share ownership schemes* are more related to questions of ownership and participation than pay.

9. COMMUNICATION

Communication is the imparting or exchange of information [23].

It is a complex subject which may be approached from numerous standpoints including (to mention a few): the elements of communication, oral and written communication, communication technology, barriers to communication, verbal and non-verbal communication, listening, formal and informal communication, communication networks and the psychology of communication.

(i) *Effective communication* occurs when the intended message of the sender and the interpreted meaning of the receiver are the same.

(ii) *Efficient communication* occurs at a minimum cost in terms of resources, including time expended.

As shown in Chapters 5 and 7 developments such as EDI and CAD are greatly increasing efficiency in the transmission and reception of information relating to purchasing and associated functions.

10. THE MANAGEMENT OF CHANGE

For examples of change it is unnecessary to look further than those which during the last two decades have taken place in respect of the purchase function itself. A summary of these changes is given in Chapter 1 (Table 2).

(a) Understanding change. Daft [24] has identified four basic types of change which affect organisations. These can be applied to purchasing or other functions:

(i) *Technology*, e.g. computerisation, EDI, CAD/CAM.

(ii) *The product or service*, e.g. purchasing was mainly an operational function charged with obtaining items for production or internal use. While still carrying out operational tasks it is now involved in the provision of strategic information and services.

(iii) Administrative changes, e.g. the movement from discrete purchasing 'departments' to cross-functional procedures such as the scanning, screening and selection of supplying partners by purchasing teams of design and production engineers, marketing, procurement, and financial specialists.

(iv) People, e.g. the need for trained purchasing professionals.

(b) Forces for change may also be categorised as:

(i) External: which create pressures on organisations to devise and implement new strategies, e.g. competition.

(ii) Internal: those from within the organisation which may be the result of changing environmental conditions, e.g. declining competitive advantage, rising production costs or outdated production facilities may create internal pressure for new corporate strategies.

(c) Resistance to change. These may also be:

(i) External: e.g. prior commitments to suppliers, tools owned by suppliers, obligations to customers, government regulations re the environment.

(ii) Internal: e.g. limited organisational resources, incompatibility with existing equipment, inadequate personnel skills or interest, opposition from trade unions.

Organisational culture comprising the leadership style of top management and the values, practices and norms of employees may be a major factor in resistance to change. *Power and internal politics* which reflect the different interests of those affected are also important sources of resistance.

(d) Implementing change. Because of factors such as those mentioned in c*(ii)* above it has been stated [25] that:

> 'Executives have learned that planning is about 10 per cent of the effort to change an organisation, whereas implementing the plan, the tougher part of the job by far, requires the remaining 90 per cent of the effort.'

(i) Readiness for change. For change efforts to be effective they must be supported by favourable conditions. Beer [26] has expressed the most important indicators of readiness for change in a rough formula:

$$C = (D \times S \times P) > X$$

where C = change, D = dissatisfaction with the current state of affairs, S = an identifiable and desired end state, P = a practical plan for achieving the desired end state, X = cost of change to the organisation.

The formula suggests that change is a function of dissatisfaction, a desired goal, a means to obtain the goal and a desired cost.

(ii) Strategies for change. These may be summarised as:

- *Force change strategy* involves giving orders and enforcing them. This has the advantage of being fast but has the disadvantages of low commitment and high resistance.
- *Educative change strategy* involves convincing people by the provision of information of the need for change. This has the advantages of higher commitment and less resistance than force change strategy but the disadvantages of being slow and difficult.
- *Rational or self-interest change strategy* attempts to convince individuals or groups that change will be advantageous. When this approach is successful change will be relatively easy. Implementation of change, however, is rarely to everyone's advantage.

(e) Organisational development (OD) has been defined as a *planned and systematic attempt to change an organisation.* The individual or group responsible for ensuring that planned change is properly implemented is an internal or external *change agent.* Initially outside consultants may be used on the grounds that they have greater objectivity and may be more acceptable to those affected. In time internal staff may take over the change agent role. Change agents may use one or more of the following techniques:

(i) Survey feedback. This process involves (1) collection of data regarding how the operation operated; (2) feedback to those from whom data was obtained on the organisational problems discovered; (3) discussion as to what the findings mean and what steps should be taken; (4) action to implement the steps required.

(ii) Team building – developing effective work teams throughout the organisation.

(iii) Sensitivity training aimed at enabling individuals to develop awareness and sensitivity to oneself and others.

(iv) Management by objectives, i.e. the facilitation of change by setting attainable goals for individuals and groups and monitoring progress towards goal achievement.

(v) Job enrichment – making basic changes in the content and responsibility of a job to provide greater responsibilities and challenge to the worker.

(vi) The 'Grid Approach'. This is an approach suggested by Blake and Mouton and described in their book *The New Managerial Grid* (1978) in which the writers define five major leadership styles and concluded that the most effective is the one that stresses concern for both output and people. The Managerial Grid provides a framework for assisting an organisation by moving to the best style.

(vii) Management development – formal efforts to improve the skills and attitudes of present and prospective managers.

(f) Kurt Lewin [27], a behavioural scientist, argues that the process of change involves three basic phases:

(i) Unfreezing efforts to make a person or organisation willing to change.

(ii) Changing – selection of techniques to implement change.

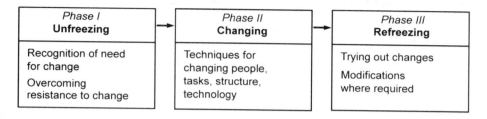

Fig 6.2 Lewin's view of the change process

(iii) Refreezing – reinforcing and supporting the change so that it becomes a relatively permanent part of organisational processes.

Lewin's view of the change process is shown in Fig 6.2.

11. TEAMWORK AND MULTIFUNCTIONAL TEAMS

Brief reference to task forces, team building, matrix structures and networks is made in Chapter 3 (**10 a–d**). There are also references to teams in relation to design (7:**5a**), value analysis (7:**8b**), quality circles (7:**14a** and **d**), negotiation (13) and capital purchases (10:3). There is also 'team buying' which combines the technical skills of the design and production functions with the negotiating and commercial skills of purchasing to determine what shall be bought and the source(s) from which an important item shall be obtained.

(a) Reasons for team formation. The formation and involvement in procurement matters in multi-skilled teams drawn from several functions is due to many factors including:

(i) The involvement of purchasing in strategic procurement decisions.

(ii) The concept of the 'supply chain' which emphasises the need to deal with work-flow in an integrated way through materials management and logistics approaches.

(iii) Only teams can take full advantage of the vastly increased information availability and ability to communicate effectively provided by information/communications technology.

(iv) The development of approaches such as MRP and JIT together with single and partnership sourcing.

(v) A recognition that, because of such developments as global purchasing, more complicated price and cost analyses, the need to integrate purchasing processes with those of manufacturing and the enhanced importance of quality, purchasing often needs to have expert advice and support in decision making.

(vi) The recognition, based on research findings, that 'Teams out-perform individuals acting alone or in large organisation groupings especially when performance requires multi-skills judgements and experiences'. [28]

(b) Teams and their aims. Teams have been defined [29] as:

Collection of people who must rely on group collaboration if each member is to experience the optimum of success and goal achievement.

'The growing consensus is that teams are the single best way to achieve the following aims:

- Integrate tasks
- Integrate information
- Maximise competence
- Manage performance
- Manage uncertainty
- Manage resources
- Increase enjoyment and reduce stress
- Total quality management and improvement.'

(c) Team building. This relates to those activities directed towards assisting the individuals who work together or have common organisational goals to combine more effectively. Initially team building involves two stages:

(i) Analysing group norms and relationships to identify any factors, especially those of the relationship between the leader (or manager/project leader) and subordinates that may consciously or unconsciously affect the effectiveness of the group.

(ii) Assisting individual members of the group to learn new ways of working together so that their group effectiveness is increased. This may involve helping individuals not only to identify problems but to smooth group relationships by learning how:

- to express disagreement without getting into win-lose situations
- to provide leadership without dominating others
- to express negative feelings in a non-condemnatory way
- to tolerate and learn from the opinions of others
- to recognise that group tension and conflict can be positive as well as negative.

Team building interventions are, therefore, typically directed towards four areas:

- *Diagnosis* involves the open discussion by the group of the performance to uncover problems that are adversely affecting group performance.
- *Task accomplishment* involves agreement on what the team exists to do, what can be realistically achieved and how it should be accomplished.
- *Team relationships* comprises identifying the role expectations and responsibilities of team members, examining what the leader expects from the group and what the group expects from its leader.
- *Team organisation* is the process of selecting the strongest available team to achieve the identified goals and determining the roles and responsibilities of each member selected.

12. MANAGEMENT STYLE AND LEADERSHIP

Leadership is an important element in motivation, communication, teamwork and the management of change.

(a) Management and leadership roles. There is a distinction between management and leadership. Managers may perform tasks radically different from those traditionally ascribed to leadership. A purchasing manager, for example, may carry out the transactional activities such as placing orders and ensuring their conformance to price, delivery and quality requirements and not be a leader. Yet leadership in the sense of directing the work efforts of other people to successfully accomplish their assigned tasks is one of the four functions frequently ascribed to management, the other three being:

- *Planning* – the process of setting performance objectives and identifying the actions needed to accomplish them.
- *Organising* – the process of dividing up the work to be done and then co-ordinating results to achieve a desired purpose.
- *Controlling* – the process of monitoring performance, comparing actual results to objectives, and taking corrective action as necessary.

Broader concepts of managerial work have been provided by Mintzberg [30] and Drucker [31]. Mintzberg states that managerial work encompasses ten roles:

- *Interpersonal roles* (leading)
  (i) Figurehead – manager as a symbol obliged to carry out social, legal and ceremonial duties.
  (ii) Leader – relationship with subordinates especially in allocating tasks, motivating, training, developing supervising and influencing.
  (iii) Liaison – development of a network of contacts outside the vertical chain of command through which information and favours can be traded for mutual benefit.

- *Informational roles* (administrating)
  (iv) Monitoring – seeking and receiving information from a variety of sources which is used to build up a general understanding of the organisation and its environment as a basis for decision making, to determine organisational values and inform outsiders and subordinates.
  (v) Disseminator – sending external information into their organisation and internal information from one subordinate to another.
  (vi) Spokesperson – transmitting information to external groups in a public relations capacity, lobbying for the organisation, informing the public about the organisation's performance plans and policies and providing information to superiors.

- *Decisional roles*
  (vii) Entrepreneur – initiating and designing controlled change in the organisation. Initiating 'improvement projects'.
  (viii) Disturbance handler – taking charge when their organisations meet

situations for which there is no predetermined response. Such situations can include conflicts between subordinates or organisations and the loss of resources or threats thereof.

(ix) Resource allocator – overseeing the allocation of all forms of organisational resources such as money, manpower (or people), machines and materials.

(x) Negotiator – taking charge in important negotiation activity with other bodies. In such negotiations, managers participate as figurehead, spokesperson and resource.

Drucker analysed the work of a manager into five basic integrated operations: (1) setting objectives; (2) organising; (3) motivating and communicating; (4) measuring and (5) developing. It should be noted that

(i) Almost all the above roles include activities that can be construed as leadership.

(ii) Not all managers perform every role.

(iii) Most roles can apply to non-managerial as well as managerial positions.

It is a useful exercise for readers to identify and provide examples of the roles undertaken by the executive in charge of purchasing in their organisations and those for which they have some personal responsibility.

(b) Management and leadership styles

(1) One of the earliest approaches to the study of leadership styles is the distinctions between autocratic, democratic and laissez-faire leadership identified by White and Lippett [32].

(2) An important aspect of leadership style is that of *power sharing*. Tannenbaum and Schmidt [33] suggest that participation and its complement, direction, are based on the amount of authority used by the superior in relation to the amount of freedom permitted to subordinates. As shown by Fig 6.3 this can be represented as a continuum from boss-centred to subordinate-centred leadership.

(3) McGregor [34] shows that behind every management decision or action are assumptions about human nature and behaviour which he referred to as Theory X and Theory Y.

Theory X assumes that the average human being dislikes work, prefers to be directed, wishes to avoid responsibility, has little ambition and above all requires security. Because of these factors most people must be coerced, controlled, directed or threatened with punishment to get them to put forward adequate effort towards achieving organisational objectives.

Theory Y assumes that 'the expenditure of physical and mental effort in work is as natural as rest or play.' People are prepared to exercise self direction and control, learn, seek responsibility, and that the capacity to exercise imagination, ingenuity and creativity is widely, not narrowly, distributed in the population.

(4) Ouchi [35] draws attention to the influence of culture in determining management style by contrasting Japanese practices with the American traditional and more bureaucratic environment. Ouchi believes that the higher employee

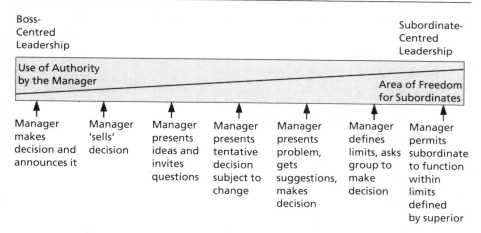

Fig 6.3 Directive versus participative leadership

motivation, quality and productivity achieved by Japanese enterprises can be attributed to:

- Decision making based on a consensus reached by managers with their subordinates
- A participative approach to decision making encouraging the interchange of information between managers and subordinates which encourages trust and democracy.
- The humanising of work which gives a feeling of significance to all employees.

(5) *Contingency approaches* emphasise that there is no one leadership style that can be consistently applied. In addition to organisational culture variables include: (1) the nature of the task; (2) the formal authority possessed by the leader; (3) the characteristics of the work group; and (4) the maturity of the subordinates. This latter factor is important. Based on the findings of Cousens (1992), Barr [36] notes the 'dramatic increase in the professional and academic qualifications of purchasing personnel' over the decade 1980–1990:

'CIPS training coupled with a substantial rise in the number of graduates entering the profession has greatly increased the overall level of buyer training. Buyers in 1980 were predominantly educated only to O-level standards; whereas in 1991 buyers were found to be predominantly degree or CIPS qualified. . . . The number of buyers who have CIPS qualifications has increased from 10% in 1980 to 35% in 1991.

These findings have implications for purchasing management. A study of hospital staff nurses [37] indicated that because of their training, cohesion with colleagues and work technology, the more educated nurses could work autonomously without leadership from the sister in charge. What seems to emerge is that where the task is clear and personnel have extensive professional training and experience the need for a purchasing manager to play a dominant leadership role is of less significance than where the converse applies.

13. STRATEGIC ASPECTS OF HRM APPLIED TO PURCHASING

(a) HRM planning. This must:

(i) Be based on the corporate plan.
(ii) Consider both external and internal factors as listed in **2** of this chapter.
(iii) Reflect the need for possible redundancy and retraining of staff as indicated by the Human Resources Audit.

(b) Recruitment and Selection

(i) Job descriptions and specifications must reflect the changed nature of purchasing as shown in 1:**9**.
(ii) Emphasis must be placed on

- an understanding of strategic issues
- the contribution of purchasing to competitive advantage and the supply chain
- understanding and experience of such approaches as JIT, TQM, MRP and EDI.

(iii) Possibly there may be a policy of graduate recruitment.

(c) Performance appraisal. This must:

(i) Be designed to meet the organisational objectives specified in **5b** of this Chapter.
(ii) Relate criteria appropriate to the job description of the appraisee.

(d) Training and development. This must:

(i) Include provisions for general management training in addition to purely functional (purchasing) aspects.
(ii) Be related to national training developments, i.e. into the CIPS examinations scheme, NVQs in Purchasing and Supply, the Management Charter Initiative.
(iii) Cater for needs arising from the concept of global purchasing, e.g. language training, import and export procedures.
(iv) Provide an understanding of functions related to purchasing, e.g. marketing, finance, production and other supply chain activities, e.g. warehousing, transportation.
(v) Be based on the analysis of the training gap for each individual.
(vi) Improve performance in specific aspects of purchasing, e.g. negotiation, price analysis, legal and financial aspects of purchasing.

(e) Pay. This should:

(i) Be considered from a value added rather than a purely cost standpoint.
(ii) Be competitive as measured by a comparison of information provided by published surveys.

(iii) Related to job grades and also make provision for the contribution made by an individual.

References

[1] Ivanovic A. *Dictionary of Personnel Management.* Peter Cullen Publishing 1988.

[2] David E Guest. *Human resource management and industrial relations. Journal of Management Studies* Vol. 24 (5) 1987, p 507 (By permission).

[3] Plumbley P. *Recruitment and Selection,* Institute of Personnel Management. 4th Ed. 1985, Ch. 1, pp 22–23.

[4] These job descriptions were kindly provided by the CIPS.

[5] Rodger A (1952). *The Seven Point Plan,* National Institute of Industrial Psychology.

[6] Munro Fraser J (1978). *A Handbook of Employment Interviewing.* 5th Ed. McDonald and Evans.

[7] Roe R A and Greuter M J M (1989). *Developments in personnel selection methodology* in R K Hambleton and J Zoal (Eds) *Advances in Testing.* Kluwer.

[8] Anderson Gordon. *Selection* in Towers B (Ed) *The Handbook of Human Resource Management* (1992). Blackwell. Chap. 9, pp 171–172.

[9] See Torrington and Hall, *Personnel Management* (1991). Chap. 19, p 208.

[10] Torrington and Hall as (9) above. Chap. 27, p 494.

[11] Stevens John, *Measuring Purchasing Performance,* Business Books, 1978, Chap 8, pp 97–110.

[12] Mansfield Bob. *Competence and standards* in Burke J W (Ed) *Competency Based Education and Training.* Falmer Press 1989, Ch. 3, p 28.

[13] NCVQ, *Guide to National Vocational Qualifications,* 1991, p 21.

[14] Published by Purcon Consultants, Aylesbury, Bucks.

[15] Published by Remuneration Economics, Survey House, 51 Portland Road, Kington-upon-Thames, Surrey, KT1 25M.

[16] Published by Reward Group, Reward House, Diamond Way, Stone Business Park, Stone, Staffordshire ST15 OSD.

[17] Martin P and Nicholls J. *Creating a Committed Workforce.* Institute of Personnel Management, 1987, Ch 1, p 3.

[18] Martin P and Nicholls J. *Creating a Committed Workforce.* Institute of Personnel Management, 1987, Ch 2, p 25.

[19] Alpander G G. *Developing managers' ability to empower employees. Journal of Management Development.* Vol 10, No 3, 1991, pp 13–24.

[20] Eccles. *The deceptive allure of empowerment. Long Range Planning.* Vol 26, No 6, 1993, p 13, 21.

[21] Armstrong M. *A Handbook of Personnel Management Practice.* 3rd Ed, Kogan Page, 1988, p 5.

[22] This table and the following explanation are based on Kesslev I. *Reward systems* in Storey J (Ed). *Human Resource Management.* Routledge, 1995, Chap 10, p 256.

[23] *Pocket Oxford Dictionary.*

[24] Daft R L. *Organisation Theory and Design.* West 1983 quoted in Thompson J L *Strategic Management.* Chapman and Hall, 1990, Chap 24, p 590.

[25] Burke W W. *Organisation Development.* 2nd Edition, Addison-Wesley, 1993, Chap 2, p 23.

[26] Beer M reported in Ovmenakis A, Harvis M and Mossholder K, *Creating readiness for large scale change. Human Relations.* Vol 46, 1993, pp 681–703.

[27] Lewin K. *Field Theory in Social Science.* Harper and Row, 1951.

[28] Kotzenback J R and Smith D K. *The Wisdom of Teams: Creating the High Performance Organisation.* Harvard Business School Press, Boston, 1993, p 91.

[29] Quoted in Gordon J R. *Organisational Behaviour.* Allyn and Bacon, 3rd Ed, 1991, Ch 5, p 211.

[30] Mintzberg H. *The Nature of Managerial Work.*

[31] Drucker P F. *Management Tasks, Responsibilities, Practices.*

[32] R White and R Lippett. *Leader behaviour and member reactions in three 'social climates'.* In Cartwright D and Zander B (Ed). *Group Dynamics: Research and Theory.* Harper and Row, 1968.

[33] Tannenbaum R and Schmidt. *How to choose a leadership pattern. Harvard Business Review.* March–April 1958, pp 95–101.

[34] McGregor D. *The Human Side of Enterprise.* McGraw Hill, 1960, Chapters 3 and 4.

[35] Ouchi W G. *Theory 2: How American Business Can Meet the Japanese Challenge.* Addison-Wesley 1981.

[36] Barr C. *A code of ethics: good, bad or indifferent?* Paper submitted to the Second Purchasing and Supply Education Research Group Conference. Bath, 1993.

[37] Sheridan J E, Vredenburgh D J and Ableson M A. *Contextual model of leadership influence in hospital units. Academy of Management Journal.* Vol 27, 1984, pp 57–58.

Progress test 6

1. In what respects does HRM differ from personnel management?

2. List the external and internal factors to be considered in relation to HR planning.

3. What are the four elements of job analysis?

4. What factors should be considered before deciding whether or not to recruit?

5. Under what headings might a job description be prepared?

6. Prepare a job description for a Buyer in a manufacturing organisation.

7. What factors relating to an individual are specified in (a) the Seven Point Plan; (b) the Five Fold Grading Scheme?

8. What are the most important functions that selection procedures must fulfil?

9. What are the main purposes of a selection interview?

10. What are the most important organisational and individual purposes of performance appraisal?

11. How may the appraisal of performance be related to purchasing?

12. What is the importance of the training gap?

13. State what you understand by each of the following in the context of NVQs:
(i) The NVQ framework; (ii) Competence; (iii) Assessment; (iv) Standards

14. What factors may have to be considered when determining the pay for a particular purchasing job?

15. From what sources may information regarding purchasing pay be obtained?

16. What are the most important strategic aspects of HRM as applied to purchasing?

17. What is meant by 'motivation'?

18. Define 'commitment' and give five examples of commitment at work.

19. What are some of the benefits claimed for 'empowerment'?

20. Give examples of individual and collective performance based pay systems.

21. What is the distinction between 'effective' and 'efficient' communication?

22. Describe the process involved in implementing change.

23. What activities are involved in 'team building'?

24. What leadership/management roles are identified by Mintzberg and Drucker?

25. Briefly describe the contributions to an understanding of leadership styles associated with White and Lippitt, Tannenbaum and Schmidt, McGregor and Ouchi.

26. The buyer of the 1990s must be 'pro-active' rather than 're-active', managerially competent rather than clerically efficient, and be more concerned with strategic rather than operational problems. Critically examine this viewpoint, with particular reference to recruitment and development of staff.

(CIPS. *Purchasing and Supply Management I – Planning Policy and Organisation* (1991))

27. Formulate a strategy for the recruitment, selection, training and development of staff for the Purchasing function.

(CIPS. *Purchasing and Supply Management I* (1992))

28. Why and in what ways is the training and development of buyers likely to change over the next decade?

(CIPS. *Purchasing and Supply Management I* (1992))

29. Explain how you would conduct a strategic review of purchasing staff and the possible development implications of such a review.

(CIPS. *Purchasing and Supply Management I* (1994))

7

SPECIFYING AND ASSURING THE QUALITY OF SUPPLIERS

1. INTRODUCTION

Before purchasing personnel can provide materials of the right quality they must have an understanding of:

(i) What quality is and the different meanings that can be attached to the term.

(ii) The importance of TQM.

(iii) How the quality required for a particular application is determined, specified, reviewed and improved.

(iv) The procedures through which quality assurance and control is implemented.

(v) The costs of quality.

(vi) The ways in which purchasing in association with internal design and production and external suppliers can play a pro-active role in the specification and implementation of quality and the control of quality costs.

2. WHAT IS QUALITY?

(a) There are numerous definitions of quality:

(1) *ISO 8402* defines quality as: *'The totality of features and characteristics of a product that bears on the ability to satisfy stated or implied needs'*

In this definition:

- *'Features and characteristics of a product'* implies the ability to identify what quality aspects can be measured, or controlled, or constitute an Acceptable Quality Level or AQL.
- *'Ability to satisfy given needs'* relates to the value of the product or service to the customer including economic value as well as safety, reliability, maintainability and other relevant features.

(2) Crosby [1] defines quality as *'conformity to requirements, not goodness'*. He also stresses that the definition of quality can never make any sense unless it is based

exactly on what the customer wants, i.e. a product is a quality product only when it conforms to the customer's requirements.

(3) Juran [2] defines quality as *'fitness for use'*. This definition implies quality of design, quality of conformance, availability and adequate field service. There is, however, no universal definition of quality. Gavin, for example, has identified five approaches to defining quality [3] and eight dimensions of quality [4]. The five approaches are:

1. *The transcendent approach*: quality is absolute and universally recognisable. This concept is loosely related to a comparison of product attributes and characteristics.
2. *The product-based approach*: quality is a precise and measurable variable. In this approach differences in quality reflect differences in the quantity of some product characteristic.
3. *The user-based approach*: quality is defined in terms of fitness for use, or how well the product fulfils its intended functions.
4. *The manufacturing-based approach*: quality is 'conformance to specifications', i.e. targets and tolerances determined by product designers.
5. *The value-based approach*: quality is defined in terms of costs and prices. Here, a quality product is one that provides performance at an acceptable price or conformance at an acceptable cost.

These alternative definitions of quality often overlap and may conflict. Perspectives of quality may also change as a product moves from the design to the marketing stage. For these reasons it is essential to consider each of the above perspectives when framing an overall quality philosophy.

Gavin's eight dimensions of quality are:

1. *Performance* – the product's operating characteristics.
2. *Reliability* – the probability of a product surviving over a specified period of time under stated conditions of use.
3. *Serviceability* – the speed, accessibility and ease of repairing the item or having it repaired.
4. *Conformance* – the degree to which delivered products meet the predetermined standards.
5. *Durability* – measures the projected use available from the product over its intended operating cycle before it deteriorates.
6. *Features* – 'the bells and whistles' or secondary characteristics which supplement the product's basic functioning.
7. *Aesthetics* – personal judgements of how a product looks, feels, sounds, tastes or smells.
8. *Perceived quality* – closely identified with the reputation of the producer. Like aesthetics, it is a personal evaluation.

While the relative importance attached to any of the above characteristics will depend on the particular item, the most important factors in commercial or industrial purchasing decisions will probably be performance, reliability, conformance, availability and serviceability.

Other factors that determine 'the right quality' for a particular application include:

(i) *Price*, since the competitive selling price of the product in which the item is to be incorporated will determine the prices paid for bought-out items.

(ii) *Customer specifications* or those laid down by statutory or similar organisations.

(iii) *Durability* also influences the quality specifications for components, e.g. if the expected life of the final product is only three years there is little point in incorporating components with a life of five years where cheaper alternatives are available. The reputation of the product must, however, be of paramount consideration.

Quality is therefore determined by balancing technical considerations such as fitness for use, performance, safety and reliability against economic factors including price and availability. It is therefore the *optimum quality* for the application that should be sought rather than the highest quality.

As the BSI has stated, in drafting quality specifications, the aim should 'always be the minimum statement of optimum (not the highest) quality in order not to increase cost unnecessarily, not to restrict processes of manufacture, not to limit the use of possible alternatives'.

(b) Reliability. As shown above, reliability is an attribute of quality. It is, however, so important that the terms 'quality and reliability' are often used together. Reliability has been defined [5] as

'a measure of the ability of a product to function successfully when required, for the period required, under specified conditions'.

Reliability is usually expressed in terms of mathematical probability ranging from 0% (complete unreliability) to 100% (or complete reliability). Failure mode and effect analysis (FMEA) performed to evaluate the effect upon the overall design of a failure in any one of the identifiable failure modes of the design components and to evaluate how critically the failure will affect the design of performance is referred to below.

3. THE IMPORTANCE OF TQM

(a) Total Quality Management (TQM) has been defined [6] as:

A way of managing an organisation so that every job, every process, is carried out right, first time and every time.

This means that each stage of manufacture or service is 100% correct before it proceeds. An alternative definition [7] is

Management philosophy and company practices that aim to harness the human and material resources of the organisation in the most effective way to achieve the objectives of the organisation.

(b) TQM principles. TQM is based on three important tenets:

(1) *A focus on product improvement from the customer's viewpoint.* The key words in this principle are 'product improvement' and 'customer product improvement'. Juran emphasised the importance of achieving annual improvements in quality and reductions in quality-related costs. Any improvement that takes an organisation to levels of quality performance previously unachieved is termed a breakthrough. Breakthroughs are focused on improving or eliminating chronic losses or, in Deming's terminology, 'common causes of variation'. All breakthroughs follow a common sequence of discovery, organisation, diagnosis, corrective action and control.

The term customer in this context is associated with the concept of quality chains which emphasise the linkages of suppliers and customers. Quality chains are both internal and external. Thus internally, purchasing is a customer of design and supplier of production. Staff within each function are also suppliers and customers. Like all chains the quality chain is no stronger than the weakest link. Without strong supplier-customer links both internally and externally TQM is doomed to failure. Quality chains are one way of outmoding the functional conflict and power tactics referred to in 3:**10**. The first step in implementing an internal value chain approach is for each function to determine answers to the following questions relating to customers and suppliers [8].

Customers
- Who are my internal customers?
- What are their true requirements?
- How do, or can, I find out what the requirements are?
- How can I measure my ability to meet the requirements?
- Do I have the necessary capability to meet the requirements? (If not then what must change to improve the capability?)
- Do I continually meet the requirements? (If not then what prevents this from happening when the capability exists?)
- How do I monitor changes in the requirements?

Suppliers
- Who are my internal suppliers?
- What are my true requirements?
- How do I communicate my requirements?
- Do my suppliers have the capability to measure and meet the requirements?
- How do I inform them of changes in the requirements?

The second step, based on answers to questions such as the above, is to define the level of service which a function, e.g. purchasing, will provide. Cannon [9] has identified four factors affecting decisions about service types and levels: (1) what the internal customer wants; (2) what the function can provide; (3) close collaboration to solve disagreements; (4) redefining both type and level of service at regular intervals. It is also important to determine the technical expertise of purchasing 'since it is this expertise which enables the function to add value to the procurement activity beyond that which the internal customer can perform without the function's assistance'.

The questions posed earlier in this section can also be reframed by substituting the word 'external' for 'internal' so that external value chains can be considered from both supply and customer angles. In the capacity of customers, purchasing organisations expect suppliers to compete in terms of quality, delivery and price. Zairi [10] states that the best approach to managing suppliers is based on JIT which from its inception has the objective of obtaining and sustaining superior performance. The other important aspect of external customer supplier value chains refers to the management of customer processes since the purpose of TQM is customer enlightenment and long-term partnerships.

(2) *A recognition that personnel at all levels share responsibility for product quality.* The Japanese concept of *Kaizen,* or ongoing improvement, affects everyone in an organisation at all levels. It is therefore based on team rather than individual performance. Thus, while top management provides leadership, continuous improvement is also understood and implemented at shop floor level. Some consequences of this principle include:

- Provision of leadership from the top
- .Creation of a 'quality culture' dedicated to continuous improvement
- Teamwork, i.e. Quality Improvement Teams and Quality Cycles.
- Adequate resource allocation.
- Quality training for employees.
- Measurement and use of statistical concepts.
- Quality feedback.
- Employee recognition.

As Zaire [11] states 'Once a culture of common beliefs, principles, objectives and concerns has been established, people will manage their own tasks and will take voluntary responsibility to improve processes they own'.   C.f. Form and discipline !

(3) *A recognition of the importance of implementing a system to provide information to managers about quality processes which enable them to plan, control and evaluate performance.*

Most of this chapter is concerned with various aspects of quality implementation.

(c) Factors which have contributed to the development of TQM

(i) Global competition for sales, profits, jobs and funds in both the private and public sectors leading to the concept of 'world class manufacturing' with the emphasis of using manufacturing to gain a competitive edge through improving customer service.

(ii) JIT and similar strategies based on the philosophy of zero defects, i.e. that it is cheaper to design and build quality into a product than attempt to ensure quality through inspection alone.

Table 7.1 The Quality Gurus

Name	Principal Book	Important Principles
Philip B CROSBY	*Quality is Free* McGraw Hill (1983)	(i) Five absolutes of quality management – (1) 'quality means conformity to requirements – not elegance'; (2) 'There is no such a thing as a quality problem although there may be an engineering or machine problem'; (3) ' It is always cheaper to do the job right first time'; (4) 'The only performance indicator is the cost of quality'; (5) 'The only performance standard is zero defects'. (ii) The 14 step quality improvement programme.
W Edwards DEMING	*Quality, Productivity and Competitive Position* MIT Press (1982)	Deming's 14 points include (4) 'End the practice of awarding business on the basis of price tag. Instead, minimise total cost. Move toward a single supplier for any one item, on a long-term relationship of loyalty and trust.'
Armand V FEIGENBAUM	*Total Quality Control* McGraw Hill (1983)	'The underlying principle of the total quality view ..... is that ..... control must start with identification of customer quality requirements and end only when the product has been placed in the hands of a customer who remains satisfied. Total Quality Control guides the co-ordinated actions of people, machines and information to achieve this goal. The first principle is to recognise that quality is everybody's job.'
Kaoru ISHIKAWA	*What is Total Quality Control? The Japanese Way.* Prentice Hall (1985)	(i) The first to introduce the concept of Quality Control Circles. (ii) Originator of Fishbone or Ishikawa diagrams now used world-wide in continuous improvements to represent cause-effect analysis. (iii) Argues that 90-95% of quality problems can be solved by simple statistical techniques not requiring specialist knowledge.
Joseph M JURAN	*Quality Control Handbook 1988* McGraw Hill (1988)	(i) Quality is 'fitness for use' which can be broken down into quality of design, quality of conformance, availability and field service. (ii) Companies must reduce the cost of quality. (iii) Quality should be aimed at controlling (1) sporadic problems or avoidable costs; (2) unavoidable costs. The latter requires the introduction of a new culture intended to change attitudes and increase company-wide knowledge.
Genichi TAGUCHI	*Introduction to Quality Engineering* Asian Productivity Association New York (1986)	(i) Defines the quality of a product as the loss imparted by the product to the society from the time the product is shipped. The loss may include customer complaints, added warranty costs, damage to company reputation, loss of market lead etc. (ii) Uses statistical techniques additional to Statistical Process Control (SPC) to enable engineers/designers to identify those variables which, if uncontrolled, can affect product manufacture and performance.

(iii) Japanese quality procedures such as *Kaizen* (unending improvement) and *Poka-Yoke* (foolproofing) and a quality culture implemented in European manufacturing units, e.g. Toyota and Nissan.

(iv) Quality philosophies associated with internationally respected experts. See Table 7.1.

4. THE SPECIFICATION OF QUALITY

The specification of quality may be considered under four headings: product and production design and re-design, specification, standardisation and value analysis.

5. PRODUCT AND PRODUCTION DESIGN AND RE-DESIGN

(a) The design process. The ultimate performance, value, reliability and sale-ability of a product is determined at the design stage. As shown by Fig 7.1 the process of design or re-design comprises several substages.

The actual design will be prepared by a specialised function responsible for ensuring that all relevant design input requirements are correctly translated into specifications, drawings, procedures and written instructions. This function is

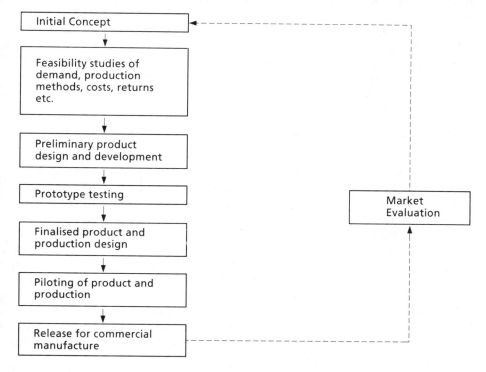

Fig 7.1 The design process

also responsible for ensuring that designs comply with legal requirements relating to such issues as safety and the environment together with all matters relating to patents.

(b) Collaboration in design. Product design is, however, a team enterprise in which the marketing, management accounting, production and purchasing functions together with suppliers are all involved in such ways as the following:

(1) *Marketing.* What are the characteristics that customers are looking for in the product, e.g. appearance, ease of operation and installation, reliability and durability, exclusiveness, etc.? What features are required to ensure that the product provides an advantage over those of competitors? What is the present and anticipated market penetration? How and through what channels will the product be marketed? Marketing will also be involved in piloting.

(2) *Management accounting.* Traditionally Western manufacturers have determined costs and set a selling price based on the costs involved. In contrast the Japanese introduced the concept of *target costing*. Target costing uses market research to estimate what the market will pay for a product with specific characteristics.

Subtracting an acceptable profit margin from the estimated selling price leaves an implied maximum per unit product target cost which is compared to an expected product cost. If the estimated cost is higher than the target cost the manufacturer involves all members of the planning team (design, engineering, production, purchasing, suppliers, marketing and management accounting) in value analysis, value engineering and production design exercises to determine how costs can be reduced to meet the desired target. If such reduction cannot be achieved either a lower profit may be accepted or the manufacturer may decide not to enter the market.

(3) *Production. Product designers* are initially responsible for determining the productability and minimum product cost.

Production designers are concerned with:

- Determining the minimum possible costs that can be obtained through material and component specifications, tolerances, joining of parts, etc.
- Specifying processes that will enable these minimum costs to be achieved while meeting the requirements of the design.
- Production designers are always subject to the constraint of available machinery and skilled operatives. Where such resources are not available then production designers will have to look at alternatives. If volume is large and the design and demand stable these alternatives may take such forms as buying in special-process technology including semi-automatic and automatic processes or special-purpose layouts. Alternatively consideration may be given to subcontracting to specialist manufacturers.
- Production designers will also be concerned with such costs as tooling, indirect labour and the non-manufacturing costs of production.

Computer integrated manufacturing (CIM) is a general term for the total integration of product design, planning and manufacturing by means of complex computer systems. The ultimate goal of CIM is the computerisation of all phases of the supply chain from the customer's initial order to its ultimate delivery.

CIM comprises several technologies including robots, automated material handling and flexible manufacturing systems which are beyond the scope of this book. Brief reference may however be made to *computer-aided design (CAD), computer-aided manufacturing (CAM) and computer-aided estimating (CAE).*

CAD, originally developed by IBM in 1960 for General Motors, is a computerised design process for creating new products or parts, altering existing ones and replacing drafting traditionally done manually. With CAD the designer uses a powerful desktop computer and computes graphics to manipulate geometric shapes. The programs provide:

- A 3-dimensional projection of any part on the screen.
- Calculations of area, volume, weight and stress.
- A data bank of existing product or part designs as what is required may only be a variation on what is already available.
- Simulation of strength and stress tests without the need for a prototype.
- Analysis of manufacturing considerations relating to the production of the item.
- Several alternative design solutions for consideration by the designer.
- The translation of the approved design into 2-dimensional drawings for use in manufacturing.
- Bills of material (BOM) parts lists or Bills of Quantities (for architectural work).

CAM utilises computers to design production processes and materials flow. CAM is therefore linked to CAD by the production of manufacturing instructions that will produce the finalised design. The integration of the two systems is known as a CAD/CAM system. Such a system is the first step to a paperless factory.

CAE refers to computerised systems for the estimation of costs including those relating to design, manufacture and, where appropriate, distribution. CAE programs enable an estimator to draw on a data bank of cost elements, perform calculations and produce a product selling price for customer quotation purposes.

CAD, CAM and CAE have numerous advantages including:

- Greatly reduced time in the production of designs, estimates and products with consequent improved utilisation of the services of skilled designers, estimators and production personnel.
- Through EDI designers and estimators can communicate directly with customer's CAD/CAM systems thereby facilitating collaboration in design and production.
- Rapid response to the request of potential customers for quotations.
- Efficient updating of parts and products with the elimination of inconsistencies between specification and drawings and finished products.
- The time frame from product conception to production can be substantially reduced.
- Simplified quality control.

(c) Purchasing and design. Some contributions of purchasing to design have already been mentioned in 3:9a. Dowlatshahi [12] has drawn attention to the differences in orientation that may arise between purchasing and design:

Purchasing orientation	*Design orientation*
(i) Minimum acceptable margins of quality, safety and performance	(i) Wide margins of quality, safety and performance
(ii) Use of adequate materials	(ii) Use of ideal materials
(iii) Lowest ultimate cost	(iii) Limited concern for cost
(iv) High regard for availability	(iv) Limited regard for availability
(v) Practical and economical parameters, specifications, features and tolerances	(v) Close or near perfect parameters, specifications, features and tolerances
(vi) General view of product	(vi) Conceptual abstraction of product quality
(vii) Cost estimation of materials	(vii) Selection of materials
(viii) Concern for JIT delivery and supplier relationship	(viii) Concern for overall product design

Dowlatshahi states that the reconciliation of these differing views is only possible in a concurrent engineering environment which he defines as:

'The consideration and inclusion of product design attributes such as manufacturability, procurability, reliability, maintainability, schedularability, marketability and the like in the early stages of product design.'

6. SPECIFICATIONS

(a) Definition types and purpose

(i) A specification is *'a statement of the attributes of a product process or service'* [13].

(ii) BS 7373 identifies five basic specification types:
- Manufacturing, build and test specifications
- Installation specifications
- Maintenance and repair specifications
- Disposal specifications
- User specifications

(iii) Specifications have two basic functions: *communication* and *comparison*. When prepared by the purchaser they inform the supplier what is required. When prepared by the supplier they provide a prospective purchaser with a description of the attributes of a product.

Specifications also provide criteria against which the products and services supplied or available can be compared.

(b) The contents of a specification. These will vary according to whether the specification is written from the standpoint of user, designer, manufacturer or seller. The specification will also vary according to the material or item concerned. For a simple item the specification may be a brief description, while in the case of a complex assembly it will be a comprehensive document, perhaps running to many pages. BS 7373 [15] recommends the following order of presentation for a specification relating to the attributes of a product, process or service.

a. Identification – title, designation, number, authority
b. Issue number – publication history and state of issue, earlier related specifications
c. Contents list – guide to layout
d. Foreword – the reason for writing the specification
e. Introduction – describes content in general and technical aspects of objectives
f. Scope – range of objectives/content
g. Definitions – terms used with meanings special to the text
h. Requirements/guidance/methods/elements – the main body of the specification
i. Index – cross-references
j. References – to national, European, international standards or other internal company specifications

The '*Requirements*' specified may relate to the following:

k. Conditions in which the item or material is to be installed, used, manufactured or stored
l. Characteristics – These may be shown by:
  i. design, samples, drawings, models, preliminary tests or investigations
  ii. properties, e.g. strength, dimensions, weight, safety, etc, with tolerances where applicable
  iii. interchangeability (functional, dimensional)
  iv. materials and their properties (including permissible variability), approved or excluded materials
  v. requirements for a manufacturing process, e.g. heat treatment (this should be specified only when critical to design considerations)
  vi. appearance, texture, finish, including colour, protection, etc.
  vii. identification marks, operating symbols on controls, weight of items, safety indications, etc.
  viii. method of marking.
m. Performance
  i. performance under specified conditions
  ii. test methods and equipment for assessing performance; where, how and by whom carried out; reference to correlation with behaviour in operation
  iii. criteria for passing tests, including accuracy and interpretations of results
  iv. acceptance conditions

v. certification and/or reporting, i.e. reports, test schedules or certificates required.

n. Life

o. Reliability, i.e. under stipulated conditions and tests and control procedures for assessing reliability

p. Control of quality checking for compliance with specification:

    i. method of checking compliance

    ii. production tests on raw materials, components, sub-assemblies, and assemblies

    iii. assurance of compliance, e.g. by suppliers' certificates or independent certification schemes

    iv. inspection facilities required by the user/designer or offered to the manufacturer/supplier

    v. instructions regarding reject material or items

    vi. instructions with regard to modification of process

    vii. applicability of quality control to subcontractors, etc.

q. Packing and protection

    i. specifications of packaging, including any special conditions in transit

    ii. condition in which the item is to be supplied, e.g. protected, lubricant free, etc.

    iii. period of storage

    iv. marking of packaging.

r. Information from the supplier to the user, e.g. instructions and advice on installation, operation and maintenance.

(c) Additional methods of specifying. The following methods may be used in association with or alternative to company or standard specifications. Each of the three methods has legal implications under the Sale of Goods Act 1979 (SGA), the Supply of Goods and Services Act 1982 (SGSA) and the Supply and Sale of Goods Act 1994 (SSGA).

As its title implies SGA applies to contracts for the supply of goods including hire purchase transactions. (It also incorporates the Sale of Goods (Implied Terms) Act 1979.) It does not, however, apply to the hire as distinct from the sale of goods or to contracts for the supply of work and materials, services, and contracts of exchange or barter which are now covered by the SGSA.

SGSA principally amends section 14 of the SAG and sections 4 and 5 and makes minor repeats in respect of both Acts.

The three additional methods of specification are:

(1) *Use of brand or trade name.* England [16] lists the following circumstances in which description by brand may be 'not only desirable but necessary':

(i) When the manufacturing process is secret or covered by a patent.

(ii) When the manufacturing processes of the vendor call for a high degree of 'workmanship' or 'skill' that cannot be exactly defined in a specification.

(iii) When only small quantities are bought so that the preparation of specifications by the buyer is impracticable.

(iv) When testing by the buyer is impracticable.

(v) When the item is a component so effectively advertised as to create a preference or even a demand for its incorporation into the finished product on the part of the ultimate purchaser.

(vi) When there is a strong preference for the branded item on the part of design staff.

The main disadvantages of branded items are:

(i) The cost of a branded item may be higher than an unbranded substitute.

(ii) Undue dependence on brands reduces the number of potential suppliers.

The SAG (s.13) and SGSA (s.3) state that where there is a sale of goods by description there is an implied condition that the goods shall correspond with the description and if the sale be by sample as well as by description, it is not sufficient that the bulk of the goods corresponds to the sample if the goods do not also correspond to the description.

(2) *By sample.* The sample can be provided either by the buyer or seller and is a useful method of specification in relation to printing and some raw materials, e.g. cloth. When orders are placed on this basis the samples on which the contract is based should be identified, labelled, and signed and retained by both parties. By section 15 of the SGA and section 5 of the SGSA as amended by the SSGA 1994 there is an implied 'term' (later defined as a 'condition') that where goods are sold by sample:

- the bulk must correspond with the sample in quality
- the buyer must have a reasonable opportunity of comparing the bulk with the sample
- the goods must be free from any defect making 'their quality unsatisfactory' (not unmerchantable) which a reasonable examination of the sample would not reveal.

(3) *By a user or performance specification.* Here the purchaser informs the supplier of the use to which the purchased item is to be put. This method is particularly applicable to the purchase of items about which the buyer has little technical knowledge.

By s.14(3) of the SGA and s.4 (4&5 of the SGSA) as amended by the SSGA, where the seller sells goods in the course of a business and the buyer, expressly or by implication, makes known to the seller any particular purpose for which the goods are being bought there is an implied 'term' that the goods supplied under the contract are of satisfactory quality. For the purpose of the SSGA goods are of satisfactory quality if 'they meet the standard that a reasonable person would regard as satisfactory, taking account of any description of the goods, the price (if relevant) and all the other relevant circumstances'. By section 2B of SSGA the quality of the goods include their state and condition and the following (among others) are, in appropriate cases, aspects of the quality of goods:

a. fitness for all the purposes for which goods of the kind in question are commonly supplied

b. appearance and finish

c. freedom from minor defects

d. safety and

e. durability.

By section 2C of SSGA the 'term' does not extend to any matter making the quality of goods unsatisfactory –

a. which is specifically drawn to the buyer's attention before the contract is made

b. where the buyer examines the goods before the contract is made which that examination ought to reveal, or

c. in the case of a contract for sale by sample, which would have been apparent on a reasonable examination of the sample.

Section 4 of the SSGA provides that, when the seller can prove that the deviation from the specification is only slight that it would be unreasonable for the buyer to reject the goods, the buyer may not treat the breach of contract as a condition entitling him to reject the goods but only as a warranty giving a right to damages arising from the breach.

Section 4 also makes a distinction between commercial buyers and consumers. If the buyer is a consumer the right to reject goods on the grounds that the quality of the goods is unsatisfactory is not affected.

Section 3(2) states that the section applies unless a contrary intention appears in or is to be implied from the contract.

As Woodroffe [17] observes:

'This time buyers must look to their own ts and cs, for a well drafted clause will enable a buyer to terminate a contract for any breach of Section 13–15 whether slight or not'.

7. STANDARDISATION

A standard differs from a specification in that while every standard is a specification not every specification is a standard. The distinction lies in the fact that a standard is a specification intended for recurrent use. Standards may be distinguished according to their subject matter, purpose and range of application.

(a) Subject matter. This may relate to an area of economic activity, e.g. engineering, and with items used in that field, e.g. fasteners. Each item may be further sub-divided into suitable subjects for standards. Thus 'fasteners' may lead to standards for screw threads, bolts and nuts, washers, etc.

(b) Purpose. Standards may relate to one or more aspects of product quality. These include:

(i) Dimensions, thus encouraging interchangeability and variety reduction, e.g.

BS 308 *Engineering Drawing Practice Part 3* relates to Recommendations for Geometrical Tolerances.

(ii) Performance requirements for a given purpose, e.g. BS 1515 covers all stressing and constructional features of fusion-welded pressure vessels necessary for a design to meet statutory requirements and those of manufacturers, users and insurers.

(iii) Safety requirements. These specify construction requirements with related methods of test, e.g. to ensure that a gas cylinder will meet a stated level of safe performance.

(iv) Environmental requirements relating to such matters as pollution, waste disposal on land, noise and environment nuisance. Environmental performance objectives and targets are covered by BS 7750.

In addition to the above, standards may also cover codes of practice, methods of test and glossaries.

Codes of practice give guidance on the best accepted practice in relation to engineering and construction techniques and for operations such as installation, maintenance and provision of services. *Methods of test* are required for measuring the values of product characteristics and behaviour and are essential for the establishment of quality and performance standards. *Glossaries* help to ensure unambiguous technical communication by providing standard definitions of the terms, conventions, units and symbols used in science and industry.

(c) Range of application. This relates to the domain in which a particular standard is applicable. Standards may be:

(i) Individual, i.e. laid down by the individual user.

(ii) Company, prepared by agreement between various functions to guide design, purchasing, manufacturing and marketing operations. Ashton [18] has drawn attention to the importance of keeping registers or databases of bought-out parts and company standards which can be referred to by codes listed in a codes register as a means of variety reduction and obviating variations in tolerances, finishes, performance and quality.

(iii) Association or trade, prepared by a group of related interests in a given industry, trade or profession, e.g. the Society of Motor Manufacturers and Traders.

(iv) National, e.g. British Standard Specifications.

(v) International. The two principal organisations producing world-wide standards are the International Electrotechnical Commission (IEC) and the International Standards Organisation (ISO). The former, established in 1906, concentrates on standards relating to the electrical and electronic fields. The latter, founded in 1947, is concerned with non-electrical standards. Both organisations are located in Geneva. In Western Europe progress is being made for the development of standards that will be acceptable both as European and as international standards. This work is being done through the European Committee for Standardisation (CEN) formed by Western European standards organisations. The demarcation of European standardisation mirrors the international arrangement with CEN covering

non-electrical aspects and the European Committee for Electrotechnical Standardisation (CENELEC) and the European Telecommunications Standards Institute (ETSI) being responsible for the others.

Different standards and specifications can often be used in conjunction.

(d) Purchasing and standardisation. Purchasing staff should be aware of the major trade, national and international standards applicable to their industry and the items bought. They should also appreciate the advantages that standardisation offers to the buyer:

(*i*) Clear specifications and the removal of any uncertainty as to what is required on the part of both buyer and supplier.

(*ii*) Standardisation helps to achieve reliability and reduce costs.

(*iii*) Saving of time and money by eliminating the need to prepare company specifications and reducing the need for explanatory letters, telephone calls etc.

(*iv*) The saving of design time may also reduce the time for production of the finished produce.

(*v*) Accurate comparison of quotations, since all prospective suppliers are quoting for the same thing.

(*vi*) Less dependability on specialist suppliers and greater scope for negotiation

(*vii*) Reduction in error and conflict thus increasing supplier goodwill.

(*viii*) Facilitation of international sourcing by reference to ISO standards.

(*ix*) Saving in inventory and cost through variety reduction (see Chapter 8). By a co-ordinated effort between purchasing, design and production one company reduced 30 different paints to 15, 120 different cutting fluids to 10, 50 different tools steels to 6, and 12 different aluminium casting alloys to 3. Standardisation and coding of items also discovered 36 different terms in use for a simple washer.

(*x*) Reduced investment in spares for capital equipment.

(*xi*) Reduced cost of material handling when standardisation is used.

(*xii*) Elimination of the need to purchase costly brand names.

(*xiii*) Irregular purchases of non-standard equipment supplies are revealed.

8. VALUE ANALYSIS AND ENGINEERING

(a) Background and definitions. Value analysis (VA) was developed by the General Electric Company (USA) at the end of World War II. One of the pioneers in this approach to cost-reduction was Lawrence D Miles whose book *Techniques of Value Analysis and Engineering* (McGraw-Hill, 1972) is still the classic on the subject. The term value engineering (VE) was adopted by the US Navy Bureau of Ships in respect of a programme of cost reduction at the design stage, aimed at achieving economies without affecting the needed performance, reliability, quality and maintainability. Miles described value analysis as:

... a philosophy implemented by the use of a specific set of techniques, a body of knowledge, and a group of learned skills. It is an organised, creative approach which has for its purpose the efficient identification of unnecessary cost, i.e. cost which provides neither quality nor use nor life, nor appearance nor customer features.

Value analysis results in the orderly utilisation of alternative materials newer processes, and abilities of specialist suppliers. It focuses engineering, manufacturing and purchasing attention on one objective – equivalent performance at lower cost. Having this focus, it provides step-by-step procedures for accomplishing its objective efficiently and with assurance.

Although the terms VA and VE are often used synonymously, they may be defined as follows:

(i) *Value analysis.* This is a systematic procedure aimed at ensuring that necessary functions are achieved at minimum cost without detriment to quality, reliability, performance and delivery. This is normally a post-production activity.

(ii) *Value engineering.* This is the application of value analysis at the pre-production or development stage.

This distinction may be summarised by the statement that VA is concerned with 'cost correction', VE with 'cost avoidance'. Since VA includes VE the former term will be used.

The keywords for an understanding of VA are *function* and *value.* The function of anything is that which it is designed to do, and should normally be capable of being expressed in two words, a verb and noun; thus the function of a pen is to 'make marks'. 'Value' is variously defined. The most important distinction is between:

(i) *Use value,* i.e. that which enables an item to fulfil its stated function.

(ii) *Esteem value,* i.e. factors that increase the desirability of an item. The function of a gold-plated pencil and a ball-point pen costing £70.00 and 50p respectively is in both cases to 'make marks'. The difference of £69.50 in the price of the former over the latter represents esteem value.

(b) Implementation of VA. The necessary implementation of VA depends on choosing the right people and the right projects.

(1) *The right people.* VA may be carried out by the following:

- A team comprising representatives from such departments as cost accounting, design, marketing, manufacturing, purchasing, quality control, research and work study.
- A specialist VA engineer where the turnover warrants such an appointment. A VA engineer often has the responsibility of co-ordinating a VA team; such a person should have:
  (i) experience of design and manufacturing related to the product(s)
  (ii) understanding of a wide range of materials, their potentials and limitations

(iii) a clear concept of the meaning and importance of 'value'

(iv) creative imagination and flair for innovation

(v) knowledge of specialist manufacturers and the assistance they can provide

(vi) the capacity to work with others and a knowledge of how to motivate, control and co-ordinate.

- Just-in-time approaches emphasise the importance of consultation with suppliers and their co-option to VA teams.

(2) *The right project.* In selecting possible projects, the VA team or engineer should consider the following:

- What project shows the greatest potential for savings: The greater the total cost the larger the potential savings – consider two hypothetical examples, A and B:

	A	B
Present cost each	10p	100p
Possible savings (10%)	1p	10p
Annual usage	100,000	1,000
Projected annual savings	£1,000	£100

Component A offers the greatest potential return from the application of VA.

- What products have a high total cost in relation to the functions performed, i.e. is it possible to substitute a cheaper alternative?
- What suggestions for projects emanate from design, production staff and suppliers?
- Are there drawings or designs that have been unchanged in the last five years?
- Is manufacturing equipment installed more than, say, five years ago now obsolete?
- What inspection and test requirements have not been changed over the last five years?
- Do single-source orders where the original order was placed more than, say, two years ago offer possibilities for savings?

Some areas of VA investigation include the following:

- Product performance, i.e. what does it do?
- Product reliability, i.e. reducing or eliminating product failure or break-down.
- Product maintenance, i.e. reducing costs of routine maintenance such as cleaning, lubrication, etc., and emergency repairs and replacement
- Product adaptability, i.e. adding an additional function or expanding the original use.
- Product packaging, i.e. improving the saleability or protection of the product.

- Product safety, i.e. eliminating possible hazards, e.g. sharp edges, inflammability.
- Product styling, i.e. the introduction of appearance-enhancing changes into the product, e.g. streamlining.
- Product installation, i.e. specifying lighter, stronger or more flexible materials or simplifying instructions
- Product distribution, i.e. making it easier to distribute, e.g. by reducing weight or better transportation.
- Product security, i.e. making the product less liable to theft or vandalism, e.g. better locks, imprinting the customer's name on easily moveable equipment.

(c) VA procedure. The 'job plan' for a VA project comprises the following stages:

(1) *Project selection* (see above).
(2) *Information stage.*

- Obtain all essential information relating to the item under consideration, i.e. cost of materials and components, machining and assembly times, methods and costs, quality requirements, inspection procedures, etc.
- Define the functions of the product, especially in relation to the cost of providing them.

(3) *Speculation stage.* Have a 'brainstorming' session in which as many alternative ideas as possible are put forward for achieving the desired function, reducing costs or improving the product. Some questions that may promote suggestions at this stage include:

- What *additional* or *alternative* uses can we suggest for the item?
- How can the item be *adapted*, i.e. what other ideas does the item suggest?
- Can the item be *modified*, especially with regard to changes in form, shape, material, colour, motion, sound, odour?
- Can the item be *augmented*, i.e. made stronger, higher, longer, thicker, developed to provide extra value, etc?
- Can the item be *reduced*, i.e. made shorter, smaller, condensed, lighter, or features omitted?
- What can be *substituted*, i.e. other materials, components, ingredients, processes, manufacturing methods, packaging?
- Can we *rearrange* the item, i.e. change the layout or design, alter the sequence of operations, interchange components?
- Can the item or aspects of the item be *reversed*, i.e. reversing roles or functions or positions, turned it upside down or front to back?
- What aspects of the product can be *combined*, i.e. functions, purposes, units, other parts, etc?

(4) *Investigation stage.* Select the best ideas produced at the speculation stage and evaluate their feasibility. When VA is organised on a team basis, each specialist will approach the project from his or her own standpoint and report back.

(5) *Proposal stage.* Recommendations will be presented to that level of management able to authorise the suggested changes. The proposals will state:

- What changes or modifications are suggested
- Statements relating to the cost of making the suggested changes, the projected savings, the period(s) over which the savings are likely to accrue.

(6) *Implementation stage.* When approved by the responsible executive the agreed recommendations will be progressed through the normal production, purchasing or other procedures.

VA checklist. The following checklist which every material component or operation must pass was prepared by the Purchasing Department of the General Electric Company (USA).

1. Does its use contribute value?
2. Is its cost proportionate to its usefulness?
3. Does it need all its features?
4. Is there anything better for the intended use?
5. Can a usable part be made by a lower cost method?
6. Can a standard product be found which will be usable?
7. Is it made on proper tooling – considering the quantities used?
8. Are the specified tolerances and finishes really necessary?
9. Do material, reasonable labour, overhead and profit total its cost?
10. Can another dependable supplier provide it for less?
11. Is anyone buying it for less?

(d) Purchasing and VA. Purchasing should be the most cost-conscious of all departments. Where no VA team exists, all buyers should be encouraged to understand and apply the approach. As a member of a VA team, purchasing can make the following contributions:

(i) Provision of information concerning:
- materials and components, e.g. alternative materials such as plastics instead of metals
- costs, e.g. material cost of bought-out components
- standards, e.g. use of a supplier's standard part instead of a special.

(ii) Suggestions for buying economies:
- economic ordering quantities
- reduction in costs of packing, handling and transportation
- purchase of assemblies other than components
- alternative reliable suppliers.

(iii) Encouraging supplier participation. This involves examining, with the suppliers, the function of the item being analysed and seeking their specialist advice as to how the cost can be reduced. Usually specialist suppliers will provide advice free in the interest of good business relationships. It may, however, be sensible to provide the supplier with some financial incentive to collaborate with VA.

9. THE IMPLEMENTATION OF QUALITY

The implementation of quality is concerned with quality control and assurance, quality systems, independent assurance, quality and reliability tools, and vendor rating.

10. QUALITY CONTROL AND ASSURANCE

(a) Quality Control (QC) has been defined [19] as

> *The operational techniques and activities that are used to fulfil requirements for quality.*

Quality Assurance (QA) differs from quality assurance and is defined [20] as

> *All those planned and systematic activities implemented within the quality system and demonstrated as needed to provide adequate confidence that an entity will fulfil requirements for quality.*

Quality control is concerned with defect *detection* and *correction* and relates to such activities as determining where, how and at what intervals inspection should take place, the collection and analysis of data relating to defects and determining what corrective action should be taken. Since defects are detected through post production inspection and are not prevented Schonberger [21] has referred to QC as the 'death certificate' approach.

(b) Quality assurance is concerned with defect *prevention* and has become synonymous with the quality systems BS 5750 and its international counterpart ISO 9000.

11. QUALITY SYSTEMS

A *quality system* is defined [21] as:

> *The organisational structure, responsibilities, procedures, processes and resources for implementing quality management.*

A quality system typically applies to, and interacts with, all activities pertinent to the quality or a product or service. As shown by Fig 7.2 it involves all phases from initial identification to final satisfaction of requirements and customer expectations.

(a) BS 5750. This series of standards has now been redesignated BS/EN 1S0 9000. The letters EN and ISO indicate that the standards have been accepted by CEN (the European Committee for Standardisation) and the ISO (the International Organisation for Standardisation). As shown by Fig 7.3 the main documents relating to the system are a vocabulary and separate standards.

The BS/EN ISO 9000 series provides the principles which are put into practice by the BSI system for the Registration of Firms of Assessed Capability. To be registered, an undertaking is required to have a documented quality system

171

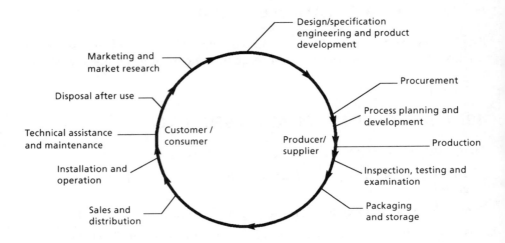

Fig 7.2 The quality loop (reproduced by kind permission of the BSI)

which complies with the appropriate parts of BS/EN 9000 and with a quality assessment schedule (QAS) which defines in precise terms the scope and special requirements relating to a specific group of products, processes or service. QASs are developed by BSI in co-operation with a particular industry after consultation with purchasing and associated interests. When an undertaking seeking

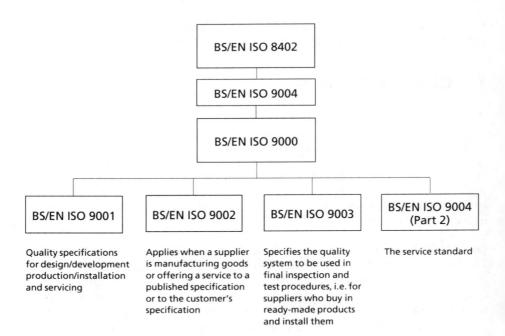

Fig 7.3 The main documents relating to BS/EN ISO 9000 standards

registration has satisfactory documented procedures, the BSI arranges for an assessment visit by a team comprising at least two experienced assessors, one of whom is normally from the BSI inspectorate. Afterwards a report confirming any discrepancies raised and the outcome of the assessment is sent to the undertaking seeking registration.

The initial assessment is followed by regular unannounced audit visits at the discretion of the BSI to ensure standards are maintained.

(b) Purchasing and BS/EN ISO 9000. BS/EN ISO 9001 defines the standard for and requirements of a quality system under twenty main headings of its Section 4 numbered 4.1 to 4.20 of which 4.6 relates to Purchasing. In the context of 4.6 the term *supplier* means the undertaking that is seeking conformance with the standard, i.e. 'us'. The terms *subcontractor* and *purchaser* refer respectively to 'our' suppliers and external customers.

Purchasing (4.6) therefore covers setting up procedures to ensure that supplies used in 'our' production processes meet requirements. The procedures include provisions relating to:

(i) Assessment of suppliers (4.6.2)
(ii) Purchasing Data (4.6.3)
(iii) Verification of Purchased Product (4.6.4).

These sections of BS/EN ISO 9001 should, however, be read in conjunction with the Guide to the above which is provided by BS EN USO 9004–1 (formerly BS 5750: Part 1) which states that, as a minimum, the quality system for purchasing should provide the following elements:

(1) *Requirements for specifications, drawings and purchase documents.* Such documents should contain data clearly describing the product ordered. Typical elements include:

- precise identification of type, class and grade
- inspection instructions and applicable issue of specifications
- quality sub-system standard to be applied.

(2) *Selection of acceptable subcontractors (suppliers).* Methods of establishing the capability of suppliers to meet the requirements of the specifications, drawings and purchase documents include, but are not limited to, any combination of the following:

- on-site evaluation of supplier capability and/or quality system
- evaluation of product samples
- past history with similar products
- test results of similar products
- published experience of other users.

(3) *Agreement on quality assurance.* Clear agreement should be developed with subcontractors (suppliers) for the assurance of products supplied. Such agreements may be achieved by

- reliance on subcontractor's quality system
- submission of specified inspection/test data and process control records with shipments
- 100% inspection testing by the subcontractor
- lot acceptance inspection/testing by sampling by the subcontractor
- implementation of a formal quality system as specified by the organisation: in certain cases a formal quality assurance model may be involved, e.g. BS EN ISO 9000
- periodic evaluation of subcontractor quality practices by the organisation or a third party
- in-house receiving inspection or sorting.

(4) *Agreement on verification methods.* Clear agreement with the subcontractor (supplier) on the methods by which conformance to requirements will be verified.

(5) *Provision for settlement of disputes.*

(6) *Receiving inspection and planning and control.* These procedures should include quarantine areas or other appropriate methods to prevent unintended use or installation of non-conforming materials.

(7) *Quality records related to purchasing.* Maintenance of such records will ensure the availability of historical data to assess subcontractor performance and quality trends. Additionally it may be useful to keep records of lot identification for the purposes of traceability.

Purchasing is therefore concerned with both registration and post-registration, i.e. audit issues relating to BS/EN ISO 9000. It also benefits from the system in that the BSI Register of Firms of Assessed Capability assists purchasing staff when sourcing by:
  (i) eliminating the need for additional supplier assessment
  (ii) simplifying buying decisions
  (iii) providing assurance that quality needs will be met, thereby increasing confidence in supplier capability.

(c) BS 7750 (1994). This relates to environmental management systems including (4.4), those for which the purchasing function has responsibility.

12. INDEPENDENT QUALITY ASSURANCE AND CERTIFICATION

Independent quality assurance and certification is of great benefit to the user, the purchaser and the manufacturer. The BSI, through its Kitemark, Safety Mark, Registered Firms and Registered Stockist Schemes which put into practice the principles of BS 5750, set out procedures by which a product's safety and a supplier's quality management systems can be independently assessed.

(a) The Kitemark. This indicates:

(i) that BSI has tested samples of the product against the appropriate British Standard and confirmed that the requirements of the standard have been met

(ii) that BSI has assessed the manufacturer's quality management system against BS/EN ISO 9000.

(iii) that both company and product are subject to continual surveillance by BSI.

(b) The Safety Mark. This indicates compliance with a British or International Standard specifically concerned with safety or with the safety requirements of a standard covering additional product characteristics. As with the Kitemark scheme, the Safety Mark Scheme includes the testing of samples and assessment of the manufacturer's quality system, followed by continual surveillance by BSI. There is also the European Safety Mark which does not claim to be a mark of safety or compliance with standards.

(c) The Registered Firm Scheme. Reference to this scheme is made above.

(d) The Registered Stockists Scheme. This provides for the registration with the BSI of stockists of electronic components, chemicals, metal fasteners, plastics, etc., having a quality management system in accordance with the scheme and applicable to all items stocked. Buyers have an assurance that all items supplied by a registered stockist will emanate from a quality-assured source. Details of approved products and licensed manufacturers are given in *The Buyers Guide* published annually by the BSI.

(e) Testing houses. About 30 third party certification bodies are members of the Association of British Certification Bodies (ABCB). A number are set up by trade associations such as the Manchester Chamber of Commerce Testing House for the Cotton Trade, Bradford Chamber of Commerce for the Wool Trade, the Shirley Institute, Manchester, and the London Textile Trading House. Certification bodies assessed by the National Accreditation Council for Certification Bodies (NACCB) are entitled to use the NACCB National Quality 'Tick'.

13. TOOLS FOR QUALITY AND RELIABILITY

It would not be practical in this book to attempt even an outline of quality control assurance and reliability techniques. In this section brief reference is made to inspection, seven simple quality control tools, benchmarking, statistical process control, and Failure Mode and Effects Analysis (FMEA) and Quality Circles. Buyers requiring further information should consult one of the many specialised quality texts and, in particular, the relevant parts of BS/EN ISO 9000.

(a) Inspection. Three aspects of interest to the purchaser are incoming inspection, source inspection and source control.

(1) *Incoming inspection.* Items are inspected on delivery according to a specified accepted quality level (AQL). The results of incoming inspections are tabulated by the quality control department and this information will be provided to purchasing so that appropriate action can be taken. Items that pass inspection will be received into the store. Rejected items may be dealt with in one of the following ways:

- Returned to the supplier at their expense for correction or replacement.
- Parts may be corrected by the purchaser and the supplier charged with the cost. This may interfere with production schedules and shop loadings.
- Where the rejected items are usable, although not strictly in accordance with the specification, the buyer may negotiate a price reduction.

One major disadvantage of incoming inspection is that a tendency may emerge for some suppliers to rely on the purchaser's inspection.

(2) *Source inspection.* The purchaser has either resident inspectors at the vendor's plant or arranges for the inspectors to visit the vendor at regular intervals.

Advantages:

- Reduction in the time -period for rejection, return, reworking and redelivery
- Inspectors become expert in dealing with the supplier's products
- The supplier's specialised inspection and test equipment can be utilised.

Disadvantages:

- Source inspection is usually more costly than incoming inspection
- The supplier's responsibility for meeting quality requirements may be reduced, i.e. responsibility is transferred to the purchaser rather than retained by the supplier.

While inspection can ensure 'conformance to specification,' it has, as Saunders [22] points out, a 'major limitation because it does not permit questions to be asked with regard to the correctness or appropriateness of the specification'.

(3) *Source control.* The emphasis is now on the reduction or elimination of inspection by the purchaser of goods received by making the supplier wholly responsible for supplying a product in accordance with a given specification and reporting inspection results to the purchaser by a test certificate or by one of the procedures specified in BS EN ISO 9004–1 (see **11b**(iii) above). In many industries, e.g. the automotive industry, suppliers are required to set up quality systems to provide for the control of incoming quality, the prevention of in-process discrepancies, timely and corrective action where required and the prevention of shipment of non-conforming products.

(b) Seven simple quality control tools. The traditional tools to help organisations to understand their processes with a view to improving their quality techniques are stated below. Readers are also advised to refer to BS EN ISO 9004–4 where further illustrations and explanations are given.

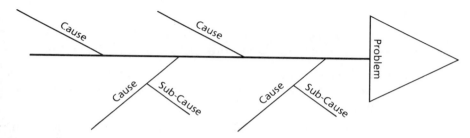

Fig 7.4 Fishbone cause and effect diagram

(1) *Cause and effect diagrams.* These are also known as Ishikawa or 'Fishbone' diagrams after Kaoru Ishikawa, a Japanese engineer, who invented the chart. As shown by Fig 7.4 such a chart resembles a fish in which the problem forms the head from which the spine extends. From the spine are other bones representing possible causes with, possibly, other bones representing sub-causes of the larger cause. This approach is useful in 'brainstorming' sessions designed to locate and identify the causes of organisational problems.

(2) *Check sheet.* A simple list of problems, errors, failures, etc. to be checked. The user puts a tick against each item checked. By examining check sheets it is possible to determine which defect error, etc. is occurring most frequently.

(3) *Control charts.* These are used to control *processes* and are associated with statistical process control involving *sampling*. As shown by Fig 7.5 time is measured on the horizontal axis which usually corresponds to the average value of the characteristic measured on the vertical axis which shows lower, mean and upper control limits. These limits are chosen so that there is a high probability (generally greater than 0.99) that, if the process is in control, sample values plotted in the control chart will fall within these limits.

Control charts are based on the principle of exceptions, i.e. they focus attention on items or results which fall outside the control limits. The causes of such exceptions can be either *random* or *special*.

Random causes affect everyone associated with the process and tend to act on the process in a predictable manner, e.g. overtime, temperature changes.

Special causes do not affect everyone and only arise because of specific

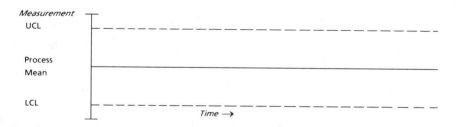

Fig 7.5 The structure of a control chart

177

circumstances and are therefore assignable causes, e.g. material variation, operator performance, tool wear.

(4) *Information flow diagrams.* These are a form of flowchart which provide a graphical representation of the steps in a process (see Chapter 5, Fig 5.5).

(5) *Histograms* indicate the shape of a data distribution. They are also known as column diagrams or bar charts in which the X axis is used for class intervals and the Y axis for frequencies.

(6) *Pareto charts.* These charts are graphical tools used for ranking causes from the most to the least significant. Pareto charts are referred to again in Chapter 8.

(7) *Scatter diagrams.* These analyse the relationship between two variables, typically causes and effects such as training and performance, education and income, cost and reliability. Shown by the scatter diagram in Fig 7.6 there is a high correlation between income and education in the sample of men interviewed.

(8) The above seven tools have been expanded by such approaches as benchmarking, statistical quality control and approaches relating to reliability such as Failure Mode and Effects Analysis (see **14** below).

(c) Benchmarking. This is an approach in which an organisation measures its performance against industry leaders in areas such as quality control and procedures. Because benchmarking can be applied to almost any activity that can be measured, e.g. waste and rejects, inventory (stock levels), purchasing performance, it is considered later in this book under Performance Measurement.

(d) Statistical process control. This is the application of statistical techniques to control a process as indicated in **b**(3) above. It uses control charts to determine if a process is in or out of control. The calculation of the mean and standard deviation and the concept of the normal curve which are the basis of control charts have many other applications including the forecasting of the probability of stock outs and are therefore dealt with as an aspect of Inventory Control in Chapter 8.

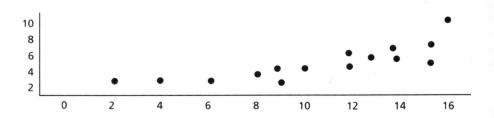

Fig 7.6 Years of post primary education sample of 17 men aged 40 showing income in relation to post primary education

14. FAILURE MODE AND EFFECTS ANALYSIS (FMEA)

(a) What is FMEA? FMEA which originated in the USA aerospace industry is an important reliability engineering technique which has the following main objectives:

- to identify all the ways in which failure can occur
- to estimate the effect and seriousness of the failure
- to recommend corrective design actions.

FMEA has been defined as [23]:

A systematic approach that applies a tabular method to aid the thought process used by engineers to identify potential failure modes and their effects.

(b) Types of FMEA. These take three forms [24]:

(i) Systems FMEA is used to analyse systems and sub-systems in the early concept and design stages. System function is the design or purpose(s) of the system and is derived from customer wants. It can also include safety requirements, government regulations and constraints.

(ii) Design FMEA is used to analyse products before they are released to production.

(iii) Process FMEA is used to analyse products before they are released to the customer.

(c) The preparation of a FMEA

(1) The Ford Motor Company which was the first of the UK motor manufacturers to request suppliers to use FMEA in their advance quality planning recommends a team approach led by the responsible System, Product or Manufacturing/ Assembly Engineer who is expected to involve representatives from all affected activities. Team members may be drawn from Design, Manufacturing, Assembly, Quality, Reliability, Service, Purchasing, Testing, Supplier and other subject experts as appropriate.

The team leader is also responsible for keeping the FMEA updated.

For proprietary designs the preparation and updating of FMEAs is the responsibility of the suppliers.

(2) With a design FMEA, for example, the team is initially concerned with identifying how a part *may* fail to meet its intended function and the seriousness of the effect of a potential failure which is rated on a ten-point scale as shown in Fig 7.7.

(3) Starting with the failure modes with the highest severity ratings the Design FMEA team then ascertains the possible causes of failure based on two assumptions:

- that the part is manufactured/assembled within engineering specifications
- that the part design may include a deficiency that may cause an unacceptable variation in the manufacturing or assembling process.

(4) The team then proceeds to ascertain

(i) the cumulative number of failures that could occur over the life of the part

(ii) design evaluation techniques that can be used to detect the identified failure causes

Effect	Rating	Criteria
No Effect	1	No effect
Very Slight Effect	2	Very slight effect on vehicle performance. Customer not annoyed. Non-vital fault noticed sometimes.
Slight Effect	3	Slight effect on vehicle performance. Customer slightly annoyed. Non-vital fault noticed most of the time.
Minor Effect	4	Minor effect on vehicle performance. Fault does not require repair. Customer will notice minor effect on vehicle or system performance. Non-vital fault always noticed.
Moderate Effect	5	Moderate effect on vehicle performance. Customer experiences some dissatisfaction. Fault on non-vital part requires repair.
Significant Effect	6	Vehicle performance degraded, but operable and safe. Customer experiences discomfort. Non-vital part inoperable.
Major Effect	7	Vehicle performance severely affected, but driveable and safe. Customer dissatisfied. Subsystem inoperable.
Extreme Effect	8	Vehicle inoperable but safe. Customer very dissatisfied. System inoperable.
Serious Effect	9	Potentially hazardous effect. Able to stop vehicle without mishap – gradual failure. Compliance with Government regulation in jeopardy.
Hazardous Effect	10	Hazardous effect. Safety related – sudden failure. Non-compliance with Government regulation.

Severity is a rating corresponding to the seriousness of the effect(s) of a potential failure mode. Severity applies only to the effect of a failure mode.

Fig 7.7 Severity rating table for design (FMEA)

(iii) what design actions are recommended to reduce the severity, occurrence and detection ratings.

The completed Design FMEA in respect of a Lighting Switch Sub-system is shown in Fig 7.8. The technique is further described in BS 5760.

(d) The advantages of the FMEA approach. These are listed by Ford as:

(i) Improved quality, reliability and safety of Ford products
(ii) Improved Ford image and competitiveness
(iii) Increased customer satisfaction
(iv) Reduction in product development timing and cost
(v) Documentation and tracking of actions to reduce risk.

(e) Some disadvantages of the FMEA approach. A study undertaken by UMIST [25] concluded that engineers still view FMEA as a hard slog; more use should be made of computerised aids to reduce the effort of preparing and updating the FMEA; the main difficulties are related to time constraints and lack of understanding of the importance of FMEA, training and commitment.

15. QUALITY CIRCLES AND TASK TEAMS

(a) Definition of quality circles. *A small group of volunteers, usually from the same work area, meeting regularly under the leadership of their immediate superior to analyse and solve problems relating to their responsibilities and, where appropriate, themselves implement solutions agreed with management.* This definition may be analysed as follows:

(i) 'A small group'. Normally a QC comprises three to twelve persons. Membership must be large enough to generate ideas and cater for absenteeism but not too large for genuine participation.

(ii) 'Volunteers'. Employee participation is voluntary.

(iii) 'From the same work area'. Unlike a VA team, which is made up of representatives from several departments, a QC usually consists of persons from the same work area. This gives the circle its identity. Exceptionally a QC may have members sharing the same problems but drawn from different departments.

(iv) 'Meeting regularly'. Meetings take place fortnightly, monthly, or more frequently as required.

(v) 'Their immediate superior'. One benefit of a QC is that the leader's role is enhanced. Circle leaders should therefore be of at least supervisory level.

(vi) 'To analyse and solve problems'. Projects may be identified either by the QC or referred to it by management.

(vii) 'Themselves implement solutions agreed by management'. All proposed solutions must be submitted to management for evaluation and approval before they are implemented.

POTENTIAL FAILURE MODE AND EFFECTS ANALYSIS (DESIGN FMEA)

Subsystem/Name   17.05.01 / Lighting Switches Subsystem   Suppliers and Plants Affected __
Design Responsibilty Lighting Department   Model Year/Vehicle(s) _____
Other Areas Involved   TBD   Engineering Release Date ____

Part Name & number Part Function	Potential Failure Mode	Potential Effect(s) of Failure	s e v	∇	Potential Cause(s) of Failure	o c c u r
(9)	(10)	(11)	8		(14)	7
Electric Switch (F9DB-999-AB) / Pass current to headlamp filament	Switch fails to pass current (Row 1)	System: Primary function will not be provided (S = 8) Other Effects: See Note in text explanation	8		1.0) Crystal fails to pass current when pressed	7
Electric Switch Crystal Material / Generate signal when pressed	1.0) Crystal fails to pass current when pressed (Row 2)	Switch fails to pass current (S = 7) Other effects: Same as Row 1 above	8		1.1) Electric crystal Material cracked 1.2) 0 degree vertical orientation not maintained (see Row 5)	7
Electric Switch Crystal Material / Generate signal when pressed	1.1) Electric crystal material cracked (Row 3)	Same as Row 2 above	8		1.1A) Surface area supporting crystal is too small	3
					1.1B) Crystal material is too brittle at -40 deg C (Row 4)	3
	1.2) 0 degree vertical orientation not maintained (Row 5)	Same as Row 2 above	8		Improper design allows switch to be improperly installed (i.e., 0 degree vertical orientation not maintained	7

			Page 1 Rows 1 through 5						
Electric Company			Prepared By _____						
1999 / Electric Vehicle			FMEA Date (Orig.) 93-05-14 (Rev.) 92 04 01						
98-07-93									

Design Evaluation Technique	Det ec	R. P. N.	Recommended Action(s)	Area/Individual Responsible & Completion Date	Action Results				
					Actions Taken	Sev	Occ	Det	R. P. N.
(16)	5	280	(19)	(20)	(21)				
Vehicle Durability Test (D = 8)			(Transfer Cause 1.0 to Failure Mode in Row 2)						
Laboratory Accelerated Life Test (D = 5)									
Buck/Assembly Test (D = 3)	3	168	(Determine root causes of 1.1 – see Rows 3 and 4 below)						
Installation Drawing (D = 5)									
Computer program (Calculate bending stresses)	5	120	Increase crystal support structure area to distribute load evenly over crystal surface (P)		Supporting surface area increased from 3 to 6 sq. mm. Rev -DD added to drawing on 93-06-18	8	2	5	80
(16)	5	120	Add lab test to detect failure mode when crystal is subjected to design load at -40 deg C (D)		Lab test added to DV Test Program on 93-06-18	8	3	3	72
Vehicle Durability Test (D = 8)									
Laboratory Accelerated Life Test (D = 5)									
Buck/Assembly Test (D = 3)	3	168	Add tab to switch housing to prevent misorientation during assembly (P)		Tab added to switch housing. Rev -DE added to dwg on 93-06-17	8	1	3	24
Installation Drawing (D = 5)									

(b) The establishment of QCs. The earliest QCs, comprising mainly shop-floor employees, were developed in Japan during the 1960s by Kaoru Ishikawa as part of a national quality drive. QCs are now concerned with projects relating to matters other than quality, such as cost reduction, safety, communications and energy conservation. The main steps in setting up QCs are as follows:

(i) Obtain the commitment of senior management to the QC concept.

(ii) Inform the trade unions of the intention to establish QCs and obtain their co-operation.

(iii) Form a steering committee chaired by a senior manager to provide guidance, direction and resources, to monitor the progress of QCs and to support the facilitator.

(iv) Appoint a facilitator responsible for initiating, co-ordinating and directing QC activities in the organisation.

(v) Provide training for QC leaders. In addition to group dynamics the content of this training may include such all-purpose techniques as the application of statistical techniques, lateral thinking and Pareto analysis.

(vi) Form the QCs. This should be done after considering what areas of the organisation might benefit from their introduction.

(c) QC objectives. These may include:

(i) Reduction of errors and enhancement of quality

(ii) Problem prevention rather than detection and correction

(iii) Reduction in product or service costs

(iv) Improved productivity

(v) Increased employee involvement, motivation, job satisfaction and commitment

(vi) Improved teamwork and working relationships

(vii) Development of employee problem-solving ability.

(d) Task teams are a variant of quality circles since they are formed to undertake a specific task or solve a specific problem. Unlike quality circles which usually comprise people from a single functional area who meet on a continuing basis, task teams involve specialists from several functions and disband when the specific task is completed. The *self-managed team* is a development of the task team approach. This moves the focus from a management-initiated drive for quality and improvement to a self-directed work team concept. A self-managed team is defined [26] as:

'A highly trained group of employees, from 6 to 18 on average, fully responsible for turning out a well defined segment of finished work. The segment could be a final product like a refrigerator or a service like a fully processed insurance claim. It could also be a complete but intermediate product or service like a finished refrigerator motor, an aircraft fuselage or the circuit plans for a television set.'

(e) Work cells. These are typified by Walker's [27] description of the development by Rover Cars. Work cells comprise about 80 persons controlled by a production manager rather than a supervisor. The production manager's responsibilities extend to employee welfare, training and education in addition to technology and production. Cell members are encouraged to suggest production and product quality improvements. While each team takes on enhanced quality responsibilities (the concept was introduced as a consequence of JIT and Minimal Inventory Control Systems) cell autonomy is restricted by such factors as the flow-time rate and orders received.

(f) Purchasing Quality Circles and Task Teams. There is nothing to prevent the establishment of a purchasing QC. Purchasing, however, is more likely to be involved as a member of a task or self-managed team. Virtually any problem that can be considered by a VA team is also suitable for the attention of a task team.

16. THE COST OF QUALITY

(a) The cost of quality may be defined as *costs of conformance plus the costs of non-conformance or the cost of doing things wrong.* The main costs of quality are set out in Table 7.2 (overleaf).

(b) Data collection. Quality costs become absorbed and hidden in various overheads unless they are separately recorded and collected. Collection of data usually involves obtaining information from a number of sources and charging expenditures against a quality or budget centre using appropriate codes. Activity costing (see Chapter 12) is one way of charging quality costs to products. Sources of cost data relating to quality include:

- Payroll analysis
- Manufacturing expense reports
- Scrap reports
- Rework or rectification authorisation/reports
- Travel expense claims
- Product cost information
- Field repair, replacement and warranty cost reports
- Inspection and 'test' records
- Material review records.

(c) Quality cost formulae or records. The collating and reporting of quality costs is stated by BS 6143 to be a shared activity between the quality and accounting functions. BS 6143 should be consulted by readers wishing for more information on quality costing systems. Briefly, this involves allocating quality costs to accountable cost centres by the use of account codes under appropriate headings. When accumulated it is possible to build up a typical quality cost element comparison as shown in Table 7.3 (overleaf).

Table 7.2 The costs of quality

Costs of Conformance	
Prevention Costs	*Appraisal Costs*
(Costs of any action taken to investigate, prevent or reduce defects and failures including:)	(Costs of assessing the quality achieved)

Prevention Costs:
- Quality engineering (or quality management, department or planning)
- Quality control/engineering including design/specification review and reliability engineering
- Process control/engineering
- Design and development of quality measurement and control equipment
- Quality planning by other functions
- Calibration and maintenance of production equipment used to evaluate quality
- Maintenance and calibration of test and inspection equipment
- Supplier assurance including supplier surveys, audits and ratings identifying new sources of supply, design evaluation and testing of alternative products, purchase order review before placement
- Quality training
- Administration, audit and improvement

Appraisal Costs:
- Laboratory acceptance testing
- Inspection tests (including 'Goods Inward')
- Product quality audits
- Set up for inspection and test
- Inspection and test material
- Product quality audit
- Review of test and inspection data
- Field (on-site) performance testing
- Internal testing and release
- Evaluation of field stock and spare parts
- Data processing inspection and test reports

Costs of Non-Conformance	
Internal failure	*External failure*
(Cost arising within the manufacturing organisation before transfer of ownership to the customer)	(After transfer of ownership to the customer)

Internal failure:
- Scrap
- Rework and repair
- Trouble shooting or defect/failure analysis
- Re-inspect, re-test
- Scrap and rework, fault of vendor, downtime
- Modification permits and concessions
- Downgrading, i.e. losses for quality reasons resulting from a lower selling price

External failure:
- Complaints
- Product or customer service, product liability
- Products rejected and returned, recall reject
- Returned materials repair
- Warranty costs and costs associated with replacement

Table 7.3 Typical example of quality cost element comparison
(reproduced with permission from BS 6143)

Segment	Element	Percentage of Total Quality Cost
Failure	Scrap	35
	Rework	11
	Re-inspection	9
	Additional operation	8
	Warranty	5
	Downgrading	2
	Others	2
	Total failure cost	72
Appraisal	Inspection and test	26
Prevention	Control of prevention activities	2
Grand Total		100

BS 6143 points out that 'Quality costs alone do not provide sufficient information for management to put them into perspective with other operating costs or to identify critical areas in need of attention'. To establish the significance of quality costs it is necessary to use ratios showing the relationships between total quality costs and the costs of prevention, appraisal and failure. Typical ratios include:

$$\frac{Prevention\ costs}{Total\ quality\ costs} \qquad \frac{Cost\ of\ supplier\ assessment}{Prevention\ costs}$$

17. PURCHASING AND QUALITY

Purchasing contributions to design have already been mentioned in 3:**9a**. References to purchasing and standardisation value analysis and BS/EN ISO 9000 are made earlier in this chapter. It may, however, be useful to summarise the numerous ways in which an effective purchasing function can contribute to specifying and assuring the quality of supplies.

(a) General

(i) Contributing to the competitive advantage of the undertaking by participating in the procurement of bought-out items at the most economical cost.
(ii) Ensuring that quality is not confused with price and grade.
(iii) Providing a high level of expertise with regard to quality to both internal and external 'customers' of the purchasing function.
(iv) Ensuring that purchasing's responsibilities in relation to quality meet with the requirements of BS/EN 9000 and BS 7750.

(b) As a support service to design and production

(v) Serving as a member of teams concerned with concurrent design, value engineering and value analysis and special projects/problems.

(vi) Advocating, where appropriate, the involvement of suppliers in design, VA, etc., teams.

(vii) Advising on costs in relation to 'fitness for purpose', e.g. lower priced alternative materials such as aluminium rather than zinc or pressure rather than gravity manufacture for die-castings.

(viii) Suggesting more economic forms of procurement, e.g. assemblies rather than components.

(ix) Providing information on the availability of items of a specified quality.

(x) Assisting, from the standpoint of quality, in drafting company specifications.

(xi) Emphasising the quality advantages of using standard specifications.

(xii) Ensuring that items of the right quality are purchased when no formal specifications exist.

(xiii) Advising on the availability of alternatives of the same quality but at a cheaper price to brand names.

(c) At the pre-ordering stage. It is suggested that the purchasing staff should take as a guide the requirements of BS EN ISO 9004–1 relating to the following (see **IIb** above):

(xiv) Selection of acceptable subcontractors (suppliers).

(xv) Agreement on quality assurance.

(xvi) Agreement on verification methods.

(xvii) Receiving inspection and planning and control.

(d) At the ordering stage

(xviii) The above BS EN ISO 9004–1 requirement relating to specifications, drawings and purchase documents.

(xix) Including in the terms and conditions of purchase appropriate terms relating to quality including provision of the settlement of quality disputes.

(e) At the post ordering stage

(xx) Vendor rating with respect to quality.

(xxi) Feedback to suppliers in respect of their quality performance and co-operation, where required, with regard to quality improvement.

(xxii) Maintenance of quality records with respect to purchased items.

(xxiii) Negotiations with suppliers in respect of items rejected as unsatisfactory.

(f) Training. To carry out the above responsibilities purchasing staff should have appropriate training in:

- An appreciation of design and production processes
- Quality control and assurance procedures and methods

- Procedures relating to reliability, e.g. FMEA
- The provisions of BS EN ISO 9000 and BS 7750.

References

[1] Crosby P B. *Quality is Free*. Mentor Books, 1980. Chap 2, p 15.

[2] Juran J M. *Quality Control Handbook*. 3rd Ed. McGraw Hill, 1974. Sect 2, p 22.

[3] Gavin D A. *What does product quality really mean? Sloan Management Review*. Fall 1984. pp 25–38.

[4] Gavin D A. *Competing in eight dimensions of quality. Harvard Business Review*. Nov-Dec 1987. No 6, p 101.

[5] Logothetis N. *Managing of Total Quality*. Prentice Hall, 1991. Chap 8, pp 216–217.

[6] DTI. *Total Quality Management and Effective Leadership*. 1991. p 8.

[7] BSS 7856. Part 1, 1992.

[8] DTI. *Total Quality Management and Effective Leadership*. 1991. p 10.

[9] Cannon S. *Supplying the service to the internal customer. Purchasing and Supply Management*. April 1995, pp 32–35.

[10] Zaire M. *Total Quality Management for Engineers*. Woodhead Publishing (1991). Chapter 9, p 193.

[11] Zaire M. *Total Quality Management for Engineers*. Woodhead Publishing (1991). Chapter 10, p 216.

[12] Dowlatshahi S. *Purchasing's role in a concurrent engineering environment. International Journal of Purchasing and Materials Management*. Winter 1992, pp 21–25.

[13] BS 7373. 1991, p3.

[14] BS 7373. 1991, pp 7–8.

[15] BS 7373. 1991, Appendix A.

[16] England WB, *Modern Procurement Management*, 5th Ed. 1970, Chap 4, p 306.

[17] Woodroffe G. *So farewell then market overt. Purchasing and Supply Management*. Feb 1995, pp 16–17.

[18] Ashton T C. *National and international standards* in Lock (Ed), *Gower Handbook of Quality Management*. 2nd Edition 1994. Chap 10, pp 144–145.

[19] BS EN ISO 8402, 1995, p 25, Sect 3.4.

[20] BS EN ISO 8402, 1995, pp 25–26, Sect 3.5.

[21] Schonberger R J. *Building a Chain of Customers*. Free Press (USA), 1990.

[22] Saunders M. *Strategic Purchasing and Supply Chain Management*. Pitman, 1994, Ch 6, p 154.

[23] Ford Motor Co Ltd. *Failure Mode and Effects Analysis Handbook* 1992, pp 22.

[24] Ford Motor Co Ltd. *Failure Mode and Effects Analysis Handbook* 1992, pp 24 and 25.

[25] Dale B G and Shaw P. *Failure Mode and Effects Analysis. A Study of the Use in the Motor Industry*. University of Manchester Institute of Science and Technology. Occasional Paper 8904. 1990.

[26] Osborn J D, Moran I, Musselwhite E and Zenger J N. *Self Directed Work Teams*. Business One – Irwin, 1990. Chap 1, p 8.

[27] Walker D. *Creative Empowerment at Rover* in Henry J and Walker D (Ed), *Managing Innovation*. Sage Publications, 1991.

Progress test 7

1. Give some definitions of quality.

2. What are the five approaches to defining quality identified by Gavin?

3. Define 'reliability'.

4. What are the basic principles of TQM?

5. What in the quality context is 'a customer'?

6. What are the stages of the design process?

7. Distinguish between CAD, CAM and CAE.

8. In what ways may the approach of purchasing to quality differ from that of the design function itself?

9. What are the basic functions of a specification?

10. What are the contents of a typical specification?

11. What additional methods of specifying goods may be used?

12. What are some advantages of standardisation from a purchasing perspective?

13. Identify some possible areas that might be the subjects of a VA investigation.

14. What are the stages of a VA exercise?

15. Distinguish between quality control and quality assurance.

16. What is a quality *system*?

17. Explain some requirements of BS EN ISO 9000 that are of significance for purchasing.

18. What are the respective advantages of incoming and source inspection?

19. Describe some simple quality control tools.

20. What are the advantages of the FMEA approach to reliability?

21. What is a Quality Circle?

22. Under what headings may quality costs be analysed?

23. What are some of the contributions that purchasing can make to quality achievement
    (i) as a support service to design and production?
    (ii) at the post ordering stage?

24. The design stage is an important element in the ability of manufacturing firms to produce goods economically. Discuss how the purchasing function and its suppliers can make a significant contribution to the lowering of product cost at this stage.
    (CIPS. *Introduction to Purchasing and Supply* (1988))

25. Many companies have moved towards the concept of 'total quality management' as the means of gaining competitive advantage in the market place. Explain the role that the purchasing department can play in this approach.
    (CIPS. *Purchasing Principles and Techniques* (1989))

26. As a Purchasing Manager you may need to assist a supplier to improve the levels of conformance to specification for components. Explain why this may be necessary and discuss three techniques which you would suggest to a supplier in such a situation.
    (CIPS. *Purchasing and Supply Management II. Provisioning* (1992))

27. Explain how value analysis and value engineering can contribute to the profitability and efficiency of an organisation. Outline a procedure for undertaking a value analysis exercise including the contribution which the purchasing function can made.
    (CIPS. *Purchasing and Supply Management II. Provisioning* (1992))

28. Describe the ways in which statistical methods can be used both in the selection of a quality capable supplier and in the maintenance of quality standards in the longer term with these suppliers.
    (CIPS. *Purchasing and Supply Management II. Provisioning* (1994))

8

MATCHING SUPPLY WITH DEMAND

The development and maturing of MRP, MRPII and JIT approaches, described later in this chapter, together with the emphasis on partnership sourcing, shorter lead times and the elimination or reduction in stock levels have brought about dramatic changes in inventory management. Nevertheless every organisation has inventories of some kind and the economics and techniques of inventory management and control are still relevant.

1. DEFINITIONS

Inventory is an American accounting term for the value or quantity of raw materials, components, assemblies, consumables, work-in-progress and finished stock that are kept or stored for use as the need arises. The term is also applied to

(i) a detailed list of goods or articles in a given place or
(ii) a stocktaking.

Inventory (or stock) control refers to the techniques used to ensure that stocks of raw material or other supplies, work-in-progress and finished goods are kept at levels which provide maximum service levels at minimum costs.

2. INVENTORY CLASSIFICATIONS

The term 'supplies' has been defined [1] as:

> *'All the materials, goods and services used in the enterprise regardless of whether they are purchased outside, transferred from another branch of the company or manufactured in house.'*

The classification of suppliers for inventory purposes will vary according to the particular undertaking. In a manufacturing enterprise, for example, inventory might be classified as:

(i) *Raw materials*: e.g. steel, timber, cloth, etc. in an unprocessed state awaiting conversion into a product.

(ii) Components and sub-assemblies: e.g. ball bearings, gearboxes, to be incorporated into an end product.

(iii) Consumables: all suppliers in an undertaking which are classified as indirect and which do not form part of a saleable product. Consumables may be sub-classified into (1) production, e.g. detergents; (2) maintenance, e.g. lubricating oil; (3) office, e.g. stationery; (4) welfare, e.g. first-aid supplies, etc.

(iv) Finished goods: products manufactured for resale which are ready for despatch.

Following supply chain usage, inventory may also be classified into:

(i) Primary inventory, i.e. raw materials, components and sub-assemblies, work-in-progress and finished goods.

(ii) Support inventories, i.e. consumables of various categories.

3. THE AIMS OF INVENTORY MANAGEMENT

(i) To provide both internal and external customers with the required service levels in terms of quantity and order rate fill.

(ii) To ascertain present and future requirements for all types of inventory to avoid overstocking while avoiding 'bottlenecks' in production.

(iii) To keep costs to a minimum by variety reduction, economical lot sizes and analysis of costs incurred in obtaining and carrying inventories.

4. THE RIGHT QUANTITY

In manufacturing or assembly-type organisations, the most important factors that determine the right quantity are as follows:

(i) The demand for the final product into which the bought-out materials and components are incorporated.

(ii) The inventory policy of the undertaking.

(iii) Whether job, batch, assembly or process production methods are applicable.

(iv) Whether demand for the item is independent or dependent (see below).

(v) The service level, i.e. the incidence of availability required. The service level required for an item may be set at 100 per cent for items where a stock-out would result in great expense through production delays or, as with some hospital supplies, where lack of supplies may endanger life. For less crucial supplies, the service level might be fixed at a lower level, e.g. 95 per cent. The actual service level attained in a given period can be computed by the formula:

Number of times the item is provided on demand
Number of times an item has been demanded

(vi) Market conditions, e.g. financial, political and other considerations that determine whether requirements shall be purchased on a 'hand-to-mouth' or 'forward' basis.

Table 8.1 Purchasing and quantities

Type of purchase	Quantities indicated by
(a) Materials or components required for a specific order or application, e.g. steel sections not normally stocked.	(i) Material specification or bill of material for the job or contract.
(b) Standard items kept in stock for regular production, whether job, batch or continuous flow.	(i) Materials budgets derived from production budgets based on sales/output target for a specified period. (ii) 'One-off' material specifications or bills of material showing quantities of each item needed to make one unit of finished product. These are then multiplied by the number of products to be manufactured. (iii) Material requisitions raised by storekeeping or stock control. (iv) Computerised reports provided at specified intervals, e.g. daily, weekly, relating to part usage, stocks on hand, on order and committed. With some programmes reordering can be automatically carried out.
(c) Consumable materials used in production, plant, maintenance or office administration, e.g. oil, paint, stationery and packing materials.	(i) Requisitions from stores or stock control or computerised inventory reports as above.
(d) Spares – these may be kept to maintain production machinery or they may be bought-out components for resale to customers who have bought the product in which the component is incorporated.	(i) Requisitions from stores or stock control. (ii) Information from sales department. (iii) Computerised inventory reports as above

(vii) Factors determining economic order quantities (see **5** below). In individual undertakings the quantity of an item to be purchased over a period may be notified to the purchasing department in several ways, as shown by Table 8.1.

5. DEMAND

Demand may be either independent or dependent.

(1) *Independent demand* for an item is influenced by market conditions and not related to production decisions for any other item held in stock. In manufacturing, only end items, i.e. the final product sold to the customer, have exclusively independent demand.

(2) *Dependent demand* for an item derives from the product decisions for its 'parents'. The term 'parent' is an item manufactured from one or more *component* items. A table, for example, is a parent made from a top, legs and fasteners. A *component* is one item that goes through one or more operations to be transformed into a parent.

Independent demand:
    (i) can only be estimated.
    (ii) although fluctuating with random market influences, usually demonstrates a continuous and definable pattern.

Dependent demand (see Fig 8.1):
    (i) derives from production decisions for its parents and can therefore be forecast.
    (ii) due to the practice of scheduling manufacturing in lots, is usually discontinuous and 'lumpy'.

Entirely different production and inventory control systems are utilised according to whether demand is being forecast or dependent (derived). Independent demand is associated with:
    Fixed Order Quantities
    Continuous and Periodic Review Systems
    A B C Analysis

Dependent demand is associated with
    Material Requirements Planning (MRP)
    Distribution Requirements Planning (DRP)
    Optimised Production Technology (OPT).

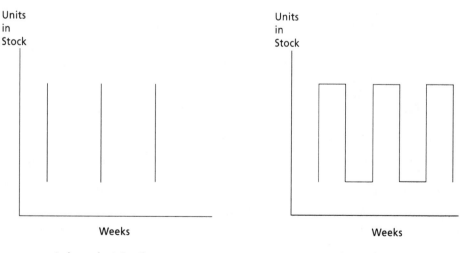

Independent-Continuous
Demand (Usage) Pattern

Dependent, 'Lumpy'
Demand (Usage) Pattern

Fig 8.1 Contrast between continuous and 'lumpy' demand

6. THE ECONOMICS OF STOCK MANAGEMENT

These are determined by an analysis of the costs incurred in obtaining and carrying inventories under the following headings.

(a) Acquisition costs. Many of the costs incurred in placing an order are incurred irrespective of the order size, e.g. the cost of an order will be the same irrespective of whether 1 or 1000 tons are ordered. Ordering costs include:

(*i*) Preliminary costs, e.g. preparing the requisition, vendor selection, negotiation
(*ii*) Placement costs, e.g. order preparation, stationery, postage, etc.
(*iii*) Post-placement costs, e.g. progressing, receipt of goods, materials handling, inspection, certification and payment of invoices.

In practice it is difficult to obtain more than an approximate idea of ordering costs since these vary with:

(*i*) The complexity of the order and the seniority of staff involved
(*ii*) Whether order preparation is manual or computerised
(*iii*) Whether repeat orders cost less than initial orders.

Sometimes the total cost of a purchasing department or function over a given period is divided by the number of orders placed in that time. This gives a completely fallacious figure since the average cost per order reduces as the number of orders placed increases which may be indicative of inefficiency rather than the converse.

(b) Holding costs. These are of two types:

(*i*) *Costs proportional to the value of the inventory*, e.g.

- Financial costs, e.g. interest on capital tied up in inventory. This may be bank rate or, more realistically, the target return on capital required by the enterprise.
- Cost of insurance.
- Losses in value through deterioration, obsolescence and pilferage.

(*ii*) *Costs proportional to the physical characteristics of inventory*

- Storage costs, e.g. storage space, stores rates, light, heat and power.
- Labour costs relating to handling and inspection.
- Clerical costs relating to stores records and documentation.

The total costs per annum under each heading will be expressed as a percentage of the monetary values or quantity of the average stock held.

(c) Cost of stockouts, e.g. the costs of being out of inventory. These comprise:

(*i*) Loss of production output.
(*ii*) Costs of idle time and of fixed overheads spread over a reduced output.

(iii) Cost of action taken to deal with the stockout, e.g. buying from a stockist at an enhanced price, switching production, obtaining substitute materials.

(iv) Loss of customer goodwill through the inability to supply or late delivery. Often costs of stockouts are hidden in overhead costs. Where the costs of individual stockouts are computed these should be expressed in annual figures to ensure compatibility with acquisition and holding costs. Costs of stockouts are difficult to estimate or incorporate into inventory models.

7. PARETO ANALYSIS

To ascertain the most economic order quantity it is necessary to find the order quantity that spreads the acquisition costs over as many units as possible without incurring uneconomical holding costs. The larger the order quantity the lower will be the ordering cost per unit. Large order quantities, however, lead to higher inventories and holding costs. Holding costs can be important and expensive when storage space is limited.

To obtain information regarding ordering and holding costs is essential for the calculation of EOQs but is in itself an expensive exercise. This expense can be reduced by concentrating on those inventory items which have the highest value. This can be done by means of ABC or Pareto analysis.

ABC analysis is the application to stockholding of Pareto's Law, derived by a nineteenth-century Italian economist who observed that a minority of the population owned the majority of his country's wealth. Applied to stocks, Pareto's Law shows that the majority of inventory value will be represented by relatively few items. While the percentages will vary between organisations, inventory will be approximately segmented in the proportions shown below.

Category (usage)	Approximate % of inventory	Approximate % of usage value
A (high value)	10	60
B (moderate value)	30	30
C (low value)	60	10

These relationships can be represented by a Pareto curve shown in Fig 8.2. The procedure for ABC analysis is:

(i) Calculate the annual usage value of each stock item (annual usage × price).

(ii) List each item in descending order of its annual purchase value.

(iii) Make cumulative totals of the number of items and of usage values.

(iv) Express items in these lists as percentages of the total number of items and totals of the usage values.

(v) Classify items into ABC categories.

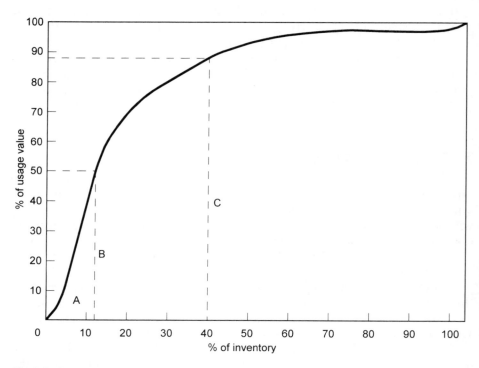

Fig 8.2 Pareto curve

Example An actual investigation revealed the following figures:

Category	No. of items	% of items	Annual usage value	% of usage value
A	367	15.00	£4,395,200	80
B	550	22.60	824,100	15
C	1523	62.40	274,700	5
	2440	100.00	£5,494,000	100.00

Without performing a complete analysis of all stocked items, ABC items can be roughly identified by the fact that if an item has a usage value of more than six times the average for all items it will be category A. An item with usage value of less than half the average for all items will probably be category C. Category B items will therefore lie between six times and half the average value.

The strictest control should be exercised over category A and, possibly, B items. These controls may include EOQs and high safety stocks. Less control will be applied to category A items.

ABC analysis draws attention to the common sense approach that it is probably not worth having elaborate controls on split pins and washers when the bulk of the inventory *value* is represented by motors, gears and diamond-tipped drills.

ABC has numerous management applications. For example, high staff turnover or absenteeism is likely to be accounted for by only a small number of workers. Other applications in the purchasing field include quality analysis, the selection of value analysis projects and vendor analysis.

8. VARIETY REDUCTION

Variety reduction can make substantial savings in inventory by standardising and rationalising the range of materials, parts and consumables kept in stock. Variety reduction can be pro-active or re-active.

(1) *Pro-active* variety reduction can be achieved by using, so far as possible, standardised components and subassemblies to make end products that are dissimilar in appearance and performance so that a variety of final products use only a few basic components. Pro-active approaches to variety reduction can also apply when considering capital purchases. By ensuring compatibility with existing machinery the range of spares carried to insure against breakdowns can be substantially reduced.

(2) *Re-active* variety reduction can be undertaken periodically by a special project team comprising all interested parties who examine a range of stock items to determine:

- the use for which each item of stock is intended
- how many stock items serve the same purpose
- the extent to which items having the same purpose can be given a standard description
- what range of sizes is essential
- how frequently each item in the range is used
- what items can be eliminated
- to what extent can sizes, dimensions, quality and other characteristics of an item be standardised
- what items of stock are now obsolete and unlikely to be required in the future.

The *advantages* of variety reduction include:

- reduction of stock holding costs
- release of money tied up in stocks
- easier specification when ordering
- narrower range of inventory
- a reduced supplier base.

9. ECONOMIC ORDER QUANTITIES (EOQs)

(a) Definition. *The EOQ is the size of order (or lot size) that minimises the total costs of acquiring and holding stock.*
The concept of EOQ is illustrated graphically in Fig 8.3.

(b) EOQ models. A model is an imitation of reality. The two EOQ models referred to below are based on the following assumptions:

(i) Uniformity of demand
(ii) Absence of any limitation imposed by stores capacity
(iii) Costs of acquisition and holding costs for a unit of material are independent of order quantity
(iv) Order and delivery quantities are equal
(v) The prices of raw materials or components are stable.

Based on these assumptions, two of the typical EOQ models that can be derived are:

- the basic EOQ model (see **(c)** below)
- the quantity discount model (see **(d)** below).

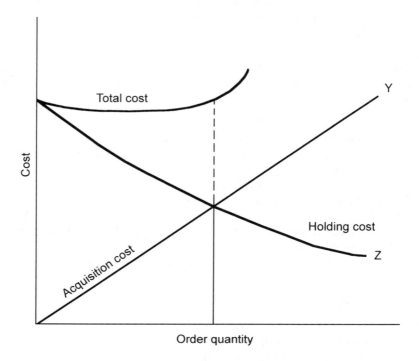

Fig 8.3 The economic order quantity

More complex models used where the demand is unknown but determinable on the basis of a probability distribution (known as *probabilistic models*) are outside the scope of this book.

(c) The basic EOQ model. This assumes that the entire quantity order is to be received at one time.

Example An undertaking has an annual usage of 6000 units of a component purchased at £2 each. Ordering costs amount to £15 per order and annual holding costs per component are £0.05.

The optimum quantity can be found by the use of formulae based on the following variables:

Q = order quantity
A = total annual usage
C = acquisition cost per order
H = holding cost as a percentage of unit price
P = price per unit.

(i) Number of orders per year:

$$\frac{\text{Annual usage in units}}{\text{Order quantity}} = \frac{A}{Q} = \frac{6000}{Q}$$

(ii) Ordering costs:

$$\frac{\text{Cost of placing order} \times \text{Annual usage in units}}{\text{Order quantity}} = \frac{CA}{Q} = \frac{£15 \times 6000}{Q}$$

(iii) Average stock in hand:

$$\frac{\text{Order quantity} \times \text{Price}}{2} = \frac{QP}{2} = \frac{Q \times £2}{2}$$

(iv) Holding cost as a percentage of unit price:

$$\frac{\text{Holding cost} \times \text{Price} \times \text{Order quantity}}{2} = \frac{£0.05 \times £2 \times Q}{2}$$

(v) Total costs:

$$\text{Ordering costs} + \text{Holding costs} = \frac{CA}{Q} = \frac{HPQ}{2}$$

The EOQ is found when Ordering costs = Annual holding costs (see Fig 8.3), i.e.

$$\frac{CA}{Q} = \frac{HPQ}{2}$$

$$\frac{£15 \times 6000}{Q} = \frac{£0.05 \times £2 \times Q}{2}$$

To solve for the EOQ simply cross-multiply the terms and isolate Q on the left-hand side of the equation:

Table 8.2 Economic order quantities

No. of orders per year	Quantity ordered (Units)	Value(£) of each order	Average stock (Units)	Average stock (£)	Cost (£) of acquisition	Holding cost (£)	Total cost (£)
1	6000	12000	3000	6000	15	300	315
2	3000	6000	1500	3000	30	150	180
3	2000	4000	100	2000	45	100	145
4	1500	3000	750	1500	60	75	135
5	1200	2400	600	1200	75	60	135
6	1000	2000	500	200	90	50	140

$$\frac{HPQ}{2} = \frac{CA}{Q} \quad \therefore HPQ^2 = 2CA \quad \therefore Q = \sqrt{\frac{2CA}{HP}}$$

Substituting

$$Q = \sqrt{\frac{2 \times £15 \times 6000}{£2 \times £0.05}} = \sqrt{\frac{180,000}{£0.10}} = 1342 \text{ units}$$

The optimum number of orders per annum can be found by transposing the above formula to give the value for:

$$\frac{A}{Q} = \sqrt{\frac{HPA}{2C}} = \sqrt{\frac{£0.05 \times £2 \times 6000}{2 \times £15}} = \sqrt{\frac{600}{30}} = \sqrt{20} = 4.47$$

Thus, 4.47 (optimum number of orders) × 1342 (EOQ) = 5999 (almost the annual usage).

Alternatively, the EOQ may be found on a trial-and-error basis by constructing a table as shown in Table 8.2. The table shows that the costs of acquisition will be at a minimum when either four or five orders are placed at a value of either £3000 or £2400 respectively. More accurately, the quantity can be expected to lie somewhere between 1200 and 1500 units.

This same result will also be obtained if the formula given below is used:

$$EOQ = \sqrt{\frac{2 \times C \times U}{H}}$$

$$= \sqrt{\frac{2 \times \text{Acquisition cost} \times \text{Annual value of units used}}{\text{Stockholding cost}}}$$

$$= \sqrt{\frac{2 \times £15 \times £12,000}{£0.05}} = \sqrt{\frac{£360,000}{£0.05}}$$

$$= £2683.3 \text{ which at £2 per unit} = 1342 \text{ units approx}$$

10. THE QUANTITY DISCOUNT MODEL

The base economic lot size is computed on the assumption that the purchase price is constant. In practice, variations in price may occur due to quantity discounts. A quantity discount is simply a reduced price (P) for the item which is purchased in larger quantities. Thus, we may have a table of discounts as follows:

Quantities	Discount price per item	Discount %
0–999	£10.00	0
1000–1999	£9.80	2
2000 and over	£9.75	2.5

Placing an order to obtain the largest quantity discount might not, however, minimise the total inventory cost. This is because, as the price per item decreases, the quantities to be bought increase so that holding costs rise.

Example Assume an annual usage (A) of 10,000 units bought at £10 each; a holding cost (I) as a percentage cost of average inventory of 20 per cent (or 0.2) and an ordering cost of £50 per order. The unit price is reduced to £9.80 and £9.75 respectively for orders of 1000–2000 units and over.
   The determination of the quantity that will minimise the total annual cost of inventory involves the following steps.

(a) Calculate the EOQ for each discount level using the formula:

$$EOQ = \sqrt{\frac{2AC}{IP}}$$

where A = annual usage
         C = holding cost as a percentage of unit price
         P = price per unit.

IP is used instead of H for the holding cost because it cannot be assumed that the holding cost is constant when the unit price per item changes with each quantity discount.
   Using the above formula the EOQ for each price level will be:

(i) $EOQ = \sqrt{\dfrac{2 \times 10,000 \times £50}{0.2 \times £10}} = 707$ units

(ii) $EOQ = \sqrt{\dfrac{2 \times 10,000 \times £50}{0.2 \times £9.80}} = 714$ units

(iii) $EOQ = \sqrt{\dfrac{2 \times 10,000 \times £50}{0.2 \times £9.75}} = 716$ units

(b) At the price of £10 there is no discount so the EOQ of 707 units needs no adjustment. The EOQs at prices of £9.80 and £9.75 are below the minimum quantities specified and will, therefore, have to be adjusted upwards to 1000 and 2000 units respectively.

(c) The third step is to find the total cost for each order quantity using the table below. The calculations in this table show the need to evaluate quantity discounts carefully. The reduced price of £9.75 actually increases the total cost of inventory as against a price of £9.80. If, however, a price of £9.70 for minimum orders of £2000 can be negotiated the total cost would be £99,190 and it would thus pay to take advantage of the discount.

1	2	3	4	5	6	7	8
				Holding			
		Average	Value of	cost of		Total	
Price per	Order	inventory	average	average	Ordering	purchase	Total
unit	size	(Units)	stock (£)	stock (£)	cost (£)	price (£)	cost (£)
£10.00	707	354	3540	708	707	100,000	101,415
£9.80	1000	500	4900	980	500	98,000	99,450
£9.75	2000	1000	9750	1980	250	97,500	99,700

Ordering cost is then calculated as follows:

$$\frac{\text{Total annual usage}}{\text{Order quantity}} \times \text{Cost per order} = \frac{10,000}{1000} \times £50 = £500$$

(d) Computer support in the calculation of EOQs. Computer programs can provide for the automatic calculation of EOQs together with such applications as automatic reordering especially of Pareto C items, generating exception reports and re-computing decision parameters.

11. LEAD TIMES

Lead time is the period taken to obtain a requirement from the time the need is ascertained to its fulfilment. It comprises the following operations:

(i) preparation of requisitions
(ii) forwarding of requisition to purchasing
(iii) processing by purchasing from enquiry to preparation of the order
(iv) transmission of order to supplier
(v) execution of order by supplier
(vi) transportation of order
(vii) receipt, inspection and storage
(viii) issue to production or sales.

Not all delays are attributable to suppliers since lead time is longer than delivery time. Steps (i) to (iii) and (vii) are controllable by the purchaser and can be improved by efficient clerical or computerised procedures, including EDI, vendor appraisal and specification of the most rapid method of transport.

It is important to recognise that consistency of lead time is more important than its actual length. Even with MRP and JIT techniques, events such as stoppage of delivery dates or receipt of defective materials require constant scrutiny to ensure that suppliers maintain consistency. In uncertain conditions it may be necessary to maintain safety stocks.

12. FORECASTING DEMAND

Before an effective system of inventory control can be implemented it is essential to analyse from records of usage what has been the trend of demand for a given item of stock over an approximate period of time with a view to forecasting future requirements. The two most common approaches are the use of moving averages and of exponentially weighted averages. These methods can, of course, be used in respect of any type of purchase and are not necessarily confined to stock.

(a) Moving averages. A moving average is an artificially constructed time series in which each annual (or monthly, daily, etc.) figure is replaced by the average or mean of itself and values corresponding to a number of preceding and succeeding periods.

Example The usage of a stock item for six successive periods was 90, 84, 100, 108, 116 and 127. If a five-period moving average is required the first term will be:

$$\frac{90 + 84 + 100 + 108 + 116}{5} = 99.6$$

The average for the second term is:

$$\frac{84 + 100 + 108 + 116 + 127}{5} = 107$$

At each step, one term of the original series is dropped and another introduced. The averages, as calculated for each period, will then be plotted on a graph. There is no precise rule about the number of periods to use when calculating a moving average. The most suitable, obtained by trial and error, is that which best smooths out fluctuations. A useful guide is to assess the number of periods between consecutive peaks and troughs and use this.

(b) The exponentially weighted average method (EWAM). The moving average method has been largely discarded for inventory applications since it has a number of disadvantages:

(*i*) It requires a large number of separate calculations.
(*ii*) A true forecast cannot be made until the required number of time periods have elapsed.
(*iii*) All data are equally weighted, but in practice, the older the demand data, the less relevant it becomes in forecasting future requirements.
(*iv*) The sensitivity of a moving average is inversely proportional to the number of data values included in the average.

These difficulties are overcome by using a series of weights with decreasing values which converge at infinity to produce a total sum of one. Such series, known as an exponential series, take the form of:

$$a + a(1 - a) + a(1 - a)^2 + a(1 - a)^3 \ldots = 1$$

where a is a constant between 0 and 1.

In practice the values of 0.1 and 0.2 are most frequently used. Where a small value such as 0.1 is chosen as the constant the response, based on the average of a considerable number of past periods, will be slow and gradual. A high value, i.e. $a = 0.5$, will result in 'nervous' estimates responding quickly to actual changes. With exponential smoothing all that is necessary is to adjust the previous forecast by a fraction of the difference between the old forecast and the actual demand for the previous period, i.e. new average forecast is:

a (actual demand) + $(1 - a)$ (previous average forecast)

Example The actual demand for a stock item during the month of January was 300 against a forecast of 280. Assuming a weighting of 0.2 what will be the average demand forecast for February?

Solution

$$0.2(300) + (1 - 0.2) (280) = 60 + 224$$

Forecast for February = 284. By subtracting the average computed for the previous month from that calculated for the current month we obtain the trend of demand.

13. FIXED ORDER AND PERIOD REVIEW SYSTEMS

Most methods of stock control fall into two main categories, fixed order point systems and periodic review (reorder-cycle) systems:

(a) Fixed order point system. This is also known as a *continuous review* system or *re-order point system*. It is also termed a two-bin system due to the fact that this approach provided a simple, non-mathematical approach to checking inventory. Under the two-bin system the stock of a particular item is segregated into two bins. Stock is initially taken from the first bin. The re-order level, when the storekeeper issues a requisition for new supplies, is when that bin becomes empty. The purchase order is therefore a fixed quantity (which can be based on an EOQ).

In practice reviews are made frequently, i.e. on a daily basis rather than upon each withdrawal.

(1) The most important control levels are calculated as follows:

Example

Normal usage:	120 items per day
Minimum usage:	60 items per day
Maximum usage:	150 items per day
Lead time:	25/30 days
EOQ (already calculated)	5500 items

(i) Re-order level = Maximum usage × Maximum lead time

$$= 150 \times 30 = 4500 \text{ items}$$

(ii) Safety or buffer level = Re-order level − Average use in maximum lead time

$$= 4500 - (120 \times 30) = 900 \text{ items}$$

(iii) Minimum level = Re-order level − Average use for average lead time

$$= 4500 - (120 \times 27.5)$$

$$= 4500 - 3300 = 1200 \text{ items}$$

(iv) Maximum level = Re-order level + EOQ − Minimum anticipated usage in lead time

$$= 4500 + 5500 - (60 \times 25)$$

$$= 10,000 - 1500 = 8500 \text{ items}$$

(2) In practice it may also be necessary to take into account items already allocated to back orders and scheduled receipts from orders already placed but not yet delivered. The inventory position (IP), i.e. the item's ability to satisfy future demand relying only on future receipts, can be calculated by the formula:

$$IP = OH + SR - BO$$

where IP = the inventory position of the item (in units)
         OH = number of units in on-hand inventory
         SR = scheduled receipts (open orders)
         BO = number of units either back ordered or allocated.

Example

Inventory on hand (OH) = 20 units
Re-order point (R) = 200 units
There are no back orders (BO)
but one open order (SR) for 400 units. Should a new order be placed?

$$IP = OH + SR - BO$$
$$= 20 + 400 - 0$$
$$= 420$$

As IP exceeds R (420 − 200) it is not necessary to re-order.

(b) Periodic review system. As the name implies in this system an item's inventory position is reviewed periodically rather than at a fixed order point.

The periods or intervals at which stock levels are reviewed will depend on the importance of the stock item and the costs of holding that item. A variable quantity will be ordered at each review to bring the stock level back to maximum (hence, the system is sometimes called the 'topping-up' system).

Maximum stock can be determined by adding one review period to the lead time, multiplying the sum by the average rate of usage and adding any safety stock. This can be expressed as:

$$M = W (T + L) + S$$

where M = predetermined stock level
   W = average rate of usage
   T = review period
   L = lead time
   S = safety stock.

Safety stock may be calculated in a similar manner to that indicated for the fixed order-point system.

Example   Assume Average rate of usage 120 items per day

Review period:	4 weeks (say, 20 days)
Lead time:	25/30 days
Safety stock:	900 items

$M = 120 (20 + 30) + 900 = 6900$ items.

If, at the first review period, the stock was 4000 items an order would be placed for 2900 items, i.e. 6900 maximum stock – actual stock at the review date.

(c) Advantages and disadvantages of fixed order and periodic review systems

Fixed order point

ADVANTAGES
- On average, stocks are lower than with the periodic review system.
- EOQs are applicable.
- Enhanced responsiveness to demand fluctuations.
- Replenishment orders are automatically generated at the appropriate time by comparison of actual stock levels against reorder levels.
- Appropriate for widely differing inventory categories.

DISADVANTAGES
- The reordering system may become overloaded if many items of inventory reach reorder level simultaneously.
- Random reordering pattern due to items coming up for replenishment at different times.
- Under conditions of varying demand or ordering costs EOQ calculations may be inaccurate.

Periodic review

ADVANTAGES	DISADVANTAGES
• Greater chance of elimination of obsolete items due to periodic review of stock.	• On average, larger stocks are required than with fixed order-point systems, since reorder quantities must provide for the period between reviews as well as between lead times.
• The purchasing load may be spread more evenly with possible economies in placing of orders.	
• Large quantity discounts may be negotiated when a range of stock items are ordered from the same supplier at the same time.	• Reorder quantities are not based on EOQs.
	• If the usage rate changes shortly after a review period, a stockout may occur before the next review date.
• Production economies due to more efficient production planning and lower set-up costs may result from orders always being in the same sequence.	• Difficulties in determining appropriate review periods unless demands are reasonably consistent.

(d) Choice of systems

(i) A fixed order point system is more appropriate if a stock item is used regularly and does not conform to the conditions of *(ii)* below.

(ii) A periodic review system is most likely to be appropriate if orders are placed with and delivered from suppliers at regular intervals (e.g. daily, monthly) or a number of different items are ordered from and delivered by the same supplier at the same time.

14. MATERIALS REQUIREMENTS PLANNING (MRP)

(a) Definition. Materials requirements planning (MRP) is a product-oriented computerised technique aimed at minimising inventory and maintaining delivery schedules. It relates the dependent requirements for the materials and components comprising an end product to time periods known as 'buckets' over a planned horizon (typically of one year) on the basis of forecasts provided by marketing or sales and other input information.

(b) A comparison of order point and MRP systems. A comparison of the two systems is made in Table 8.3.

(c) MRP terminology

(i) A *Bill of Materials* or BOM contains information on all materials, components, subassemblies required to produce each end item.

(ii) An *end item* or master scheduled item is, as stated in 5(i) above, the final product sold to the customer. Inventory for end items from the accounting standpoint will either be work in progress or finished goods.

Table 8.3 Comparison of fixed order point and MRP systems

Stock replenishment systems	MRP systems
(a) Assumes that demand for an item is *independent,* i.e. unrelated to other *inventory items*	Based on the recognition that demand for an item may be *dependent,* i.e. related to the demand for other inventory items.
(b) Deriving from (a) above the emphasis is on the individual *part*	Deriving from (a) above, the emphasis is on the *end product* into which related parts are incorporated.
(c) Assumes average usage rates with gradual depletion of inventory until it is replenished by the next delivery	Recognises that usage rates may be erratic or 'lumpy' depending on demand for the end product.
(d) Quantities required are specified on the basis of *historical* demand	Quantities required are specified on the basis of *future* demand.
(e) Demand for inventory items is forecast	Demand for inventory items is not forecast but precisely determined from the master production schedule for the end product.
(f) Orders placed when triggered by a re(c)order point signal using data relating to the costs of ordering and stocking	Orders for items placed when triggered by a time-based signal. Time phasing uses lead-time information and need dates.
(g) Safety stocks are maintained for all inventory items	Safety stocks are theoretically only maintained in respect of the end product. Factors such as stoppage of delivery dates or defective material may, in practice, necessitate safety stocks in some cases.

(*iii*) A *parent* also referred to in 5(ii) is an item manufactured from one or more component items.

(*iv*) A *component* is one item that goes through one or more operations to be transformed into a parent.

(*v*) An *intermediate item* is one that has at least one parent and one component. Intermediate items are classified as work in progress.

(*vi*) A *sub-assembly* since it is 'put together', as distinct from other means of transformation, is a special case of intermediate item.

(*vii*) A *purchased item* is one that has no components because it comes from a supplier but has one or more parents. For accounting purposes inventory of purchased items is regarded as raw materials.

(*viii*) *Part commonality* is the extent to which a component (part) has one or more parents. This concept is related to standardisation. Thus a standard ball bearing may have numerous parents.

(*ix*) *Usage quantity* relates to the number of units of a component required to make one unit of its parent.

(*x*) A *'bucket'* is a time period to which MRP relates, e.g. one week.

(d) Applications of MRP. While having elements common to all inventory situations, MRP is most applicable where:

(*i*) The demand for items is dependent
(*ii*) The demand is discontinuous, i.e. 'lumpy' and non-uniform
(*iii*) In job, batch and assembly or flow production, or where all three manufacturing methods are used.

(e) The aims of MRP

(*i*) To synchronise ordering and delivery of materials and components with production requirements.
(*ii*) To achieve planned and controlled inventories and ensure that required items are available at the time of usage or not much earlier.
(*iii*) To promote planning between the purchaser and the supplier to the advantage of each. The forward projection of orders, for example, can assist suppliers to reduce lead time and production costs and minimise the inventory costs of the purchaser.
(*iv*) To enable rapid action to be taken to overcome material or component shortages due to emergencies, late delivery, etc.

A simple example of the synchronising aims of MRP may be given. Suppose an end product X is assembled from four components, A,B,C,D, which are requisitioned on a reorder-point system using safety stocks on the basis of providing a 90 per cent 'off-the-shelf' service level. Product X clearly cannot be assembled without all four components being available. Each component will be available 90 per cent of the time, but not the same 90 per cent. The probability of all four items being available simultaneously is

$$0.9 \times 0.9 \times 0.9 \times 0.9 = (0.9)^4 = 66 \text{ per cent}$$

In other words, for 34 per cent of the time there will be a shortage. Items of inventory will, therefore, be in stock which have to be paid for and incur loss of interest and possibly losses through pilferage, etc. To raise the service level we would have to have a heavier investment in safety stocks.

MRP aims to ensure that items are available when wanted and not before, and in this way to minimise inventory and maintain delivery schedules.

(f) MRP inputs and outputs. The inputs and outputs of an MRP system are shown in Fig 8.4 and may be explained as follows:

(1) *Forecasts* of demand for the end product will be provided by the marketing function. The overall demand for the materials or components comprising the end product will be augmented by orders for spares and other orders not related to the regular production plan which will have to be treated as additions to the forecast production requirements.

(2) *The master production schedule(s)* (MPS) uses the inputs from marketing and

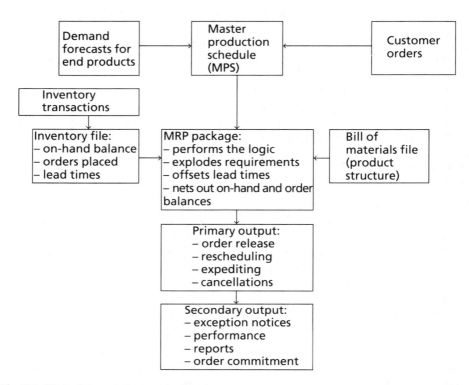

Fig 8.4 Materials requirement planning

sales to forecast demand for quantities of the final product over a planned time horizon subdivided into periods known as 'time buckets' (see Fig 8.5). These buckets are not necessarily of equal duration. Without the MPS(s), MRP cannot generate requirements for any item.

(3) *The bill of materials file* (BOM), also known as the product structure, lists all the items that comprise each assembly and sub-assembly that make up the final product or end item. Each BOM is given a level code according to the following logic:

Level 0   The final product or end item not used as a component of any other product
Level 1   Direct component of a level 0 item
Level 2   Direct component of a level 1 item
Level n Direct component of a level $(n - 1)$ item

Assume the demand for product X is 30 units. Each unit of X requires three units of A and 2 of B. Each A requires one C, one D and 3 Es. Each B requires one E and one F. Each F requires three Gs and two Cs. Thus the demand for A,B,C,D, E,F and G is completely dependent on the demand for X. From the above information we can construct a BOM or product structure for the related inventory requirements as in Fig 8.6.

Week	1	2	3	4	5	6	
Product X	30		14		10	8	Time buckets
Product Y		38	13	30	13	13	Time horizon

Fig 8.5 Master production schedule

(4) *The inventory file* comprises the records of individual items of inventory and their status. The file is kept current by the on-line posting of inventory events such as the receipt and issue of items of inventory or their return to store.

(5) *The MRP package* uses the information provided by the MPS, BOM and inventory files to:

(i) Explode or cascade the end product into its various assemblies, sub-assemblies or components at various levels. Thus the number of units of each item needed to produce 30 units of product X would be:

Part A = 3 × no. of Xs	(3) (30)	= 90
Part B = 2 × no. of Xs	(2) (30)	= 60
Part C = 1 × no. of As + 2 × no. of Fs	(1) (90) + (2) (60)	= 210
Part D = 1 × no. of As	(1) (90)	= 90
Part E = 2 × no. of As + 1 × no. of Bs	(2) (90) + (1) (60)	= 240
Part F = 1 × no. of Bs	(1) (60)	= 60
Part G = 3 × no. of Fs	(3) (60)	= 180

Thus to produce 30 units of X we shall need 90 units of A, 60 units of B, 210 units of C, 90 units of D, 240 units of E, 60 units of F and 180 units of G.

(ii) Offset for lead time. Lead times for each item must be fed into the system. Subtracting the lead time from the date of the net requirement so as to position the planned order release date in advance of the timing of the net requirement it covers is called *offsetting the lead time*.

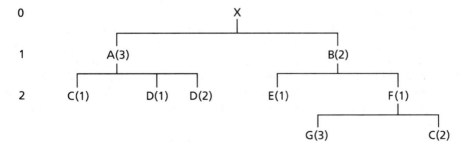

Fig 8.6 Product structure for X

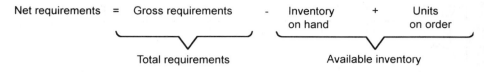

Fig 8.7

(iii) Net out on-hand and on-order balances using the equation in Fig 8.7. In an MRP system net requirement quantities are always related to some date or period, i.e. they are time phased (as shown by Fig 8.5). The primary outputs of the MRP system are:

(1) Order release instructions for the placement of planned (i.e. future) production or purchasing orders

(2) Rescheduling instructions notifying the need to advance or postpone open orders to adjust inventory coverage to net requirements

(3) Expediting instructions in respect of overdue orders

(4) Cancellation or suspension instructions in respect of open orders.

MRP systems have also the capacity to produce much secondary data.

(g) Manufacturing resource planning (MRP II). What is known as MRP II has wider implications than materials planning outlined in the above description of MRP I. MRP II is concerned with virtually any resource entering into production, including manpower, machines and money in addition to materials. For this reason the word 'resource' is usually substituted for 'requirements' when referring to MRP II.

MRP II is a *closed loop* system. In a closed loop system there is automatic feedback from the manufacturing or production functions to the ultimate production plan or master production schedule, followed by automatic adjustment of the input to correct or modify the system.

Manufacturing resource planning has been defined by the American Production and Inventory Control Society as:

A system built around materials requirements planning and also including the additional planning functions of production planning, master production scheduling and capacity requirements planning.

Further, once the planning phase is complete and the plans have been accepted as attainable, the execution functions come into play. These include the shopfloor control functions of input-output measurements, detailed scheduling and despatching, plus anticipated delay reports from both the shop and the vendors, purchasing, follow-up and control, etc. The term 'closed-loop' implies that not only is each of these elements included in the overall system but also that there is feedback from the execution functions so that the planning can be kept valid at all times.

Both MRP I and MRP II have many detailed aspects which cannot be covered in this book. Readers seeking further information should refer to specialist texts.

15. DISTRIBUTION REQUIREMENTS PLANNING (DRP)

(a) Definitions. DRP is an inventory control and scheduling technique that applies MRP principles to distribution inventories. It may also be regarded as a method of handling stock replenishment in a multi-echelon environment.

An echelon is defined by Chamber's Dictionary as

'A stepwise arrangement of troops, ships, planes etc'.

Applied to distribution the term 'multi-echelon' means that instead of independent control of the same item at different distribution points using EOQ formulae, the dependent demand at a higher echelon (e.g. a central warehouse) is derived from the requirements of lower echelons (e.g. regional warehouses). DRP is useful for both manufacturing organisations, such as car manufacturers that sell their cars through several distribution points, e.g. regional and local distributors, and purely merchandising organisations, e.g. supermarkets (see Fig 8.8).

All levels in a DRP multi-echelon structure are dependent except for the level that serves the customer, i.e. the retailer in the above illustration.

(b) DRP and MRP. DRP has been described as the mirror image of MRP. Some of the contrasts between the two approaches are set out in Table 8.4.

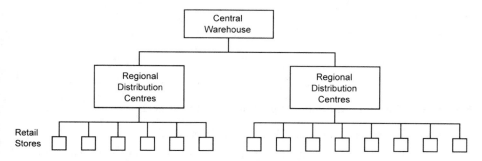

Fig 8.8 A supermarket multi-echelon distribution system

Table 8.4 Comparison of MRP and DRP

MRP	*DRP*
• Bills of Materials applies time phased logic to components and sub-assemblies to products in the MOM network.	• Bills of Distribution (the network) uses time phased order point logic to determine network replenishment requirements.
• An 'explosion' process from a master production schedule to the detailed scheduling of component replenishments.	• An 'implosion' process for the lowest levels of the network to the central distribution centre.
• Goods in course of manufacture.	• Finished goods.

MRP and DRP approaches have, however many common aspects

(i) As planning systems, neither uses a fixed or periodic review approach.
(ii) Both are computerised systems.
(iii) Just as MRP has been expanded into MRP II so DRP has been expanded into DRP II (distribution resource planning).
(iv) DRP utilises record formats and processing logic consistent with MRP.

The last point is the most important of all since it provides the basis for integrating the database throughout the whole supply chain from purchasing through to distribution. Both MRP and DRP therefore contribute to a logistics system as shown in Fig 8.9.

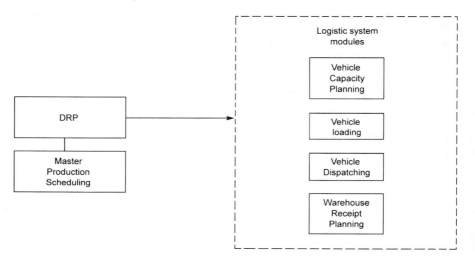

Fig 8.9   Distribution requirements planning and logistics [2]

Thus as Vollmann, Berry and Whybark observe [2]:

'Distribution requirements planning serves a central role in co-ordinating the flow of goods inside the factory with the system modules that place the goods in the hands of the customers. It provides the basis for integrating the Manufacturing Planning and Control (MRP) system from the firm to the field.'

(c) DRP planning. The fundamental document used in distribution planning is the DRP display. This document time phases across the planning horizon which is typically divided into weeks. A hypothetical example of a DRP display is shown in Fig 8.10. It is assumed:

Time horizon	10 weeks
Balance on hand at start	175 items
Safety stock	50 items
Lead time	2 weeks
Order quantity	250 items

The above records gathered from a number of distribution points will be passed to the next higher stage in the echelon. The aggregates of the regional echelons

Balance	Period (week)									
Week	1	2	3	4	5	6	7	8	9	10
Gross requirement	60	60	80	75	70	60	80	70	90	95
Scheduled receipts			250			250			250	
Balance (projected on hand quantity) 175	115	55	225	150	80	270	190	120	280	185
Planned orders	250			250			250			

Fig 8.10   DRP display or record

will be passed to the central warehouse and from there, in a full logistics system, to the factory. This process is referred to as an 'implosion'. This is different from the MEP manufacturing concept of 'explosion' where a finished product is broken down into its components. The process, however, is the same but reversed.

From the example in Fig 8.10 it can be seen that

(i) The emphasis in DRP is on scheduling rather than ordering.

(ii) This is a time-phased order point (TPOP) system. (Time phasing is 'the scheduling of inventory requirements and replenishments by need date over a specified time horizon' [3].)

(iii) For a given period, net requirements = (gross requirements + safety stock) – (scheduled receipts + projected on hand for the previous period).

(iv) Replacement stock is ordered one lead time prior to the period in which the gross requirements will eat into the safety stock.

(v) The projected on hand quantity is revised at the end of each quarter. For a given period, projected on hand = projected on hand of the prior period + scheduled receipts – gross requirements.

(vi) The planned order quantity becomes a gross requirement on the same time period for the parent supply centre at the next level.

16. JUST-IN-TIME PURCHASING

(a) Definitions. Just-in-time (JIT) purchasing has been defined by Lee White [4] as *'an inventory control philosophy whose goal is to maintain just enough material in just the right place at just the right time to make just the right amount of product'*. More concisely, JIT is *'the exact adjustment of production to quantity and time held'*.

(b) The development of JIT. The JIT concept originated in Japan in the 1950s when the Toyota Motor Company developed a system known as *Kanban* to meet customer demand for various vehicle models with minimum delivery delays. *Kanban* in Japanese means 'ticket' and refers to an information system in which instructions relating to the type and quality of items to be withdrawn from the preceding manufacturing process are conveyed by a card. JIT is a 'demand pull' system in which manufacturing planning begins with the final assembly line and works backwards, not only through the various manufacturing processes, but also to the vendors and subcontractors supplying materials and components. The exact quantity to replace the items withdrawn to meet the requirements of one manufacturing stage are provided by the preceding process. The aim is that by limiting production and assembly to what is actually needed, both materials and work-in-progress inventories can be eliminated or significantly reduced.

JIT has several versions known by such names as ZIPS (Zero Inventory Production Systems), MAN (Materials as Needed), DOPS (Daily Overhead and Perfect Supply) and NOT (Nick-of-Time). In all such cases the essential requirement is that supplies must be delivered frequently in relatively small quantities 'just-in-time' for use.

(c) JIT and purchasing. For JIT to work, two things must happen:

- All parts must arrive where they are needed, when they are needed and in the exact quantity needed
- All parts that arrive must be usable parts.

Where these are not achieved, JIT may easily become 'just-too-late'.

In achieving these requirements, purchasing has the responsibilities summarised below.

(i) Liaison with the design function. The emphasis should be on *performance* rather than *design* specifications. Looser specifications enable suppliers to be more cost effective by being more innovative with regard to the quality/function aspect of supplies. In JIT purchasing, value analysis is an integral part of the system and should include suppliers.

(ii) Liaison with suppliers to ensure that they understand thoroughly the importance of consistently maintaining lead times and a high level of quality.

(iii) Investigation of the potential of suppliers within reasonable proximity of the purchaser to increase certainty of delivery and reduction of lead time.

(iv) Establishing strong, long-term relationships with suppliers in a mutual effort to reduce costs and share savings. This will be achieved by the purchaser's efforts to meet the supplier's expectations with respect to:

- continuity of custom
- a fair price and profit margin
- agreed adjustments to price when necessary
- accurate forecasts of demand
- firm and reasonably stable specification
- minimising order changes
- smoothly timed order releases
- involvement in design specifications
- prompt payment.

(v) Establishment of an effective supplier certification programme which ensures that quality specifications are met before components leave the supplier so that receiving inspections are eliminated.

(vi) Evaluation of supplier performance and the solving of difficulties as an exercise in co-operation.

(d) Benefits of JIT. The potential benefits of JIT to an organisation, and its purchasing function in particular, have been summarised by Schonberger and Ansari [5] as follows:

(i) Part costs – low scrap costs; low inventory carrying costs.

(ii) Quality – fast detection and correction of unsatisfactory quality and ultimately higher quality in purchased parts.

(iii) Design – fast response to engineering change requirements.

(iv) Administrative efficiency – fewer suppliers; minimal expediting and order release work; simplified communications and receiving activities.

(v) Productivity – reduced rework; reduced inspection; reduced parts-related delays.

(vi) Capital requirements reduced inventories of purchased parts, raw materials, work in progress and finished goods.

(e) Possible disadvantages of JIT. Some organisations have experienced problems with JIT for the following reasons:

(i) Faulty forecasting of demand and inability of suppliers to move quickly to changes in demand.

(ii) JIT required the provision of the necessary systems and methods of communication between purchasers and suppliers ranging from vehicle telephones to EDI. Problems will arise if there is inadequate communication both internally, i.e. from production to purchasing, and externally from purchasing to suppliers and vice-versa.

(iii) Organisations with, ideally, no safety stocks are highly vulnerable to supply failures.

(iv) Purely stockless buying is a fallacy; lack of low-cost C class items can halt a production line as easily as a failure in the delivery of highly priced A class items.

(v) The advantages of buying in bulk at lower prices may outweigh the savings negotiated for JIT contracts, since suppliers may increase their prices to cover costs of delivery, paperwork and storage.

(vi) JIT is not generally suitable for bought-out items having a short life cycle and subject to rapid design change.

(vii) JIT is more suitable for flow than batch production and may require a change from batch to flow methods with consequent changes in systems required to support the new methods.

(viii) Even mass production manufacturers produce a substantial percentage of components by number, if not value, on batches as well as a small number of high value components on dedicated flow lines.

(ix) Apart from suppliers, JIT requires a total involvement of people from all disciplines and the breaking down of traditional barriers between functions within an organisation. This may involve a substantial investment in organisational development training.

(x) Rhys, McNabb and Nieuwenhuis [6] have drawn attention to Japanese transport factors arising from some resiting of suppliers at greater distances from purchasers (although these are normally still nearer to users than in Europe), road congestion and lighter vehicles, i.e. for every one vehicle required in Europe two or three are required in Japan. In consequence JIT in Japan is now 'neither lean nor green'. Nieuwenhuis [7] makes the following comparison of Japanese and European approaches in terms of vehicle use for a given road.

Japan	Europe
More journeys	Fewer journeys
More journey time	Less journey time
More traffic congestion	Less traffic congestion
Greater fuel use	More fuel efficient
More vehicles needed	Fewer vehicles needed
More air pollution and road damage	Less air pollution and road damage
Shorter distances	Longer distances

A consideration of these factors leads the above writers to conclude that:

(1) During the 1990s we shall see a far-reaching restructuring of Japanese supply systems, whereby some features of JIT will be retained. Overall, however, JIT as we have come to know and admire it will die.

(2) Rather than the wholesale adoption of pure JIT in Europe, we are more likely to see a convergence taking place of the Japanese and European approaches to supply systems, whereby the Europeans should see some benefits from the greater adoption of JIT principles in terms of reduced costs and greater integration of the supply network. The Japanese manufacturers, on the other hand, will be forced to adopt more European systems of supply, with a possible increase in costs.

The conclusion must be that careful appraisal of all the factors involved including transport costs and environmental issues, should precede a decision to implement JIT.

(f) JIT and MRP

(i) JIT serves production line manufacturing industry where the product range is small, often with a high element of common parts, and with an assembly programme fixed for several months ahead. MRP serves a batch or job production environment where the aim is to translate customer's orders into a master production schedule consistent with stock in hand and suppliers' lead times and the explosion of a bill of materials, so that scheduling can be built around critical items in terms of lead times.

(ii) JIT tends to be used for higher usage items. Lower usage, large, expensive items tend to be controlled by MRP.

(iii) JIT is a 'demand pull' system. MRP is a system in which material is *pushed* through the production line.

(iv) JIT and MRP are often complementary and can be made to work together.

It is sometimes stated that MRP is a good planning but a poor execution system, while JIT has limited planning capability but is an excellent execution tool. The combined effect of operating an MRP system and a simplified JIT environment often provides the best solution.

17. OPTIMISED PRODUCTION TECHNOLOGY (OPT)

Developed in Israel, OPT claims, like JIT, to minimise inventories of materials and work in progress and manufacturing lead times, particularly with regard to batch or continuous production.

(i) The aim of OPT is to increase profitability by simultaneously increasing throughput and reducing inventory. (Throughput is not the same as output, but is the revenue from sales.) A basic tenet is that if an item cannot be sold it should not be manufactured.

(ii) Market forecasts are scheduled backwards from the required delivery dates.

(iii) Based on utilisation, manufacturing resources are classified as critical or non-critical, known respectively as bottlenecks and non-bottlenecks. A bottleneck is the slowest machine or resource in the manufacturing chain. Time lost at a bottleneck is time lost to the whole system. Time saved at a bottleneck has no real significance, i.e. when a bottleneck feeds a non-bottleneck the output of the second machine is governed by the number of components that reach it from the first machine. Vice versa, where the non-bottleneck feeds the bottleneck, the first machine is limited only by its own capacity and so produces an output that simply accumulates in front of the bottleneck.

(iv) OPT computerised programs, therefore, simultaneously program for continuous production while regulating the output of non-bottlenecks just in time to keep the bottlenecks supplied. While bottlenecks are, therefore, the key to increasing throughput, non-bottlenecks are the key to reducing inventory.

(v) The aim is, therefore, to relieve and remove bottlenecks until the whole production line is 'balanced'.

(vi) It is claimed that OPT is easier and less disruptive to implement than JIT, since attention can be directed to remedying bottlenecks rather than to the wholesale introduction of a new system.

18. LOT SIZING

Manufacturers or distributors must decide what quantity or lot size of an item to produce or purchase. Lot sizing may be static or dynamic.

Fixed order sized or EOQ systems are static, i.e. the same quantity is maintained each time an order is issued.

Planned order release systems as with MRP and DRP which provide for a different quantity each time an order is issued are dynamic. A comparison of the two systems is given in Table 8.4 (p.216).

Dynamic lot sizes can be determined:

(1) By a *lot for lot rule*, i.e. the lot size order covers the gross requirements for a single order or period; there is, thus, no forward buying beyond these parameters. Tersine [8] states that this approach

- minimises inventory holding costs
- is suitable for very expensive items or items with a highly discontinuous demand where a high level of inventory control must be exercised
- is well suited to high volume, continuous assembly production.

It does, however, ignore order placement or set-up costs.

(2) By the *periodic order quantity rule* in which when an order is placed its lot size must be enough to cover the requirements for X weeks. The lot size or periodic order quantity (POQ) is determined by the formula

$$POQ = GR + SS - B$$

where GR = gross requirement for X weeks beginning with the week of placement
   SS = any desired safety stock
   B = projected balance from previous week.

19. SAFETY STOCKS AND SERVICE LEVELS

(a) Safety stock is needed to cover shortages due to the agreed lead time being exceeded or the actual demand exceeding that anticipated. A service level is the ability to meet the demands of internal and external customers from stock. As stated earlier the service level percentage can be computed as

$$\frac{\text{Number of times the item is provided on demand}}{\text{Number of times an item has been demanded}}$$

(b) As shown by Fig 8.11, safety stocks and service levels are inter-related. Thus by increasing the investment in inventory from 1 to $1 + x$ we can increase the service level from S to S_1. A further investment from $1 + x$ to $1 + 2x$ will increase the service level from S_1 to S_2. It should be noted, however, that:

(i) For single items an extra investment in inventory will always increase customer service levels.
(ii) Conversely larger safety stocks and service levels mean an increase in inventory investment.
(iii) For total inventory it is not possible to achieve 100% service levels. High service levels for all items may be uneconomical and cost-prohibitive.

(c) With JIT the emphasis is on low or zero inventory achieved by removing uncertainty regarding supply. Safety stock is regarded as a cost adding factor and, as such, to be eliminated.

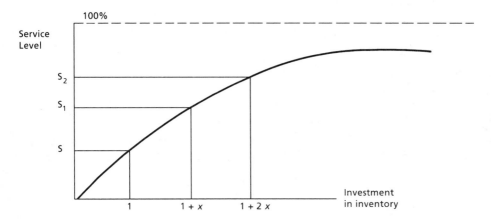

Fig 8.11 Service level inventory trade-off curve

(d) As shown above, a high safety stock implies a low stock-out risk and high service levels of all items are uneconomic. It is, therefore, normally necessary to ascertain by means of an ABC analysis the items for which the stock-out costs would be high. For such items it is also necessary to determine what is an acceptable risk of stock-out and fix order quantities and safety stocks on this basis. The service level or percentage of total demand in excess of average that must be met can be achieved by the use of a constant, usually derived from the statistical concepts of the normal curve, the mean and the standard deviation.

(1) *The normal curve.* The curve which would probably result from the plotting of a series of observations such as lead times, demand quantities, late deliveries, etc., would probably approximate to the bell-shaped, normal distribution shown in Fig. 8.12. The area under the curve represents total probability (100 per cent).

(2) *The mean.* This is calculated by dividing the sum of all the values of a variable by the number of cases.

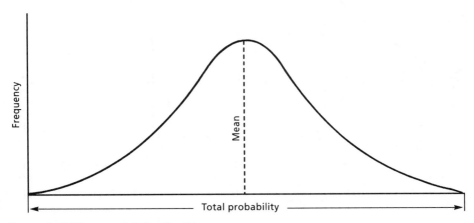

Figure 8.12 The normal distribution curve

(3) *The standard deviation.*

$$\sigma = \sqrt{\left[\frac{\Sigma\chi^2}{N} - \left(\frac{\Sigma\chi}{N}\right)^2\right]}$$

where σ = the standard deviation
Σ = the sum of
χ = the values of the variable
N = the number of cases.

Example The lead times, in days, of the last six orders placed for a stock item have been 25, 30, 32, 24, 23 and 28. Find the mean and the standard deviation.

χ	χ^2
25	625
30	900
32	1024
24	576
23	529
28	784
$\Sigma\chi = 162$	$\Sigma\chi^2 = 4438$

$$\therefore \sigma = \sqrt{\left[\frac{4438}{6} - \left(\frac{162}{6}\right)^2\right]} = \sqrt{[739.6 - 729]} = \sqrt{10.6} = 3.3$$

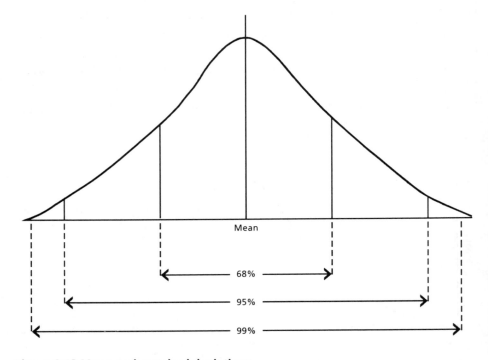

Mean

68%

95%

99%

Figure 8.13 Mean and standard deviations

Table 8.5 Probabilities table

Standard deviation σ	Service level %	Probability of a stock-out %
1.00	84.1	15.9
1.05	85.3	14.7
1.10	86.4	13.6
1.15	87.5	12.5
1.20	88.5	11.5
1.25	89.4	10.6
1.30	90.0	10.0
1.35	91.2	8.8
1.40	91.9	8.1
1.45	92.7	7.3
1.50	93.3	6.7
1.55	94.0	6.0
1.60	94.5	5.5
1.65	95.1	4.9
1.70	95.5	4.5
1.75	96.0	4.0
1.80	96.4	3.6
1.85	96.8	3.2
1.90	97.1	2.9
1.95	97.4	2.6
2.00	97.7	2.3
2.25	98.8	1.2
2.50	99.4	0.6
2.75	99.7	0.3
3.00	99.9	0.1

Standard deviation = 3.3 (say 3 days)

Mean = 162/6 = 27

From tables showing normal curve areas it can be shown that, if a measurement is one standard deviation above or below the mean, the normal curve area between − 1 and + 1 is 0.3413 + 0.3413 = 0.6826. This means that if a distribution can be approximated closely with a normal curve, about 68 per cent of cases fall within one standard deviation from the mean. Similarly, 95 and 99 per cent of all the cases fall within two and three standard deviations respectively. This can be represented as in Fig 8.13.

From these deviations a probabilities table can be constructed as in Table 8.5.

(e) Reorder levels and safety stocks. The above probabilities can be used to calculate reorder levels and safety stocks to ensure a specified degree of security against stock-out. Apart from independent and dependent demand there are two cases to consider, i.e. where demand is constant and where demand is variable.

(1) *Constant demand.* Suppose we have a stock item for which the constant demand is 100 units per day with 27 and 3 days as respective estimates of the mean and standard deviation of all possible lead times. It is desired to place order quantities to ensure that the probability of a stock-out occurring is no greater

than 2.3 per cent, i.e. a service level of 97.7 per cent. From the probability table we see that the relevant K is 2 (this means that there will only be a 2.3 per cent chance of experiencing lead times greater than two standard deviations above the mean lead time of 27 days) to meet the above requirements. The lead time can now be calculated from the formula:

Lead time = $L + (K\sigma l)$

where L = the average lead time deviation; K the probability of stockout; and σl the standard deviation of lead time; i.e. lead time is calculated as 27 + (2 × 3) or 33 days.

In 33 days the demand will be 33 × 100 units = 3300 units, and this will be the reorder level. The average lead time, however, is 27 days, in which time 2700 units will be required. The difference between 3300 items ordered and the 2700 units required for the mean lead time, i.e. 600 units, will be the safety stock.

(2) *Variable demand.* Demand may also vary as well as lead time. Using the other figures in the above example let us assume that demand has a mean and standard deviation of 100 and 10 items respectively. To compute the reorder level under these conditions we need to know:

(i) The average lead time demand
(ii) The standard deviation of the lead time demand. This latter figure is obtained from the formula

$$\sigma ld = \sqrt{[L\sigma d^2 + \bar{d}\sigma l^2]}$$

where L = average lead time
$\bar{d}$ = average demand
σd^2 = variance of demand (variance is the square of the standard deviation)
σl^2 = variance of the lead time

The standard deviation of the lead time demand will be:

$$\sigma ld = \sqrt{[(27 \times 10^2) + (100^2 \times 3^2)]} \text{ items}$$
$$= \sqrt{[2700 + 90{,}000]} = \sqrt{92{,}700}$$
$$= 304.5$$

Using the same confidence level as before we can calculate the reorder level by taking

Expected (average) lead-time demand
+ (2 × standard deviation of lead-time demand)
= (27 × 100) + (2 × 304.5)
= 2700 + 609 = 3309

The safety stock factor element will be 609 items.

20. SPECIAL INVENTORY FACTORS

The emphasis of this chapter has been on minimising stock levels consistent with a given level of customer service and the avoidance of production disruption.

There are, however, special circumstances in which it may be desirable to allow stocks to rise or fall above previously determined maximum or minimum levels.

Particularly with sensitive commodities, anticipated world shortage due to natural factors, e.g. a poor wheat harvest, industrial action, e.g. a strike by Canadian nickel miners, or political uncertainty may cause companies to maximise their stocks particularly of 'bottleneck' materials which, if unavailable, would disrupt production.

Stocks may also be increased or reduced in anticipation of a rise in prices or a stop in the value of money due to inflation. Here the total costs associated with holding stocks may be less than the anticipated rise in raw material prices.

Such decisions cannot be made by the application of formulae but require decision making based on environmental information and the exercise of sound procurement judgement.

References

[1] Compton HK and Jessop D. *Dictionary of Purchasing and Supply Management*. Pitman, 1989, p 135.
[2] Adapted (with permission) from Vollmann, Berry and Whybark, *Manufacturing Control Systems*, 2nd Edition, Irwin, 1988, Chap 19, p 798.
[3] Tersine RJ. *Principles of Inventory Management* (3rd edn.) Elsevier Science Publishing NY, 1988. Chap 10, p 430.
[4] White L. '*JIT – what is it and how does it affect DP? Computer World*, June 1985, pp 41–42.
[5] Schonberger RJ and Ansari A. *Just-in-Time purchasing can improve quality. Journal of Purchasing and Materials Management*, Spring 1984.
[6] Rhys DG, McNash and Nieuwenhuis P. *Japan hits the limits of Just-in-time. EIU, Japanese Motor Business*, December 1992, pp 81–89.
[7] Nieuwenhuis P. *Environmental implications of Just-in-Time supply in Japan – lessons for Europe. Logistics Focus*. Vol 2, No 3, 1994, pp 2–4.
[8] Tersine RJ. *Principles of Inventory Management* (3rd edn.), Elsevier Science Publishing NY, 1988. Chap 10, p163.

Progress test 8

1. Define the terms 'inventory' and 'inventory control' .

2. What are the main classifications of inventory?

3. State the principal aims of inventory management.

4. How may the quantities required be indicated for (i) materials required for a specific order, (ii) standard items, (iii) consumables?

5. Distinguish between independent and dependent demand.

6. Give three examples in each case of (i) acquisition costs (ii) cost of stock-outs.

7. Explain ABC analysis.

8. Describe how you would attempt to implement a programme of variety reduction.

9. What are the assumptions underlying EOQs?

10. State the basic EOQ formula.

11. What operations are involved in 'lead time'?

12. How can moving and exponentially weighted averages help in forecasting demand?

13. How under a fixed order point system are reorder and minimum and maximum stock levels computed?

14. Describe how maximum stock is calculated using a periodic review system?

15. Distinguish between the respective advantages and disadvantages of fixed order and periodic review systems.

16. What are the aims of MRP?

17. How does MRP differ from MRP I?

18. Define and explain DRP.

19. What are the potential benefits and disadvantages of JIT?

20. What is OPT?

21. Explain the 'lot for lot' rule and the periodic quantity rule

22. How are safety and service stocks related?

23. *Just in Time* production methods are being used increasingly to reduce inventory levels and to shorten delivery lead times, yet in some cases, the introduction of JIT has not achieved either objective and has been generally disappointing. Discuss this viewpoint.
    (CIPS. *Purchasing and Supply Management III – Logistics* (1991))

24. You have been asked to compile a glossary of terms for inclusion in the manual to be issued to the staff of a newly formed supplies department. Write the actual entries you would include for the following terms:

(a) Materials Management
(b) Just in Time Management
(c) Materials Requirements Planning
(d) Logistics.
(CIPS. *Introduction to Purchasing and Supply Management* (1992))

25. The growing use of JIT and MRP has resulted in a trend away from keeping safety stocks. Examine the effects this has upon the importance of the expediting function.
(CIPS. *Introduction to Purchasing and Supply Management* (1992))

26. It has been argued that the widespread adoption of the JIT philosophy has rendered the more traditional approaches to inventory control obsolete. Discuss this argument and indicate with reasons whether you believe it or not.
(CIPS. *Purchasing and Supply Management III – Logistics* (1992))

27. Just-in-Time (JIT) is a widely advocated strategy, and experience in Japanese organisations suggests that there are many benefits to be gained from it. As a Purchasing Manager in the UK discuss the benefits and dangers of the introduction of JIT system to the provisioning function in the UK.
(CIPS. *Purchasing and Supply Management II – Provisioning* (1992))

28. The almost universal adoption of the JIT philosophy has made the EOQ model obsolete. Explain, with reasons, whether or not you agree with this statement.
(CIPS. *Purchasing and Supply Management III – Logistics* (1993))

29. Identify the major constituency of stock holding cost and demonstrate how these may be minimised through the use of appropriate techniques.
(CIPS. *Introduction to Purchasing and Supply Management* (1993))

30. The minimum level of Inventory Record Accuracy for the successful operation of an MRP system is 95% and many of the companies at the forefront of MRP consistently operate at levels of 98% or higher (O Wight). Explain this statement and its significance within an MRP environment, and suggest ways in which such levels of Inventory Record Accuracy can be achieved.
(CIPS. *Purchasing and Supply Management II – Provisions* (1993))

31. Explain how a logistics manager might assess the efficiency and effectiveness of the inventory control function. Include in your answer a discussion of any 'tensions' that exist, for example high service levels versus low stock levels, and how these might be resolved.
(CIPS. *Purchasing and Supply Management III – Logistics* (1994))

Further exercises

1. Calculate the EOQ
   Annual quantity required = 600,000
   Cost of ordering = £11 per order
   Cost of carrying = £20 per unit   (*Ans.* 8124 rounded)

2. A supermarket divides large blocks of cheese into pieces of approximately 500g before displaying these for sale. A sample of the pieces cut by one shop assistant has the following distribution:

Grammes	Number of Blocks
450 but under 470	15
470 but under 490	20
490 but under 510	35
510 but under 530	18
530 but under 550	12

   (a) Calculate the mean and standard deviation of this sample
                                          (*Ans.* Mean 4984; Std. deviation 24.11)

   (b) Calculate the median of this sample.   (*Ans.* 498.86)

3. The delivery times for the most recent 50 orders from a supplier are tabulated below:

Delivery time in days	Number of deliveries
5 and under 9	6
9 and under 13	12
13 and under 17	17
17 and under 21	10
21 and under 25	5

   (a) Calculate the mean and the standard deviation of this sample of delivery times. Give your answers correct to one decimal place.
                                          (*Ans.* Mean 14.7; Std. deviation 4.6)

   (b) Calculate the median delivery time.   (*Ans.* 14.6)

4. The volume of liquid in a sample of 60 containers is shown below:

Volume (ml)	Number of containers
over 970 and under 980	5
over 980 and under 990	10
over 990 and under 1000	14
over 1000 and under 1010	15
over 1010 and under 1020	12
over 1020 and under 1030	4

   (a) Calculate the median of this sample.   (*Ans.* 1001)

   (b) Calculate the mean and standard deviation of this sample.
                                          (*Ans.* Mean 1000.2; Std. deviation 13.722)

9

SOURCING

1. INTRODUCTION

Sourcing of supplies is undertaken at the strategic, tactical and operational levels of an undertaking.

(a) Strategic sourcing is concerned with top-level decisions relating to high-profit/high-supply-risk strategic items and low-profit/high-supply-risk bottle-neck items (see Table 2.1, p.24). It is also concerned with the formulation of long-term purchasing policies relating to such matters as single and partnership sourcing, reciprocal and intra-company purchasing, purchase of capital equipment and ethical considerations such as environmental issues.

(b) Tactical and operational sourcing is concerned with medium and lower level decisions relating to high-profit/low-risk leverage and low-profit/low-risk non-critical items. It is also concerned with short-duration adaptive decisions as to how and from where specific supplies requirements are to be met. Thus, suggestions may be made to top management regarding temporary deviations from strategic decisions. Although strategically it may have been decided to purchase rather than make a certain component or assembly in conditions of slack work or the inability of suppliers to meet an unexpected demand within a prescribed time it may be tactical to make rather than buy.

Strategic sourcing has been defined [1] as *the process of creating a value-adding (or optimal mix) of supply relationships to provide a competitive advantage.*

It is important, however, that purchasing staff at the tactical and operational levels should also be aware of their roles in providing support services relating to sourcing which are value adding and contribute to the competitive advantage of their enterprise.

Sourcing can be considered under three headings: (1) sourcing information(2–6); (2) sourcing strategies (7–19) and (3) sourcing decisions (20–21).

Sourcing information relates to (1) the analysis of market conditions; (2) procurement directives; and (3) the assessment and development of appropriate suppliers.

2. ANALYSIS OF MARKET CONDITIONS

(a) What is a 'market?' The term *'market'* can mean:

(i) A place where goods and services are bought and sold, e.g. the European Economic Community is a market created by agreement between the participating countries to reduce barriers to the movement between them of labour and capital.

(ii) Large groups of buyers and sellers of wide classes of goods, e.g. the consumer goods market, the capital market.

(iii) Demand and supply for a single class of commodity, e.g. the steel market, the cotton market.

(iv) The general economic conditions relating to the supply of goods and services applying at a particular time. Of special importance to purchasing is the distinction between a 'buyers' and a 'sellers' market (see also p.31).

(b) Why is the analysis of market conditions important to sourcing? Analysis of market conditions:

(i) Helps in forecasting the long-term demand for the product of which bought-out materials, components, assemblies, etc. are part. It has therefore an identity of interest with market research.

(ii) Assists in forecasting the price trends of bought-out items and how material costs are likely to affect production costs and selling prices. The need for cheaper prices may influence sourcing decisions.

(iii) Indicates what alternative goods and supply sources are available, e.g. might it be more economical to source abroad?

(iv) Gives guidance on the security of supply sources. This is particularly important with sensitive commodities sourced abroad.

(v) Fig 2.2 indicates the importance of long, medium and short term market data in relation to such sourcing issues as make or buy decisions, volume insurance, vendor selection and product standardisation.

(c) What sources of information relating to market conditions are available? Information relating to market conditions may be obtained from:
– *Primary data*, i.e. field research which can use one or more approaches such as observation, analysis of internal records, e.g. sales trends and order book levels, visits to suppliers, questionnaires.
– *Secondary data*, i.e. statistics and reports issued by external organisations. It would be impractical to do more than list a few such publications.

(1) *International sources.* For the researcher in the UK a good starting point is the Export Market Information Centre, 123 Victoria St., London SW16 6RB. This library contains all the major international statistical sources.

(2) *Government sources.* Full details of publications can be obtained from one of the branches of HMSO. The most important sources include:

- *The Annual and Monthly Abstracts of Statistics*
- *Economic Trends*
- *The Census of Production*
- *The Department of Employment Gazette*
- *British Business* published weekly by the Department of Trade and Industry
- *Business Monitors* – the P series covers a wide sector of industrial activities.

(3) *Non-Government sources.* These include:

- The Economist Intelligence Unit
- Chambers of Commerce
- Professional Associations. Of particular importance to procurement staff is *Procurement Weekly* available on subscription from the Chartered Institute of Purchasing and Supply. This is the only weekly journal in the UK dealing with purchasing and supply matters. Each issue includes a weekly authoritative guide to the prices of over 100 key materials together with their movement over the previous year and current trends, events in the commodities market, wholesale price indices and Government initiatives and legislation with their implications for purchasing.
- The Press, e.g. *The Economist, The Financial Times* and the 'quality' daily and Sunday newspapers.
- Economic forecasters, e.g. the Confederation of British Industries publishes *Economic Situation Report.* Oxford Economic Forecasting has a range of publications including: *UK Economic Prospects; World Economic Prospects, UK Industrial Prospects; European Economic Prospects.*

(4) All this information should be used intelligently. Harold Macmillan once observed that using official statistics is like planning a train journey with last year's train guide. Remember that statistics are inevitably historic. When using forecasts:

- Treat long-term forecasts with special caution
- When possible look at a range of forecasts
- Do not rely too heavily on the specific numbers predicted. As the Bank of England has stated [2]:

    Forecasts will never be precisely accurate. Their value lies not in their powers of prediction. Rather they are guideposts against which future developments in the economy can be evaluated.

3. PROCUREMENT DIRECTIVES

A directive is a general instruction. Typical directives relating to sourcing include:

(a) European directives. Public procurement in the European Community takes place in the context of the World Trade Agreement on Government Procurement and directives issued by the European Commission.

(1) *The Agreement on Government Procurement* signed in Marrakesh on 15 April 1994 became operative on 1 January 1996. It follows closely the lines of the existing EC rules and covers the procurement of supplies, works and services by public bodies at both central and local government level, as well as procurement by public bodies in the port, airport, water, urban transport and electricity sectors.

(2) The European Commission has currently (1995) issued six directives. These directives are:

(i) Supplies directive: covering the purchase or hire of goods by public bodies, i.e. central, regional and local government and certain other non-commercial bodies such as health and education authorities.

(ii) Works directive: covering the procurement of building and civil engineering projects by public bodies.

(iii) Utilities directive: covering the procurement of both supplies and works by public and private purchasers in the energy, water, transport and telecommunications sectors (operative from 1 January 1993 with some exceptions for Greece, Portugal and Spain).

(iv) Services directive: covering the procurement by public bodies or services (operative from 1 July 1993).

(v) Compliance directive: under which aggrieved suppliers may seek legal redress in the event of an infringement of the national provisions which implement the Supplies or Works directives.

(vi) Remedies: the equivalent directive relating to the Utilities directive.

From the above it will be seen that 'public procurement' covers not only government departments but also public authorities such as the police, education authorities and local authorities. With the implementation of the Utilities directive which covers, among others, 'utilities which possess "special or exclusive rights" in the water, transport, telecommunications and energy sectors', many private sector entities in the UK and abroad will also be covered. These include BT, BP, the water companies and British Rail. The implementation of the directives relating to services will widen the field still further, for example, to tendering for business travel.

The directives aim to extend public sector purchasing across national boundaries and require bodies subject to such directives to:

(1) Advertise in the EC *Official Journal* all purchasing requirements in excess of a stated 'threshold' expressed in ECUs and net of VAT. The current sterling values of these thresholds should be obtained from the *Official Journal* of the EC (OJEC). Purchasers subject to World Trade Agreement are obliged to give reasons for not selecting tenderers or for awarding contracts to others.

(2) Tender for, and award contracts, following advertisement on the basis of non-discrimination between suppliers from different EC countries and on the basis of obtaining the best value for money.

(3) Procedures for the placing of public contracts may be 'open', 'restricted' or 'negotiated'. *Open* procedures mean those national procedures whereby all

interested service providers may submit a tender. *Restricted* procedures mean those national procedures whereby only those service providers invited by the authority may submit a tender. *Negotiated* procedures mean those national procedures whereby authorities consult service providers of their choice and negotiate the terms of the contract with one or more of them. The minimum periods to be allowed for the receipt of tenders are: *Open* procedures – not less than 52 days from the date of the despatch of the notice published in the *Official Journal* of the European Communities and in the TED data bank of the intention of the contracting authority to place a public service contract in excess of the stated threshold. *Restricted* and *Negotiated* procedures – not less than 37 days from the date of despatch of the notice. These times may, under prescribed conditions, be reduced to 36 days for open procedures. For restricted and negotiated procedures, where urgency renders impracticable the time limits specified, the contracting authorities may fix the following time limits: (A) a time limit for receipt of request to participate which shall not be less than 15 days from the date of despatch of the notice; (B) a time limit for the receipt of tenders which shall not be less than 10 days from the date of the invitation to tender.

(b) Central and Local Government directives. Guidance rather than directives relating to Government purchasing is provided by the Consolidated Guidelines on Public Procurement and the statements of good professional practice issued by the Central Unit on Procurement set up by the then Prime Minister, Margaret Thatcher, in 1986 to obtain Value for Money improvements in non-war-like purchasing of goods and services.

The Consolidated Guidelines lay down general principles such as [3]:

> (*i*) 'Purchasers should base all procurement of goods and services on value for money i.e. quality (or fitness for purpose) and delivery against price. Value for money should be judged on whole life costs, not simply initial costs.'
> (*ii*) 'Goods and services should be acquired by competition unless there are convincing reasons to the contrary.'

There are currently (1995) 52 CUP Guidance Notes.

While Central Government spending is based on the principle of obtaining value for money, purchasing by local authorities is subject to mandatory compulsory competitive tender. This principle when embodied in local authority standing orders has the force of a directive.

(c) Company directives. These may take the form of instructions issued by top management that particular items of supply must for reasons of strategy or in pursuance of agreements be obtained from a specified source, e.g. directives relating to intra-company and reciprocal purchasing.

4. SOURCES OF SUPPLY

Three main questions may be considered under this heading: (1) who can supply?; (2) supplier assessment; (3) supplier rating.

Who can supply? Sources of information relating to potential suppliers:

(1) *Catalogues.* The value of catalogues depends on:

(*i*) The information they contain, e.g. some contain valuable technical information

(*ii*) The ease with which the information in them can be found

(*iii*) The format of the catalogue. One survey reported that users would rather have one thick catalogue than several thin catalogues each devoted to a single line.

(2) *Trade directories,* e.g. *Kompass, Rylands, Buyers Guides,* etc. These are useful for:

(*i*) New product requirements

(*ii*) Unusual or occasional special requirements

(*iii*) Emergency items.

(3) *Yellow Pages.*

(4) *Databases* (as stated in Chapter 7). Databases can provide up-to-date information and may be space-saving substitutes for large reference collections. Some important databases relevant to purchasing include: *The Gale Directory of Databases, Vol 1 On-line Databases, Reuters Metal Service, 3T Telecom Gold and Prestel, Kompass On-line, Pergamon Infoline.* Details of how access may be obtained to various databases can be obtained from the *Director of On-line Databases Britline; Directory of British Databases (EDIP Ltd).*

(5) *Salespersons.* The usefulness of salespersons is related to their knowledge of the product they are seeking to promote. Sales staff are often able to provide useful service information regarding suppliers, e.g. items other than those manufactured by their own undertaking.

(6) *Exhibitions.* These provide an opportunity for comparing competing products and meeting representatives of suppliers. Exhibition catalogues usually provide details of the main suppliers in a particular field and should be retained for reference purposes.

(7) *Trade journals.* The text of these journals provides the buyer with information regarding new products, substitute materials, etc., while the trade gossip keeps the buyer informed about changes in the policies of suppliers and in their personnel.

(8) *Informal exchange of information between buyers.*

(9) *Information provided by prospective suppliers.* The following headings are used by a leading engineering company in a questionnaire designed to elicit further information from undertakings wishing to be placed on their approved suppliers list:

General

- Name of company
- Office address and telephone number

- Works address and telephone number
- Date established
- Whether part of a group and, if so, which
- Whether a private or a public limited company
- Authorised and issued share capital
- Annual turnover for last three years
- Current order book value.

Personnel
- Names and responsibilities of directors
- Names and responsibilities of executives
- Number of employees – office/works/site
- Shop area – covered/uncovered.

Experience
- Products/services for which orders are solicited
- Details of any previous orders placed by the purchases
- Details of any other companies/undertakings supplied which the prospective vendor wishes to mention.

Facilities
- Drawing office/development facilities including CAD/CAM
- Details of major plant and equipment
- Communication facilities, e.g. EDI
- Name, signature and official position giving the above information and date of completion of questionnaire.

5. SUPPLIER ASSESSMENT AND APPRAISAL

(a) Supplier appraisal may arise when a prospective vendor applies to be placed on the buyer's approved list or in the course of negotiation when the buyer wishes to assure himself that a supplier can meet requirements reliably. Appraisal is, therefore, an important part of quality assurance. Supplier appraisal will be of particular importance:

- where potential suppliers do not hold BS5750 or its equivalent
- where the items to be purchased are of critical importance
- where it is intended to adopt a policy of single sourcing based on partnership purchasing.

Supplier appraisal can be undertaken by a combination of the following:

(i) Desk research using published or unpublished data already in existence, e.g. company reports, balance sheets, references, strike record, etc. Desk research is particularly applicable when evaluating the financial situation of a prospective supplier.

(ii) Field research, the purpose of which is to obtain further data regarding the technical production and managerial capacities of a prospective supplier by a visit to his works.

Field research is best undertaken on a team basis, first to enable each member of the team to evaluate the supplier from a specialist viewpoint; secondly, to share responsibility for the decision to approve or reject the supplier. Desk research should always precede field research. If the team have 'done their homework' they know what questions should be asked and can appraise the veracity of the answers given. Where visits are undertaken regularly a standard 'supplier appraisal form' can be prepared. This ensures that no important questions are overlooked and provides a permanent record of the visit and the reasons for the decision reached.

(b) *Checklist for supplier visits.* The following checklist indicates areas which warrant particular attention by procurement staff when making appraisal visits to potential suppliers:

(1) *Personal attitudes.* An observant visitor can sense the attitudes of the supplier's employees towards their work and this provides an indication of the likely quality of their output and service dependability. The state of morale will be evident from:

(i) an atmosphere of harmony or dissatisfaction among the production workers
(ii) the degree of interest in customer service on the part of supervisory staff
(iii) the degree of energy displayed and the interest in getting things done
(iv) the use of manpower – whether economical with everyone usually busy or extravagant and costly with excess people doing little or nothing.

(2) *Adequacy and care of production equipment.* Close observation of the equipment in a plant will indicate whether it is:

(i) modern or antiquated
(ii) accurately maintained or obviously worn
(iii) well cared for by operators or dirty and neglected
(iv) of proper size or type to produce the buyer's requirements
(v) of sufficient capacity to produce the quantities desired.

The presence or absence of ingenious self-developed mechanical devices for performing unusual operations will be indicative of the plant's manufacturing and engineering expertise.

(3) *Technological know-how of supervisory personnel.* Conversations with foremen, shop superintendents and others will indicate their technical knowledge and their ability to control and improve the operations or processes under their supervision.

(4) *Means of controlling quality.* Observation of the inspection methods will indicate their adequacy to ensure the specified quality of the product. Attention should be given to:

(i) whether the materials received are chemically analysed and physically checked *(ii)* frequency of inspection during the production cycle

(iii) employment of such techniques as statistical quality control

(iv) availability of statistical quality control.

(5) *Housekeeping.* A plant which is orderly and clean in its general appearance indicates careful planning and control by management. Such plant inspires confidence that its products will be produced with the same care and pride in their quality. The dangers of breakdown, fire or other disasters will also be minimised, with a consequent increased assurance of continuity of supply.

(6) *Competence of technical staff.* Conversations with design, research or laboratory staff indicate their knowledge of the latest materials, tools and processes relating to their products and on anticipated developments in their industry.

(7) *Competence of management.* All the above areas are, in essence, a reflection of management and therefore indicate its quality. Particularly in the case of a new supplier, an accurate appraisal of executive personnel is of paramount importance.

6. SUPPLIER PERFORMANCE RATING

(a) Purpose. To evaluate the performance in respect of one or more of the factors, price, quality, delivery and service of an actual supplier.

(i) To provide the buyer with objective information in which judgements relating to source selection can be based.

(ii) To enable the buyer to provide the supplier with an indication of his or her performance rating and where improvements, if any, are required.

(b) Subjective rating. All buyers make subjective appraisals of supplier performance. Such appraisals may be adequate for low-cost, routine items although they have the following deficiencies:

(i) They are 'in the head' of the individual buyer and are lost should he leave.

(ii) They often have a 'halo' effect, i.e. a tendency to be biased in favour of a supplier by some quite irrelevant impression or estimate (good or bad) of that supplier.

(c) Quantitative ratings. The aim of such ratings is to remedy the deficiencies of subjective ratings. The disadvantages of such procedures are as follows:

(i) The high cost of collecting the data on which ratings are based. With quality rating, for example, this may relate to the costs of defect prevention, detection and correction, involving considerable sub-analysis of what is involved under each heading. (The introduction of computers has, however, made the collection of data easier. In any event, such rating should only be attempted in respect of critical or high-cost items using the Pareto approach.)

(ii) Ratings may give the impression of scientific accuracy while, in fact, they are no more accurate than the assumptions on which they are based.

(iii) Supplier performance is often affected by circumstances outside the control of the vendor.

(d) Vendor rating forms. Rating forms can be used to assess the overall competency of a supplier with a view to determining whether:

(i) to grant preferred supplier status
(ii) to work with the supplier to develop and improve performance
(iii) to abandon the vendor as a source of supply.

Extracts from the 14-part Suppliers' Guide to the Supplier Assessment and Ranking System of a leading engineering enterprise are shown below:

(i) As shown in Fig 9.1, suppliers are assessed and ranked under five performance headings: (1) Quality; (2) Delivery; (3) Commercial; (4) Technology; and (5) Management. In addition, suppliers are encouraged to undertake self-appraisal using the blank forms included in the Guide.
(ii) The Categorisation of overall scores is shown in Table 9.1. To achieve Preferred Supplier status, scores in all categories must fall within the 'Satisfactory' and 'Adequate' ranges. Any 'Unsatisfactory' scores will be followed up and reviewed and, if not improved within acceptable timescales, may lead to deselection. A guide to classification based on scores is given with target scores for preferred suppliers with whom we intend to place long-term business identified.
(iii) It would be impracticable to show the methods of scoring under all five headings. The guidelines with the scoring schemes for Delivery Performance and Commercial Performance are, however, shown in amended forms in Tables 9.2 and 9.3

The advantages of the system include the following:

(i) Feedback on performance is provided to suppliers. The importance of such communication is highlighted by Egan [4]:

When in 1980, Jaguar started to knobble component suppliers for poor performance of their product, they (component suppliers) were often surprised, because until that time no one had bothered to give them feedback of this kind and they, therefore, could be partly forgiven for believing that everything in the garden was rosy. I say partly because component suppliers did very little to find out how their products performed in service.

Table 9.1   Supplier performance and ranking system categorisation of overall scores

		Preferred	*Adequate*	*Unsatisfactory*
1	QUALITY	18–20	10–17	0–9
2	DELIVERY	16–20	8–15	0–7
3	COMMERCIAL	18–20	12–16	0–11
4	TECHNOLOGY	18–20	10–16	0–8
5	MANAGEMENT	16–20	10–14	0–8
	Target totals	86–100	50–85	0–49

Supplier Self Assessment Record

	Satisfactory	Adequate	Unsatisfactory
1.0 QUALITY			
1.1 Undeclared Non-conformance			
1.2 Declared Non-conformance			
1.3 Responsiveness			
1.4 Administration			
CATEGORY TOTAL			
2.0 DELIVERY			
2.1 Arrears			
2.2 Tailback			
2.3 Promise Credibility			
2.4 Early Delivery			
2.5 Responsiveness			
CATEGORY TOTAL			
3.0 COMMERCIAL			
3.1 Cost Reduction			
3.2 Competitiveness			
3.3 Risk Share			
3.4 Administration			
CATEGORY TOTAL			
4.0 TECHNOLOGY			
4.1 Process Control			
4.2 Computing Links			
4.3 Manufacturing Strategy			
4.4 Capital Investment			
4.5 Product Capability			
CATEGORY TOTAL			
5.0 MANAGEMENT			
5.1 Task			
5.2 People			
5.3 Delegated Authority			
CATEGORY TOTAL			
OVERALL TOTAL			

Fig 9.1 Performance assessment and ranking system

Table 9.2 Supplier assessment and ranking system delivery performance

| 2.0 | DELIVERY PERFORMANCE | SCORE |

2.1 Arrears

Calculated as follows at the time of the assessment.

Value of late orders
Average weekly value of orders placed

This provides a coarse measure of equivalent weeks-worth of late deliveries to X Company, by value.

	< 1 week	8
Satisfactory	1.5 weeks or less	6
Adequate	1.6–2 weeks	2
Unsatisfactory	>2 weeks	0

2.2 Tailback

Calculated as follows at the time of the assessment:

$$\left[\frac{\text{(No of schedules > 3APs late x 10) + (No of schedules 3 APs late x 6) +}}{\text{Total Number of Schedules}}\right] \times 50$$

(No of schedules 2 APs late x 3) + (No of schedules 1 AP late x 1)

	<10	6
Satisfactory	<20	4
Adequate	20–30	2
Unsatisfactory	>30	0

At this stage, no attempt is being made to smooth or 'average' data - results represent a snapshot of performance at the time of the assessment.

2.3 Promise Credibility

Satisfactory – Always meets commitments	2
Adequate – Occasional failures	1
Unsatisfactory – High level of X Company expediting required, credibility poor	0

2.4 Early Delivery

Measures delivery performance to order due-dates.

| Zero more than 2 weeks early | 2 |
| Deliveries more than 2 weeks early | 0 |

2.5 Responsiveness

Measures degree of responsiveness to delivery queries, problems or promises.

Satisfactory –	Rapid and complete response, anticipates and avoids need for progressing.	2
Adequate –	Occasional late or incomplete responses; scope for improvement	1
Unsatisfactory –	Frequently requires progressing, is often late and/ or incomplete with replies or delivery data	0

Table 9.3 Supplier assessment and ranking system commercial performance

3.0	**COMMERCIAL PERFORMANCE**	
	Measures both initiative and response to cost reduction requirements.	
	Satisfactory - Positive, responsible, meets targets and frequently comes forward with worthwhile initiatives	5
	Adequate - Generally meeting overall requirements.	3
	Unsatisfactory - Unresponsive, unable to meet targets	0
3.2	**Competitiveness**	
	Ability and willingness to compete against world-class opposition to secure X Company orders.	
	Satisfactory - Industry leader, aggressive competitor, regularly winning new orders (50% of bids).	5
	Adequate - Marginally competitive, wins some new orders (> 25% but < 50% of bids).	3
	Unsatisfactory - Limited ability to compete and win orders (typically < 25% of bids). Likely to be seeing progressive decline in overall X Company business levels	0
3.3	**Risk Share**	
	Willingness to share risk on X Company programmes, e.g. absorption of non-recurring costs such as tooling, and provision of development sets.	
	Satisfactory - Fully responsive.	5
	Adequate - Usually prepared to contribute, some degree of compromise normally involved.	3
	Unsatisfactory - Unwilling to share risk.	0
3.4	**Administration**	
	Degree of professionalism in dealing with X Company quotations, orders, contracts etc.	
	Satisfactory - Accurate, timely, reliable.	5
	Adequate - Some administrative delays or problems experienced by X Company, but satisfactorily resolved.	3
	Unsatisfactory - Frequent need for X Company expediting or protracted timescales for resolving problems.	0

(ii) The assessment provides a framework for discussion between purchaser and supplier and can be used to the benefit of each in achieving improvements.

(iii) The scores of competing suppliers within a defined family group of parts are used to rank the individual vendor in priority order. The vendor knows that this will determine his position on the purchaser's database and will directly influence the allocation of orders.

(iv) The headings in the scheme can be used to appraise potential as well as ranking the performance of actual suppliers.

7. THE SUPPLIER BASE

The supplier base relates to the range, location and characteristics of vendors from whom the external supply requirements of an undertaking are obtained. The supplier base of an enterprise may be described in several ways as broad or narrow, national or international, diversified or specialised. Supply base strategies are determined by many considerations including the size of the undertaking, whether it is a controlling or subsidiary undertaking, the location of its markets and whether it is engaged in jobbing, batch, mass or flow production. Sourcing strategies are broadly concerned with such issues as make or buy decisions, single or multiple sourcing and international procurement. Other sourcing considerations relate to partnership sourcing, supplier development, reciprocity and countertrade, intra company trade, sub-contracting and purchasing from small or large and local suppliers.

8. MAKE OR BUY STRATEGIES

Probert [5] states that make or buy is *'at the centre of a company's manufacturing strategy since it has a key effect in determining the shape of manufacturing operations and affects many other aspects of company performance'*. Make or buy is not merely an economic decision but also requires a joint manufacturing and procurement involvement.

(a) Levels of make or buy decision making. Probert [5] identifies three levels of make or buy decision-making, all of which are linked to overall company strategy.

(i) Strategic make or buy provides:
- the rationale for investment in long-term manufacturing strategy
- the framework for shorter-term tactical and component decisions.

(ii) Tactical make or buy deals with the issue of temporary capacity imbalance:
- Changes in demand may make it impossible to make everything in-house even though this may be the preferred option
- Conversely a fall in demand may cause the undertaking to bring in-house, work previously outsourced if this can be done without damaging supplier relationships.

(iii) Component make or buy decisions made ideally at the design stage relate to whether a particular product component should be made in-house or bought in.

(b) Cost factors in make or buy decisions

(1) *Marginal cost.* Accurate make or buy decisions often require the application of marginal costing. Marginal cost comprises materials, direct labour, direct expenses and *variable* factory, administrative and selling overheads. Fixed overheads are omitted from the cost computation.

The difference between the marginal cost approach and that normally adopted can be shown by an example.

Example

	£
Direct material	60
Direct wages	30
Direct expenses	10
Prime cost	100
Works overhead	
(100 per cent on direct wages)	30
Works cost	130
Office overhead	
(20 per cent on works cost)	26
	156
Selling overheads £14 per item	14
Cost of sales	170
Net profit	30
Normal selling price	200

Assume:
(1) that works overheads are 60 per cent fixed and 40 per cent variable
(2) that office overheads are constant
(3) that selling expenses are 50 per cent fixed and 50 per cent variable.
Then the *marginal* cost would be:

	£	
Direct materials	60	
Direct wages	30	
Direct expenses	10	
	100	
Works overhead	12	(i.e. 40 per cent of £30)
Selling overheads	13	(i.e. 50 per cent of £26)
	125	

Any price over £125 represents a *contribution* to fixed overheads. If fixed overheads totalled £75,000 a selling price of £200 would represent a contribution of £75 per item to fixed overheads and it would be necessary to sell 1000 items before the undertaking would *break even*. If, however, the selling price were reduced to £150 it would be necessary to sell 3000 units before reaching the *break-even point* since the contribution per item would be only £25.

In make or buy decisions it is necessary to compare the vendor's price with the marginal cost of making, plus the loss of contribution of work displaced.

Example A component, *X*, can be bought for £350 per 1000. The marginal and total costs of *X* are £240 and £400 per 1000 respectively. To make *X* would involve the use of machinery needed for the production of *Y*, the marginal and selling costs of which are £500 and £800 per 1000. Cost data shows that for every 1000 *X* items made, 250 fewer of *Y* will be produced. Is it more profitable to make or buy component *X*?

Marginal cost of *X* per 1000	£240
Add lost contribution on *Y*	
£800 – £500 = £300	
£300 ÷ 1000 = £0.3 each	
£0.3 × 250	£75
Cost of making *X*	£315

The profit per 1000 on making over buying *X* will therefore be £35.

(2) *Opportunity cost.* This is the maximum earning that might have been obtaned if the production facilities used in making had been applied to some alternative use.

Example An undertaking manufactures 100,000 of item *X* at a total cost of £120,000 and a marginal cost of £100,000. Item *X* could be bought out for £1.50 each. The decision whether to make in or buy out depends on the cost of foregoing the opportunity to make something else. If the production capacity could be used to make an item with a contribution of £0.75 each then the position would be:

Making	*Buying but production capacity not used*	*Buying less opportunity cost*
£100,000	£150,000	£150,000
		– £75,000
		£75,000

(3) *Learning.* Learning curves are dealt with in Chapter 12. When components are bought from a specialist manufacturer there may be little opportunity for learning. When the items are new, however, the costs of both making and buying may have to be adjusted for a learning factor. In comparing made in and bought out prices, therefore, learning is a factor that must, where applicable, be considered.

(c) Other considerations in make or buy decisions. Apart from those mentioned above a number of other quantitative and qualitative factors must be considered in deciding whether to make or buy.

(i) *Quantitative factors* in favour of *making* include:
- Chance to use up idle capacity and resources
- Potential lead time reduction
- Possibility of scrap utilisation
- Greater purchasing power with larger orders of a particular material

- Large overhead recovery base
- Exchange rate risks
- Cost of work is known in advance.

(ii) Quantitative factors in favour of *buying* include:
- Quantities required too small for economic production
- Avoidance of costs of specialist machinery or labour
- Reduction in inventory.

(iii) Qualitative factors in favour of *making* include:
- Ability to manage resources
- Commercial and contractual advantages
- Worries are eliminated regarding such matters as the stability and continuing viability of suppliers or possible repercussions of changes in supplier ownership
- Maintaining secrecy.

(iv) Qualitative factors in favour of *buying* include:
- Spread of financial risk between purchaser and vendor
- Ability to control quality when purchased from outside
- Availability of vendor's specialist expertise, machinery and/or patents
- Buying, in effect, augments the manufacturing capacity of the purchaser.

(d) Making the make or buy decision. From the above it is clear that irrespective of whether it relates to the strategic, tactical or component levels, many quantitative and qualitative factors have to be considered when arriving at make or buy decisions.

A simple procedure designed to answer the question 'are we competitive?' is shown in Fig 9.2.

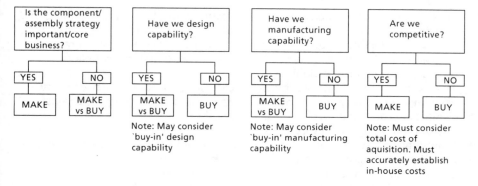

Fig 9.2   Decision processes for make or buy
(by permission of the Society of British Aerospace Companies)

9. SINGLE AND MULTIPLE SOURCING

(a) Single sourcing. This has become an important issue as the result of such developments as:

- Partnership sourcing (Lamming [6] points out that partnership does not necessitate single sourcing)
- Total Quality Management
- JIT.

Single sourcing should be distinguished from *sole* sourcing where, because of monopoly conditions, it is only possible to order from one supplier.

Quayle [7], in an extensive review of the literature, distinguishes between short and long term single and multiple sourcing. The advantages and disadvantages of each, based on Quayle's work, are set out in Table 9.4.

Table 9.4 Advantages and disadvantages of short and long term single sourcing

Advantages	Disadvantages
Short term	
• Lower costs and prices, because of economies of scale arising from the allocation of the buyer's total requirements to one supplier, one set of tooling costs and lower administration costs	• Lack of security of supply – 'all the eggs in one basket'
• Communication can be improved and the supplier has greater certainty of the volume of business to be transacted	• The reduction of competitive pressures
Long term	
• All the benefits of partnership sourcing (see 9:11)	• Possible loss of access to information[8] about new products, market trends and current prices due to lack of regular contact with multiple suppliers
• Reduced product variation: a single source of supply leads to improved processes and reduced variability	
• Better planning and control arising from improved communications permits improved logistics operations and less inventory	• Overpayment (due to lack of ready ability to play one supplier against another)
• Collaboration between buyer and supplier triggers product and process innovations and provides a climate in which suppliers are prepared to make the necessary investments in fixed assets and people	• Exposure to the supplier's problems (e.g. lack of product should the supplier suffer a strike)
• Working with a supplier on a long-term basis reduces administrative costs and develops a closer understanding of the supplier's business	• Vulnerability to supplier opportunism manifested in such ways as missed delivery dates, deficient quality, reneging on promises and price increases

(b) Multiple sourcing. The conventional purchasing wisdom is that multiple sourcing provides:

- an insurance against a breakdown in supplier
- an incentive to suppliers to maintain a high level of performance.

Multiple sourcing may be undertaken provided the business placed with each vendor is large enough to be attractive.

One approach is a 60/40 percentage allocation on the grounds that the smaller supplier has an incentive to increase market share while the larger vendor is aware of the threat posed by the competitor.

The advantages and disadvantages of short and long term multiple sourcing as identified by Quayle are shown in Table 9.5.

(c) Single vs. multiple sourcing. An analysis of single as against multiple sourcing strategies seems to indicate that neither has a dominant advantage. Probably the conclusion is that the decision to single or multi-source is situational and depends on the conditions obtaining for a particular purchaser with

Table 9.5 Advantages and disadvantages of short and long term multiple sourcing

Advantages	Disadvantages
Short term	
• Increased security of supply	• Loss of economies of scale because of lower volumes of business received by each supplier. Extra tooling and administrative expenses arise through dealing with more suppliers
• Competitive pressures can be increased by varying the amount of business flowing to each of the contracted suppliers	
• Contact with several suppliers enables buyers to compare performance and keep in touch with developments in more than one supplier	• Suppliers have increased uncertainty regarding expected levels of business thus making planning more difficult
	• Supplier may be less willing to communicate about developments for fear of information being passed on to competitors.
Long term	
• The award of long-term contracts even on a multi-sourcing basis brings certainty and an increase in supplier responsiveness	• Some suppliers may be cautious of working on the same products as competitors
• Long-term contracts can be used to reward desirable performance and behaviour	
• The long-term nature of an agreement may be more significant in encouraging a progressive relationship than the adopting of a single sourcing approach	

a particular supplier at a particular time. There is also the fact that single or multiple sourcing is not necessarily a straight choice and that dual sourcing and other variants may be feasible alternatives. In practice, many factors including purchasing procedures (e.g. JIT, MRP, etc.) cost, location and performance will be considered. In evaluating such factors, vendor rating helps in making an objective choice. There is, however, no simple answer.

'Aggregating your business with one supplier should give you a better prices, reduce any unnecessary tooling costs and should improve the service you receive. Alternatively, the resulting competition from dividing up your business between two or three suppliers could give you a better deal. A well-motivated single source supplier may be a more secure one in difficult trading conditions. Alternatively, a second source could give you greater security in the event of an accident or other upheaval at your main supplier. Good arguments can often be found on both sides, but the trend today among successful firms is towards reducing rather than expanding the supplier base'[9].

10. INTERNATIONAL SOURCING

(a) Terminology. Birou and Fawcett [10] distinguish between *international sourcing, multinational sourcing, foreign sourcing* and *strategic global sourcing*. They define the first three terms as *'buying outside the firm's country of manufacture in a way that does not co-ordinate requirements among world-wide business units of a single firm'*. Strategic global sourcing is defined as *'the integration and co-ordination of procurement requirements across world-wide business units, looking at common items, processes, technologies and suppliers'*.

Stevens [11] points out that global sourcing involves integration in two respects – the internationalism of purchasing and the adoption of a strategic orientation for all resource management. Global sourcing is associated with multinational companies such as Ford, Chrysler and Xerox.

(b) Why do organisations source internationally? Reasons for international sourcing include:

(i) Changes in the business environment. Carter and Narasimhan [12] identify such challenges as
- Intense international competition
- Pressure to reduce costs
- Need for manufacturing flexibility
- Shorter product development cycles
- Stringent quality standards
- Ever changing technology.

(ii) Factors relating to the needs or competitiveness of the particular enterprise:
- Domestic non-availability, e.g. commodities, rubber, cotton, etc.
- Insufficient domestic capacity to meet demand
- 'Insurance' reasons, i.e. buying abroad to maintain continuity of supplies due to shortages or strikes

- Competitiveness of overseas sources, e.g. lower prices, improved deliveries, better quality
- Reciprocal trading and counter trade due to policy reasons or government pressures due to balance of payments considerations
- Access to worldwide technology
- To obtain penetration of a growth market, e.g. Toyota sources from the Pacific Rim not only to achieve lower costs but to enter markets with restrictive quotas by increasing the local content component of the cars.

(c) Information regarding sourcing abroad. Because of the complexity of buying abroad the buyer will have to acquire specialist knowledge regarding:

(i) The country from which he intends to buy, i.e. its economic and political conditions and policies with regard to export subsidies

(ii) The supplier from whom he intends to buy, i.e. capacity, financial position, reputation, and reliability

(iii) The legal and commercial considerations and procedures involved in buying abroad, e.g. ordering, transportation and payment.

Such information may be obtained from the following:

(i) Visits to the proposed overseas supplier

(ii) References furnished by the proposed overseas supplier

(iii) Importers – an undertaking new to sourcing abroad may be wise to use an importer until some expertise in buying abroad has been obtained

(iv) Commercial attaches, and other government departments of foreign nations

(v) The Department of Trade and Industry

(vi) Shipping and forwarding agents

(vii) The banks

(viii) Chambers of commerce, especially the London Chamber of Commerce Information Department

(ix) Directories, e.g. *Kompass, Jaeger and Waldman* and the English-language edition of *Wer Liefert Was (Who Supplies What)*

(x) Specialist enquiry agents, e.g. Dun and Bradstreet, offer a product-finding service and credit checks on prospective suppliers

(xi) Details of goods imported into the UK, the country of origin and their value are given in the UK Trade and Navigation accounts published monthly, and also yearly in summary form by HMSO.

(d) Difficulties in buying abroad. Many buyers are reluctant to buy abroad because of the difficulties that can arise due to the following:

(i) Contact with the supplier is more difficult.

(ii) The time required for negotiation is generally longer than with home suppliers.

(iii) Currency difficulties. Among matters to be resolved are the following:

- In what currency is price quoted and payment to be made? If possible this should be in sterling.

- Precautions against currency fluctuations, e.g. forward buying of currency.
- How payment is made, e.g. by a letter of credit, sight draft, authority to pay, etc.

  Note: A letter of credit is a written instrument issued by a bank (referred to as the issuing bank) at the request of its customer (the importer) in which the bank obligates itself to pay the seller (the exporter) against presentation of a draft and documents which evidence shipment and meet all the terms and conditions stipulated in the credit. Letters of credit may be *revocable* or *irrevocable,* the latter being a legally binding obligation that cannot be amended or cancelled without the consent of all parties to the transaction.

- What Bank of England or other regulations apply

(iv) Legal difficulties. It is necessary to determine *(inter alia)* the following:
- What law shall govern the transaction, i.e. that of the importing or exporting nation. In general this will be the law of the country in which the contract is made.
- Arrangements for arbitration.
- Terms and conditions applicable to cancellation, deliveries and delays and the passing of property.
- Protection of buyer against infringements of patents.
- Protection of buyer against product liability.

(v) Redress of complaints, i.e. the return to the supplier of goods rejected or damaged in transit. The recovery of damages is awarded to the buyer by the courts or arbitration. (It is useful to ascertain what assets, if any, the supplier has in the buyer's country since these can be restrained by the courts in payment of damages due.)

(vi) Delays in delivery due to weather, cargo transfer, dock strikes and customs action

(vii) Transportation, including the terms of delivery

(viii) Important duties and insurance

(ix) Documentation, e.g. bills of lading, certificates of origin and customs entry forms that are unnecessary in the home trade.

(x) Price rises due to increased costs incurred by the supplier, and the basis on which these shall be computed or allowed.

(xi) Specifications, especially where there are differences in units of measurement.

(e) Key elements in successful sourcing abroad. Birou and Fawcett [13] on the basis of information obtained from 149 purchasing and management executives affiliated to the USA National Association of Purchasing Management, state that the four factors in international sourcing which participants considered most important are:

(i) Top management support
(ii) Developing communication skills

(iii) Establishing long-term relationships
(iv) Developing the skills unique to international sourcing.

Four other factors rated as being above average in importance are:

(v) Understanding of international opportunities
(vi) Knowledge of foreign business practices
(vii) Foreign supplier certification/qualification
(viii) Planning for international sourcing.

To these might now be added the importance of world-wide information systems. Of particular importance is obtaining expert assistance in the development and implementation of an international sourcing strategy. Approaches to obtaining such expertise include:

(i) Training of in-house staff
(ii) Finding experts familiar with purchasing in specific geographical areas
(iii) Establishment of overseas buying offices
(iv) Use of international subsidiaries
(v) Employment of an import broker or merchant.

11. PARTNERSHIP SOURCING

(a) Definition and objectives

(i) Partnership purchasing has been defined by Partnership Sourcing Ltd [14] as:

'A commitment to both customers and suppliers, regardless of size, to a long-term relationship based on clear, mutually-agreed objectives to strive for world-class capability and competitiveness'.

(ii) Objectives. Griffiths [15] states that reasons for seeking partnerships can include improvements in:

* design
* quality
* delivery and completion times
* production costs
* operating costs
* stock levels
* cash flow
* skill and resource availability

For case studies of partnership sourcing in action see the Partnership Sourcing booklet *Partnership Sourcing* (1991) which contains case studies relating to Glaxo, Heath Springs, IBM, Kodak, Laing Homes, Nissan and Tesco.

(b) A comparison of traditional and partnership sourcing

Traditional	Partnership
(i) Emphasises competitiveness and self-interest on the part of both purchaser and supplier.	Emphasises co-operation and a community of interest between purchaser and supplier
(ii) Emphasis on 'unit price' with lowest price usually the most important buyer consideration.	Emphasis on total acquisition costs (TAC) including indirect and hidden costs, e.g. production hold-ups and loss of customer goodwill through late delivery of material and components. Lowest price is never the sole buyer consideration.
(iii) Emphasis is on short-term business relationships.	Emphasis on long-term business relationships with involvement of supplier at the earliest possible stage to discuss how buyer requirements can be met.
(iv) Emphasis on quality checks with inspection of incoming supplies.	Emphasis on quality assurance based on total quality management and zero defects.
(v) Emphasis on multiple sourcing	Emphasis on single sourcing although it is not, of necessity, confined to single sourcing. It will, however, reduce the supplier base.
(vi) Emphasis on uncertainty regarding supplier performance and integrity.	Emphasis on mutual trust between purchaser and supplier.

(c) What types of supplier relationships are suitable for partnership sourcing?

Partnership Sourcing [16] has identified seven types of supplier relationships that may be suitable for partnership, namely:

- *High spend* – the 'vital few'
- *High risk* – items and services which are vital irrespective of their monetary value
- *High hassle* - vital supplies which are technically complex to arrange and take a lot of time, effort and resource to manage
- *New services* – new products or services which may involve possible partners
- *Technically complex* – involving technically advanced or innovative suppliers where the cost of switching would be prohibitive
- *Fast changing* – areas where knowing future technology or trends or legislation is critical
- *Restricted markets* – markets which have few reliable or competent suppliers where closer links with existing or new suppliers might improve supply security.

(d) The advantage of partnership sourcing

To the purchaser	To the supplier
(i) Purchasing advantage through: quality assurance; reduced supplier base; assured supplies through long-term agreements; ability to plan long-term improvement rather than negotiating for short-term advantage.	*Marketing advantage* through: stability through long-term agreements; larger share of orders placed; ability to plan ahead and invest; ability to work with key customers on product and/or service.
(ii) Lower costs through: co-operative cost reduction programmes, e.g. EDI; supplier participation in new designs; lower inventory through better production availability; improved logistics.	*Lower costs* through: co-operative cost reduction programmes; participation in customer design; lower inventory through better customer planning; improved logistics; simplification or elimination of processes; payment on time.
(iii) Strategic advantage through: access to supplier's technology; a supplier who invests; shared problem-solving and management.	*Strategic advantage* through: access to customer's technology; a customer who recognises the need to invest; shared problem-solving and management.

(e) Implementing partnership sourcing

(1) *Identifying purchased items potentially suitable for partnership sourcing*

- High-spend items and suppliers – Pareto analysis may show that a small number of suppliers account for a high proportion of total spend
- Critical items where the cost of supplier failure would be high
- Complex items involving technical and innovative supplies where the cost of switching sources would be prohibitive
- 'New buy' items where supplier involvement in design and production methods is desirable from the outset.

(2) *Sell the philosophy of partnership sourcing to:*

- Top management – demonstrating how partnership sourcing can improve quality, service and total costs throughout the organisation
- Other functions likely to be involved, e.g. accounting (will need to make prompt payments); design (will need to involve suppliers from the outset); production (will need to schedule supply requirements and changes)
- Stress the advantages in **(d)** above.

(3) *Define standards that potential suppliers will be required to meet.* These will include:

- A commitment to total quality management

- BS 5750 (ISO 9000 certification or equivalent)
- Existing implementation or willingness to implement appropriate techniques, e.g. JIT, EDI, etc.
- In-house design capability
- Ability to supply locally or world-wide as required
- Consistent performance standards with respect to quality and delivery
- Willingness to innovate
- Willingness to change, flexibility in management and workforce attitudes.

Partnership Sourcing Ltd state [17] :

Remember that people are key. It is people who build trust and make relationships work. Are the people right? Is the chemistry right?

Partnership is two-way: if one of your customers was evaluating your business on the same criteria that you are using on suppliers, would you qualify? If not, perhaps you should think again about your minimum entry standards.

(4) *Select one or a few suppliers as potential suppliers.* Do not attempt to launch too many partnerships at once.

(5) *Sell the idea of partnership to the selected suppliers.* Stress the advantages in **(d)** above.

(6) *If a commitment to partnership sourcing is achieved,* determine on the basis of joint consultation what both parties want from the partnership and

(i) Decide common objectives such as:
- Reduction in total costs
- Adoption of total quality management
- Zero defects
- On-time payment
- JIT or on-time deliveries
- Joint research and development
- Implementation of EDI
- Reduction or elimination of stocks.

(ii) Agree performance criteria for measuring progress towards objectives, e.g.:
- Failure in production or with end users
- Service response time
- On-time deliveries
- Stock value
- Lead time and stability
- Service levels.

(iii) Agree administrative procedures.
- Set up a steering group to review progress and ensure development
- Set up problem-solving teams to tackle particular issues
- Arrange regular meetings at all levels with senior management steering the process

(iv) Formalise the partnership. This should be on the basis of:
- A simple agreement
- Letters of intent
- A simplified legal contract.

(7) *Review and audit the pilot project.*
   (i) Review against objectives
   (ii) Quantify the gains to the business as a whole
   (iii) Report back to senior management on what has been achieved.

(8) *Extend the existing partnership.*
   (i) Extend existing agreements
   (ii) Commit to longer agreements
   (iii) Get involved in joint strategic planning.

(9) *Develop new partners for the future.*

(f) Problems of partnership sourcing

(i) Termination of relationships – aim should be to part amicably, preferably over a period of time through an agreed separation plan.
(ii) Business shares, i.e. possible domination by the customer or overdependence on the supplier. These issues need to be explored by joint consultation.
(iii) Confidentiality – where prospective partners are also suppliers to competitors.
(iv) Complacency – avoidance requires regular review of competitiveness through regular meetings of multi-functional buying team.
(v) Attitudes – traditionally adversarial buyers and sales people will require retraining to adjust to the new philosophy and environment.
(vi) Contractual – where for reasons of falling sales, recession, etc., forecasts have to be modified. 'Agreements' should therefore be 'letters of intent' and the forecasts should be updated regularly.

12. FORMING SUCCESSFUL PARTNERSHIPS

Research at UMIST concludes [18] that to form successful partnerships, undertakings must take into account the commercial realities of their trading relationships and act consistently at all levels of the organisation.

(1) The realities of a trading relationship are:
- Objectives in critical areas will almost always be in conflict at the highest level, no two companies' strategies can be identical for long – that is why they are separate companies.
- Co-operation endures only as long as there is mutual competitive advantage.
- An effective relation is less likely where there is an imbalance of power.

(2) Successful partnership depends on consistency throughout the organisation 'unless the company is aligned to support supply chain development, it is all too easy for one part of the organisation to subvert the good intentions of another'.

(3) The UMIST report observes that a company cannot leap straight to high-level strategic intervention and that the level at which it is capable of forming links depends on its degree of internal readiness. A four-part stages of excellence model is offered:

- At Stage I a company has entrepreneurial energy but lacks management control and consistency which must be achieved to pass to Stage II.
- Stage III companies have moved beyond control which eventually becomes stifling, to focus on quality and customer satisfaction.
- At Stage IV the company 'breaks down functional barriers to become a process-based organisation externally focused on providing value to the customer'.

(4) Matching up the two dimensions of levels and integration as shown in Fig 9.3 defines a range of integration options:

(i) 'Companies with a sound functional foundation have a basis for integration at *transaction* level, providing efficiency improvements through e.g. EDI.'
(ii) Firms which have well developed cross-functional processes internally may have scope for integration at *process* level, i.e. the re-engineering of linking processes across companies to eliminate duplicated activities. Examples include: automatic stock replacement, invoiceless payment based on consumption and direct delivery to the assembly line.
(iii) Those firms that have mastered functional and process integration can choose to integrate at *strategic* level, forming an extended enterprise to secure competitive advantage for the supply chain as a whole rather than the individual parts. The UMIST research observes that this stage 'most closely resembles conventional ideas of partnership, but firms should recognise that the relationship may have a finite life span as external factors or changes in corporate interests cause supply chain strategies to diverge'.

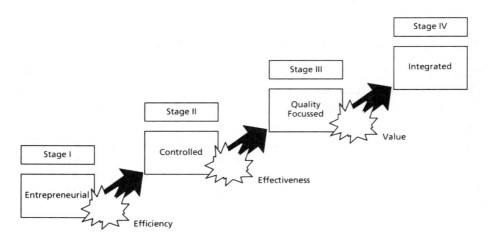

Fig 9.3 Stages of excellence
(reproduced by kind permission of A T Kerney Ltd from *Partnership and Power Play* as **12**(3) in the text)

(iv) Supplier development. This is concerned with assisting actual and potential suppliers to meet the requirements of the purchasing organisation. One important aspect is that of extending the resources of a larger company to a smaller vendor which has demonstrated a willingness to meet the buying requirements of the purchaser. Such support can take several forms including:

- financial, e.g. loans for purchase of equipment or special payment arrangements
- management support, e.g. advice on production control
- shared facilities, e.g. inspection equipment
- purchasing assistance, e.g. placing the purchasing facilities of the buyer at the disposal of the supplier.

Supplier development may be considered as a special aspect of partnership sourcing and subcontracting.

13. RECIPROCAL TRADE

(a) Definition. Reciprocity is defined as: *'Mutual or correspondent concession of advantages or privileges, as forming a basis for commercial relations' (Shorter Oxford Dictionary).* Reciprocity is often referred to a 'selling through the order book' when a policy is adopted of giving preference to those suppliers who are also customers of the buying undertaking.

(b) Types of reciprocity

(i) External, i.e. suppliers have no relationship to the buying undertaking.
(ii) Internal, i.e. supplier and buyer are both members of the same group.
(iii) Two-way reciprocity, e.g. A, a tyre manufacturer, agrees to buy fork-lift trucks from B on condition that B buys tyres from A.
(iv) Multi-reciprocity, e.g. A is a large foundry seeking to sell castings to B, a manufacturer of mechanical handling equipment. B agrees to buy from A on condition that the latter buys sand from C, a mining and quarrying company which is is a substantial customer of B.

(c) Factors in reciprocity. Reciprocity is influenced by:

(i) The economic climate; pressures for reciprocal agreements increase in times of depression.
(ii) The type of product. Reciprocal dealing is greater where both supplier and buyer are producers of standard, highly competitive products. It does not arise where a buyer has no alternative but to buy from a given supplier.

(d) Advantages of reciprocity

(i) Both supplier and buyer may benefit from the exchange of orders.
(ii) Both supplier and buyer may obtain a greater understanding of mutual problems, thus increasing goodwill.
(iii) More direct communication between suppliers and buyers may eliminate

or reduce the need for intermediaries and the cost of marketing or procurement operations.

(e) Disadvantages of reciprocity. Where price, delivery and quality are at least equivalent to that offered by other suppliers then it is common sense for the buyer to give preference to customers of his undertaking. These conditions apply infrequently and in practice reciprocity may have the following consequences:

(i) Costs may increase due to the reduced competitive position of the buyer without compensating benefits

(ii) Sales must increase substantially to provide an equivalent saving on purchases (see 1:4)

(iii) Selling through the order book uses purchasing to perform a market function. Credit may accrue to marketing while the performance of purchasing may be adversely affected

(iv) Marketing effort may become slack

(v) Disputes may arise where the respective values of purchases and sales become substantially different

(vi) The opportunity to buy cheaper, better-quality alternatives may be denied to the buyer who is tied by a reciprocal agreement

(vii) Business may be taken from satisfactory suppliers

(viii) Difficulties may arise in finding alternative suppliers in an emergency

(ix) In practice it is often difficult to terminate reciprocal relationships without friction

(x) The morale of the buying staff may be adversely affected.

Reciprocity in the last analysis is a top management decision. The buyer should respond to pressures to enter into such relationships by setting out in writing the advantages and disadvantages of any proposals made.

14. COUNTERTRADE

(a) This is a form of international reciprocal trading in which an order is placed by a purchaser with a supplier in another country on condition that goods to an equal or specified value are sold in the opposite direction.

Product lines most frequently countertraded are aeroplane parts and products, industrial equipment, communications and electronic products, transportation/navigational equipment and chemicals.

(b) Forms of countertrade. Carter and Gagne [19] identify five distinct types of countertrade:

(1) *Barter/swaps* – a one-off direct, simultaneous exchange of goods or services between trading partners, without a cash transaction. The term 'swap' is used when goods are exchanged to save transportation costs.

(2) *Counter purchase* occurs when a company in country X sells to a foreign country Y, on the understanding that a set percentage of the sale proceeds will

be spent on importing goods produced in country Y. Both trading partners agree to fulfil their obligations within a fixed time period and to pay for the major part of their respective purchases in cash.

(3) *Buy-back/compensation* occurs when the exporter agrees to accept, as full or partial payment, products manufactured by the original exported product, e.g. Occidental Petroleum negotiated a deal with the USSR under which they would build several plants in the Soviet Union and receive partial payment in ammonia over a twenty-year period.

(4) *Switch trading* refers to the transfer of unused or unusable credit balances in one country to overcome an imbalance of money by a trading partner in another country. Country X sells goods of a certain value to country Y. Country Y credits country X with the value of the goods which X can use to buy goods from Y. Country X, however, does not wish to buy goods from Y. X therefore sells the credits to a third party trading house at a discount. The trading house then locates a country or company wishing to buy goods from Y. In return for a small profit the trading house sells the credits to the country or company wishing to buy from Y.

(5) *Offset.* This is similar to counterpurchase except that the supplier can fulfil the undertaking to import goods or services of a certain percentage value by dealing with any company in the country to which the original goods were supplied.

(c) The advantages and disadvantages of countertrade. These have been identified by Forker [20] as shown below:

Advantages	Disadvantages
(i) Acceptance of goods or services as payment can: • avoid exchange controls • promote trade with countries with inconvertible currencies • reduce risks associated with unstable currency values (ii) Overcoming the above financial obstacles enables countertrading enterprises to: • enter new or formerly closed markets • expand business and sales volume • reduce the impact of foreign protectionism on overseas business (iii) Countertrade has enabled participants to: • make fuller use of plant capacity • have longer production runs • reduce unit expenses due to greater sales volume • find valuable outlets for declining products.	(i) Countertrade negotiations tend to be longer and more complex than conventional sales negotiations and must, sometimes, be conducted with powerful government procurement agencies. (ii) Additional expenses, e.g. brokerage fees and other transaction costs, reduce the profitability of countertrade deals. (iii) There may be difficulties with the quality, availability and disposal of goods taken as payback. (iv) Countertrade may give rise to pricing problems associated with the assignment of values to products/commodities received in exchange. (v) Offset customers can, later, become competitors. (vi) Commodity prices can vary widely during the lengthy periods of countertrade negotiation and delivery.

(d) Countertrade and purchasing. One advantage of countertrade not mentioned above is that a multi-national company can use its purchasing power to forge strong supplier links as a means of exploiting sales opportunities in a foreign country. Thus, with what is termed 'reverse countertrade' an enterprise can present actual or potential foreign trading partners with their current and future sourcing requirements. When the availability of these requirements has been established the feasibility of selling its own goods abroad can be raised. Purchasing can play a major part in countertrade by:

(i) Identifying low-cost sources of supply that may be exploited on a countertrade basis.

(ii) Providing negotiating expertise when discussing countertrade arrangement with prospective foreign suppliers.

(iii) Ensuring that goods to be purchased under countertrade arrangements are of the right quality.

(iv) Finding internal uses for countertrade materials.

(v) Developing long-term strategic countertrade partnerships.

(vi) Recognising that countertrade can be a major source of low-cost quality materials that will provide a competitive advantage over those to whom such sources are not available.

15. INTRA-COMPANY TRADING

This applies to large enterprises and conglomerates where the possibility arises of buying certain materials from a member of the group. This policy may be justified on the grounds that it ensures the utilisation and profitability of the supplying undertaking and the profitability of the group as a whole. It may also be resorted to in times of recession to help supplying subsidiaries to cover their fixed costs.

Policy statements should give general and specific guidance to the procurement function regarding the basis on which intra-company trading should be conducted. General guidance may be expressed in a policy statement such as the following:

> Company policy is to support internal suppliers to the fullest extent and to develop product and service quality to the same high standards as those available in the external market.

Specific guidance may direct buyers to:

(i) Purchase specified items exclusively from group members regardless of price.

(ii) Obtain quotations from group members which are evaluated against those from external suppliers with the order being placed with the most competitive source whether internal or external.

Difficulties can arise where intra-company trading involves import or export considerations.

16. SUBCONTRACTING

(a) Reasons for subcontracting. The buyer encounters problems of subcontracting in two main areas:

(i) Where the buyer's organisation is the employer or client entrusting work to a main contractor who, in turn, subcontracts part of the work. This is the case with most construction contracts.

(ii) Where the buyer's organisation is the main contractor and subcontracts work for such reasons as:

- overloading of machinery or labour
- to ensure completion of work on time
- lack of specialist machinery or specialist know-how
- to avoid acquiring long-term capacity when future demand is uncertain
- subcontracting is cheaper.

(b) Organisation for subcontracting

(i) When subcontracting is a regular and significant part of the activity of an undertaking it may be desirable to set up a special subcontracting section either within or external to the purchasing department.

(ii) Arrangements must be made for adequate liaison between all departments connected with subcontracting, i.e. design, production control, erection and site staff, inspection, finance, etc.

(iii) Friction over who should negotiate with the select suppliers sometimes develops between purchasing and design or technical departments. This can be avoided by a proper demarcation of authority and responsibility, purchasing having a power of commercial veto and design, etc, a technical veto.

(c) Selection of subcontractors. This is essentially a sourcing problem and most of the factors listed in Chapter 8 apply. It may be necessary to check whether external approval of the selected subcontractor is necessary, as in government contracts or where a specific subcontractor has been specified by the client.

(d) Liaison with subcontractors. Matters to be considered include the following:

(i) Planning, to ensure that the subcontractor can complete by the required date. Techniques such as PERT are of assistance.

(ii) Ensuring that the subcontractor is supplied with the most recent copies of all necessary documentation including drawings, standards and planning instructions.

(iii) Arranging with the subcontractor for the supply by the main contractor of materials, tooling, specialist equipment, etc, and the basis on which this shall be charged.

(iv) Control of equipment and materials in the possession of subcontractors.

(v) Arrangements for returns at stocktaking of free-issue material in the possession of the subcontractor.

(vi) Arrangements for visits to the premises of the subcontractor by progress and inspection staff employed by the main contractor.

(vii) Arrangements for transportation, especially where items produced by the subcontractor require special protection, e.g. components with a highly finished surface.

(viii) Payment for any ancillary work to be performed by the subcontractor, e.g. painting on of part numbers.

(e) Legal factors. These will depend on the circumstances of the specific contract. All major contracts for subcontracting should be vetted by the legal department of the main contractor. Where the buyer's undertaking is the client entrusting work to a main contractor, it is useful to remember the following general principles:

Unless the contract has been placed on the basis, express or implied, that the work will be wholly performed by the main contractor, the client will have no authority to prevent the subcontracting of part of the work (this will not apply to contracts for personal service). If, therefore, the client wishes to specify particular subcontractors or to limit the right of the main contractor to subcontract, these matters must be negotiated when the order is placed. With construction contracts, tenderers are sometimes required to state what parts of the work will be subcontracted.

17. LOCAL SUPPLIERS

What is 'local' must be determined bearing in mind such factors as ease of transport and communication. The advantages of using local rather than distant suppliers include the following:

(i) Closer co-operation is facilitated between buyer and suppliers based on personal relationships.

(ii) Social responsibility is shown by 'supporting local industries' and thus contributing to the prosperity of the area.

(iii) Reduced transportation costs.

(iv) Improved availability in emergency situations, e.g. road transport can be used to collect urgently needed items. The potential importance of localised confidence in the maintenance of lead times increases where a JIT system is adopted.

(v) The development of subsidiary industries situated close to the main industry and catering for its needs is encouraged.

The main principle in deciding where to place orders must, however, be what is best for the buying undertaking.

18. SMALL OR LARGE SUPPLIERS

Advantages claimed for *small* suppliers include:

- closer attention to buyer's requirements – many large suppliers, however, recognise that smaller accounts often grow
- relationships, especially at executive level, are more personal
- response to requests for special assistance from the buyer can be more rapid than with a large undertaking.

It is government policy to encourage the development of small firms and to improve the access of such undertakings to public sector business, not, however, by favouring small firms at the expense of competitiveness. The CIPS has issued *A Guide to Practice* when buying from small firms. This recommends, *inter alia*, that larger organisations should:

(a) Facilitate access by small firms by publishing the names of the larger organisation's purchasing staff and details of its organisation structure.

(b) Confirm orders in sufficient time to allow small firms to meet completion dates.

(c) Provide assistance to small suppliers, especially by means of:

(i) prompt payment, thereby easing liquidity problems
(ii) secondment of staff to deal with such problems as quality control design and specification
(iii) supply of materials either as a free issue or at a price which the small firm would not have been able to negotiate itself.

If a large organisatiom merely wants to tender for price comparison purposes the small company should be informed and in certain circumstances the cost of tendering should be paid.

(d) Limit over-dependence by a small supplier on them by setting a ceiling to the percentage of sales taken which, exceptional circumstances apart, should not be exceeded.

(e) Through a written purchasing policy, state its policy towards small suppliers.

(f) Be aware of and consider ameriorating the harmful impact which centralised purchasing *may* have on small local suppliers.

Advantages claimed for *large* suppliers include:

(1) Reserve capacity to undertake extra work and cope with emergencies is usually greater
(2) Special facilities and knowledge can be made available to the buyer
(3) There is less danger of the supplier becoming too reliant on the buyer's business.

19. OUTSOURCING SERVICES

(a) Outsourcing of support services is closely related to facilities management and is being increasingly adopted in respect of such activities as catering, cleaning, information technology management, pensions, printing, public relations, recruitment and security.

Beauchamp [21] states that outsourcing agencies are unlikely to have the level of expertise to undertake high technology strategic *procurement* involving top level and specialist advice to senior management. It is, however, feasible to outsource high-work-load, lower-skill *purchasing* activities such as those associated with one-off and repeat orders, locally and nationally purchased items, low-value or low-value/high-volume acquisitions and all the associated administration.

In this context the Central Unit on Purchasing [22] distinguishes between:

(*i*) Purchasing agents – who act on behalf of an organisation to buy goods and services from suppliers.
(*ii*) Supplies agencies or stockists – which are agencies who contract to supply a variety of goods and services but do not act as the agent of employing organisation.

Purchasing agents may be used:

(*i*) to perform all the organisation's purchasing
(*ii*) to handle specific projects
(*iii*) to handle low value purchase orders
(*iv*) to provide direct call off contracts, i.e. where the user orders direct and pays the supplier.

(b) The benefits of outsourcing services. The main benefit identified by organisations that have adopted outsourcing is the freeing of management time to concentrate on core business operations. Other benefits are shown in Fig 9.4.

(c) The problems of outsourcing. Outsourcing is not, however, without its problems and it can be up to two years before an organisation starts to benefit from any savings and in some cases the whole process is cost neutral. Some of the problems of outsourcing are shown in Fig 9.5.

(d) Contracting for outsourcing. Lacity and others [24] point out that one of the biggest mistakes that organisations can make is signing supplier's standard contracts, since in virtually every supplier-written contract studied they discovered hidden costs. They also recommend that whenever possible organisations should negotiate short-term contracts. For outsourcing purchasing sound advice is given in the CUP Guidelines referred to in [22].

20. SOURCING DECISIONS

Sourcing decisions involve a consideration of: (a) factors influencing buying decisions; (b) buying centres; (c) buying situations; and (d) factors in deciding where to buy.

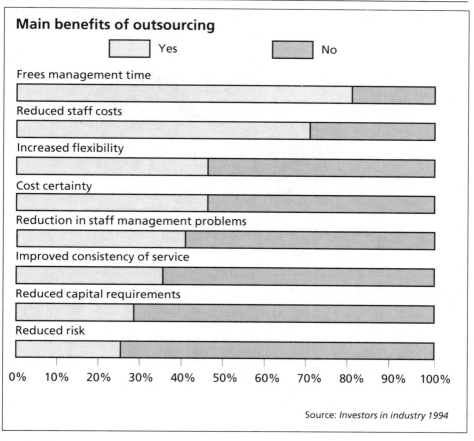

Main benefits of outsourcing

☐ Yes   ▨ No

Frees management time

Reduced staff costs

Increased flexibility

Cost certainty

Reduction in staff management problems

Improved consistency of service

Reduced capital requirements

Reduced risk

0% 10% 20% 30% 40% 50% 60% 70% 80% 90% 100%

Source: *Investors in industry 1994*

Fig 9.4   Main benefits of outsourcing
(taken from Carrington [23])

(a) Factors in deciding where to buy. Webster and Wind [25] classify factors influencing industrial buying decisions into four main groups as shown in Table 9.6.

It is of interest that Webster and Wind, writing in 1972, make no reference to the linkage between purchasing and overall strategies and procurement decisions aimed at enhancing the competitive advantage of the buying organisation such as the decision to source abroad.

(b) The buying centre. This is the buying decision-making unit of an organisation and is defined by Webster and Wind [26] as 'all those individuals and groups who participate in the purchasing decision process and who share some common goals and the risks arising from the decisions'. The buying centre is a temporary, often informal, group which can change in composition and functions from purchase to purchase.

The composition of the buying centre can be analysed as follows:

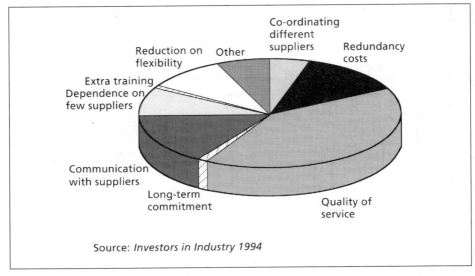

Source: *Investors in Industry 1994*

Fig 9.5   Problems of outsourcing
(from [23])

(i) By individual participants or job holders, e.g. the managing director, chief purchasing officer, engineer, accountant, etc.

(ii) By organisational units, e.g. departments or even individual organisations, as when a group of hospitals decide to standardise on equipment.

(iii) The buying centre comprises all members of the organisation (varying

Table 9.6   Factors in industrial buying decisions

Environmental	Organisational	Interpersonal	Individual
These are normally outside the buyer's control and include: (a) the level of demand (b) the economic outlook (c) interest rates (d) technological change (e) political factors (f) government regulations (g) competitive development	Buying decisions are affected by the organisation's system of reward, authority, status and communication, including organisational: (a) objectives (b) policies (c) procedures (d) structures	Involving the interaction of several persons of different status, authority, empathy and persuasiveness who comprise the *buying centre*	Buying decisions are related to how individual participants in the buying process form their preferences for products and suppliers, involving the person's age, professional indentification, personality and attitude towards the risks involved in their buying behaviour

from three to twelve) who play any of the five roles in the purchasing decision process, namely:

- *Users* – who will use the product or service and often initiate the purchase and specify what is bought.
- *Influencers* – such as technical staff who may directly or indirectly influence the buying decision in such ways as defining specifications or providing information on which alternatives may be evaluated.
- *Buyers* – who have formal authority to select suppliers and arrange terms of purchase. Buyers may help to determine specifications but their main role is to select vendors and negotiate within purchase constraints.
- *Deciders* – who have either formal or informal authority to select the ultimate suppliers. In routine purchasing of standard items the deciders are often the buyers. In more complex purchasing the deciders are often other officers of the organisation.
- *Gatekeepers* – who control the flow of information to others, e.g. buyers may prevent sales persons from seeing users or deciders.

(c) The buying situation. Robinson, Faris and Wind [27] relate the involvement of buying in deciding where to buy to the situation as follows:

(i) New task. Buyers and their departments are not involved in the early stages of new purchase decisions because it is generally accepted that the technical problems associated with new purchases must be solved before detailed commercial considerations of where to buy can be made.

(ii) Modified rebuy. Buyers take a leading role both as initiator of the change and the final arbiter of the purchase decision.

(iii) Straight rebuy. Buyers are the key decision-takers providing no technical differentiation is present. Decisions regarding repeat orders are usually made by purchasing staff rather than the head of the purchasing department.

Buying decisions also relate to product classifications. The survey *How British Industry Buys* (1967) showed that the leading role in deciding which supplier obtained the order, in surveying sources of supply and in soliciting quotations was undertaken by the purchasing department for materials and components but by general or operating management where plant and equipment is concerned.

Increasingly, however, sourcing decisions are being made in a team or buying centre basis due to:

(i) The increased involvement of procurement in strategic as well as tactical and operational decision making.

(ii) The integration of purchasing into materials management and logistics functions.

(iii) The movement towards single and partnership sourcing.

(iv) The increasing complexity of purchasing including global sourcing where many factors including political, currency and similar considerations enter into the purchasing decision.

(v) The desirability of spreading responsibility to high-risk purchasing decisions.

(vi) The need to evaluate the risks and potential contribution to profitability of new materials, products technology and suppliers.

21. FACTORS IN DECIDING WHERE TO BUY

Assuming that the decision is taken that a product should be bought out rather than made in, many factors determine where the order is placed and by whom the decision is made. Such considerations include:

(a) General consideration

(i) How shall the item be categorised, i.e. capital investment, manufacturing material or parts, operating, supply, or MRO item?
(ii) What are our current and projected levels of business for the item?
(iii) Is the item a 'one off' or a continuing requirement?
(iv) Is the item unique to us or in general use?
(v) Are we currently buying the item or have we bought it before?
(vi) If it is being currently bought, or has been bought before, from what source was it obtained?
(vii) Is/was the present/previous supplier satisfactory from the standpoints of price, quality and delivery?
(viii) Having regard to the value of the order to be placed is the cost of searching for an alternative supply source justified?
(ix) What internal customers may wish to be consulted on the sourcing of the item?
(x) Within what time scale is the item required?

(b) Strategic consideration

(i) What supply source will offer the greatest competitive advantage from the standpoints of:
* Price
* Differentiation of product
* Security of supplies and reliability of delivery
* Quality
* Added value through specialisation, production facilities, packaging, transportation, after-sales services etc.

(ii) Is the source one with whom we would like to:
* Single source
* Share a proportion of our requirements for the required item
* Built up a long-term partnership relationship
* Discuss the possibilities of supplier development
* Subcontract?

(iii) Does the supply source offer any possibilities for
* Joint product development
* Reciprocal or countertrade?

(iv) What relationships has the supplier with our competitors?

(v) Is it desirable that, at least part, of our requirements should be sourced locally for political, social responsibility or logistical reasons.

(vi) What risk factors attach to the purchase? Is the product (1) high profit impact/high supply risk; (2) low profit impact/high supply risk; (3) high profit impact/low supply risk; (4) low profit impact/low supply risk?

(c) Product factors

(i) What critical factors influence the choice of suppliers? Chisnall [28] reports a research finding that seven critical factors were found to influence buyers in the British valve and pump industry in the choice of their suppliers of raw materials: delivery reliability, technical advice, test facilities, replacement guarantee, prompt quotation, ease of contact, and willingness to supply range. These attributes helped to reduce the risk element in purchase decisions.

(ii) What special tooling is required? Is such tooling the property of the existing supplier or the vendor?

(iii) To what extent are learning curves applicable to the product? Are these allowed for in the present and future prices?

(iv) Is the product 'special' or 'standardised'?

(v) In what lot sizes is the product manufactured?

(vi) What is the estimated product life cycle cost?

(vii) Is the product one that can be leased as an alternative to buying?

(d) Supplier factors. Such factors are those normally covered by supplier appraisal and vendor rating exercises; see **4** and **5** earlier in this chapter.

(e) Personal factors. These relate to the psychological and behavioural aspects of those involved in making organisational buying decisions. Sheth [29] identified three principal components that combine to explain a purchasing decision outcome: expectations of the individual decision participants, the number of individuals involved and approaches to conflict resolution.

(i) Factors that determine participant expectations about the ability of suppliers and products to meet requirements.
- Background of individuals, e.g. education, job orientation, lifestyles.
- Active information, search information, e.g. sources and amount available.
- Information distortion due to the goals, values and differing experiences of individual buying centre members.
- Satisfaction with past purchases.

(ii) Factors that determine the number of individuals involved
- *Product factors:*
  - Time pressure
  - Perceived risk
  - Type of purchase

- *Company factors:*
  - Orientation
  - Size
  - Degree of centralisation

- *Approaches to conflict resolution among those involved:*
  - Problem solving
  - Persuasion
  - Bargaining
  - Politicking

Sheth also recognises that situation factors such as strikes at the supplier's factor, mergers and a sudden glut or shortage in the global supply of a critical commodity can also influence purchasing decisions.

References

[1] Killen K H and Kamauff J W. *Managing Purchasing.* Irwin Publishing, 1995. Ch. 1 p 7.

[2] Bank of England Quarterly Bulletin, February 1994

[3] Public Purchasing Policy Consolidated Guidelines.

[4] Egan J. *Benefits of total quality : a vehicle manufacturer's view* quoted in Lascelles D M and Dale B G *The buyer-supplier relationship in total quality management. Journal of Purchasing and Materials Management.* Summer 1989 pp 10–19.

[5] Probert D R. *Make or buy – your route to improved manufacturing performance. DTI Managing in the 90s series* 1995

[6] Lamming R. *Beyond Partnership: Strategies for Innovation and Supply.* Prentice Hall, 1993. Chap 6 p 171.

[7] Quayle M. *Change partners and dance. Purchasing and Supply Management.* Feb 1995 pp 32–35.

[8] Quayle M. *Changing a supplier – how do they do that? Purchasing and Supply Management.* January 1995 pp 26–30.

[9] DTI *Building a Purchasing Strategy* 1993 pp 11–12.

[10] Birou L M and Fawcett S E. *International purchasing, benefits, requirements and challenges. International Journal of Purchasing and Supply.* Spring 1993 pp 28–37.

[11] Stevens J. *Global purchasing in the supply chain. Purchasing and Supply Management.* Jan 1995 pp 22–25.

[12] Carter J R and Narasimhan R. *Purchasing in the international marketplace. Journal of Purchasing and Materials Management.* Sept 1990 pp 2–11.

[13] Birou L M and Fawcett S E. *International purchasing, benefits, requirements and challenges. International Journal of Purchasing and Supply.* Spring 1993 pp 28–37.

[14] Partnership Sourcing Ltd. *Making Partnership Sourcing Happen.* p 4.

[15] Griffiths F. *Alliance partnership sourcing – a major tool for strategic procurement. Purchasing and Supply Management.* May 1992 pp 35–40.

[16] Partnership Sourcing Ltd. *Creating Service Partnerships* 1993 p 7.

[17] Partnership Sourcing Ltd. *Making Partnership Sourcing Happen.* p 4.

[18] A T Kerney Ltd and University of Manchester Institute of Science and Technology (UMIST). *Partnership or Power Play.* UMIST Occasional Paper 1994 p18. This research was undertaken by Drs S New and S Young.

[19] Carter J R and Gagne J. *The do's and don'ts of Countertrade. Sloan Management Review.* Spring 1988 pp 31–37.

[20] Forker L B. *Purchasing's views on countertrade*. International Journal of Purchasing and Materials Management. Spring 1992 pp 10–19.

[21] Beauchamp M. *Outsourced everything else? Why not purchasing? Purchasing and Supply Management*. July 1994 pp 16–19.

[22] Central Unit on Purchasing. *CUP Guidance: 28 Contracts with a Private Sector Purchasing Agent*.

[23] Carrington L. *Outside chances*. Personnel Today. 8 Feb 1994. p 34.

[24] Lacity M C, Willcocks L P and Feeny D F. *IT outsourcing: maximise flexibility and control*. Harvard Business Review. May-June 1995 pp 84–93.

[25] Webster F E and Wind Y J. *Organisational Buying Behaviour*. Prentice Hall, 1972. pp 33–37.

[26] Webster F E and Wind Y J. *Organisational Buying Behaviour*. Prentice Hall, 1972. p 6.

[27] Robinson P J, Faris C W and Wind Y. *Industrial Buying and Creative Marketing*. Allyn and Bacon, 1967. p 14.

[28] Chisnall P M. *Strategic Industrial Marketing* (2nd edn.). Prentice Hall, 1989. Ch 3 pp 82–83.

[29] Sheth J N. *A model of industrial buyer behaviour*. Journal of Marketing. October 1978 pp 50–56.

Progress test 9

1. Distinguish between 'strategic', 'tactical' and 'operational' sourcing.

2. Why is an analysis of market conditions important to sourcing?

3. From what sources can information relating to market conditions be obtained?

4. What, in the context of purchasing, are 'directives'?

5. From what sources can information relating to potential suppliers be obtained?

6. List some of the areas to which you would give attention when making an appraisal visit to a potential supplier.

7. What are the advantages and disadvantages of vendor rating?

8. What is meant by the Supplier Base?

9. What factors may determine make or buy decisions?

10. State the advantages and disadvantages of (a) single and (b) multiple sourcing.

11. For what reasons may an enterprise source internationally?

12. What difficulties may be encountered in sourcing abroad?

13. Define the term 'partnership sourcing' and compare traditional and partnership sourcing.

14. Define the term reciprocal trade and discuss its advantages and disadvantages.

15. What is countertrade and how may purchasing be involved?

16. For what reasons may an enterprise subcontract part of a contract to other organisations?

17. State some matters on which it is essential that close relationships should be maintained with subcontractors.

18. What are some advantages of using local suppliers?

19. What is a buying centre and what roles may its members play in the purchasing decision process?

20. What factors may need to be considered when deciding where to buy?

21. Advocating the use of *world class suppliers* implies worldwide sourcing. Discuss the possible gains for the buyer from sourcing on a worldwide basis, and outline the difficulties which may be encountered.
   (CIPS *Purchasing and Supply Management II Provisioning* (1992))

22. Partnership Sourcing is a term which has recently achieved considerable prominence. Identify and discuss the benefits and difficulties likely to face both buyer and seller when attempting to establish such an arrangement.
   (CIPS *Introduction to Purchasing and Supply Management* (1992))

23. The criteria on which a successful purchaser should be judged spring from his ability to 'shop around and select good suppliers and not on his ability to shop around for cheap buys' (Lord Rayner). Critically evaluate this statement.
   (CIPS *Introduction to Purchasing and Supply Management*(1993))

24. Evaluate the view that 'all things being equal', preference should be given to local suppliers.
   (CIPS *Introduction to Purchasing and Supply Management* (1993))

25. Name five important sources of information regarding suppliers and their capabilities, showing clearly the importance and relevance to effective supply management of each source.
   (CIPS *Introduction to Purchasing and Supply Management* ((1994))

26. Discuss the view that the buyer should 'clearly identify his motives and only source from overseas when all the potential domestic sources have been thoroughly evaluated.

    (CIPS *Introduction to Purchasing and Supply Management* (1994))

27. Reciprocal trading has important implications for the purchasing activity. Explain the nature of such a policy, and its likely effects on the activity.

    (CIPS *Purchasing and Supply Management I Planning, Policy and Organisation* (1994))

28. What benefits is partnership sourcing likely to bring to both buying and supplying organisations? Highlight some of the key areas for concern in such a relationship.

    (CIPS *Purchasing and Supply Management I Planning, Policy and Organisation* (1994))

10

CONTRASTING APPROACHES TO SUPPLY

1. INTRODUCTION

The considerations that apply to the purchase of products, as distinct from services, can be contrasted according to the nature of the product, the type of production and the principal use to which a purchased item will be put. We can also distinguish between purchasing of consumer, industrial and re-sale items.

- *Consumer products* used in this context to refer to goods purchased by individuals and households for personal consumption are outside the scope of this book.
- *Industrial products* are purchased by organisations for use in the production of other products to make profits or achieve other objectives.
- *Re-sale products* are purchased by organisations in order to resell them at a profit.

The present chapter is concerned with industrial products, consumables or maintenance, repair and operating CMRO supplies and goods for resale.

2. INDUSTRIAL PRODUCTS

These may be sub-divided into

- Capital investment items
- Production materials.

3. CAPITAL INVESTMENT ITEMS

What is capital equipment?

(a) From the *marketing* standpoint, Marrian [1] has distinguished between six types of industrial equipment:

(i) Buildings: permanent constructions on a site to house or enclose equipment and personnel employed in industrial, institutional or commercial activities.

(ii) Installation equipment (capital equipment, plant): essential plant, machinery or other major equipment used directly to produce the goods and services of producing organisations.

(iii) Accessory equipment: durable major equipment used to facilitate the production of goods and services or to enhance the operations of organisations. Installation and accessory equipment often coincide but there is a distinction. Aircraft purchased by an airline, for example, would be installation equipment; aircraft purchased by a manufacturing organisation to facilitate the movement of executive personnel would be accessory equipment.

(iv) Operating equipment: semi-durable minor equipment which is movable, used in but not generally essential to the production of goods and services, e.g. special footwear, goggles, brushes and brooms.

(v) Tools and instruments: semi-durable or durable portable minor equipment and instruments required for producing, measuring, calculating, etc., associated with the production of goods or services, e.g. word processors, all tools, surgical instruments, timing devices, cash registers, etc.

(vi) Furnishings and fittings: all goods and materials employed to fit buildings for their organisational purposes but not that equipment used specifically in production, e.g. carpets, floor coverings, draperies, furniture, shelving, counters, benches, etc.

(b) From the *accountancy* standpoint, expenditure on capital equipment results in the acquisition of fixed rather than current assets. One useful definition of capital expenditure is 'All expenditure which is expected to produce benefit to the firm over a period longer than the accounting period in which the expenditure was incurred'.

(c) Characteristics of capital expenditure. Expenditure on capital equipment differs from that on materials and components in many ways, including the following:

(i) The cost per item is usually greater.

(ii) The items bought are used up gradually in facilitating production rather than as a part of the end product.

(iii) Capital expenditure is financed from long-term capital or from appropriations of profit rather than from working capital or charges against profit.

(iv) Tax considerations such as capital allowances and investment grants have an important bearing on whether to purchase capital equipment and the timing of such purchases.

(v) Government financial assistance towards the cost of capital equipment may be available, e.g. where a manufacturing organisation is located in a development area.

(vi) The purchase of capital equipment is often postponable, at least in the short term.

(vii) The decision to buy capital equipment often results in consequential decisions relating to sales, output and labour. In the latter case, consultations with the appropriate unions may be necessary.

The terms and conditions of purchase may have to be adapted to meet the circumstances arising from the acquisition of capital equipment.

The purchase of capital equipment is therefore usually a more complex procedure than that involved in the case of materials and components, a large proportion of which are repeat purchases.

(d) Factors to be considered in buying capital equipment. Apart from the mode of purchase, finance and the return on the investment made, the factors to be considered include the following:

(i) Purpose. What is the prime purpose of the equipment?

(ii) Flexibility. How versatile is the equipment? Can it be used for purposes other than those for which it was primarily acquired?

(iii) Standardisation. Is the equipment compatible with any already installed, thus reducing the cost of holding spares?

(iv) Life. This usually refers to the period before the equipment will have to be written off due to depreciation or obsolescence. It is, however, not necessarily linked to the total life span if it is intended to dispose of the asset before it is obsolete or unusable.

(v) Reliability. Breakdowns mean higher costs, loss of goodwill through extended deliveries and possibly high investment in spares.

(vi) Durability. Is the equipment sufficiently robust for its intended use?

(vii) Product quality. Defective output proportionately increases the cost per unit of output.

(viii) Cost of operation. Costs of fuel, power and maintenance. Will special labour or additional labour costs be incurred? Is discussion with the unions advisable?

(ix) Cost of installation. Does the price include cost of installation, commissioning and training of operators?

(x) Cost of maintenance. Can the equipment be maintained by own staff or will special agreements with the vendor be necessary? What estimates of maintenance costs can be provided before purchase? How reliable are these?

(xi) Miscellaneous. These include appearance, space requirements, quietness of operation, safety and aspects of ergonomics affecting the performance of the operator.

(e) Life cycle costing (Terotechnology) is an important aspect of capital expenditure. Life cycle costing is further considered in Chapter 12.

4. BUYING USED EQUIPMENT

Used equipment available from dealers' auctions or direct purchase from a previous owner may be an alternative to buying new.

(a) Advantages

(i) Often cost is substantially lower than new.

(ii) Used equipment may be more readily available.

(iii) Used equipment, especially when reconditioned or rebuilt, may have a long life and be protected by guarantees or warranties.

(iv) It may be economical to buy low-priced used equipment when it would not pay to acquire new.

(v) A used machine may be compatible with others already in use, thus reducing the costs of carrying spares.

(vi) It is often possible to inspect used equipment in use under actual working conditions.

(b) Precautions. Although protection is given by the Sale of Goods, Trades Description and Misrepresentation Acts, the purchaser of used equipment should work on the principle of *caveat emptor* (let the buyer beware). Some questions that a prospective buyer of used equipment should ask include the following:

(i) Is a history of the equipment available?

(ii) Is there any indication of age such as a serial number?

(iii) How well has the equipment been maintained?

(iv) Are spares readily available? Will they continue to be?

(v) How does the price asked for used equipment compare with the cost of buying new?

(vi) Are the vendors well established? Have they a sound reputation?

(vii) What special terms and conditions, if any, apply to the purchase?

(viii) Do any guarantees or warranties supersede the protection given under the Sale of Goods Act?

(ix) What trials, tests or approval period will the vendor allow?

(x) Will the vendor permit an inspection by an independent assessor?

(xi) What will be the cost, where appropriate, of dismantling, transporting and re-erecting/installing equipment?

5. EVALUATING CAPITAL INVESTMENTS

Although this is the province of the management accountant, buyers should have an awareness of the methods of appraising expenditure on capital items. Three highly simplified examples of these approaches (pay-back, average rate of return and two applications of discounted cash flow) are briefly considered.

(a) Pay-back. This is the time required for cash returns to equal the initial cash expenditure.

Example An enterprise buys two machines each costing £20,000. The net cash flows after operating costs and expenses but not allowing for depreciation are expected to be as shown:

Year	Cash flow Machine A (£)	Cash flow Machine B (£)
1	5,000	4,500
2	5,000	4,500
3	5,000	4,500
4	5,000	4,500
5	5,000	4,500
6	–	4,500
7	–	4,500
	£25,000	£31,500

Pay-back $\dfrac{£20,000}{5,000} = 4$ years or $\dfrac{£20,000}{4,500} = 4.4$ years

The example shows both the principle and fallacy of the pay-back approach. Machine A has the better pay-back since the initial cost is recovered in a shorter time. Machine B has an inferior pay-back but the return extends over two further years.

The pay-back method, because of its simplicity, is probably the most popular method of investment appraisal. With this approach the emphasis is on risk rather than profitability, i.e. the risk with machine B is somewhat greater because it has a longer pay-back period.

(b) Average rate of return (prior to tax). This method aims to assess the average annual net profit after depreciation and other cash outlays as a percentage of the original cost. Three simple calculations are required:

(1) The annual rate of depreciation. This is calculated by the 'straight line' method namely:

$$\frac{\text{Cost} - \text{Residual value}}{\text{Estimated life}}$$

Assuming that machines A and B each had an estimated residual value of £1,000, their annual depreciation rates would be:

$$\text{Machine A} = \frac{£20,000 - £1,000}{5} = £3,800$$

$$\text{Machine B} = \frac{£20,000 - £1,000}{7} = £2,174$$

(2) Deduct depreciation from the average annual profit:

Machine A = £5,000 − £3,800 = £1,200

Machine B = £4,500 − £2,714 = £1,786

(3) Express net annual profit after depreciation as a percentage of the initial cost:

$$\text{Machine A} = \frac{£1,200 \times 100}{£20,000} = 6 \text{ per cent}$$

$$\text{Machine B} = \frac{£1,786 \times 100}{£20,000} = 8.93 \text{ per cent}$$

This method shows that the investment in machine B is the most profitable and allows comparison with the returns anticipated from alternative investments.

(c) Discounting. Discounting is the opposite process to compounding. The latter shows the extent to which a sum of money invested now will grow over a period of years at a given rate of compound interest. Thus £100 invested now at 10 per cent compound interest will be worth £110 in one year's time and £121 at the end of two years.

Discounting shows the value at the present time of a sum of money payable or receivable at some future time. This present value can be obtained by dividing the amount now held by that to which it would have grown at a given rate of compound interest, i.e.

$$\frac{£100}{£110} = 0.909 \quad \text{or} \quad \frac{£100}{£121} = 0.8264$$

These present values are *discount factors* and state that £100 at the end of one year at 10 per cent is now worth £0.9091 or £0.8264 at the end of two years. In practice the discount factors would be obtained from present value tables which give the following for £1 at 10 per cent and 12 per cent respectively:

Years	10%	12%
1	£0.9091	£0.8923
2	£0.8264	£0.7972
3	£0.7513	£0.7118
4	£0.6830	£0.6355
5	£0.6209	£0.5674
6	£0.5645	£0.5066
7	£0.5132	£0.4523

Net present value and yield methods illustrate two of a number of approaches based on discounted cash flow.

(d) Net present value (NPV). In this method the minimum required return on the capital investment is determined. The present value of anticipated future cash flows is that discounted at this rate. If the sum of these discounted cash flows exceeds the initial expenditure then the investment will be given a higher return than forecast. Using the figures given above and a minimum required rate of 10 per cent the discounted cash flows for machines A and B would be:

Machine A:

Year	Cash return	10% factor	Net present value
1	£5,000	£0.909	£4,545
2	£5,000	£0.826	£4,130
3	£5,000	£0.751	£3,755
4	£5,000	£0.683	£3,415
5	£5,000	£0.621	£3,105
6	–	–	–
7	–	–	–
	£25,000	–	£18,950

Machine B:

Year	Cash return	10% factor	Net present value
1	£4,500	£0.909	£4,090
2	£4,500	£0.826	£3,717
3	£4,500	£0.751	£3,880
4	£4,500	£0.683	£3,073
5	£4,500	£0.621	£2,795
6	£4,500	£0.565	£2,542
7	£4,500	£0.513	£2,309
	£31,500		£22,406

Machine A has a total return less than the initial expenditure of £20,000, i.e. less than the 10 per cent required. In contrast Machine B will exceed the given figure. This approach is very useful in evaluating which of two alternative investment propositions to adopt.

(e) Yield. In this connection, 'yield' has been defined as the 'rate of interest which discounts the future net cash flows of a project into equality with its capital cost'. To find the yield expected, cash flows are discounted at varying rates until a rate is found at which the present value of both the initial and anticipated returns are approximately equal. In the above example, the return from Machine B is in excess of 10 per cent. With the aid of present value tables we would discover by a series of trial and error computations that the yield would be between 12 per cent and 13 per cent, ascertained as follows:

Year	Cash return	10% factor	Net present value
1	£4,500	£0.892	£4,014
2	£4,500	£0.797	£3,586
3	£4,500	£0.712	£3,204
4	£4,500	£0.636	£2,862
5	£4,500	£0.567	£2,556
6	£4,500	£0.507	£2,282
7	£4,500	£0.452	£2,034
	£31,500		£20,538

Taxation and tax allowances, difficulties in forecasting future trends, interest rates and depreciation are some of the factors that have to be considered in practice when evaluating capital expenditure. These and other aspects of the evaluation of capital expenditure are discussed at length in specialist texts.

6. SELECTING SUPPLIERS OF CAPITAL ITEMS

A Department of Trade and Industry Committee on Terotechnology provided the following checklist for purchasing personnel for use when selecting a supplier or before placing an order for capital equipment [2].

(a) When selecting a supplier:

- Check that the specification of the asset to be acquired is clear and unambiguous.
- Check that it covers all relevant aspects of life-cycle performance.
- Will it permit intending suppliers to prepare realistic estimates for costs and delivery?
- Check that modifications to the specification (if any) proposed by intending suppliers have been fed back to the originators of the relevant part of the specification and actioned, if necessary, by amendment and reissue of the specification
- Have intending suppliers proposed any trade-off between initial purchase price and estimated life-cycle costs, e.g. will payment of a higher price permit a significant reduction in total outgoings?
- Have they provided adequate information on forecast costs and availability of service and/or critical spare parts during the expected life of the asset?

(b) Before placing an order:

- Check that the information provided by intending suppliers is adequate for making or confirming the decision to acquire the asset in question (i.e. does it provide an adequate response to your enquiry); this applies equally to custom-built and catalogued items.
- Check that your company corporate plan includes the life-cycle of an asset and makes financial provision for it.
- Check that the purchase specification is a clear and complete statement of your requirements.
- Check that the supplier's conditions of sale are not at variance with your short- and long-term requirements.
- Check that the specification has been agreed by all those who will be connected with installation, commissioning, operation, maintenance and safety.
- Have you consulted the quality department manager or engineer on quality aspects of the specification?
- Check the vendor ratings of the intending suppliers.
- Check the intending supplier's warranties and forecasts of availability of service and critical spare parts.
- Check that the quantity and quality of the information supplied with the

asset will be adequate for operation, overhaul and repair during its expected life.

(c) After delivery: check that procedures and formalities concerned with acceptance of the asset have been completed correctly.

7. LEASING

(a) What is leasing? A lease has been defined by the Equipment Leasing Association as '*A contract between lessor and lessee for hire of a specific asset selected from a manufacturer or vendor of such assets by the lessee*'. The lessor retains ownership of the asset. The lessee has possession and use of the asset on payment of specified rentals over a period.

Leasing can be distinguished from hiring (including plant and contract hire). In hiring the intending user selects from the specialised stock already held by the hiring organisation which usually charges a fixed tariff. In leasing, the intending user selects from a manufacturer or vendor of the required asset. A lease is then negotiated, often on tailor-made terms, with the lessor who acquires the asset chosen at the request of the lessee. The unique feature of leasing is that it enables the lessee to acquire the use of capital equipment by making payments out of revenue. It is estimated that leasing now accounts for over 10 per cent of UK investment in capital equipment. Cars and commercial vehicles, computers, contractor's plant, containers, locomotives and rolling stock, machine tools, office equipment and furniture and telecommunications equipment are a few of the assets that may be leased.

(b) Types of lease. Leasing situations fall into two broad categories, namely financial and operating leases.

(i) *Financial leases.* With these the lessor has no commercial interest in the transaction other than as a supplier of finance. The lessor pays for the asset and thereby becomes its owner. The rental paid to him by the lessee will cover the capital cost of the asset together with a service charge to cover the lessor's overheads, interest charges and an element of profit. The lessee will also be responsible for insurance, servicing and maintenance. The purpose of this type of lease is thus to enable the lessee to obtain finance, the asset being the security.

(ii) *Operating leases.* These are undertaken mainly by manufacturers or suppliers as a means of marketing their products which are often highly specialised or technical, e.g. computers. In operating leases the asset is not wholly amortised during the obligatory period (if any) of the lease and the lessor is also responsible for the servicing, maintenance and updating of the equipment. This type of lease is often a more realistic alternative to outright purchase since it enables the lessee to avoid some of the risks of ownership, such as obsolescence.

(c) The advantages of leasing

(i) Leasing provides certainty. Costs are known in advance and the financial accommodation cannot be withdrawn once the contract is signed.

(ii) Leasing reduces the need to tie up capital in fixed assets. By means of a lease the use of an asset can be obtained without capital outlay.

(iii) Leasing is concerned only with rentals and not with grants, allowances, depreciation or other calculations.

(iv) Leasing provides a medium-term source of capital which may not be readily available elsewhere.

(v) Leasing pays for equipment out of pre-tax expenditure rather than after-tax profits. The rentals payable by the lessee are wholly allowable expenses against the lessee's assessment for corporation tax.

(vi) Leasing enables the suitability of equipment to be assessed over a predetermined trial period.

(vii) Replacement decisions are made easier. Ownership of an asset can sometimes have the psychological effect of locking the owner into the use of an asset which should be replaced by a more efficient piece of equipment.

(viii) Leasing provides a hedge against the risk of obsolescence.

(ix) Leasing is also a hedge against inflation. The use of the asset involved is obtained immediately. The payments are met out of future earnings and are made in fixed money terms, with real costs falling over the years.

(d) Disadvantages of leasing. Some of the benefits listed above will not apply in larger organisations able to obtain capital on equal terms with the lessor and with a steady flow of taxable profit enabling them to obtain the capital allowances available under the current Finance Act for themselves. For such organisations leasing will be more costly than buying. Other disadvantages include the following:

(i) A fixed obligation to pay rental is created which may be an embarrassment in depressed conditions.

(ii) The flexibility to dispose of obsolete equipment before the end of the lease may be reduced.

(iii) Leasing does not provide the prestige of ownership.

(e) Leasing or buying. In practice, the decision to lease or buy is complex depending on operating, legal and financial considerations.

(i) Operating factors relate to the advantages of a trial period before purchase, the immediate availability of cost-saving equipment, the period for which assets are required and the hedges provided against obsolescence and inflation.

(ii) Legal factors are important since leasing agreements are one-sided in that most risks are transferred to the lessee. The lessee should therefore carefully examine the terms and conditions of the contract, especially with regard to such aspects as limitations on the use of the equipment and responsibilities for its insurance, maintenance, etc. Where possible, improved terms should be negotiated.

(iii) Financial factors are usually crucial in deciding whether to lease or buy. These include:

- The opportunity cost of capital, i.e. what the purchase price of the equipment would earn if used for other purposes or invested elsewhere.
- The discounted cost of meeting the periodical rental payments over the period of the lease. Note that 'flat' interest rates, calculated on the initial amount owing rather than on the average amount owed, can be misleading.

Example (Taken from *The Lease-buy Decision*, BIM)

	Leased cost i.e. 20 payments of £75 per quarter over 5 years	*Excess cost of leasing over purchase*	*Annual flat rate of interest*
Cash price of asset			
£1000	*£1500*	*£500 or 50%*	*50% ÷ 5 = 10%*

The true rate, however, is just over 20.4 per cent per annum, as can be seen from the following table.

Quarterly periods	Balance brought forward	Repayment in advance £	Interest 20.4064% compound £	Balance carried forward £
1	1000.00	−75.00	43.95	968.95
2	968.95	−75.00	42.48	936.43
3	936.43	−75.00	40.94	902.37
4	902.37	−75.00	39.32	866.69
5	866.69	−75.00	37.62	829.31
6	829.31	−75.00	35.85	790.16
7	790.16	−75.00	33.98	749.14
8	749.14	−75.00	32.04	706.18
9	706.18	−75.00	29.99	661.17
10	661.17	−75.00	27.85	614.62
11	614.62	−75.00	25.62	564.64
12	564.64	−75.00	23.27	512.91
13	512.91	−75.00	20.81	458.72
14	458.72	−75.00	18.23	401.95
15	401.95	−75.00	15.54	342.49
16	342.49	−75.00	12.71	280.20
17	280.20	−75.00	9.75	214.95
18	214.95	−75.00	6.65	146.60
19	146.60	−75.00	3.40	75.00
20	75.00	−75.00	0.00	0.00
		−£1,500.00	£500.00	

Ignoring tax, the lessee will be indifferent on cost grounds whether to lease or buy if the opportunity cost of capital is about 20.4 per cent. If the cost of capital exceeds 20.4 per cent then leasing will be cheaper in NPV terms. If less, then leasing will be the most expensive proposition.

8. THE BUYER AND CAPITAL INVESTMENT PURCHASES

Research findings indicate that:

(i) Capital equipment is more likely to be bought centrally than products of relatively continuous consumption such as materials and component parts.
(ii) Purchasing decisions relating to capital items will be made by a buying centre, with the ultimate user, such as the production manager in the case of machinery, playing a dominant role.
(iii) The greater the technical nature and complexity of an item the greater the influence of technical staff in the buying decision.

A respected professional buyer can, however, do more than contribute a list of possible vendors to buying centre decisions. Other contributions may include:

(i) Emphasis on life cycle considerations relating to capital purchases.
(ii) Countering prejudice of users in favour of one make of capital equipment which may exclude considerations of more innovative or competitive equipment available from other manufacturers.
(iii) Provision of commercial, contractual and negotiating expertise.
(iv) Identification of alternatives to the purchase of new machines, e.g. availability of second-hand items, leasing, sub-contracting.

9. PRODUCTION MATERIALS

Risley [3] has classified materials and parts for use in manufacture under three headings:

(a) Raw materials primarily from agriculture and the various extractive industries: minerals, ores, timber, petroleum and scrap as well as dairy products, fruits and vegetables sold to a processor.

(b) Semi-finished goods and processed materials to which some work has been applied or value added. Such items are finished only in part or may have been formed into shapes and specifications to make them readily usable by the buyer. These products lose their identity when incorporated into other products. Examples include: metal sections, rods, sheets, tubing, wires, castings, chemicals, cloth, leather, sugar, paper.

(c) Component parts and assemblies. Completely finished products of one manufacturer which can be used as part of a more complex product by another manufacturer. These do not lose their original identity when incorporated into other products. Examples include: bearings, controls, gauges, gears, wheels, transistors, radio and TV tubes, car engines and windshields.

10. RAW MATERIALS

(a) Characteristics. Raw materials are:

(i) Often 'sensitive' commodities.
(ii) Frequently dealt with in recognised commodity markets.
(iii) Safeguarded in many organisations by backward integration strategies.

(b) Sensitive commodities. Sensitive commodities are raw materials (copper, cotton, lead, zinc, tin, hides and rubber), the prices of which fluctuate daily. Here the buyer will aim to time purchases to obtain requirements at the most competitive prices. The main economic and political factors which influence market conditions are:

(i) interest rates, e.g. minimum lending rate
(ii) currency fluctuations, e.g. the strength of sterling
(iii) inflation, e.g. the effect of increased material and labour costs
(iv) government policies, e.g. import controls or stockpiling
(v) 'glut' or shortage supply factors, e.g. crop failure
(vi) relationships between the exporting and importing country, e.g. oil as a political weapon.

(c) Information regarding market conditions. The main sources of information regarding present and future market conditions for a commodity such as copper are as follows:

(i) Government sources, i.e. the Department of Trade and Industry.
(ii) Documentary sources. These may be 'general', e.g. *The Financial Times*, or specialised', e.g. *World Metal Statistics* published by the World Bureau of Metal Statistics, or the *Metal Bulletin.*
(iii) Federations, e.g. the British Non-ferrous Metals Federation or the International Wrought Copper Council.
(iv) Exchanges. These include independent research undertaken by brokers and dealers into metal resources and the short- and long-term prospects for the commodity.
(v) Analysts. These include economists and statisticians employed by undertakings to advise on corporate planning and purchasing policies and external units such as the Commodities Research Unit.
(vi) Databanks. Can provide up-to-date information and may be space-saving substitutes for large institutions.
(vii) Chambers of Commerce, e.g. the London Chamber of Commerce.

The task of the buyer is to evaluate information and recommendations from the above sources and put forward appropriate policies which fall broadly into two classes: hand-to-mouth and forward buying.

(d) Hand-to-mouth buying. This is buying according to need rather than in quantities that are the most economical. Circumstances in which this policy may be adopted are where prices are falling or where a change in design is imminent and it is desirable to avoid large stocks.

(e) Forward buying. This applies to all purchases made for the purpose of increasing stocks beyond the minimum quantities required to meet normal production needs based on average delivery times. Forward buying may be undertaken:

(i) to obtain the benefit of EOQs

(ii) when savings made by buying in anticipation of a price increase will be greater than the interest lost on increased stocks or the cost of storage

(iii) to prevent breakdowns in production due to occurrences such as strikes or stockpiling to avoid shortages

(iv) to secure materials for future requirements when the opportunity arises, e.g. some steel sections are only rolled at infrequent intervals.

Forward buying can apply to any material or equipment. A particular aspect of forward buying applicable to commodities is dealing in 'futures'.

11. FUTURES DEALING

A commodity such as copper may be bought direct from the producer or on a commodity market. The latter provides the advantages of futures dealing. The London markets are divided into two main areas: metals and soft commodities. The non-ferrous metal markets in copper, tin, lead, zinc and silver operate at the London Metal Exchange (LME). The soft commodity markets dealing in cocoa, coffee, sugar, vegetable oils, wool and rubber are situated at the Corn Exchange building.

(a) Functions of exchanges

(i) to enable customers, merchants and dealers to obtain supplies readily and at the competitive market price. On the LME, for examples, contracts traded are for delivery on any market day within the period of three months ahead, except for silver which can be dealt in up to seven months ahead.

(ii) to smooth out price fluctuations due to changes in demand and supply

(iii) to provide insurance against price fluctuations through the procedure known as 'hedging' (see below).

(b) The purpose of and conditions for futures dealing. The purpose of futures dealing is to reduce uncertainty arising from price fluctuations due to supply and demand changes. This reduction in uncertainty benefits both producers and consumers. The producer can sell forward at a sure price; the consumer can buy forward and fix material costs in accordance with a predetermined price. Manufacturers of copper wire, for example, might be able to obtain an order based on the current price of copper. If they think the price of copper may rise before they can obtain their raw materials they can immediately cover their copper requirements by buying on the LME at the current price for delivery three months ahead, thus avoiding any risk of an increase in price.

For futures dealing to be undertaken the following conditions must apply:

(i) The commodity must be capable of being stored without deterioration for a reasonable period

(ii) The commodity must be capable of being graded for the purpose of providing a basis for description in the contract

(iii) The commodity must be tradable in its raw or semi-raw state

(iv) Producers and consumers must approve the concept of futures dealing

(v) There must be a free market in the commodity, with many buyers and sellers, making it impossible for a few traders to control the market and thus prevent perfect competition.

(c) Some terms used in futures contracts

(i) *Arbitrage.* The (usually) simultaneous purchase of futures in one market against the sale of futures in a different market to profit from a difference in price.

(ii) *Backwardation.* The backwardation situation exists when forward prices are less than current 'spot' ones.

(iii) *Contango.* A contango situation exists when forward prices are greater than current 'spot' ones.

(iv) *Force majeure.* The clause which absolves the seller or buyer from the contract due to events beyond his control, e.g. unavoidable export delays in producing countries due to strikes at the supplier's plant. *Note*: there is now no *force majeure* clause in a London Metal Exchange contract. Customers affected by a *force majeure* declared by a producer or refiner can always turn to the LME as a source of supply. Equally, suppliers can deliver their metal to the LME if their customers declare *force majeure*.

(v) *Futures.* Contracts for the purchase and sale of commodities for delivery some time in the future on an organised exchange and subject to all the terms and conditions included in the rules of that exchange.

(vi) *Hedging.* Hedging is the use of futures contracts to insure against losses due to the effect of price fluctuations on the value of stocks of a commodity either held or to be acquired. Basically this is done by establishing a position in the futures market opposite to one's position in the physical commodity. The operations of hedging can be described by a simplified example.

Example
(1) On 1 June, X (a manufacturer) buys stocks of copper value £1000 which he or she hopes to make into cablewire and sell on 1 August for £2000, of which £750 represents manufacturing costs and £250 profit.

(2) Price of this copper falls by 1 August to £750 so that he or she sells at £1750, i.e. he or she makes no profit.

(3) To insure against the situation in (2) the manufacturer, on 1 June, sells futures contract in copper for £1000.

(4) In August if the price remains stable he or she will buy at this price thus making a profit of £250 on his or her futures contract, which will offset any loss on manufacturing.

If the price rises to £1250 he or she will lose on his or her futures contract but this will be offset by gains on manufacturing. While trading refers to actual physical copper trading, a futures transaction is really dealing in price differences and the contract would be discharged by paying over or receiving the balance due.

(vii) Spot price. The price for immediate cash payment.
(viii) Spot month. The first deliverable month for which a quotation is available in the futures market.

12. METHODS OF COMMODITY DEALING

Dealing in commodities is a highly complex activity involving the possibility of heavy gains or losses. An undertaking buying large quantities of a commodity will therefore employ a specialist buyer who has made a specialist study of the commodity and its markets. Often commodity buying will be a separate department distinct from other purchasing operations. Where quantities or the undertaking are smaller a broker may be retained to procure commodity requirements, in effect subcontracting this aspect of purchasing.

Other approaches are designed to enable non-specialists to undertake commodity buying with the minimum of risk. These include:

(a) Time budgeting or averaging. This is an application of hand-to-mouth buying, in which supplies of the commodity are bought as required and no stocks are held. As supplies are always bought at the ruling price, losses are divided, but, of course, the prospect of windfall gains are obviated. This policy cannot be applied if it is necessary to carry inventory.

(b) Budgeting or £-cost averaging. This approach is based on spending a fixed amount of money in each period, e.g. monthly. The quantity purchased therefore increases when price falls and reduces when the price rises.

Example Assume the monthly requirements for commodity X are 100 tonnes, the average price of which, from experience, is estimated at £100. We therefore budget to spend £100 × 100 = £10,000 monthly. The price fluctuates as shown below.

Date	Cost per tonne	Amount spent	Tonnes purchased
Jan	£98	£10,000	102.04
Feb	£97	£10,000	103.09
March	£95	£10,000	105.26
April	£96	£10,000	104.16
May	£95	£10,000	105.26
June	£93	£10,000	107.52
July	£92	£10,000	108.69
Aug	£95	£10,000	105.26
Sept	£97	£10,000	103.00
Oct	£100	£10,000	100.00
Nov	£102	£10,000	98.03
Dec	£104	£10,000	96.15
		£120,000	1238.46

Average cost per tonne, total cycle $= \dfrac{£120,000}{1238.46} = £96.89$

Purchases over the total cycle exceed requirements by 38.46 tonnes.

There is thus an average saving of £3.11 per tonne.

(c) Volume timing of purchases. This approach is based on forward buying when prices are falling and hand-to-mouth buying when prices are rising. Its success depends on accurate forecasting of market trends.

Example Assume that the price of a commodity with a constant monthly requirement of 100 tonnes is between £100 and £120 per tonne. The buyer is authorised to purchase up to 3 months' supply.

In January, market intelligence is that the current price of £100 is likely to rise over the next three months to £120. An order is therefore placed for 300 tonnes at £100 per tonne.

In early March intelligence is that over the next 3 months, April-June, the price of £120 will further rise to £135. A further 300 tonnes are ordered at £120 per tonne. In early June it is forecast that prices will fall. For July, August, September and October we therefore buy one month's supply at £130, £125, £120 and £110 respectively. In September the forecast is of a further rise to £125. We therefore place a forward order for 3 months at £110.

The savings from forward buying on the upswing and hand-to-mouth buying on the down swing is shown below.

Date	Quantity Purchased Tonnes	Price Paid per Tonne £	Market Price per Tonne £	Actual Cost £	Market Cost £
Jan	100	100	100	10,000	10,000
Feb	100	100	110	10,000	11,000
Mar	100	100	120	10,000	12,000
April	100	120	125	12,000	12,500

Continued from previous page

Date	Quantity Purchased Tonnes	Price Paid per Tonne £	Market Price per Tonne £	Actual Cost £	Market Cost £
May	100	120	130	12,000	13,000
June	100	120	135	12,000	13,500
July	100	130	130	13,000	13,000
Aug	100	125	125	12,500	12,500
Sept	100	120	120	12,000	12,000
Oct	100	110	110	11,000	11,000
Nov	100	110	120	11,000	12,000
Dec	100	110	125	11,000	12,500
	1200			136,500	145,000

$$\text{Average price paid per tonne over year} = \frac{£136,500}{1200} = £113.75$$

$$\text{Average market price per tonne} = \frac{£145,000}{1200} = £120.83$$

$$\text{Saving over total period} = \frac{\text{Average market price} - \text{Average price paid}}{\text{Average market price}}$$

$$= \frac{£120.83 - £113.75}{120.83} \times 100 = \frac{7.08}{120.83} \times 100 = 5.86\%$$

13. COMPONENT PARTS AND ASSEMBLIES

These may be either standard, e.g. a ball bearing, or specific, e.g. a casting made to the design of a particular customer. Standard components are, generally, readily available and have the advantages listed in 7:7.

Specific components:
(i) offer opportunities for liaison between design and purchasing regarding material costs, suppliers and alternatives
(ii) may be jointly developed by purchaser and supplier
(iii) may involve detailed negotiation over such aspects as tooling costs, learning curves, etc.
(iv) should always be subject to value analysis
(v) raise make-or-buy issues
(vi) can often be combined into sub-assemblies.

14. PRODUCTION MATERIALS AND BILLS OF MATERIALS

Bills of Materials (BOMs) are also referred to in 4:3c. A BOM:

(i) Lists all the components, including the quantities of each required to produce one unit of the finished product.

293

(ii) Enables a production schedule to be 'exploded' into a list of required items of all types, i.e. raw materials, components, assemblies, etc.

(iii) Enables the total number of each item needed for a production order to be checked against inventory to enable purchasing to determine:
- What items are in stock
- What items are not in stock and require to be purchased.
- What items and quantities need to be purchased to replenish stock.
- What is the 'net inventory', i.e. total inventory for each item minus the requirements of that item for a particular job.

(iv) BOMs can be either *single-level* or *indented*. A single-level BOM comprises only those subordinate components that are immediately required, i.e. *not* the components of the components, e.g. 5 wheels for a car. An indented bill of materials is a listing of the components from the end item all the way down to each item comprising the component and the total components in the product. Thus for a car an indented BOM would be

Item: 30,122 Wheel (5 required)
123 Wheel pressing $(1 \times 5$ required)
124 Tyres $(1 \times 5$ required)
082 Nuts $(4 \times 5$ required)
125 Cover $(1 \times 5$ required)

(v) A fully indented BOM is often used by production engineers to determine how the product is to be physically assembled and by management accountants for cost implosions.

(vi) A *bill of material processor* is a computer software package that organises and maintains linkages in the BOM files. It is the BOM processor that is used in MRP to pass the planned orders for a parent part to gross requirements for its components.

15. CONSUMABLES

(a) These are sub-divided by Risley [4] into operating supplies and maintenance, repair and overhaul items.

(i) Operating supplies are defined as 'consumable items used in the operations of the business enterprise', for example: stationery and office supplies, machine oil, fasteners, insecticides, fuels, small tools, packaging and wrapping materials.

(ii) Maintenance, repair and overhaul (MRO) items are defined as 'items which are needed repeatedly or recurrently to maintain the operational efficiency of the business', for example: electrical supplies, caretaking requirements, lubricants, paint, plumbing and a wide variety of repair parts or spares for plant and equipment.

These items have the following characteristics:

(b) Characteristics of consumables. Consumables and MRO items are, generally:

(i) Low cost, low risk items (with the exception of 'critical' items, e.g. some spares).
(ii) Pareto category C items.
(iii) Revenue items, usually relating to one financial period in contrast to capital items relating to many financial periods.
(iv) 'Called off' by the actual consumers against orders negotiated with approved suppliers by the purchasing function.
(v) Independent demand items suitable for fixed order and periodic stock control systems.
(vi) Purchased by one of the simplified procedures for small orders described in 4:**6**.
(vii) Linked to maintenance policies in the case of MRO items.

(c) Maintenance and replacement policies. Breakdowns and repairs can never be totally avoided but regular, systematic and thorough maintenance will reduce their number and consequential costs such as lost production, idle time and hold ups in respect of other production items. Pareto analysis can provide a useful guide as to where maintenance attention should be placed, i.e.

(i) Class A or critical items which are essential parts of the machine or system, whose failure would result in total breakdown with high repair and consequential costs.
(ii) Class B or major components but where failure would not result in stoppage of the total system.
(iii) Class C or minor components, the failure of which would not, in the short term, affect the overall process or system.

There are five approaches to planned maintenance aimed at keeping equipment or facilities in good operating condition:

- *Inspection* by visual means on a regular, planned basis.
- *Breakdown (or corrective) maintenance.* This approach actually waits for the item to breakdown and it is then repaired.
- *Preventive maintenance.* This is an overall approach that combines inspection, repair and regular servicing, based on a detailed plan.
- *Planned replacement.* This policy sets fixed times or dates when components or machines will be replaced irrespective of their condition.
- *Breakdown replacement.* This is a positive policy particularly appropriate for small items where maintenance costs would be disproportionately high or items that rapidly become obsolete.

(d) Purchasing and consumables. Apart from negotiating the actual purchase of consumables and MRO items the purchasing function can:

(i) Liaise with maintenance staff to ensure that information regarding the cost, availability and delivery times is available especially in respect of 'critical' items.
(ii) Advocate a policy of standardisation to avoid holding a variety of 'critical' spares.

(iii) Suggest alternatives, e.g. outsourcing of catering and cleaning can obviate the need to hold stocks of food and cleaning materials.

(iv) Minimise administrative and storage costs by the application of small order procedures and direct requisitioning by users against 'call-off' contracts, etc.

(v) Analyse proposed maintenance contracts offered by suppliers and advise whether or not these should be accepted.

16. CONSTRUCTION SUPPLIES AND BILLS OF QUANTITIES

(a) Construction supplies. These differ in a number of respect from supplies purchased for manufacturing and service undertakings.

(i) Construction supplies are purchased for use on a site which may be distant from the office from which orders are placed or even in another country altogether.

(ii) Many construction supplies have a high bulk relative to their value, e.g. bricks, steel. Because of the high cost of transport it is desirable that construction supplies are procured as near as possible to the site where they will be used.

(iii) With many construction schemes the purchasing department will probably be asked to negotiate agreements for electricity, gas and water supplies and, occasionally, for sewage or effluent disposal.

(iv) Specification of construction supplies will often be on the basis of

- Instructions given by the client to an architect or civil engineer.
- Architects specifications

These specifications are often stated in the Bill of Quantities.

(v) In the interests of security it is important that purchased supplies should be delivered to site as closely as possible to the time they will be used.

(vi) Because of the remoteness of the site from the contractor's office, procedures for the recording of supplies received and issued will have to be agreed between the contractor's purchasing department and site engineer.

(vii) Some construction supplies may be 'free issue' supplies, i.e. items provided by the client for use in connection with a construction project that is being undertaken on the client's behalf.

(viii) Subcontracting is an important aspect of purchasing for construction contracts, e.g. contracts for foundations, drainage, air conditioning, lift installation, ventilation, structural steelwork, etc.

(ix) Some construction supplies involve intra-company purchasing. Thus a construction company may also own stone, sand and gravel quarries which supply other companies within the group.

(x) Supplies may be transferred from one site or construction contract to another. It is therefore important to know what supplies are available at each site.

(xi) Some discretion to arrange for the supply of materials and services must

be allowed to the site engineer, e.g. discretion to hire plant for use in connection with a contract from a local plant hire undertaking. All such orders should be notified to the contractor's purchasing department to ensure that orders are placed and amounts due to suppliers duly paid.

(b) Bills of quantities

(1) *Definition. Bills of quantities are documents, prepared by quantity surveyors from drawings and specifications prepared by architects or engineers, setting out as priceable items the detailed requirements of the work and the quantities involved.*

(2) *Contents of bills of quantities.* Bills of quantities are usually formidable documents running to many pages and incorporating schedules of conditions of contract in addition to the specifications of labour and materials required for the particular construction project. A typical bill of quantities will fall into six main sections:

Section 1 Preliminary items and general conditions. This will set out the terms and conditions of the contract and responsibilities of the contractor, architect and other parties involved in the contract together with provision for the settlement of disputes arising from the contract.

Section 2 Trade preambles. This sets out the general requirements relating to such aspects of a construction contract as:
- Excavation and earthwork
- Concrete work
- Brickwork and blockwork
- Roofing
- Woodwork
- Structural steelwork
- Metalwork
- Plumbing installation
- Foul drainage above ground
- Holes/chases/covers/supports for services
- Electrical and heating installations
- Floor, wall and ceiling finishes
- Glazing
- Painting and decorating.

Section 3 Demolition and spot items. Foundation work

Section 4 General alteration and refurbishment work

Section 5 Provisional sums and contingencies.

} Set out the quantities of work to be done

Section 6 Grand summary.

Typical extracts from Sections 2 and 4 relating to plumbing installation are shown in Figs 10.1 and 10.2.

(3) *The purpose of bills of quantities.* Bills of quantities:

	SECTION 2	Trade Preambles
Clause	**PLUMBING INSTALLATION**	

R1 | **General**
Before pricing the Specification, Contractors tendering are requested to visit the site, peruse the drawings and make themselves fully conversant with the nature of the works for which they are tendering.

HOT AND COLD WATER

GENERAL INFORMATION/REQUIREMENTS

R2 | THE INSTALLATION
- Drawing reference: See Architect's layout.
- Cold water: Mains fed.
- Hot water - direct system(s): Unvented direct water storage cylinder.
  Heat sources(s): Immersion heaters
  Control: Thermostat on immersion heater.
- Other requirements: Remove existing pipework.
    Allow for general builders work.

R3 | ELECTRICAL WORK in connection with the installation is not included, and will be carried out by the Electrical contractor. Provide all information necessary for the completion of such work.

R4 | SERVICE CONNECTIONS are covered elsewhere by a Provisional Sum.

R5 | FUEL FOR TESTING: Costs incurred in the provision of fuel for testing and commissioning the installation are to be included in Clause B40 Section 1.

GENERAL TECHNICAL REQUIREMENTS

R6 | PIPELINE SIZES: Calculate sizes to suit the probable simultaneous demand for the building and to ensure:
- A water velocity of not more than 1.3 m/s for hot water and 2.0 m/s for cold water.
- Suitable discharge rates at draw-off points.
- A filling time for the cold water storage cistern of not more than 1 hour(s).

R7 | INSTALLATION GENERALLY:
- Install, test and commission the hot and cold water systems so that they comply with B.S. 6700, water supply bye-laws, and the requirements of this section to provide a system free from leaks and the audible effects of expansion, vibration and water hammer.
- All installation work to be carried out by qualified operatives.
- Store all equipment, pipework components and accessories in original packaging in dry conditions,
  Protect plastics pipework from prolonged exposure to sunlight. Wherever practicable retain protective wrappings until Practical Completion.
- Securely fix equipment, components and accessories in specified/approved locations, parallel or perpendicular to the structure of the building unless specified otherwise, using fixing brackets/mountings, etc. recommended for the purpose by the equipment manufacturer.
- In locations where moisture is present or may occur, use corrosion resistant fittings/fixings and avoid contact between dissimilar metals by use of suitable washers, gaskets, etc.
- All equipment, pipework, components, valves, etc. forming the installation to be fully accessible for maintenance, repair or replacement unless specified or shown otherwise.

Fig 10.1 Extract from bill of quantities

Item	PLUMBING INSTALLATION			
			£	p

GENERAL

A Bring to site and remove from site on completion)
all plant required for the work in this section.   )   Item

B Maintain on site all plant required for the work
in this Section   ..   Item

*Installation as shown in the following sections
to be carried out to the Architects drawings
and Specification*

C Soil and waste pipes.   ..   Item

D Hot and cold water supply including all fittings
and rising mains.   ..   Item

E Dry riser installation.   ..   Item

F Sanitary fittings.   ..   Item

G Allow for carrying out all Builder's work in   )
Connection with the Plumbing Installations as   )
described including cutting and forming chases,   )
cutting and forming holes, forming ducts   )
through walls and floors, timber support battens,   )
all dire stopping to walls and floors and everything)
necessary to complete the whole of the works to   )
the reasonable satisfaction of the Architect.   )   Item

H Allow for testing and commissioning to plumbing   )
installation including obtaining any certificates to)
be handed to the Architect.   )   Item

J Hand to the Architect at Practical Completion of   )
the Works copies of the manufacturer's operation   )
and maintenance instructions together with two   )
sets of 'as fitted' drawings   )   Item

**PLUMBING INSTALLATIONS
CARRIED TO SUMMARY FOLIO NO. 4/63**

£

Fig 10.2 Extract from bill of quantities

- Enable tenderers to show against each item on the unpriced bill of quantities a price per unit covering labour, materials, overhead and profit. When totalled in the 'Grand Summary' the items will provide the tender price for the contract.
- Enable the quantity surveyor, on receipt of the successful tender, to ensure that the contractor has made no serious errors that could cause complications at a later date.
- Avoid the inclusion by the tenderer of a large amount for contingencies.
- Assist in verifying the valuation of variations due to changes in design requested or agreed by the client after the contract has been placed.

(4) *Purchasing and construction contracts.* The purchasing function will be involved at both the tendering and implementation stages. At the tendering stages the purchasing function will provide estimators with prices for materials and subcontracted work on which the tender can be based. Since tendering is highly competitive the prices obtained by purchasing can determine whether a tender is competitive or otherwise. Of particular importance will be:

- Ensuring that transport costs for materials are kept low by purchasing built items from sources as near as possible to the point of use.
- Negotiating with subcontractors.
- Obtaining the best quality commensurate with the life of the item where tenderer/contractor has discretion over what is bought.
- Effecting suitable delivery arrangements to ensure that supplies are delivered to site as near as possible on time to their use in the project.
- Negotiation of quantity and trade discounts.
- Control of all purchasing undertaken by site engineers etc.
- Control of surplus supplies and transfer to other contracts where it is economical to do so.

17. GOODS FOR RESALE IN WHOLESALING AND RETAILING

(a) Definitions

(i) Merchandising enterprises are wholesalers or retailers that buy completed products for resale. They are therefore different from manufacturing enterprises that engage in activities involving the physical conversion or transformation of inputs into finished products.

(ii) Wholesalers sell to retailers, other wholesalers or to individual users but not in significant amounts to ultimate consumers.

(iii) Retailers are involved in selling, renting and providing products and services to ultimate consumers for personal, non-business use.

(b) Forms of wholesaling. Wholesaling may be undertaken either by independent wholesaling intermediaries or by manufacturers who sell directly to retailers through sales branches, or depots or renting space in independently owned warehouses. Wholesalers may be:

(*i*) *General merchandisers* – carrying a broad assortment of goods.

(*ii*) *Speciality merchandisers* – carrying an extensive assortment of goods within a specified range of products.

(*iii*) *Rack jobbers* – who replenish display racks in retail stores with goods sold on a consignment or sale or return basis.

(*iv*) *Cash and carry* – sell to buyers who visit the warehouse, pay cash for purchases and take away the goods bought.

(*v*) *Drop shippers* – solicit orders from retailers which they arrange to be delivered directly from the manufacturer. These are strictly agents rather than wholesalers.

(c) Wholesaling functions. Wholesalers carry out logistical, transactional and facilitating functions.

(*i*) *Logistical functions*
- Breaking of bulk, i.e. buying in bulk from the manufacturer and selling in smaller quantities to retailers.
- Storing merchandise in convenient locations.
- Transportation of merchandise to retail outlets.

(*ii*) *Transactional functions*
- Buying goods including importing.
- Sales calls on retailers.

(*iii*) *Facilitating functions*
- Provision of sales services to manufacturers.
- Provision of market information and research to retailers.
- Occasionally preparation of goods for sale by grading, blending, etc.
- Assisting the cash flow of both manufacturers and retailers by paying the former promptly and granting credit to the latter.

(d) Forms of retailing. British retailers are usually grouped into three main categories [5]:

- Independent retailers, including small chain stores with nine or fewer branches.
- Multiple retailers with ten or more branches but excluding retail co-operative societies.
- Retail co-operative societies.

Within these categories retail outlets can be classified into store and non-store.

(*i*) *Store retailers* include:

- *Speciality stores* – carrying a wide assortment of a narrow range of products, e.g. books, pharmaceuticals, clothing
- *Department stores* – carrying a wide variety of product lines each of which is operated as a separate department.

- *Supermarkets* – large, low-cost, low-margin, high-volume, self-service stores carrying a wide variety of food and other household products.
- *Superstores and Hypermarkets* – larger than supermarkets and a wider range of goods including furniture, appliances, clothing. These offer discount prices and operate like warehouses.
- *Service businesses* – where the product line is actually a service, e.g. banks, restaurants, dry-cleaners, travel agents.
- *Catalogue showrooms* – selling a wide selection of high-mark-up, fast-moving, brand-name goods at discount prices.

(ii) Non-store retailers include:

- *Direct mail* – send out letters, samples, offers, etc. to people on their mailing lists.
- *Mail order* – send out either general merchandise or speciality mail order catalogues to agents or customers.
- *Telemarketing* – the use of free call numbers to receive orders from television and radio advertisements or unsolicited phone calls to prospective customers.
- *Door to door retailing* – products such as Avon cosmetics, Tupperware.
- *Automatic vending* – cigarettes, beverages, records, etc.

(e) Retailing functions. Retailing is the final link in the distributive chain and, as Baker [6] points out, is responsible for several important marketing functions including:

(i) The physical movement and storage of goods.
(ii) The transfer of title to goods.
(iii) The provision of information to consumers concerning the nature and uses of goods.
(iv) The standardisation, grading and final processing of goods.
(v) The provision of ready availability.
(vi) The assumption of risk concerning the precise nature and extent of demands.
(vii) The financing of inventory and extension of credit to customers.

(f) Trade enterprises. Van Weele [7] uses the term 'trade companies' to refer to all types of wholesale and retail undertakings. Not all such undertakings are, however, companies. Accordingly the term trade enterprises will be used for convenience for the remainder of this aspect of purchasing.

(g) Buying in trade enterprises. This is similar in many respects to buying for industrial organisations. The standard purchasing definition of purchasing as 'buying the right quality in the right quantity at the right price from the right source' is, in fact, widely attributed to Gordon Selfridge, the founder of the famous London store.

Evans [8], however, has drawn attention to some differences between industrial and retail buyers:

(i) Industrial buyers are generally told what to buy and in what quantities. Retail buying roles include merchandise selection and range building.

(ii) Industrial buyers tend to analyse the supplier's material and labour costs and then negotiate with the supplier on an acceptable contribution to his fixed costs and profit. Retail buyers negotiate down to a cost price which provides an acceptable selling price and target margin.

(iii) Industrial buyers in appropriate industries use 'just-in-time' agreements as a means of improving return on capital employed. Retail buyers generally find JIT to be inappropriate and find a consignment stock approach of greater relevance. With the consignment stock approach the supplier retains ownership of the goods until they have been sold to the customer by the retailer. The supplier therefore only receives payment when the goods are sold, an arrangement which helps the retailer to try new lines without investing in stock.

Other special characteristics of buying in trade enterprises include:

(i) Purchasing and selling are closely integrated – 'Goods well bought are half sold'.

(ii) Due to the extra responsibilities mentioned in *(i)* and *(ii)* above buying in trade enterprises is a high profile activity.

(iii) Because of short lead times and stock turnover the outcome of purchasing decisions in trade enterprises is easy to assess. 'We know on Friday whether Monday's purchases were good or not'.

(iv) Different buying considerations apply according to whether the goods to be purchased are 'staple', i.e. in regular demand, or 'fashion' in which case demand is subject to 'sales cycles'. The four stages of a sales cycle are (1) *distinctiveness* when the product is custom made or produced in small quantities; (2) *copying* when additional manufacturers produce larger quantities of the product; (3) *mass fashion* when the concept has become very popular and manufacturers are geared up to mass production; (4) the decline stage when consumers start moving to other fashions. Some products are also 'seasonal'.

(v) Merchandise inventories must be adequate to prevent loss of sales and customer goodwill through stockouts but small enough to reduce losses through excessive holding costs and the need for markdowns.

(vi) Developments such as bar coding and EPOS (Electronic Point of Sale) (see 5:**12** and **15**) are helping to reduce stocks, improve service levels and integrate warehouse and branch inventory policy.

(h) The aims of buying for trade enterprises. These include

(i) To meet customer demands satisfactorily.

(ii) To improve profits and improve returns on capital.

(iii) To negotiate purchases on the most favourable terms and against predetermined profit margin targets.

(iv) To 'bring some excitement into the store' by the introduction of new lines, sales promotion, etc.

(v) To manage stock positively by optimising investment in inventory,

minimising slow-selling merchandise and keeping in mind the relationship between stocks and sales in achieving profit goals.

(i) The qualities of a trade buyer. Evans [9] in a controversial statement declares that 'It is an undeniable fact that retail buyers are more entrepreneurial than their industrial counterparts' and states 'as a sweeping generalisation that they tend to be more creative, profit conscious and better negotiators'. Cox and Brittain [10] suggest that retail buyers should be able to

(i) Recognise customer needs, even though customers themselves are unaware of them.
(ii) Know thoroughly the merchandise they deal with, maintaining a balanced assessment.
(iii) Be good judges of quality.
(iv) Be good judges of resaleability.
(v) Be able to recognise new and profitable lines ('Flair' is required particularly in textiles, toys and other fashion goods).
(vi) Liaise effectively with suppliers, stores management and other sections of the merchandising and marketing departments, e.g. advertising, sales promotion.
(vii) Plan effectively in numerate terms.

McGoldrick [11] states that because of the complexity of retail buying decisions buyers need to be 'effectively able to assimilate large volumes of information, be highly competent in the mathematical appraisal of supplier's terms and also be effective communicators and negotiators'.

Trade buying is a subject area in its own right. For this reason and because of the many forms that trade enterprises can take it is impracticable to do more than refer to three further aspects of purchasing in trade enterprises, namely: who buys?, what to buy and how much to buy.

(j) Who buys? As with their industrial counterparts purchasing in trading enterprises may be centralised or decentralised. The former is associated with buying for wholesalers and independent retailers, the latter with multiple stores and co-operative societies. Some enterprises also use the services of external buying organisations. Within such forms of organisation buying may be undertaken by:

(1) *The owner* – as in small single trader enterprises.

(2) *Specialist individual buyers* who possess the qualities outlines in **(h)** above. Such buyers may be:
  • responsible for both the buying and selling and therefore the profit of a centre, branch, department, etc.
  • responsible only for buying on the premise that it is desirable to separate the buying and selling functions.

(3) *A buying team.* This is similar to a buying centre in an industrial enterprise (see 9:**20**). At Marks and Spencer, for example, the buying team includes a selector, merchandiser, technologist and distributors or allocators.

The *selectors* choose cloth, design and style and are responsible for offering an attractive choice to customers. They travel extensively keeping abreast of the latest fashion trends, carry out comparative shopping to monitor competitors and work closely with both manufacturers and the company's design departments.

The *merchandisers* are responsible for negotiating prices, estimating the quantities and scheduling the production with manufacturers and suppliers. They determine the budget for a range, its distribution to stores and are constantly reacting to changing sales patterns to keep sales as high and stock as low as possible.

The *technologists* develop and monitor specifications and quality control systems. They are technical advisers to the selectors and merchandisers and to manufacturers who may run into production problems.

The *distributors* allocate finished goods to stores on the basis of estimated future sales in relation to the available stock. This function is becoming increasingly automated as computers take over.

Once a range is formulated within the department's budget the merchandiser decides which manufacturers will produce particular lines and styles. Merchandisers know how much each manufacturer can cope with or have the special skills required. The merchandiser agrees a production programme with the manufacturer, detailing quantities required and delivery dates and contracts are signed.

The organisation of a typical buying group at Marks and Spencer is shown in Fig 10.3.

(k) What to buy. This is a complex subject. Decisions on what to buy tend to centre on:

(1) *The market to be served*, i.e. expensive, middle range or inexpensive merchandise or a mixture of the three. Factors to be considered in deciding the quality of merchandise to be carried include:

- The market to be targeted, i.e. what quality is demanded.
- Competition in the market.
- The store image and location
- Stock turnover required.
- Profitability.
- Whether the stock manufacturer's brands are supported by national advertising, deal brands or both.
- The need to employ skilled knowledgeable sales staff if quality products are to be sold.
- Customer perceived goods and benefits, e.g. inexpensive merchandise tends to be bought primarily for its functional uses. High quality merchandise is bought for additional reasons such as prestige, style, exclusiveness, etc.

(2) *Innovation*, i.e. the extent to which new goods and lines should be marketed. Factors to be considered in deciding whether or not to stock new products include:

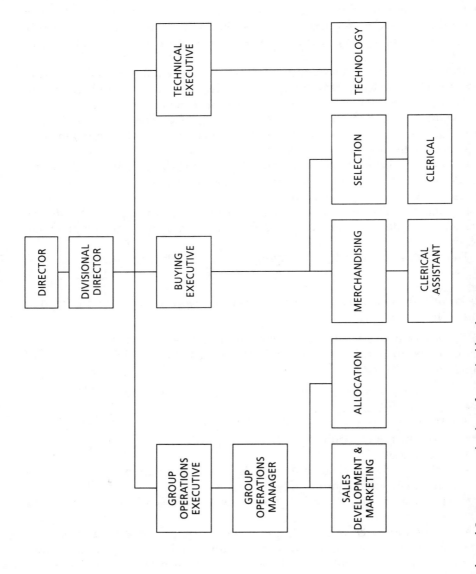

Fig 10.3 Marks and Spencer organisation of a typical buying group

- The market to be targeted, e.g. conservative or progressive.
- Potential for sales growth.
- Fashion trends and the stage at which a product has reached in the sales cycle.
- Effect of new goods on existing products. In general old goods should be dropped when sales are low.
- Competition – whether the store should 'take the lead' or follow competitors.
- Store image – innovativeness should be consistent.
- Risk including investment costs, opportunity cost and supplier relations.
- Profitability – potential short and long term returns.

(3) *The width and assortment of goods to be stocked.* Assortment strategies may be:

- Wide and deep – many categories of goods and a large assortment in each category.
- Wide and shallow – as above but with a limited assortment in each category.
- Narrow and deep – few categories of goods but a large assortment in each category.
- Narrow and shallow – few categories of goods and a limited assortment in each category.

(4) *Product knowledge of what goods are available and the extent to which stock requires replenishment.* Such information can be obtained from:

- Information provided by manufacturers, wholesalers or agents through their representatives.
- Trade exhibitions and seminars.
- Trade journals.
- Observation of what is being sold by competitors.
- Customer enquiries.
- Historical data obtained from past experience or the analysis of statistical trends.
- On-line information provided by EPOS technology.

(l) Brands. A brand name is any word or device (design, shape, sound or colour) that is used to distinguish one company's products from a competitors [13]. Branding aims to:

(i) Give a product a character or image firstly, through the name then through the packaging and thirdly through advertising.
(ii) Create a monopoly or at least some form of imperfect competition so that the brand owner can obtain some of the benefits which accrue to a monopoly particularly those related to decreased price competition.

Mercer [14] points out that the 'brand', whatever its derivation, is a very important investment for any organisation. Rank Hovis McDougall, for example, value their international brands at anything up to twenty times their annual earnings.

Brands may be:

(i) *Manufacturer brands* produced and controlled by manufacturers and supported by manufacturer advertising.

(ii) *Dealer brands* which have names designated by wholesalers or retailers. These are more profitable to retailers, and less expensive to customers and lead to retailer rather than manufacturer loyalty. Dealer brands are exclusive and cannot be sold by competing retailers. Where the retailer has a strong identity, e.g. Marks and Spencer St Michael clothing, this own brand may be able to compete against the strongest brand leaders.

(iii) *Generics*. These are unbranded goods which have little or no expensive advertising or packaging and are generally the least expensive to the customer. In the case of drugs manufacturers, brands and generics may be identical in quality.

Trade buyers, especially in the retail sector, have to decide what mix of manufacturer and dealer brands and generics to stock.

(m) How much to buy. Two important concepts are planned purchases and 'open to buy'.

(1) *Planned purchases*. These may be calculated for a particular period by either of the following formulae:

Planned purchases   =   Planned sales + Planned reductions + Planned increase in stock, or – Planned decrease in stock.

Planned purchases   =   Planned stock at end of period + Planned sales + Planned reductions – Stock in hand at beginning of period.

To use either formula the buying team will have to have decided in money terms or value:

(i) Anticipated sales for the period

(ii) Stock in hand at the beginning of the period.

(iii) Desired stock in hand at the end of the period.

(iv) Planned reductions in the value of stock, i.e. 'markdowns' due to errors in buying, or stores promotional policies, e.g. 'sales to attract custom'.

(v) Planned initial mark-ups.

Examples

Formula 1 – For October 19.....

Planned sales		£20,000	
Planned reductions, i.e.		£2,000	
Markdowns	£1,800		
Shortages	200		
			£22,000
Stock in hand 1 October		£22,000	
Planned stock 31 October		£44,000	
Planned increase in stock			£4,000
Planned purchases			£26,000

Formula 2 – Also applied to October

Planned stock 31 October	£44,000
Planned sales	£20,000
Planned reductions	2,000
Total	£66,000
Stock in hand 1 October	£40,000
Planned purchases	£26,000

(2) *Open to buy.* This may be defined as *the amount or value of merchandise in terms of retail prices or at cost which a buyer is open to receive into stock during a certain period on the basis of the formulated plans.* It may be regarded as the difference between planned purchases and purchase commitments already made by a buyer for a given time period, usually a month. It is therefore the amount that the buyer has left to spend during the period. Obviously the amount to buy balance is reduced whenever a purchase is made. Open to buy is always recorded at cost.

Example Assume the planned purchases for October are £26,000 at *retail price.* Purchases already made amount to £18,000. The open-to-buy figure at retail value is therefore £8,000. To calculate the open-to-buy figure at cost price, the figure of £8,000 must be multiplied by the trader's merchandise costs (or cost of goods sold) as a percentage of selling price. If we assume these to be 60% then:

$$\text{Open-to-buy at cost price} = £8{,}000 \times \frac{60}{100} = £4{,}800$$

The open-to-buy approach has two significant strengths:

(*i*) It avoids under- or over-buying by establishing a specified relationship between stock in hand and planned sales.

(*ii*) It helps a trader to adjust merchandise purchases to reflect changes in sales and markdowns.

(*iii*) But sometimes the open-to-buy figure must be exceeded when actual demand exceeds sales forecasts.

References

[1] Marrian J. *Marketing characteristics of industrial goods and buyers* in Wilson (Ed) *The Marketing of Industrial Products.* Hutchinson 1965, Ch 2, pp 10-23.

[2] Department of Trade and Industry. *Terotechnology Check List No 4 for Purchasing Personnel,* June 1976. (Now out of print).

[3] Adapted from Risley G. *Modern Industrial Marketing.* McGraw Hill, 1972. pp 24–25.

[4] Adapted from Risley G. *Modern Industrial Marketing.* McGraw Hill, 1972. pp 24–25.

[5] Barker M J. *Marketing.* 4th edition, Macmillan, 1990, Ch 10. p 164.

[6] Barker M J. *Marketing.* 4th edition, Macmillan, 1990, Ch 10. p 158.

[7] Van Weele A J. *Purchasing Management.* Chapman and Hall, 1994. Ch 15, p 248.

[8] Evans E. *Retail buying. Journal of Retail and Distribution Management,* Sept/Oct 1989, pp 15–16.

[9] Evans E. *Retail buying. Journal of Retail and Distribution Management,* Sept/Oct 1989, pp 15–16.

[10] Cox R and Brittain. *Retail Management,* Pitman, 1991. Ch 10, p 110.
[11] McGoldrick P J. *Retail Marketing.* McGraw Hill, 1990, Ch 7. pp 189–190.
[12] Marks and Spencer, *Textiles, Spinning a Yarn* (undated).
[13] Berkowitz E N, Kevin R A and Rudelius W A. *Marketing.* Irwin, 1989. Glossary p 687.
[14] Mercer D. *Marketing.* Blackwell, 1993. Ch 6, pp 275–276.

Progress test 10

1. Give examples of six types of industrial equipment.

2. What are the main characteristics of capital expenditure?

3. List some advantages of buying used equipment.

4. Describe 'pay-back', 'average rate of return' and 'net present value' as means of evaluating capital investments.

5. What factors should be considered when selecting a supplier of capital equipment?

6. Define 'leasing'.

7. What are the advantages and disadvantages of leasing?

8. What are 'sensitive commodities'?

9. Explain what is meant by 'futures dealing'.

10. What is 'hedging'?

11. Distinguish between '£ cost averaging' and 'volume timing of purchasing' in connection with commodity dealing.

12. What is a BOM and what are its purposes?

13. How may consumables be classified?

14. Describe the contributions other than their actual acquisition that the purchasing function can make in respect of consumables and MRP items.

15. In what respects do construction supplies differ from supplies purchased for use in manufacturing and service undertakings?

16. Define and outline the contents of a bill of quantities..

17. What are the main types of (a) wholesalers and (b) retailers?

18. Discuss some of the differences between retail and industrial buyers..

19. What qualities are important in a trade buyer?

20. Define the term 'brand name'.

21. State one formula for the calculation of planned purchases.

22. Explain the open-to-buy approach to trade purchases.

23. Explain the relative advantage of buy, hire or lease when considering the acquisition of any major item of road transport equipment.
(CIPS. *Purchasing and Supply Management III, Logistics* (1992))

24. Explain the different criteria which need to be considered by a retail buyer in selecting new products.
(CIPS. *Retail Merchandise Management* (1992))

25. Explain the difficulties which face a fashion retailer in achieving the desired balance between the costs of holding stock and the costs of running out of stock.
(CIPS. *Retail Merchandise Management* (1992))

26. Explain the reasons why it may be claimed that retail EPOS systems are crucial to protecting margins and providing a competitive edge.
(CIPS. *Retail Merchandise Management* (1992))

27. Assess the importance of new product decisions by a retail buyer.
(CIPS. *Retail Merchandise Management* (1993))

28. The supermarket retailer and the grocery retailer are faced with a large and ever growing range of products and supplies. Explain the factors which need to be considered in the selection of an acceptable supplier.
(CIPS. *Retail Merchandise Management* (1994))

29. Your company is considering the purchase of a new item of plant, the capital cost of which is approximately £10,000. The item would be expected to have a useful life of 5 years and to produce an average income of £3,000 a year after deduction of operating and maintenance costs. Its residual value after 5 years would be nil.
   (a) Describe the possible methods which you would use in order to evaluate whether or not your company should proceed with the investment.
   (b) State which method you would recommend should be used, giving your reasons.
   (c) Show how you would allow in the evaluation for the fact that the

figures, especially those for earnings, are only estimates and could be wrong.

(CIPS. *Project and Contracts Management* (1994))

30. A regional supermarket chain plans to introduce a limited range of private brands. Explain the factors to be considered in the selection of this range of merchandise.

(CIPS. *Retail Merchandise Management* (1994))

11

CONTROLLING PRICES AND COSTS

1. PRICE

Price can be defined as the value of a commodity or service measured in terms of the standard monetary unit. In comparing two quotations, price enables us to appraise the relative value offered by each supplier.

Economic theory shows that demand and supply are balanced by the influence of price, the equilibrium price indicating the point at which demand and supply are equal. The equilibrium price can be represented diagrammatically as in Fig 11.1 in which $D_1 - D_1$ is the demand curve indicating quantities demanded at various prices, $S_1 - S_1$ is the supply curve indicating quantities demanded at various prices, and P_1 is the equilibrium price where demand and supply will be balanced.

At a particular moment in time the market price may differ from the equilibrium price because the effect of temporary influences may not have had the chance to work themselves out, but when these factors have stabilised, a normal, i.e. equilibrium, price will apply. In the above analysis the shape of the demand

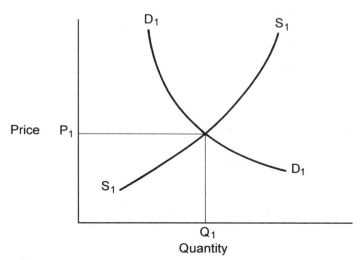

Fig 11.1 Equilibrium curve

and supply curves will be influenced by 'elasticity' or the degree of responsiveness of demand or supply to changes in price. Where a slight change in price will cause a substantial change in demand, then demand is said to be *elastic*. Demand is *inelastic* where a substantial change in price makes little difference to the amount demanded.

$$\text{Price elasticity of demand} = \frac{\% \text{ change in quantity demanded}}{\% \text{ change in price}}$$

Demand is likely to be less elastic where the following conditions obtain:

(*i*) There are few or no substitutes or competitors.

(*ii*) There is 'buyer inertia', i.e. buyers are slow to change their buying habits and search for alternative sources or lower prices.

(*iii*) Buyers do not notice or fail to challenge the higher price.

If demand is elastic suppliers will consider reducing their price since a lower price will result in enhanced revenue.

2. THE CONDITIONS FOR PERFECT COMPETITION

The above theory is based on the concept of 'perfect' competition. For perfect competition to exist the following conditions must apply:

(*i*) The item dealt in must be homogeneous so that a buyer is indifferent regarding the seller from whom he makes his purchase, e.g. an absence of trade or proprietary names.

(*ii*) The item must be easily transportable from one place to another.

(*iii*) There must be many buyers and sellers so that the former cannot artificially restrict demand or the latter supply.

(*iv*) There should be an absence of preferential treatment or discrimination of or against buyers and sellers.

(*v*) Easy communication must exist between buyers and sellers so that they are immediately aware of what is happening anywhere in the market.

Under perfect competition there is only one price at which the entire quantity available can be sold.

3. IMPERFECT COMPETITION AND MONOPOLY

While perfect competition applies in the commodity markets as outlined in Chapter 9, most buyers operate under conditions of imperfect competition. Under imperfect competition there is no single selling price for an item. Imperfect competition may take several forms according to the number of suppliers and the ease with which additional suppliers may enter the market. The most common forms of imperfect competition are:

Type	No. of suppliers	Entry of suppliers into the market
(a) Monopoly	One	No entry
(b) Oligopoly (*oli*, the Greek word for a few)	Few	Limited entry
(c) Monopolistic competition	Many	Competition between suppliers

It would be impracticable to deal with the effect of each of these conditions on demand, supply and price, and, in any case, a full treatment is contained in any standard textbook of economics. Buyers should remember that even a monopolistic supplier is not all-powerful. He or she can control the price or the quantity sold but not both, and is thus subject to the 'sovereignty' of the consumer. If he or she overexploits their monopoly power they will provoke a search for alternative products. Monopolies and restrictive trading may also give rise to intervention by central government.

4. UK COMPETITION LEGISLATION

Buyers should be aware of current legislation which provides machinery for the scrutiny of certain structural and uncompetitive situations which may operate against the public interest. These relate mainly to monopolies, mergers and restrictive trade practices.

(a) Monopolies. Under the Fair Trading Act 1973 the Secretary of State and the Director of Fair Trading have discretionary powers to refer to the Monopolies and Mergers Commission the supply or acquisition of goods and services in the UK where it appears that a monopoly situation exists. In general, a monopoly situation qualifying for investigation exists where a company or a group of companies accounts for at least 25 per cent of the relevant market, whether as buyer or seller.

If, as a result of their investigation, the MMC find that a monopoly situation exists and has particular effects adverse to the public interest, the Trade Secretary may exercise his wide-ranging powers to make an order for the company to cut its prices and/or implement the Commissioner's recommendations.

(b) Mergers. Also under the Fair Trading Act 1973 the Secretary of State may refer to the MMC for investigation mergers, if they are in contemplation or during the six months after they have taken place, where the gross value of assets being transferred exceeds £5 million or where the merger would create or enhance 25 per cent or more of the relevant market in the UK or a substantial part of the UK.

(c) Restrictive trade practices. The Restrictive Trade Practices Act 1976 (as supplemented by the Restrictive Trade Practices Act 1977) provides for the registration and subsequent judicial investigation by the Restrictive Practices Court of agreements between two or more persons carrying on business in the

UK in the supply of goods or services under which certain types of restriction are accepted. These restrictions include such matters as prices to be charged, terms and conditions of supply, and persons or areas to be supplied.

Any agreement which contains relevant restrictions must be registered with the Director General of Fair Trading before the date on which any restriction accepted under the agreement takes effect.

Heavy penalties can be imposed for contempt of court arising from the breach of an undertaking given to the Restrictive Practices Court. In December 1980 the British Steel Corporation was fined £50,000 and ordered to pay substantial costs. In an earlier case four manufacturers of concrete pipes were fined a total of £185,000 with estimated costs of £500,000 for breaking undertakings not to fix prices nor to tender collusively.

(d) The Competition Act 1980. This Act, which applies to companies with an annual turnover of more than £10 million or companies with a smaller turnover controlling more than 25 per cent of the market, *inter alia*, provides:

> for the control of anti-competitive practices in the supply and acquisition of goods and the supply and securing of services; to provide for references of certain public bodies and other persons to the Monopolies and Mergers Commission, to provide for the investigation of prices and charges by the Director General of Fair Trading; ... to amend and provide for the amendment of the Fair Trading Act 1973; to make amendments with respect to the Restrictive Trade Practices Act 1976.

An anti-competitive practice is defined in section 1(I) as 'a course of conduct which ... has or is intended to have or is likely to have the effect of restricting, distorting or preventing competition in connection with the production, supply or acquisition of goods in the United Kingdom or any part of it or the supply or securing or services in the UK or in any part of it'.

Examples of contracts or arrangements which may have anti-competitive effects include [1]:

> *(i) Exclusive supply arrangements.* A supplier agrees to supply only one customer, usually in a certain geographical area. The customer may, in turn, agree not to compete with the supplier's other customers in their exclusive territories.
> *(ii) Exclusive purchasing contracts.* A customer agrees to deal exclusively with a single supplier. Contracts which do not specify exclusivity, but require customers to buy a specified proportion of their requirements, or even a specified quantity in a given period, may also have anti-competitive effects.
> *(iii) Long-term supply contracts.* Such contracts which do not contain an exclusivity term can have a similar effect if customers are faced with onerous termination terms.
> *(iv) Restrictive terms.* Such terms occur in agreements which prevent or restrict customers from dealing with the contracted supplier's competitors, or where loyalty rebates and discounts inhibit them from switching business to another supplier.
> *(v) Selection distribution systems.* A supplier deals only with a certain number

of distributors, or only those who can meet set criteria on such matters as stock-holding levels or post sales service.

(vi) Tie-ins. A tie-in exists when a supplier of one product or service (the typing item) insists that customers must buy all or part of their requirements of another product or service (the tied item) from the same source.

(vii) Restrictions on the supply of parts or other inputs required by competitors.

(viii) Restrictive licensing policies. Such policies generally arise in connection with the licensing of intellectual property rights (patents, copyrights, trade marks, etc.) but they can occur more generally with the licensing of technology and know-how.

In broad outline the Office of Fair Trading will be able to investigate any company with the turnover or share of the market indicated above if it considers that that company is pursuing an anti-competitive trade practice. The formal investigation by the Office of Fair Trading may then be followed by a full-scale investigation by the Monopolies and Mergers Commission. After the Commission has completed the investigation the Trade Secretary may exercise his wide-ranging powers including the power to make an order for the company to cut its prices and/or implement the Commission's recommendations.

EEC competition legislation. Reference to such legislation is made in 9:**3**.

5. PRICE INFORMATION

Apart from commodity prices which are reported daily in newspapers such as *The Financial Times,* there are a number of ways in which a buyer can obtain information regarding prices, including catalogues and price lists; trade journals; databases; soliciting quotations; and tendering.

(a) Catalogues. Prices stated may be 'asking' prices and be subject to trade, cash or quantity discounts. A disadvantage is that catalogue prices rapidly become dated. Unless the catalogue is revised and reissued frequently, it will be necessary to ensure that price details are amended to prevent their being misleading.

(b) Trade journals. These provide useful, and often essential, information on prices applicable to particular commodities and industries. *Procurement Weekly,* published by the Chartered Institute of Purchasing and Supply, gives information regarding UK prices and price trends for a wide range of materials.

(c) Databases. For changeable factors such as price and availability on-line databases can provide up-to-date information and may be space-saving substitutes for large reference collections.

(d) Soliciting quotations. Prices are obtained by sending an enquiry to a number of selected suppliers. On receipt the quotations are compared, possibly using a

Contract No ....
Specification No ....
Title of Item ....

Client ....
Requisition No ....
Quantity reg ....

Drawing No ....
Enquiry No ....
Delivery reg ....

	Estimate	Vendor I	Vendor II	Vendor III	Vendor IV
Date of quotation					
Quotation ref					
Quotation valid to					
Price ex Works					
Price for packing					
Price for delivery					
Price for tooling					
Other extras					
Total price					
Terms for payment					
Delivery					
Comments					

Selected supplier ....
....
Name ....
Reason(s) for selection ....
....

Buyer ....
Date ....
Quotation discussed with ....
....

Fig 11.2 Quotation analysis form

quotation analysis form as illustrated in Fig 11.2. Factors in the evaluation of quotations are listed below.

(e) Tendering. This is described in Chapter 12.

6. PRICING AGREEMENTS

An important aspect of purchasing is the negotiation of the price to be paid to the supplier. Negotiation is the subject of Chapter 13 but it is useful to look at some factors that both suppliers and purchasers will consider when arriving at selling and buying prices respectively.

(a) Suppliers will consider:
(i) Their position in the market ranging from a monopoly position in which there is no product differentiation and the *seller* (subject to Government control) sets the price to pure competition in which the *market* sets the price.
(ii) The nature of demand for the product, i.e. is it elastic as will be the case where there are substitutes, or inelastic where demand is not affected by the price.
(iii) What the market or a particular purchaser will pay, i.e. charging what the market will bear.
(iv) Prices charged by competitors in general; higher prices can only be charged where it can be shown that the higher price is justified by product differentiation or other added value.
(v) The supplier's need for the business.
(vi) The potential long-term value of the purchaser to the supplier in terms of continuity of orders, promptness of payment, etc.
(vii) Is the product 'standard' or a 'special'.
(viii) The order volume – long production runs make lower prices possible.
(ix) The stage of the product in its life-cycle. In general, the earlier a product is in its life cycle, the higher will be the price.

(b) Purchasers will consider:
(i) The risk attached to the purchase and the method of pricing.
(ii) The position of the purchaser in the market: where the supplier is in a monopoly position the purchaser must, as previously stated, exploit the fact that except for products with an inelastic demand, the monopolist can control either the price or the quantity demanded, but not both.
(iii) The number of suppliers in the market and the possibility of alternative products.
(iv) Prices paid by competitors. This information may be difficult to obtain.
(v) Whether learning curve factors are applicable to the product.
(vi) What is the relationship between price and value in terms of competitive advantage.
(vii) The period for which the price is to be agreed.

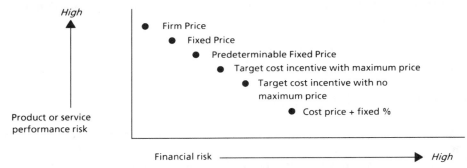

Fig 11.3 Risks of different pricing arrangements to the purchaser
(adapted from Behan [2])

(viii) What is a reasonable price based on a price analysis.

(ix) What quantities are likely to be involved over what period.

(x) What may be considered a 'fair price' from both the purchaser's and supplier's viewpoints.

All the above factors influence the selling or purchase price of a product. In practice price agreements are basically of two types, namely firm and cost type. As shown by Fig 11.3 firm and cost type agreements are at opposite ends of a continuum with a number of intermediate pricing arrangements aimed at reducing the risks to the purchaser.

(c) Firm price agreements are not subject to any provision for variation. Such agreements are most advantageous to purchasers since:

(i) All risks are borne by the supplier and the purchaser knows from the start what is to be paid.

(ii) Suppliers have the maximum incentive to produce efficiently and complete the work on time.

All cost savings *below* the price are kept by the supplier.

All costs incurred *above* the price are met by the supplier.

(iii) A minimum of administration is involved, e.g. auditing of costs.

The only possible disadvantage is that an unscrupulous supplier/contractor may attempt to enhance profits or reduce losses by 'taking it out of the job' to the long-term detriment of the product.

(d) Cost price agreements in which a fixed percentage is added to the production or construction cost are the most disadvantageous to the purchaser since:

(i) All financial risks accrue to the buyer.

(ii) Such agreements are difficult to administer since the suppliers' cost schedules require to be checked by financial and management accountants and possibly other specialist staff such as engineers, architects, quantity surveyors, etc.

7. VARIATIONS TO FIRM AND COST PRICE AGREEMENTS

In practice, factors such as the escalation in material costs, through inflation or wage rises, the duration of the contract, the need to provide incentives or the difficulty of measuring the work to be done make it desirable to reduce the risks to both purchaser and supplier by making variations to both firm and cost type contracts.

Some possible variations to firm and cost type agreements are shown in Table 11.1.

Table 11.1 Variations to firm and cost price agreements

Type of agreement	Characteristics	Application
(a) Fixed price	Once determined, price remains fixed until completion of the contract apart from changes in the scope of the contract.	Standard items from stock or for short-term production.
(b) Redeterminable fixed price	Fixed price is finally determined at an agreed point in the contract (e.g. 30 per cent completion) in the light of actual experience of production costs. The price may be retrospective to the commencement of the contract and prospective to completion.	Where development and production proceed concurrently.
(c) Target cost with maximum price	The maximum price is fixed including an agreed profit. Any reductions in cost are shared on an agreed percentage basis between purchaser and supplier.	Where target cost can be fixed with reasonable certainty but exact costs cannot be determined when contract is placed.

Example
Target price = £11 including £1 profit. Ceiling price = £12 with no profit. Cost savings shared 80%/20% between supplier and purchaser

Cost	Profit	Price
£11.00	–	£11.00
£10.00	£1.00	£10.80
£9.00	£2.00	£10.60
£8.00	£3.00	£10.40

(d) Target costs without maximum price	No maximum price is fixed. Excess or reduced costs over target costs are shared between supplier and purchaser in agreed proportions.	Contracts extending over any period of time during which the supplier may require to be compensated for costs incurred over target or rewarded for cost savings.

Example

Target cost per item = £10 with a profit of £1. Increases or excesses above or below this target cost shared equally between supplier and vendor.

Target/Actual Cost	Profit/Loss	Price
£10.00 (Target)	£1.00	£11.00
£11.00	£1.00	£11.50
£9.50	+£1.50	+£10.75

8. PRICE ANALYSIS

Definition. Price analysis is the breaking down of a quoted price into its constituent elements for the purpose of determining the reasonableness, or otherwise, of the proposed charge. The reasonableness of the proposed charge is an analysis of the quoted price to ensure that it covers the costs of an efficient producer and allows a fair profit commensurate with the risks involved in undertaking the work. An analysis of price can be based on:

(*i*) Cost experience of the buyer's undertaking, e.g. when subcontracting items previously manufactured

(*ii*) Cost estimates prepared by the estimating or cost department of the buyer's undertaking

(*iii*) Cost information provided by the vendor

(*iv*) As a joint exercise undertaken by the purchaser in association with the supplier.

Price analysis has the following advantages:

(*i*) It provides the buyer with a guide as to what he or she ought to pay.

(*ii*) It highlights possible mistakes in quoting on the part of the vendor, i.e. where the price is exceptionally low or high.

(*iii*) It provides a basis for subsequent negotiation that can often benefit both vendor and buyer, i.e. cost reduction leading to price reduction.

(*iv*) Management accounting provides a number of approaches that can be applied to price analysis including Life Cycle Costing, Target Costing, Absorption Costing, Activity Based Costing and Standard Costing. These approaches are discussed in Chapter 12. Marginal costing and its application to make or buy decisions is dealt with in 9:**8b**.

9. PRICE VARIATION AND ADJUSTMENT

(a) **Price variation.** Prices may vary between suppliers and at different times due to the following factors:

(1) *Quantity considerations.* Quantity discounts are often given as an incentive to the buyer to give the vendor a larger share of the available business. The vendor may also pass on to the buyer a proportion of savings accruing from large quantities such as reductions in production, selling, transport and administration costs.

(2) *Payment considerations.* Cash discounts are given as an incentive to prompt payment, enabling the vendor to reduce borrowing and the risk of bad debts. Buyers do not always appreciate the true value of cash discounts. It would be necessary for the bank rate to exceed 36.1 per cent before it would pay an undertaking to forego a cash discount of 2.5 per cent monthly account. Cash discounts also offer scope for negotiation. A cash discount of 3.5 per cent for 7 days is preferable to 2.5 per cent monthly.

(3) *Time considerations.* Vendors may sometimes offer discounts to encourage buying in slack trading periods or for buying 'out of season'.

(4) *Quality considerations.* These reflect the cost of producing from more expensive materials, to higher standards of accuracy or from a 'brand name'.

(5) *Distribution considerations.* Trade discounts are given to compensate suppliers or buyers for undertaking distributive functions. Manufacturers of original equipment give trade discounts since their market is widened both by the initial sale and the subsequent business in spares.

(6) *Transport considerations.* The meaning of the terms given in Table 11.1 should be known and understood.

(b) **Price adjustment formulae.** Examples of methods of price variation have been given in 7 above. Contract price adjustment (CPA) formulae have been developed for certain industries. The CPA formula originally developed by the British Electrical and Allied Manufacturers Association (BEAMA) was the prototype for similar formulae used by other trade associations, local and central government departments, etc. The fundamental principle of the BEAMA formula is to calculate the variation of labour and material costs in relation to the incidence of expenditure and manufacture throughout the contract period. In the case of electrical machinery the procedure is as follows:

(*i*) Contract price is divided: 47.5 per cent labour, 47.5 per cent materials and 5 per cent fixed portion.
(*ii*) Material costs are variated by reference to indices published by the Central

323

Statistical Office at two points in time, i.e. the tender date and the average of the indices between the two-fifths and four-fifths points of the contract period.

(iii) Labour costs are variated by reference to a labour index published by BEAMA and based on a Department of Employment figure of average earnings modified to include statutory payments made by the employer. Adjustments in labour costs are made by considering the labour index at the date of tender and the average of labour indices published for the last two-thirds of the contract period.

(iv) Variations in the cost of materials and labour can, therefore be calculated by the formula

$$P = P_0 \left(0.05 + 0.475 \frac{M_1}{M_0} + 0.475 \frac{L_1}{L_0} \right)$$

where P = Final contract price.

P_0 = Contract price at date of tender.

M_1 = Average of producer price index figures of material and fuel for basic electrical equipment commencing with the index last published before 2/5 of the contract period.

M_0 = Producer price index figure of material and fuel purchased for basic electrical equipment commencing with the index last published before the date of tender.

L_1 = Average of BEAMA labour cost index figures for electrical engineering published for the last 2/3 of the contract period

L_0 = BEAMA labour cost index figure for electrical engineering published for the month in which the tender date falls.

Example

(1)	Contract price	£200,000
(2)	Tender date	6 January 1994
(3)	Date of order	12 February 1994
(4)	Date of despatch or taking over	21 June 1995
(5)	Contract period between (3) and (4)	494 days
(6)	Date at one-third of contract period	27 July 1994
(7)	Date at two-fifths of contract period	29 August 1994
(8)	Date at four-fifths of contract period	14 March 1995
(9)	Labour costs index at tender date (LO)	364.6
(10)	Average of labour cost indices for period (6) to (4) (LI)	383.1
(11)	Department of Industry Index figures of Materials used in Electrical Machinery/Industries last published before tender date (MO)	107.0
(12)	Average of Department of Industry Index figures commencing with Index last published before date at (7) and ending with the index last published before date at (8) (MI)	113.7

(13) Labour adjustment:

$$\frac{(10) - (9) \times 47.5}{(9)} = \frac{18.5 \times 47.5}{364.6} = \qquad\qquad 2.4102\%$$

(14) Materials adjustment:

$$\frac{(12) - (11) \times 47.5}{(11)} = \frac{6.7 \times 47.5}{107.0} = \qquad\qquad 2.9743\%$$

(15) Total percentage adjustment for labour and materials
(13) + (14): $\qquad\qquad$ 5.3845%

(16) Total price adjustment:

$$\frac{(1) \times (15)}{100} = \frac{£200,000 \times 5.3845}{100} = \qquad\qquad £10,769$$

(c) Procedure for price adjustments. The procedure adopted for dealing with price increases should include the following:

(i) Adjustments should, wherever possible, be authorised by a single responsible official.
(ii) Adjustments should be notified to all interested departments, e.g. design, estimating, etc.
(iii) Adjustments should be confirmed in writing.
(iv) Where standard costing is in operation a procedure for monitoring price adjustments and variances against standard materials costs will be necessary.
(v) Where adjustments are calculated in accordance with an agreed formula the base date of both the original contract and the circumstances giving rise to an adjustment should be clearly identified.
(vi) Suppliers should be asked to provide data to justify price increases, e.g. an increase of 10 per cent on labour costs only justified 1 per cent on the total price.

Where the vendor and buyer cannot reconcile the request for a price adjustment the latter may consider such strategies as:

- alternative suppliers
- alternative materials
- make or buy
- value analysis
- longer-term contracts requiring longer notification of adjustments
- where the supplier is in a monopoly position the buyer may, as a last resort, take the matter to the Restrictive Practices Court.

10. CURRENCY MANAGEMENT

(a) Currency and rates of exchange. Currency is the official medium of exchange or money of a country. Since each sovereign state has a currency, e.g. the American Dollar, German Deutsche Mark, Japanese Yen, a payment from one country to another requires to be made in terms of a *rate of exchange* between their currencies. The exchange rate between two currencies therefore represents a price. Exchange rates fluctuate due to a number of factors including:

(i) Economic news affecting confidence in the economy of a particular country.

(ii) Balance of payments considerations, e.g. if British demands for American goods and dollars exceeds American demand for British exports the demand for dollars would rise and the rate of exchange for sterling would depreciate.

(iii) Interest rates. Funds of international investors will, providing the currency is considered stable, move to centres where high interest rates prevail.

(iv) Inflation. Inflation rate is an indicator of a country's economic well being. A large increase in the rate of inflation will adversely affect exchange rates.

(v) Political and social factors. These include strikes, civil war and changes of government.

(vi) Central bank intervention. While the factors listed in *i-iv* above *help* to determine exchange rates, the stability of a particular currency is often supported by action taken by the country's central bank. Thus, where exchange rates are declining, the central bank will enter the foreign exchange market to buy the national currency and sell foreign currency from its reserves. Conversely, where the national currency is appreciating too rapidly, the central bank will sell the home and buy foreign currencies.

(b) Currency and international sourcing. In Chapter 9 currency is listed as one of the difficulties likely to be encountered when sourcing internationally. The principal problems are potential price rises or reductions arising from fluctuations in exchange rates, as in the following example:

X a British company contracts to buy a machine from Y an American manufacturer on three months' delivery for 200,000 dollars. The current 'spot' rate of exchange is 1.75 dollars to the £, i.e. a price in sterling of £114,285. During the period, the exchange rate becomes 1.50 dollars to the £ so that the sterling price of the machine rises to £133,333. Unless the British company has taken action to safeguard against an adverse exchange rate it will therefore be faced with an increase of £19,048.

(c) Currency management. In the context of purchasing, Carter and Vickery [3] identify two major categories of currency management strategies which they term *macro* and *micro*. Macro strategies precede micro strategies. Both strategies rely on forecasts of the likely trend of exchange rates. Such forecasts can be obtained from:

- professional forecasting services
- the banks
- close monitoring of rates and influences on the part of the buyer.

(1) *Macro-level strategies* affect the sourcing decision itself or pertain to the volume timing of purchases.

- *Supplier selection in global sourcing.* As Carter and Vickery observe [3]:

Because of volatile exchange rate fluctuations, two equally capable suppliers from different countries who quote the same US dollar equivalent price at a particular point in time can end up generating significantly different costs for the buyer over the extended life of a requirements contract.

- *Volume timing of purchases.* This is covered in 10:7c where it is shown that a policy of forward buying when prices are falling and hand-to-mouth buying when prices are rising can result in significant savings.

By using exchange rate information in the above ways a purchasing manager can effect significant savings and help to make his company's products more competitive in the global marketplace.

(2) *Micro-level strategies.* These are typically used to protect the buyer from the rise of exchange rate fluctuations as instanced in **10b** above. These include:

(i) Payment in sterling. If a British buyer can arrange for this to be done all exchange risks are transferred to the seller. Conversely payment in a foreign currency means that all exchange rate risks are borne by the buyer. In the example given in **10b** the US manufacturer will receive 200,000 dollars irrespective of exchange rate movements.

(ii) Negotiation of special exchange risks contract terms, e.g. that price increases or decreases will be shared between exporter and importer in agreed proportions.

(iii) Forward buying of currency (risk avoidance). Forward buying will take place when exchange rates are expected to rise. The transaction will be effected through the purchaser's bank. A forward exchange contract can be defined as 'a binding contract between a bank and its customer for the purchase or sale of a specified amount of a particular foreign currency at an agreed future date at a rate of exchange fixed at the time the contract is made' [4].

The agreed future date may be 'fixed' or 'optional'. With fixed contracts the purchase or sale of currency will take place on a specified date. 'Optional' contracts enable the bank's customer to make the transaction on any day within the specified future period. Although different periods can be arranged, forward exchange rates are normally quoted for periods of 1, 3 and 6 months ahead. The forward rates are quoted in terms of either a premium or a discount to the 'spot' rate. The spot rate is a rate of exchange for a transaction which is to be carried out within two working days of the deal. Details of forward rates can be found in the *Financial Times.*

The purpose of a forward contract is to enable a buyer to calculate with certainty the sterling cost of a purchase which is to be paid for in an overseas currency on a specified future date.

(iv) Purchasing futures contracts (risk minimisation). A financial future resembles a forward exchange contract in that it is a contract to buy or sell a stated currency at a specified future date with the price agreed at the time of the deal. Unlike the forward market which is limited to large customers, i.e. banks, the futures market is accessible, through a broker, to anyone needing hedging facilities. The London International Financial Futures Exchange was set up in 1982 as a centre for trading in financial contracts. One of the purposes of such trading is to give businesses protection against exchange rate fluctuation risks.

If, in the period before payment is due, the price at which futures were bought rises, the buyer will sell the contract and use the profit to make up the difference when the goods are actually paid for. Conversely, if the currency value of the futures contract falls the buyer will sustain a loss on the sale of the futures contract which will be offset, at least in part, because the price actually paid in sterling will be less. Unlike a forward exchange contract this hedging mechanism does not completely remove the risk of foreign exchange fluctuations but it does reduce such risk.

(v) Payment in Euro-currency. A Euro-currency is a currency outside the control of the authorities of the country of which it is the currency. The ECU (European Currency Unit) is the common unit of currency for conversion purposes not only among EEC countries but also with many non-member countries including over 60 African, Caribbean and Pacific (ACP) nations who are signatories to the Lomé Convention.

11. INCOTERMS

Incoterms refer to the set of international rules for the interpretation of the chief terms used in foreign trade contracts first published by the International Chamber of Trade in 1936 and amended in 1953, 1967, 1976, 1980 and 1990. Although the use of Incoterms is optional, such terms can reduce difficulties encountered by importers and exporters such as uncertainty as to the law of what country will be applicable to their contracts, difficulties arising from inadequate information and difficulties arising from interpretation. If, when drawing up a contract, buyer and seller specifically refer to one of the IC Incoterms, they can be sure of defining their respective responsibilities simply and safely, thus eliminating any possibility of misunderstanding and subsequent dispute. Thus, while Incoterms do not enter into the contract of sale automatically in the same way as national, local or international conventions, they may be incorporated into the contract in five ways, i.e. the custom of the trade; standard forms; statutory rules, e.g. Sale of Goods Acts; implied terms and by express intention.

Earlier editions of Incoterms focused on the carriage of goods by sea. Later revisions have reflected the increasing use of other modes of transport in international trade and also the increasing tendency for goods to be sold on delivered terms. The 1990 *Incoterms* covers 13 terms divided into four groups. The first group has only one trade term; the others designated F, C and D have 3, 4 and 5 respectively.

Table 11.2 Incoterms

Group	Terms	Meaning
E	EXW	EX WORKS – DEPARTURE (… named place)
F (Seller must hand over the goods to a nominated carrier.	FCA	FREE CARRIER (… named place)
Free of risk and expense to the buyer)	FAS	FREE ALONGSIDE (… named port of shipment)
	FOB	FREE ON BOARD (... named port of shipment)
C (Signified the seller must bear certain	CFR	COST AND FREIGHT (…named port of destination)
Costs even after the critical point for the division of risk of loss or danger to	CIF	COST, INSURANCE AND FREIGHT (…named port of destination)
goods has been reached)	CPT	CARRIED PAID TO (… named place of destination)
	CIP	CARRIAGE INSURANCE PAID TO (… named place of destination)
D (Signified the goods must arrive at a	DAF	DELIVERED AT FRONTIER (… named place)
stated **D**estination)	DES	DELIVERED EX-SHIP (... named port of destination)
	DEQ	DELIVERED EX-QUAY (... named port of destination)
	DDU	DELIVERED DUTY UNPAID (... named place of destination)
	DDP	DELIVERED DUTY PAID (... named place of destination)

References

[1] These examples are taken from *Monopolies and Anti-competitive Practices*. Office of Fair Trading 1995.

[2] Behan P. *Purchasing in Government*. Longman, 1994. Ch 5, p 57.

[3] Carter J R and Vickery S K. *Currency exchange rates: their impact on global sourcing*. *Journal of Purchasing and Materials Management*. Fall 1989, pp 19-25.

[4] Cowdell P. *Finance of International Trade*. Hutchinson, 1988, Ch 1, p 2.

Progress test 11

1. How is price determined under conditions of perfect competition?

2. What are the conditions for perfect competition?

3. What UK legislation regulates monopolies, mergers and restrictive trade practices?

4. Give examples of contracts or arrangements which may have anti- competitive effects.

5. What are the main sources of price information?

6. What are the main factors considered by (a) suppliers and (b) purchasers when arriving at selling and buying prices respectively?

7. Distinguish between 'firm' and 'cost-price' agreements.

8. State some variations that may be made to fixed and cost type agreements.

9. Define the term 'price analysis'.

10. For what reasons may prices for an item vary between suppliers and at different times?

11. Give an example of 'price adjustment'.

12. Why do exchange rates vary between different currencies?

13. Distinguish between macro and micro currency management.

14. What are 'Incoterms'?

15. When there is uncertainty regarding future costs, it may prove difficult for the buyer to obtain fixed prices on long-term contracts. Explain why this is the case and assess, utilising worked examples, two of the alternatives to fixed price contracts available to the buyer in such situations.
    (CIPS. *Purchasing and Supply Management II, Provisioning* (1990))

16. A company based in the United Kingdom buys industrial machinery from a supplier based in Utopia. The goods are to be sold on to the UK firm's customer in Xanadu.
    The agreed purchase price between the UK buyer and the Utopian supplier is 200,000 Utopian Dollars; the agreed sale price between the UK seller and the Xanadu customer is 150,000 Xanadu Francs.

Some three months later, when the goods are ready for shipment, the Sterling/Utopian Dollar exchange rate has moved from 2.4 Dollars to the Pound to 2.3 Dollars to the Pound; the Xanadu Franc/Sterling exchange rate has also moved, from 1.6 Francs to the Pound to 1.8 Francs to the Pound.

Ignoring all other factors (such as duties, transport costs, etc) calculate

(a) The difference between the original purchase and sale price (answer in sterling)

(*Ans.* £10,417 profit)

(b) The difference between the purchase and sale price after three months (answer in sterling)

(*Ans.* £3,623 loss)

(c) The difference between answers (a) and (b) above

(*Ans.* £14,000)

(d) As international buyers what lessons can we learn from the above?

(CIPS. *International Purchasing* (1994))

12
SUPPORT TOOLS

1. TENDERING

(a) Definition. *A purchasing procedure whereby potential suppliers are invited to make a firm and unequivocal offer of the price and terms which, on acceptance, shall be the basis of the subsequent contract.*

(b) Types of tender

(i) Open tenders: prospective suppliers are invited to compete for a contract advertised in the press, the lowest tender generally being accepted, although the advertisers usually state that they are not bound to accept the lowest or any tender.

(ii) Restricted open tenders: prospective suppliers are invited to compete for a contract, the advertising of which is restricted to appropriate technical journals or local newspapers.

(iii) Selective tenders: tenders are invited for suppliers on an 'approved list' who have been previously 'vetted' regarding their competence and financial standing.

(iv) Serial tenders: prospective suppliers are requested either on an open or selective basis to tender for an initial scheme on the basis that, subject to satisfactory performance and unforeseen financial contingencies, a programme of work will be given to the successful contractor, the rates and prices for the first job being the basis of the rest of the programme. Advantages claimed for this system include:

- Contractors are given an incentive to maintain a high performance level
- Savings in cost and time by eliminating pre-contract negotiations for each stage of a programme
- Teams of employees and plant can be moved to successive jobs without disruption
- Supplier security of contract should enable purchasers to negotiate keener prices.

(v) Negotiated tenders: a tender is negotiated with only one supplier so that competition is eliminated. This type of contract is unusual. In the case of a local authority it would require the waiving of standing orders.

(c) The application of tendering. Although tendering is sometimes used to obtain prices by private sector undertakings, particularly in respect of construction and service contracts, it is in the public sector that tendering is most used to ensure the principles of public accountability. Section 135 (3) of the Local Government Act 1972, for example, states:

> Standing orders made by a local authority with respect to the supply of goods or materials for the execution of works shall include provision for securing competition for such contracts and for regulating the manner but may exempt from any such provision contracts for a price below that specified in standing orders and may authorise the authority to exempt any contract from such provision when the authority is satisfied that the exemption is justified by special circumstances.

These provisions have been extended by:

(i) The Local Government, Planning and Land Act 1980, which controls the authority of local authorities to award contracts to direct works organisations without fair competition. There is a statutory requirement that contracts exceeding a prescribed amount can only be placed following tenders from at least three parties.

(ii) The Local Government Act 1988 extends the concept of compulsory competitive tendering (CCT) and requires such authorities as local authorities, police authorities and development corporations to open up opportunities for contracting to the private sectors.

(iii) The Local Government Act 1992 extends the principle of CCT to tendering for the provision of professional or technical services to local authorities.

Under EC Directives it is expected that the majority of public contracts will use open tender procedures. Restricted procedures will apply only where

- the contract value does not justify the procedural costs of an open tender
- the product required is highly specific in its nature.

'Negotiated' tenders will normally only be allowable:

- where because bids were irregular or unacceptable, no suitable supplier has been found by open or restricted tender procedures
- where such procedures have resulted in no tender being received
- where the required product is manufactured purely for research and development or experimental purposes
- where, for technical or artistic reasons or the existence of exclusive rights, there is only one supplier
- where, for urgent reasons, the time limits laid down by competitive tendering cannot be complied with
- where additional deliveries by the original supplier are required, either as part replacement or to extend existing supplies or equipment or where a change of supplier would result in non-compatible equipment or technical differences in terms of operation or maintenance. Contracts of this type should generally not exceed three years.

(d) Tendering procedure. In public purchasing, procedures are usually codified within standing orders which usually prescribe a cash limit above which tenders must be invited, the forms of contract to be used, and to whom and under what circumstances responsibility may be delegated, e.g. to senior officers. In general, the procedure for open tendering involves:

(*i*) The issue of a public advertisement inviting tenders.

(*ii*) Full and identical specifications being issued to each prospective contractor, who is required to submit his tender in a sealed and identifiable envelope by a prescribed date.

(*iii*) On the date arranged for the opening of tenders appointed officers from the purchasing department and an external department, e.g. Treasurer's Department, will attend.

(*iv*) Tenders will be initialled, listed and entered on an analysis sheet showing details of prices, rates, carriage charges, delivery, settlement terms and other information necessary for their evaluation.

(*v*) Late tenders are not considered and are usually returned unopened.

(*vi*) Standing Orders frequently give delegated powers to chief officers or the officer in charge of the purchasing function to place orders against tenders up to a specified value. For contracts exceeding this amount, delegated authority is given provided the lowest tender to the specification is accepted; where the acceptance of the lowest tender is not recommended, Standing Orders may require the consent of a prescribed committee chairman (e.g. Policy and Finance) before the tender is accepted.

(e) The **disadvantages of tendering** are:

(*i*) Contractors may quote a price that is too low, leading to subsequent disputes if goods or services supplied are unsatisfactory.

(*ii*) Tendering is unsuitable for certain contracts. With plant contracts, for example, consultation with one or more of the more favourable tenderers is often essential to clear up technical points. These often result in the tenderer making suggestions that will result in cheaper running and maintenance costs. The extent to which technical changes can be allowed without affecting the validity of open competition is a matter of difficulty.

(*iii*) Tendering procedure is too slow for emergencies – this is usually recognised by Standing Orders.

(*iv*) Where tenders are accepted on the principle of the lowest price, credit may not be given to suppliers for past performance.

(*v*) Tendering procedure, particularly with open tendering, may be expensive from the standpoint of clerical, stationery and postage costs.

(*vi*) Tendering is expensive to the contractor. For this and reason (*v*) selective tendering is usually preferable.

2. DEBRIEFING

The Central Unit on Procurement (CUP) has pointed out [1] that 'debriefing candidates not selected for a bid list and unsuccessful tenderers is recommended in the Treasury's Public Purchasing Policy: Consolidated Guidelines'. Government departments are also subject to specific requirements for debriefing on contracts for supplies, works and priority services under EC rules and the GATT Agreement on Government Procurement. The GATT Agreement provides, *inter alia*, that [2]

> *Subject to Paragraph 9 below* (this relates to disclosure of confidential information) *upon request by an unsuccessful tenderer, the procuring entity shall promptly provide that tenderer with pertinent information concerning the reasons why the tender was not selected, including information on the characteristics and the relative advantages of the tender selected, as well as the name of the winning tenderer.*

The practice of debriefing might be adopted by private sector purchasers.

(a) The benefits of debriefing. Debriefing can be costly. It is often best done verbally rather than by written communication. The Treasury recommends [3] that government departments should balance the resource costs against the likely benefits. The benefits accruing to a purchasing organisation from adopting a policy of responding to requests from unsuccessful tenderers for debriefing information include:

(i) Establishing a reputation as a fair, honest, 'open' and ethical client.

(ii) Providing unsuccessful tenderers with some benefit from the time and money spent on preparing their tenders. This is likely to be of most value to smaller and newer suppliers. It will help all tenderers to be more competitive in the future.

(b) Debriefing topics. The CUP lists the following [3]:

(i) Cost – actual prices or rates offered in tenders are confidential and should never be disclosed. It is permissible, however, to disclose a prospective supplier's ranking in the tender list. The CUP observes that '*if the tenderer was the lowest bidder in cost terms but not selected on VFM this need not be disclosed: it is unlikely to lead to constructive debate. The interviewee could, however, be told that although the price was competitive, other factors were more significant in the award decision'.*

(ii) Schedules – exceptionally long production and/or construction schedules.

(iii) Design – deficiencies, higher operating costs.

(iv) Organisation/administration weaknesses.

(v) Experience – where the experience of the tenderer is deemed to be inadequate for the demands of the contract.

(vi) Personnel – where numbers, experience and quality of personnel including management are deemed inadequate.

(vii) Facilities/equipment – outdated equipment or facilities.

(viii) Subcontracting – too much reliance on subcontractors and inadequate control arrangements.

(ix) Cost and schedule control inadequacies.

(x) Industrial relations – where the tenderer has an unsatisfactory record and no plans for improvement.

(xi) Quality management – where control procedures relating to materials, methods, systems and people are deemed unsatisfactory.

(xii) Contract terms – where these differ fundamentally from those of the client.

(xiii) After-sales service – inadequate arrangements for servicing or the supply of spares.

3. POST-TENDER NEGOTIATION (PTN)

The disadvantages of traditional tendering procedures have indicated the importance of post-tender negotiation. PTN is defined by the CIPS as:

> *'Negotiation after receipt of formal tenders and before the letting of contract(s) with the Supplier(s) Contractor(s) submitting the lowest acceptable tender(s) with a view to obtaining an improvement in price, delivery or content in circumstances which do not put other tenderers at a disadvantage or affect adversely their confidence or trust in the competitive tendering system.'*

Post-Tender Negotiation, issued by the Central Unit on Purchasing, points out that, if it is not considered unethical for a supplier to tender at the highest level that it is considered the purchaser will pay, the converse is that it is not unethical for buyers to challenge the prices tendered.

PTN may relate to any of the areas listed in Chapter 13. CUP has stated [4] that post-tender negotiation can apply to almost any order or contract, although care should be taken to ensure that the cost of negotiation does not outweigh any resultant savings. In particular post-tender negotiation is recommended for:

- all orders potentially worth £100,000 or over
- where the final bid evaluation does not present overwhelming evidence for one tenderer
- where there is doubt regarding quality or performance or where clarification of terms and conditions is required
- all supply agreements made for a period of 12 months or longer.

CUP also identifies eight common areas for direct price negotiation:

(i) where single-tender action has been authorised

(ii) where it is known or suspected that price-fixing or cartel arrangements are operating

(iii) where tender prices appear grossly inflated over known or reliably estimated market prices or the price(s) paid for similar or identical items

(iv) where despite competitive tendering a particular supplier is consistently successful in obtaining the contract

(v) where the enquiry is based on a functional or development specification rather than a detailed specification

(vi) where the purchaser needs to justify selections by testing the market

(vii) where the quantity to be ordered justifies splitting requirements between more than one supplier

(viii) to evaluate whether market conditions are in the buyer's favour or otherwise.

CIPS has issued a statement on PTN in which the following criteria and controls are offered for consideration:

(a) Criteria

(i) The value of the contract, potential for savings and the cost to the buyer of conducting PTN against the likely saving in price.
(ii) Is there time to conduct PTN without delaying the completion date for the contract?
(iii) Effect on the future supply position.
(iv) Is the contract affected by regulations such as EC directives and CATT, which require equality of treatment of potential suppliers?
(v) Is it or would it be considered ethical?

(b) Controls

(i) Who will authorise PTN in particular cases and how will that person relate to the person authorised to award the contract?
(ii) Who will take part in and who will lead the negotiations?
(iii) Who will award the contract?
(iv) What documentation is needed to record events before, during and after PTN, and does this provide a satisfactory audit trail?
(v) How will the conduct and results of PTN be reviewed and by whom?

4. FORECASTING TECHNIQUES

Forecasting techniques are methods that can be used to predict future aspects of a business operation. Such methods can be classified as either quantitative or qualitative.

(a) Quantitative, based on an analysis of historical data appertaining to a time series and, possibly, other related time series. The most used quantitative approaches are:

(1) *Moving averages.* Moving in the sense that as new data becomes available it replaces the oldest data in the equation

$$\text{Moving average} = \sum \frac{(\text{most recent data values})}{n}$$

(2) *Exponential smoothing.* The use of a weighted average of past time series as the forecast in the equation:

$$F_{t+1} = aY_1 + (1-a)F_1$$

where F_{t+1} = forecast of the time series for period $t+1$
    Y_1 = actual value of the time series in period t
    F_1 = forecast of time series for period t
    a = smoothing constant $(0 \le a \le 1)$

Moving averages and exponential smoothing are also described in 8:**11**.

(3) *Trend projection*. This extrapolates (to extrapolate is to estimate from observed tendencies) from a time series of data over a given number of periods. If we consider the monthly usage of a product, for example, the trend may be up, down or zero dependent on whether the demand is expanding, contracting or stationery.

(b) Qualitative forecasting methods generally use the judgement of experts to make predictions. Qualitative forecasts are closely related to the planning approaches described in Chapter 2, namely:

- Life cycle analysis
- Scenario planning
- Systems modelling
- Strategic issue management
- Delphi method.

5. TECHNIQUES OF INVESTMENT APPRAISAL

Top management, assisted primarily by the management accountant, has the responsibility of identifying the best assets for an enterprise to acquire for the achievement of its goals and objectives. Barfield, Raiborn and Kinney [5] state that making such an identification requires answers to four questions:

(1) *Is the activity worthy of an investment?* An activity's worth is measured by *cost benefit analysis*. Cost benefit analysis involves three basic steps:

- Computing the total costs associated with a decision.
- Estimating the total benefits arising from the decision. Often the benefits cannot be quantified in monetary terms, e.g. the refurbishment of an office will not directly improve employee productivity but may do much for morale.
- Comparing the total costs with total anticipated benefits.

(2) *Which assets can be used for the activity?* This involves consideration of monetary and non-monetary information for each asset such as initial cost, estimated life, scrap value, raw material and labour requirements, operating costs, output capability, service availability, maintenance cost and revenues (if any) to be generated.

(3) *Of the available assets for each activity, which is the best investment?* Deciding which asset is the best investment requires the use of one or more of the evaluation techniques described in 10:**3f**, namely:

- Pay-back
- Average rate of return
- Net present value.

(4) *Of the 'best investments for all worthwhile activities', in which ones should the enterprise invest?* Since investment resources are limited the enterprise must decide which of several competing assets and activities to fund. This requires the application of sophisticated investment appraisal techniques which allow for the fact that since capital decisions are based on assumptions relating to future occurrences an amount of risk is involved. Such advanced appraisal techniques are outside the scope of this book.

Rough guides to choosing the best investments are however provided by:

- Ranking investment possibilities in terms of *anticipated profitability* based on their net present value.
- Ranking investment projects in terms of *capital rationing*. Capital rationing means that there is an upper limit on the amount of capital available for asset acquisition. Within this amount, money can be allocated according to the following priorities:
  - Required by legislation, e.g. pollution control equipment.
  - Essential to operating, e.g. assets without which production could not continue.
  - Non-essential but income generating, e.g. assets which could provide increased productivity or cost savings.
  - Optional improvements, e.g. those which do not produce cost savings or revenue improvements but which make the enterprise run more smoothly, e.g. office refurbishment.
  - Miscellaneous, e.g. 'pet projects' of managers.

6. APPLICATION OF COSTING TECHNIQUES

No buyer can afford to be unaware of the various cost accounting approaches to make or buy decisions, negotiation, price appraisal and purchasing performance to mention just four such applications. Relevant approaches include life cycle costing, target costing, absorption costing, activity based costing and standard costing. Marginal cost as applied to make or buy decisions is considered in 9:**8b**.

7. LIFE CYCLE COSTING

The concept of life cycle analysis with its stages of development, growth, maturity, decline, and withdrawal was introduced in 2:**3**. As stated in 10:**3d** life cycle costing is an important factor in making decisions relating to capital expenditure.

(a) Definition. Life cycle costing has been defined by the Chartered Institute of Management Accountants (CIMA) [6] as:

The practice of obtaining over their life time the best use of the physical assets at the lowest cost to the entity (Terotechnology). This is achieved through a combination of management, financial, engineering and other disciplines.

The term *'Terotechnology'*, coined in 1970, is derived from the Greek verb *tereo* and means literally 'the art and science of caring for things'.

Life cycle costs are therefore those associated with acquiring, using, caring for and disposing of physical assets, including feasibility studies, research, development, design, production, maintenance, replacement and disposal, as well as the associated support, training and operating costs incurred over the period in which the asset is owned.

(b) The importance of life cycle costing

(1) Unless life cycle implications are taken into consideration there is a danger that initial cost on delivery will be used as the sole criterion when selecting a physical asset. This simplistic approach can, however, have detrimental implications for the total life cycle cost of the item.

(2) Life cycle costing is of particular importance for products liable to rapid technological style changes. From the standpoint of producers rapid technological change may mean that revenue from sales may be insufficient to make the original investment in design and development worthwhile. From the buyer's viewpoint the asset may, to a greater or lesser extent, be obsolete before the amount invested in its purchase has been recouped.

(3) Purchasing executives concerned with the acquisition of capital items are therefore advised to:

- ensure that specifications include reference to factors which have a bearing on the cost of ownership of an asset, e.g. maintenance, availability of spares
- create a communication bridge with the supplier regarding developments in the particular field
- treat initial costs as only one of many factors that contribute to total life cycle costs
- ensure that all factors which may have implications for the total life cycle costs are given due consideration before recommending the purchase of a particular asset.

(c) Life cycle costing methodology. This involves four basic steps:

(1) *Identify all relevant costs.* As shown in Fig 12.1 these are initially broken down into (1) acquisition and (2) operation and maintenance costs and then further categorised under each heading.

(2) *Calculate costs over the anticipated life of the asset of all elements identified in (1) above.* Such costs may be:

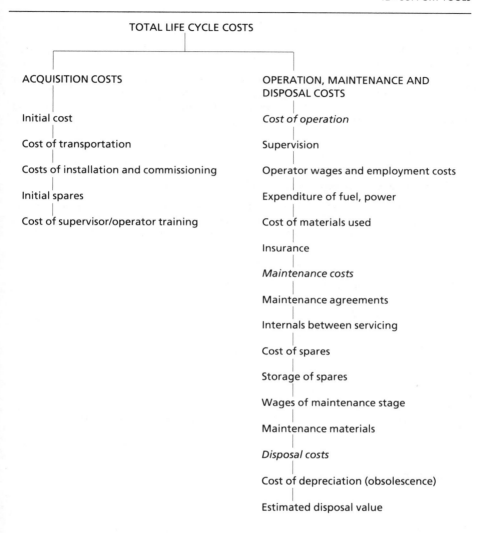

Fig 12.1 Life cycle costing breakdown structure

- Known rates – e.g. operator wages, maintenance charges
- Estimated rates based on historical figures or other empirical date
- Guesstimates – based on informed opinion.

(3) Use *discounting* to adjust future costs to the present, i.e. the time when the purchase decision is made. This reduces all options to a common base thereby ensuring fair comparison. Discounting is described in 10:**5c**.

(4) Draw conclusions from the cost figures obtained by the above procedure.

(d) An example of LCC. The following example of life cycle analysis is reproduced by kind permission of the Treasury and the Copyright Unit of HMSO [7].

EXAMPLE OF AN LCC ANALYSIS

A department has a requirement for 50 photocopiers capable of producing 40,000 copies per month from each copier.

There are 2 copiers that fully meet the department's technical specification together with the quality requirements. The anticipated life of the copier is 5 years.

The metered cost per copy offered by the suppliers includes maintenance charges and all consumables. The two proposals are as follows:

	Copier A	Copier B
Unit price for an order of 50	£10,745	£8,625
Metered cost/copy fixed in cash terms for 5 years	0.9p	1.9p

To ascertain the most cost-effective acquisition in through life cost terms an LCC analysis is carried out. A Discount Rate of 6 per cent in real terms (i.e. after adjusting for inflation) is used in the analysis which gives the following discounting factors:

Year 0	1
Year 1	0.943
Year 2	0.890
Year 3	0.840
Year 4	0.792

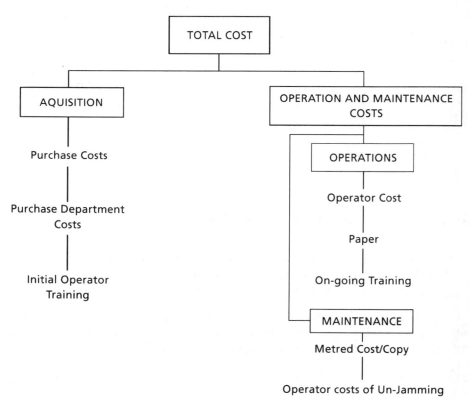

Fig 12.2

The following example sets out the steps involved in this procedure. All costs are expressed at year '0' prices. Staff costs and consumables will almost certainly rise in line with inflation. But any costs which will remain the same in cash terms over the five years will need to be adjusted to year '0' prices using a forecast of inflation which your finance division will be able to give you. In this example, inflation is assumed to be 4 per cent per year. It is also assumed that the machines are deployed at separate locations around the building, not as part of a continuous flow print room. In the case of the latter, it would be necessary to allow for some standby facility to maintain the required level of output.

STEP 1: Produce a cost breakdown structure (Fig 12.2)

STEP 2: Produce a cost estimate

Acquisition		Copier A	Copier B
Purchase costs		£537.25k	£431.25k
Purchase department costs			
(2 man/weeks)		£2.5k	£2.5k
(Operator training time required per copier)		(3 hrs	2 hrs)
Total training cost			
(2 operators per copier)			
at £10 per hour × 50 copiers		£3k	£2k
Total acquisition cost		£542.75k	£435.75k

Operation (5 years)		Copier A	Copier B
Operator cost		£k	£k
Year 0		600	600
Year 1		565.8	565.8
Year 2		534.0	534.0
Year 3		504.0	504.0
Year 4		475.2	475.2

.... (£5 per 1000)		£k	£k
Year 0		120	120
Year 1		113.2	113.2
Year 2		106.8	106.8
Year 3		100.8	100.8
On-going training		95.0	95.0
		1.5	1
Total operation cost		£3216.3	£3215.8

Maintenance (5 years)			Copier A	Copier B
Metered cost per copy			0.9p	1.0p
Adjusted at	Copier A	Copier B	Then discounted	
4% per year			at 6%	
	£k	£k	£k	£k
Year 0	216.0	240.0	216.0	240.0
Year 1	207.7	230.8	195.7	217.4
Year 2	199.7	221.9	177.7	197.2
Year 3	192.0	213.3	161.3	179.2
Year 4	184.6	205.1	146.2	162.5

Operator/supervisor cost of un-jamming		
Mean number of copies between jamming		
(source: previous experience)	5000	3000
Average down-time	0.5 hr	1 hr
5 year cost at £10/hour	£k	£k
Year 0	24	80
Year 1	22.6	75.4
Year 2	21.4	71.2
Year 3	20.2	67.2
Year 4	19.0	63.4
Total maintenance cost	£1004.1	£1353.7
Total 5 year LCC	**£4.831m**	**£5.080m**

Analysis The example shows that the acquisition cost is far exceeded by the maintenance costs. The cost of operation although large is committed by the decision to buy the copier and is not affected by the choice. Therefore, it was unnecessary to discount these costs as they apply equally to both options.

The maintenance costs show the major cost drivers over which the procurer has some control. Not only are the meter costs important but also the time expended by the operator in unjamming the machine.

Before the decision can be fully assessed the options should be evaluated in performance terms. The prime criterion for copiers of equal performance is availability for use. This can be calculated as follows:

$$\text{Availability} = \frac{\text{UPTIME}}{\text{TOTAL TIME}}$$

With the following data:

	Copier A	Copier B
Total possible availability	176 hrs	176 hrs
Downtime for replacement of consumables/month/copier (company brochures)	3 hrs	4 hrs
Downtime for operator un-jamming/month/copier (user experience)	4 hrs	13.3 hrs
Downtime for maintenance engineers/month/copier (expert opinion)	5.4 hrs	10.8 hrs
Average downtime/month/copier	12.4 hrs	28.1 hrs
Uptime	176 – 12.4	176 – 28.1
Total time	176	176
Availability	93%	84%

STEP 3: Draw conclusions

Copier A although over £100,000 more expensive to buy is some £349,000 cheaper to own when considered in LCC terms over 5 years (i.e. the difference between the operation and maintenance costs of copiers A and B). Additionally, Copier A being a higher quality machine with better reliability than Copier B is on average 9 per cent more available than its competitor, or viewed alternatively, Copier B would be unavailable for twice as long as Copier A. The additional investment in purchase will be more than recouped during the life of the copiers.

8. TARGET COSTING

(a) Definition. Target costing is defined by CIMA as:

A product cost estimate derived from a competitive market price. Used to reduce costs through continuous improvement and replacement of technologies and processes. [8]

(b) Target cost procedures

(1) Target cost, as explained in 7:5b(ii), is simply Target price – Target profit.

(2) Target costing is:

- Proactive and forward looking rather than reactive and historical as is the case with standard costs.
- Dynamic since target costs are revised not only in the design and development stages but throughout the life cycle of a product or service. The emphasis on continuous improvement implies that target costs over this period are expected to decrease.

(3) Market driven in the sense that targets are fixed by reference to the costs of competitors.

(4) Linked closely to the concept of *Functional Analysis*. A function is that which a product or service is designed to do, e.g. the function of a pen is to make a mark. Functional analysis [9] 'contributes to cost management by eliminating or modifying functions of the product or service'. Alternatively functional analysis can, on occasion, lead the designer to add new functions if the target profit is greater than the target cost generated by the additional functions.

Component X		
Estimated life cycle	5 years	
Estimated annual sales	40,000	
Estimated total sales over life cycle	200,000	
Initial target sales price per unit	£342 (50% on target cost)	
	TARGET COSTS	
	Per Unit	Total Life Cycle
Design and development	£12.50	£2,500,000
Production	£125.50	£25,100,000
Packaging	£10.00	£2,000,000
Marketing	£35.00	£7,000,000
Transportation	£25.00	£5,000,000
Post sale service	£10.00	£2,000,000
	£218.00	£43,600,000

Fig 12.3

(5) Functional analysis is undertaken by a team comprising representatives of design, engineering, production, purchasing, marketing and management functions, to determine how costs can be managed to meet the desired target.

(6) An initial target cost statement prepared by the supplier would resemble the format shown in Fig 12.3.

(7) Each cost element will be considered by the team to ascertain how target costs can be modified or the competitiveness of the product can be enhanced by:

- Improved design specifications
- Improved production techniques
- Alternative materials
- Eliminating or combining functions
- Control of packaging, marketing and transportation costs
- Reduction in after-sales service through improved reliability.

(c) **Target costing and purchasing.** Target costing is primarily associated with the search for competitiveness by product manufacturers and service providers. It is, however, an approach that can be utilised by purchasing particularly in relation to negotiation in such ways as the following:

(i) Providing suppliers with a target price that the purchaser is prepared to pay.

(ii) Identifying, in association with a supplier, the means by which the target price may be achieved including a fair profit.

(iii) Incorporating improvements into the product or price at agreed intervals or when a contract is due for renewal.

(iv) Providing suppliers with an estimate of the life cycle of parent products in which bought-out components or assemblies will be incorporated. It is then possible to estimate the total demand that a supplier may expect to receive over a defined period of time. This total demand can be used to negotiate quantity discounts, price reviews and learning allowances.

9. ABSORPTION COSTING

(a) **Definition.** Approaches such as life cycle and target costing are approaches to price comparison and price control and reduction rather than day-to-day costing methods. Probably the simplest and best understood method of cost ascertainment is absorption costing defined by ICMA as [10]:

A principle whereby fixed as well as variable costs are allotted to cost units and total overheads are absorbed according to activity level.

The term may be applied where (a) production costs only or (b) costs of all functions are so allotted.

(b) **The elements of cost.** Cost is the amount of expenditure incurred on a given thing. Costs can be classified in several ways, according to the purpose for which they are required. The most usual classifications are into:

(i) Direct costs comprising direct wages, materials and expenses that can be allocated to specific cost units or centres.

(ii) Indirect costs comprising expenses, i.e. indirect wages, materials and expenses, that cannot be allocated but which can be apportioned or absorbed by cost units or centres.

Costs can also be classified as:

(i) Fixed, i.e. a cost which tends to be unaffected by variations in volume of output

(ii) Variable, i.e. a cost which tends to vary directly with variations in volume of output

(iii) Semi-variable, i.e. a cost which is partly fixed and partly variable.

(c) Price composition. The price quoted will therefore be built up as follows:

Direct costs	*Materials, labour and expenses*	*Prime cost*
	+	
Indirect costs	*Works or factory expenses (Production overheads)*	*Work costs*
	+	
	Office and administrative expenses (Establishment overheads)	*Cost of production (Gross cost)*
	+	
	Selling and distribution expenses (Selling overheads)	*Cost of sales (Selling cost)*
Net profit		*= Selling price*

By price analysis the buyer, with the assistance of his design, production and financial colleagues, will be able to arrive at a reasonably close estimate of the prime cost of a bought-out item. There will, however, be less precision in arriving at estimates of indirect costs and profit. The preparation of such an estimate is an essential preliminary to negotiation. When presented to a vendor, the estimate puts the prospective supplier in the position of having to explain why the buyer's estimate is wrong or providing cost data to support his or her quotation.

The questions that the buyer might raise in analysing the prices quoted by vendors will be peculiar to the particular item or job. Some examples of questions applicable to each of the elements that constitute selling price indicate the approach.

(d) Material costs. These comprise the Quantity of material × Purchase price of material.

(i) What material is used, i.e. would an alternative material reduce costs?

(ii) What standardisation is possible?

(iii) Is it possible for the buyer to purchase materials on behalf of the vendor at cheaper cost?

(iv) What weight of material has been allowed for?

(v) What scrap allowances are included?

(vi) Has scrap any resale value?

(e) Labour costs. These comprise Time × Wage rates.

(i) What time allocations have been made?

(ii) Has any allowance been included for idle time?

(iii) What element of overtime is included?

(iv) Has any allowance for 'learning' been included? (see 12:**13**)

(v) What production methods will be used?

(f) Indirect costs. All material, labour and expense costs which cannot be identified as direct costs are termed indirect costs and are usually separated into:

(1) *Production overheads:* i.e. indirect production *material* (e.g. lubricating oil, spare parts for machinery); indirect *labour* (e.g. supervisory and maintenance wages); and indirect *expenses* (e.g. factory rates and insurance).

(2) *Administration overheads:* e.g. management, secretarial and office services and related expenditure.

(3) *Selling overheads:* i.e. costs incurred in securing orders (e.g. salesmen's salaries, commissions and travelling expenses). Overheads may be

(i) Allocated: i.e. charged against an identifiable cost centre or unit. (A cost centre is a location, function or item of equipment in respect of which costs may be ascertained and related to cost units for control purposes, e.g. the drawing office, the purchasing department.)

(ii) Apportioned: spread over several cost centres on an agreed basis (e.g. rates and lighting may be apportioned on the basis of floor area or space occupied respectively).

(ii) Absorbed: charged to cost units by means of rates separately calculated for each cost centre. In most cases the rates are predetermined.

(g) Production overhead costs. These are usually absorbed in one of six ways shown by the following example:

Total overhead for period	=	£24,000
Total units produced in period	=	180
Total direct labour hours for period	=	3200
Total direct wages	=	£6,400
Total direct material used	=	£12,000
Total machine hours	=	£4,800

From the above the following overhead absorption rates can be calculated:

(i) Cost unit OAR= $\frac{£24,000}{180}$ = £133.33 overhead per unit produced

(ii) Direct labour OAR = $\frac{£24,000}{3200}$ = £7.50 per labour hour

(iii) Direct wages OAR $= \dfrac{£24,000}{£6,400} = 375\%$ or £3.75 per £ of wages

(iv) Direct material OAR $= \dfrac{£24,000}{£12,000} = £2$ or 200% of materials

(v) Machine hours OAR $= \dfrac{£24,000}{£4,800} = £5$ per machine hour

(vi) Prime cost OAR $= \dfrac{£24,000}{£6,400 + £12,000} = 130\%$ or £1.30 per £ of prime use

(h) Non-production costs. These are typically absorbed on an arbitrary basis such as:

$$\text{Administration overheads} = \frac{\text{Administration costs}}{\text{Production cost}}$$

$$\text{Selling overheads} = \frac{\text{Selling + Marketing costs}}{\text{Sales value or production cost}}$$

Price analysis in relation to overheads should therefore involve such questions as:

(i) What is the basis on which indirect costs are allocated, apportioned or absorbed?

(ii) To what extent can the fixed overhead element per unit be reduced by increased quantities?

(iii) What is the vendor's break-even point per item or contract?

(iv) What is the proportion of selling and administrative overhead as a proportion of production cost?

(v) Attention should also be given to marginal and activity costing approaches as described in 9:**8b** and 12:**10**.

(i) Profit. The vendor is entitled to a fair profit, since this is the reason he accepts the order. Profit expectation may also provide an incentive to do the work efficiently. The following seven points should be considered when analysing a vendor's anticipated profits:

(i) Competitive price. Buyer who offers lowest price should be allowed what profit he can make providing this is not excessive.

(ii) Initial orders. A high profit may be necessary on initial orders to persuade the vendor to undertake the risks of a new line or production.

(iii) Size or order. Higher profit may be justified on a small order.

(iv) Amount of value added to a product. Vendors who produce all the components incorporated in a product generally make larger profits than assemblers of purchased parts.

(v) Management expertise required. High profits may be required to keep vendors with products requiring a high degree of designer production expertise

interested in the buyer's business. Subcontracted items usually require less skill and therefore lower profits.

(vi) Risks assumed by vendor. The greater the risk the higher the allowable profit.

(vii) Efficiency of vendor. A vendor who has demonstrated reliability with regard to quality and delivery should not be lost because his prices do not allow him adequate profit.

10. ACTIVITY-BASED COSTING (ABC) AND MANAGEMENT

(a) Definition. *A cost attribution to cost units on the basis of benefit received from indirect activities, e.g. ordering, setting up, assuring quality* [11].

(b) The distinction between absorption based and ABC costing

(i) Within traditional absorption costing, overhead costs are assigned to products, services, jobs or other cost objects using one of the approaches indicated in **9g** and **h** above. Overhead costs are applied in proportion to production volume.

(ii) With ABC an overhead is applied to cost objects according to the activities and resources consumed.

(c) Terminology. The following key terms are used in relation to ABC.

(1) An *activity* in this context is a repetitive action performed in fulfilment of business functions, e.g. designing, purchasing, production set up, assembly, quality control, packaging and shipping.

(2) A *resource* comprises costs which support activities. The purchasing activity, for example, incurs costs for salaries and benefits, office space, computer time, travelling, training, etc. Thus, as Lapsley, Llewellyn and Falconer state [12]:

> *Activities consume resources*
> *and*
> *Products (or services) consume activities*

(3) A *cost object.* This can be almost anything in respect of which costs are incurred, e.g. products, services, units, batches, jobs, customers, sales territories, etc.

(4) A *cost driver* is a factor that has a direct cause-effect relationship to a cost; activities creating cost drivers may be either:

(*i*) resource drivers or
(*ii*) activity drivers.

Resource drivers assign costs to activities thereby forming activity cost pools each containing their appropriate share of resource costs. A number of costs pools can be assigned to an activity cost centre.

(5) An *activity cost centre* is a segment of the production or service process for which management wants to separately ascertain the costs of the activities performed., e.g. purchasing, production, marketing. Activity centres should be created where a significant amount of overhead cost is incurred and several key activities are undertaken.

(6) *Direct cost inputs* as a traditional costing comprise direct labour and direct material and, sometimes, direct technology.

(d) A simple example of ABC. As shown by Fig 12.4, ABC involves the following steps:

(i) Total overhead costs for a given period are computed either prospectively from budgets or retrospectively from departmental and general ledger records.
(ii) A project team is formed by top management to plan and implement the ABC system. The team, normally led by the management accountant, may comprise representatives of the design, production, purchasing/logistics, marketing and financial accounting functions.
(iii) The estimated or actual total overheads will be divided into service and production categories. Functional managers will then be interviewed and asked questions such as the following:

What activities does your function undertake?
What activities are undertaken by each member of staff in the function?
What are the outputs of each activity?
What equipment and supplies are used for each activity?
What overtime is worked?
Why does idle time occur?

This activity analysis describes what is done by the enterprise and each function within the enterprise, i.e. how resources including time and effort are spent and what inputs and outputs are involved.
(iv) The team will then assign resource costs to activity cost centres and cost pools using first stage resource drivers as shown in Fig 12.4 (for simplicity only three resources, salaries, office costs and computers, are shown).
(v) Second stage activity drivers, e.g. number of purchaser orders, items stored, deliveries made, will be chosen. These will normally be outputs and are used to assign the cost pools to cost products as shown in Fig 12.3.
(vi) A Bill of Activities will be prepared for each product as shown in Table 12.1. This enables the unit cost of each product using ABC to be ascertained.

(e) The application of ABC. Burch [13] states that ABC is especially appropriate in companies where:

(i) Competition is high.
(ii) Product mix is diverse in batch sizes, physical sizes, degree of complexity and raw material characteristics.

Table 12.1 Bill of Activities of products X and Y for the period ended 31 March 19....

Activity Cost Pool	Second Stage Driver Rate	Product X = 20,000 Units Activity Cost Driver Quantity	Activity Cost	Unit Cost	Product Y = 12,000 Units Activity Driver Quantity	Activity Cost	Unit Cost
Purchasing	£264 per order	800	£211,200	£10.56	1200	£316,800	£26.400
Storage	£200 per item stored	600	£120,000	£6	800	£160,000	£13.33
Distribution	£10,625 per delivery	200	£212,500	£10.63	120	£127,500	£10.63
Accounting	£200 per a/c	904	£180,800	£9.04	1356	£271,200	£22.60
Factory Administration	£1,000 per factory hour	1100	£1,100,000	£55.00	1500	£1,500,000	£125.00
Set ups	£2,000 per set up	100	£200,000	£10.00	200	£400,000	£33.34
			£2,024,500			£2,775,500	

	Unit Cost
Activity Costs per unit	£101.23
Direct materials cost per unit £65	£65.00
Direct labour cost per unit £25	£25.00
Total costs per unit	£191.23

(Product Y Unit Cost column)

	Unit Cost
Activity Costs per unit	£231.30
Direct materials cost per unit £65	£127.50
Direct labour cost per unit £25	£46.20
Total costs per unit	£405.00

With traditional absorption costing the overhead rate per unit produced would be £4,800,000 ÷ 32,000 = £150 per unit. The costs would therefore be:

	Product X	Product Y
Direct materials	£65.00	£127.50
Direct labour	£25.00	£46.20
Overhead	£150.00	£323.70
	£240.00	£497.50

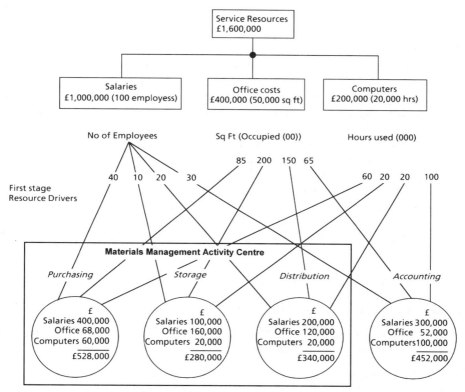

Allocation of Service Resources to Cost Pools

Fig 12.4

(iii) Product life cycles are short, i.e. three years or less.

(iv) Collection and manipulation of data are performed by an integrated computer-based information system (ICBIS).

(f) Activity based costing and purchasing. Barker [14] states that purchasing is 'a key activity for using ABC' and points out that 'much of the literature uses the purchasing and supply function to illustrate how to apply ABC.' Barker identifies a number of ways in which ABC can be implemented within purchasing including:

(i) The attribution of purchasing function costs to products.

(ii) Provision of information which can be utilised in relation to make or buy and sourcing decisions. Ness and Cucuzza report [15] that the introduction of ABC at Chrysler showed that the actual costs of some low volume parts were as much as 30 times greater than the stated costs. This made clear that the company would be much better off outsourcing these parts and making more high volume parts.

(iii) Analysis of the total acquisition cost of purchased items 'may give buyers the information to prove what they have long suspected: paying more often costs less'.

ABC can also:

(iv) Highlight procurement activities that do not add value to products, e.g. inspection and storage and which activities should be cut.

(v) Identify ways in which savings in procurement costs can contribute to the competitive advantage of the enterprise, e.g. reduction in the number of suppliers and transactions, elimination of unnecessary purchasing documentation, improve design with fewer and standardised parts.

(vi) Control of the overall procurement function by regarding it as an activity centre in which all purchasing activity related cost pools are aggregated. This may provide data on drivers and rates which allows comparisons to be made across functions and with potential external suppliers.

(vii) ABC has the potential to make a significant contribution to TQM since costs are a key factor in any decision.

11. STANDARD COSTING

(a) Definition. Standard costing is defined by ICMA [16] as:

A control technique which compares standard costs and revenues with actual results to obtain variances which are used to stimulate improved performance.

Standard costing is therefore a technique of comparisons – the actual with the standard. This approach is used mainly in undertakings engaged in repetitive production and assumes the use of materials or components whose design, quality and specifications are standardised. The standard cost of materials comprises:

(b) Quantity. Normally this is derived from technical and engineering specifications, frequently as indicated in the Bill of Materials. Standard quantities normally include allowance for normal losses due to factors such as scrap, breakages, evaporation and the like.

(c) Price. Prices used are the forecast expected prices, normally the latest prices at which the item can be obtained from approved sources in the quantities estimated for the relevant budget period. Another approach which takes into account that an item may have to be bought from several suppliers is to base prices on the average expected to be paid over the period under consideration.

(d) Variance. The difference between the standard and actual cost is termed a *variance*. The most important material variances are those relating to price and usage and are calculated by the following formulae:

(1) *Direct materials price variance.* The difference between the standard price and actual purchase price for the actual quantity of material. It can be calculated at the time of purchase or the time of usage. Generally the former is preferable. The direct materials price variance can be calculated by the formula:

(Actual purchase quantity × Actual price)
– (Actual purchase quantity × Standard price)

(2) *Direct materials usage variance.* The difference between the standard quantity specified for the actual production and the actual quantity used, at standard purchase price. The direct material usage variance can be calculated by the formula:

(Actual quantity used for actual production × Standard price)
– (Standard quantity for actual production × Standard price)

(3) The sum of the usage and price variances gives the *direct materials total variance* defined as:

The difference between the standard direct material cost of the actual production volume and the actual cost of direct material.

Example Assume the *standard* quantities and prices of the direct materials used for product X are 75 kg at £3.75 per kg.

The *actual* usage and price were 74 kg at £3.85 per kg.

Then direct materials price variance =
  (74 kg × £3.85) – (74 kg × £3.75) = £284.90 – £277.50
an *adverse* variance of £7.40.

The direct material usage variance =
  (74 kg × £3.75) – (75 kg × £3.75) = £277.50 – £281.25
a *favourable* variance of £3.75.

The direct materials total variance will therefore be:

Adverse direct materials price variance =	£7.40
Favourable direct material usage variance =	£3.75
	£3.65 (Adverse)

It is also possible to calculate *direct materials yield and mix variances* in respect of production processes involving the mixing of various materials. For information on these variances and their calculation, reference should be made to any cost accounting text.

(e) Causes of material price variances

(i) Actual prices are higher or lower than budgeted.
(ii) Quantity discounts may be lost or gained by buying in smaller or larger quantities than expected.
(iii) Prices paid may be affected by buying higher or lower qualities than anticipated.
(iv) Buying substitute material or from stockists due to the non-availability of planned material.

(f) Causes of material usage variance

(i) The actual production yield from the material is greater or less than planned.
(ii) The amount of scrap or shortage is greater or less than expected.

Standard costing is an application of the management principle of exceptions. Where a variance exceeds a prescribed level it will be analysed with a view to identifying controllable and uncontrollable factors. Particularly with regard to prices, standard costs provide a widely used measure of purchasing effectiveness.

12. BUDGETS AND BUDGETARY CONTROL

(a) Definitions. ICMA provides the following [17]:

(i) Budget. A plan quantified in monetary terms, prepared and approved prior to a defined period of time, usually showing planned income to be generated and/or expenditure to be incurred during that period and the capital to be employed to attain a given objective.

(ii) Budgetary control. The establishment of budgets relating the responsibilities of executives to the requirements of a policy, and the continuous comparison of actual with budgeted results, either to secure by individual action the objective of that policy or to provide a basis for its revision.

(b) Purchasing budgets. These are derived from the sales and production budgets and will be divided into:

(1) A *materials budget* based on

(i) Whole units of products to be completed in the budget period converted into individual direct material requirements expressed in terms of physical quantities and monetary expenditure.
(ii) The company's end inventory policy based on the availability of materials and components. An example of a materials/components budget is given below.

Example

Material/components for budget period 1995–96

Material (units)	A	B	C	D	E	F	G
Stock in hand 1 April 1995	20,000	25,000	16,000	3,500	9,800	7,500	28,600
Required stock 31 March 1996	18,000	27,000	15,000	4,000	9,000	8,000	25,000
Standard price per unit	£0.06	£0.35	£1.20	£3.25	£0.90	£2.00	£1.20

Procurement budget for the period
1 April 1996 – 31 March 1996

Material (units)	A	B	C	D	E	F	G	Total
Required stock 31 March 1996	18,000	27,000	15,000	4,000	9,000	8,000	25,000	
Budgeted usage during period	125,000	150,000	18,000	24,000	18,000	22,000	137,000	
Totals	143,000	177,000	33,000	28,000	27,000	30,000	162,000	
Stock in hand 1 April 1995	20,000	25,000	16,000	3,500	9,800	7,500	28,100	
Items to be purchased	123,000	152,000	17,000	24,500	17,200	22,500	133,900	
Std. price per unit	£0.06	£0.35	£1.20	£3.25	£0.90	£2.00	£1.20	
Value of budgeted purchases (£)	73,800	53,200	20,400	79,625	15,480	45,000	160,680	448,185

(2) A *purchasing department operating budget* covering projected expenditure for the budget period on salaries, training, computer time, travelling, entertainment, office space occupied, stationery, etc.

While budgetary control and standard costs are interrelated, the former can be operated in enterprises where the latter is difficult to apply. The value of budgeting is, however, enhanced when it is used with standard costing.

13. LEARNING CURVES

(a) Definition. *A learning curve (sometimes termed a 'skill acquisition or experience curve') is a graphical representation of the rate at which skills or knowledge is acquired over a period of time.*

(b) The basis of the learning curve. 'Skill to do comes by doing'. A task is performed more quickly with each subsequent repetition until a point is reached where no further improvement is possible and performance levels out. In industry, cost reduction arising from 'learning' is due to

(i) less time required for the operative to 'weigh-up' the job
(ii) improved speed and proficiency in performing the actual operations
(iii) reduction in scrap and rectification
(iv) improved operational sequences
(v) improved tooling as a result of production experience
(vi) the application of value engineering and analysis
(vii) larger lot sizes with reduced setting-up costs.

Learning curves are therefore developed on the basis of the following assumptions [18]:

(i) The direct labour required to produce the $(n + 1)$th unit will always be less than the direct labour required for the nth unit.

(ii) Direct labour requirements will decrease at a declining rate as cumulative production increases.

(iii) The reduction in time will follow an exponential curve.

(c) The learning curve theorem. This states that each time the number of production units is doubled, the cumulative average labour hours per unit declines by a specific and constant percentage of the previous cumulative average.

More simply it means that with an 80% learning curve each doubling of the *cumulative* total output of a product will take 20% less time. Thus the second unit will take only 80% of the first, the fourth unit only 80% of the second, the 100th unit, 80% of the 50th and so on. For an 80% learning curve we have therefore the table as shown in Table 12.2.

With the aid of a table of Conversion Factors for the Cumulative Average Number of Direct Labour Hours per unit we can find the average time per unit for selected cumulative production quantities. Thus for the cumulative production of 2 units the time would be 180/2 hours per unit = 90 hours. Table 12.2 gives extracts from a table of conversion factors.

It should be noted that learning curves vary according to:

(i) The complexity of the operation – the learning rate for simple products is less pronounced than for more complex items because the opportunity to improve work is greater with the latter.

(ii) The opportunity to reduce direct labour hours on machine-paced operations is limited because the output rate is controlled by the machine.

(iii) Learning will be affected by the introduction of automation or improved equipment. Because of the variability in learning rates it is necessary, when a number of operations are involved in manufacturing a part, to prepare an aggregate learning curve by multiplying the percentage of the total task for a given operation by the learning rate for that operation. The learning rate for all the operations involved will then be aggregated.

Table 12.2

Cumulative production	Cumulative average hours per unit	Ratio to previous cumulative average
1	1.00	80%
2	0.80	80%
4	0.64	80%
8	0.51	80%
16	0.41	80%
32	0.33	80%
64	0.26	80%
128	0.21	80%

Example The manufacture of a product involves four operations.

Operation	Improvement rate	Percentage of task
1	90%	30%
2	92%	20%
3	85%	20%
4	80%	30%

The aggregate learning curve slope will be:

$$(0.92 \times 0.30) + (0.92 \times 0.20) + (0.85 \times 0.20) + (0.80 \times 0.30)$$
$$= 0.28 + 0.18 + 0.17 + 0.24 = 0.87$$

(d) Drawing the learning curve. The cumulative average hours per unit could be plotted on arithmetic graph paper, when they would appear as shown in Fig 12.5.

In practice, log-log paper is used (see Fig 12.6) because it has the following advantages:

(i) All lines will be approximately straight
(ii) The cumulative total can be plotted within the confines of the paper
(iii) For forecasting, a ruler can be laid on the actual line and the results read off.

(e) The application of learning curves. The greatest potential for savings through learning curve analysis lies in high-cost items, items with a high direct labour content, and items which lie at the beginning of the curve.

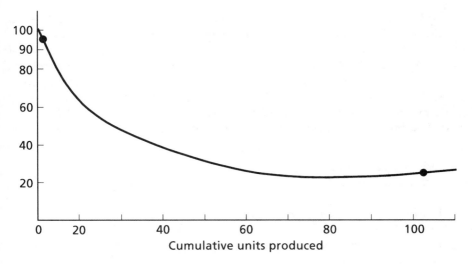

Fig 12.5 Arithmetic scale

359

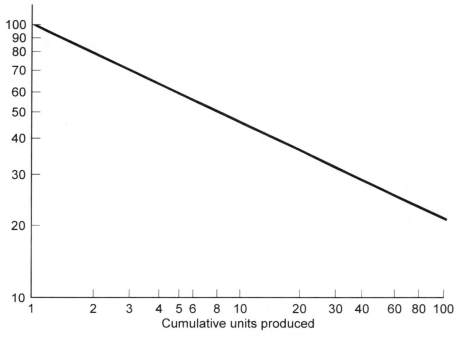

Fig 12.6 An 85% learning curve on log-log scale

(1) *Price determination*. The learning curve approach indicates the areas in which to concentrate on a price analysis in order to obtain the greatest savings. The method of using learning curves to renegotiate the price for a repeat order can be shown by an example.

Example Two hundred items were purchased at £100 each. A repeat order for an additional 200 is under negotiation. Analyse the supplier's costs based on the following information: £2,000 was spent on tools, half of which was written off on the first order. Raw material costs per item were £40 on the first order but will now be £45. The supplier has given a 10 per cent wage rise to his labour force. Direct labour costs amounted to £50 on the first order. The supplier made no profit on the first order and considers he is entitled to a profit of at least 10 per cent. Assuming a 90 per cent learning curve, what should the new price be?

	£
Original price per item	100
Deduct tooling cost	10
	90
Deduct cost not subject to learning, i.e.	
raw material	40
Balance subject to learning	50
Add wage increase, 10%	5
	55

90% of £55	49.50
Add half cost of tooling	10.00
Add material costs	45.00
	104.50
Add 10% profit	10.45
Price per item for repeat order	114.95

(2) *Make or buy decisions.* In comparing the costs of making and buying, the effect of learning on each production run should be determined and taken into consideration as well as the quantity under consideration.

(3) *Delivery times:* The principle can be illustrated by a further example:

Example A contract is placed for 100 units of a component. By allocating 7200 labour hours, the manufacturer expects to produce 10 units in the first month. Assuming that an 80 per cent learning curve applies, how long should it take to complete the order?

Month	Capacity (labour hours)	Cumulative average values (80% learning curve) (from tables)	Units produced	Cumulative total
1	7200	1.00	10	10
2	7200	0.08	16	26
3	7200	0.70	21	47
4	7200	0.64	25	72
5	7200	0.59	26	98

The contract should take just over 5 months, and not 10 months as might be expected from a constant output of 10 units which would be the case if no learning took place.

(f) When not to use learning curves

(i) When learning is not constant, i.e. where a straight line cannot be fitted to the data reasonably accurately.
(ii) Where the direct labour content of the job is small.
(iii) Where the cost/volume does not justify the high expense of periodic time studies or job costing required to obtain the data from which the learning curve is constructed.
(iv) When production is largely automated so that human input is relatively small.

14. PROJECT MANAGEMENT

(a) Definitions

(i) Project. In the present context a project may be defined as:

An activity (or usually, a number of related activities) carried out according to a plan in order to achieve a definite objective within a certain period of time and which will cease when the objective is achieved [19].

(ii) Project management. The function of evaluating, planning and controlling a project so that it is finished on time, to specification and within budget [20].

(b) Types of project. Lock [21] classifies projects under four headings:

(i) Civil engineering, construction, petrochemical, mining and quarrying projects. These are normally undertaken at a site, exposed to the elements and remote from the contractor's office.
(ii) Manufacturing projects aimed at the production of a piece of equipment or machinery, ship, aircraft, land vehicle, or some other item of specially designed hardware.
(iii) Management projects, i.e. operations involving the management and co-ordination of activities to produce an end result that is not identifiable principally as an item of hardware or construction, e.g. relocation of offices, installation of a new computer system.
(iv) Research projects aimed at extending the boundaries of current scientific knowledge which carry high risk because the outcomes are uncertain.

(c) Purchasing and project management. Although not always designated as such, a project manager will have responsibility for the overall direction and control of a particular project and the staff involved. Such staff may be organised on

(i) a *matrix* basis
(ii) a *functional* or team basis.

Matrix structures and their advantages and disadvantages are described in 3:**10c**. Teamwork is discussed in 6:**11**.

Under either form of organisation, however, purchasing may contribute to ensuring that the project is 'finished on time, to specification and within budget' in such ways as the following:

(i) Liaising at each stage with appropriate members of the project organisation (e.g. the project manager, architects, designers, consultants, quantity surveyors, site engineers) with regard to the specification, procurement and scheduling of materials, equipment and services required in connection with the contract.
(ii) Agreeing where, and by whom, purchasing will be undertaken. Lock [22] points out that:

'The purchasing agent could be an independent organisation, the contractor's purchasing department, or even the client's own purchasing department. There can also be various combinations of these arrangements. In international projects the client's purchasing department might issue purchase orders to local suppliers, with the contractor's head office dealing with other suppliers world wide (possibly operating through purchasing agents overseas where their location and local experience provides for greater efficiency)' *(iii)* Advising on the most economic approaches to procurement, e.g. purchase or lease of capital equipment.

(iv) Assistance with the preparation of tender specifications and negotiation with subcontractors. Typical parts of a project to be subcontracted include:

- Brickwork
- Civil engineering
- Drainage
- Electrical installations
- Heating and ventilation
- Painting and decorating
- Pipework
- Plumbing
- Structural steelwork.

(v) Evaluating tenders and post-tender negotiation.

(vi) Placing of orders and subcontracts and ensuring that the terms and conditions are appropriate to the particular contract.

(vii) Expediting orders placed to ensure deliveries meet scheduled requirements.

(viii) Inspecting materials received and maintenance of quality records.

(ix) Dealing with requests from suppliers and subcontractors for price variances.

(x) Controlling 'free issue' supplies, i.e. items provided by the customer or client for use in connection with the project. A glass manufacturer might, for example, provide the glass for use in a contract for a new office building.

(xi) Certifying payment of invoices for goods and services provided by external suppliers and subcontractors.

15. SCHEDULING

Of the above contributions one of the most important is that of ensuring that materials and equipment are on site to obviate delays in meeting the scheduled times for the completion of each part of the project. Two useful scheduling tools are Gantt charts and Networks.

(a) Gantt charts. Devised by Henry L Gantt in 1917 they depict across time the occurrence of the activities comprising a project. An example of a Gantt or bar chart is shown in Fig 12.7.

Gantt activity progress charts:

(i) Show at a glance what project activities are behind schedule (e.g. Activities 2 and 6), on time (Activities 1 and 4) and ahead of schedule (Activities 3 and 5).

(ii) Can facilitate the co-ordination of activities and labour. Activities represented by overlapping bars can be performed concurrently to the degree that they overlap. Activities shown by non-overlapping bars must be performed in the sequence indicated. Thus Activity 4 cannot be started until the completion of Activity 1. Activity 4 can, however, be performed concurrently with Activities 3 and 5.

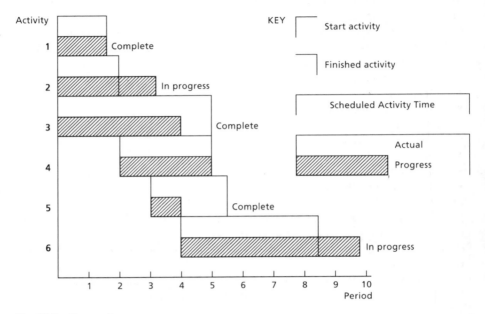

Fig 12.7 Gantt chart

(iii) Gantt charts are most useful in scheduling a series of unrelated activities. Where many activities must be correlated network analysis is more appropriate.

(b) Network analysis. A network has been defined [23] as a convenient method of showing the logical sequence of activities in a project. The two most commonly used network techniques are CPM (Critical Path Method) and PERT (Project Evaluation and Review Technique). One major advantage of these approaches to network analysis is the ease with which they can be computerised.

A *network diagram* comprises:

(1) Arrows . These represent *activities.* Activities are operations, jobs, processes, etc. which consume time and resources.

(2) *Circles or nodes which represent events.* An event is a specific situation or occurrence that indicates a point in time but does not consume time. Events mark the beginning and end of an activity.

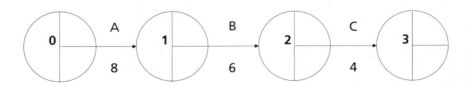

- An event occurs when all the activities leading into a circle have been completed.
- Events are assumed to move sequentially from left to right.
- By what is known as the IJ rule the end of an activity must be given a greater number than the event at the beginning of an activity.
- By convention an activity is written in capitals above the arrow. The numbers indicating the beginning and end of the activity are written in the left-hand half of the circle and the expected time required to perform the activity is written underneath the arrow.

(3) *The critical path.* A 'path' is a sequence of connected activities leading from a starting event 0 to a completion event. In practice there may be many paths through a network all of which have to be travelled in order to complete the project. It is therefore essential to ascertain the total time required to travel each path. This is because it is the longest path that determines the total time to complete the project. This longest path is termed the *critical path*. If activities on the longest path are delayed then the entire project will be delayed. Conversely if it is necessary to reduce the completion time for a project it will be necessary to reduce the time for some of the critical path activities.

On a large project such as the construction of a hospital there may be a great many paths and it is almost impossible to derive the critical path without the help of a computer program. Critical path analysis is, in itself, a complex subject and within the constraints of a non-specialist book it is impracticable to do more than provide a very simple example illustrating the basic procedure and some of the concepts involved.

(4) *Critical path procedure.* This involves the following steps:

Step 1. Draw up a list of activities that comprise the project showing the immediate predecessor activities for each activity and estimated completion times.

Activity	Immediately Preceding Activity	Estimated Completion Time (Weeks)
A	–	5
B	–	6
C	B	4
D	AC	3
E	C	4
F	DE	14
		36 (weeks)

Step 2. Draw a network depicting the activities, immediate predecessors and estimated completion times identified in Step 1 (see Fig 12.8).

In Fig 12.8 the dotted line from 3-4 indicates a *'dummy activity'*. If we had drawn an arrow from D to E this would have indicated that E had to be preceded by activities A and D. E, however, only needs to be preceded by C. We therefore preserve the logic of the network by drawing dotted lines from 3 to 4. This dotted

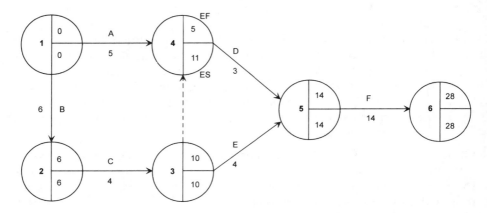

Fig 12.8

line has no activity above it and no time below. This is because a dummy activity consumes no time. If, in a table of activities and preceding activities, an activity occurs more than once in the 'preceding activity' column it will be necessary to introduce dummies. If an activity occurs n times in the preceding activity column then $(n - 1)$ dummies will have to be drawn from its end event.

Step 3. Using the network and the activity time estimates, determine the earliest start (ES) and earliest finish (EF) times for each activity by making a forward pass through the network.

$$EF = ES + t$$

where t is the expected time for the activity.

The EF for Activity A = 0 + 5 = 5 weeks.

For Activity B the EF = 0 + 6 = 6 weeks. Thus for event 1 the EFs are 5 and 6 weeks respectively (activities A – B complete). For other events the EF will be:

Event	EF	
2	6 + 4 = 10 weeks	(Activity C complete)
3	6 + 4 + 4 = 14 weeks	(Activity E complete)
4	5 + 3 = 8 weeks	(Activity D complete)
5	6 + 4 + 4 + 14 = 28 weeks	(Activity F complete)

Consider event 5 above. This cannot start until activities D and E are completed. The completion times are respectively A – D = 8 weeks; B + C + E = 14 weeks. The EF time for event 5 is clearly 14 weeks. The EF is written in the upper right segment of the event circle or node.

Step 4. Using the project completion time identified in Step 3 (28 weeks) as the latest finish time for the last activity (F), make a backward pass through the network to find the latest start (LS) and earliest finish (EF) times for each activity.

$$LS = LF - t$$

where t is the expected time for the activity. The EF for event 5 is 28 weeks; the ES for that event is $28 - 14 = 14$ weeks.

Event	LF	
4	$(14 - 3) = 11$ weeks	(Activity D start)
3	$(14 - 4) = 10$ weeks	(Activity E start)
2	$(10 - 4) = 6$ weeks	(Activity C start)
1	$(6 - 6) = 0$ weeks	(Activity B start)
1	$(5 - 5) = 0$ weeks	(Activity A start)

The latest start times are written in the lower right hand segment of the starting circle or node.

Step 5. Find the 'float' time for each activity.

Float is the length of time for which an activity can be delayed without affecting the scheduled completion time for the project. There are several types of 'float' but the two most important are *total float* and *free float*.

(a) *Total float* is defined [24] as:

The amount by which an activity can be delayed if all its preceding activities take place at the earliest possible times and following activities are allowed to wait until their latest possible times.

Total float can be obtained from the formula:

$$LF = EF - t$$
where t is the activity duration

Consider Activity A in Fig 12.8. The earliest time it can start = 0 weeks; the latest time in which it must be completed is 11 weeks if the project is to meet the scheduled time of 28 weeks. There is therefore 11 weeks to complete activity A. The activity itself is expected to take 5 weeks. The total float for activity A is 6 weeks.

(b) *Free float* is defined [25] as:

The amount of float available when all preceding activities take place at their earliest possible times and following activities can also take place at their earliest possible times.

Free float = the earliest possible end-event time *minus* the earliest possible start event time *minus* the activity duration.

Consider activity D. The earliest possible end event time is 14 weeks; the earliest possible start event time is 5 weeks and the activity duration is 3 weeks. Free float is therefore

$$14 - 5 - 3 = 6 \text{ weeks}$$

Step 6. Use the information from steps 4 and 5 to develop an activity schedule indicating the activities with zero slack. These are the critical path activities.

Activity Schedule

Activity	Start Event	Time	Earliest Start	Earliest End	Latest Start	Latest End	Float	Critical
A	1	5	0	5	0	11	6	
B	1	6	0	6	0	6	0	*
C	2	4	6	10	6	10	0	*
D	4	3	5	14	11	14	6	
E	3	4	10	14	10	14	0	*
F	5	14	14	28	14	28	0	*

The critical activities are therefore

$$+ B + C + E + F = 6 + 4 + 4 + 14 = 28 \text{ days}$$

Items on the critical path need to be closely monitored since if an activity slips one day the whole project will be delayed one day. Activities not on the critical path are of less importance.

(c) Network analysis and cost. Time is not the only consideration associated with project management. The cost is of equal importance. What is known as PERT/Cost is a technique used to plan, schedule and control project costs and ensure adherence to a specified budget. Basically this involves identifying all the costs associated with a project and then developing a schedule of when the costs are expected to occur. As with other budgets actual are compared with budgeted costs at prescribed intervals, e.g. the end of each activity, and appropriate action taken. Attention to critical activities also indicates how, by the introduction of additional resources, it may be possible to shorten completion times. The cost of introducing such resources has to be weighed against the projected savings. If, for example, a project has high daily fixed costs it may be profitable to take on extra labour, buy or hire equipment or subcontract part of the work to reduce the completion time.

(d) CPM and PERT. CPM and PERT use much of the same terminology and techniques. Both aim to show the logical sequence of activities in a project.

CPM, however, was developed mainly for use in industrial projects where activity times could be estimated with reasonable accuracy. In contrast PERT was devised in the late 1950s in connection with the Polaris missile project where the times could not be forecast because the associated activities had not been previously encountered. Unlike CPM which provides only one time estimate for each activity, PERT provides three, namely:

(i) Normal (m), the most realistic assessment of the time required, without allowing for unforeseen contingencies

(ii) Pessimistic (p), the longest times that will be required, allowing for all foreseeable contingencies

(iii) Optimistic (o), the shortest duration within which the activity can be accomplished if all circumstances work out favourably.

These three times are used to calculate expected time on the basis of the following weighted average

$$\frac{4m + p + o}{6}$$

(e) Network analysis and purchasing

(i) Generally network analysis is applicable to large, complex, long-running projects such as construction contracts and to subcontracted work.

(ii) Network analysis provides purchasing with an overview of the complete project and the significance of the contribution of purchasing to its successful completion.

(iii) Network analysis is a team activity to which purchasing contributes essential information such as the availability of materials and the duration of lead times.

(iv) The network enables purchasing to compare actual with promised deliveries and to take early expediting action on 'slippage' to prevent delays in delivery having a cumulative effect on the whole project.

(v) Purchased items can be scheduled for delivery in the right sequence and to the right location, e.g. materials for construction projects can be delivered direct to site immediately before use, thus reducing the possibility of loss through theft or deterioration.

(vi) In subcontracted work progress payments can be linked to the completion of specified events.

(vii) Networks can be used to control expenditure on long-running contracts. Computer printouts can show:

- actual costs incurred at a given date
- estimated costs for the rest of the project
- statements of future expenditure, e.g. purchase orders outstanding.

16. MODELS AND SIMULATION APPROACHES

(a) Definitions

(1) *Model*. Today scientists use the term *'model'* rather than law or theory to describe the conceptual framework they have erected to describe a particular aspect of reality. Thus Newton's Law of Gravitation is a mathematical model which describes the gravitational interactions of bodies.

(2) *Simulations* are constructions of mathematical models to represent the operation of real-life processes or situations. The object of a simulation is to explore

the effect of different policies on the model to deduce what might happen in reality without going to the expense or risk of trial and error in actuality.

(3) *Operational research.* This is defined by the UK Operational Research Society as:

> *The application of the methods of science to complex problems arising in the direction and management of large systems of men, machines, materials and money in industry, business, government and defence. The distinctive approach is to develop a scientific model of the system incorporating measurement of factors, such as chance and risk, with which to predict and compare the outcomes of alternative decisions, strategies or controls. The purpose is to help management determine its policy and action scientifically.*

In this context 'research' has the narrower meaning of 'the application of new mathematical models, methods and techniques to the solution of business or other problems'.

The above definition emphasises:

(i) that OR is concerned with problems of organisation and allocation of resources comprising men, machines, materials, and money to achieve a specified objective
(ii) that a model of the system can be built
(iii) that OR is a service to management
(iv) that alternative decisions can be evaluated against some measure of effectiveness.

(b) OR procedures. The application of quantitative techniques to management practice is known as operational research. The major phases of an OR project have been identified as follows:

(i) Statement of the problem to which a solution is required.
(ii) Construction of a mathematical model as an analogue (i.e. a symbolic model or simulation) of the real system. The general form of an OR model is:

$$E = f(x_1, y_1)$$

where E represents the effectiveness of the system, and x and y the controllable variables and non-controllable variables in the system respectively.
(iii) Deriving an optimum solution from the model either *analytically*, i.e. by the manipulation of the mathematical model, or *numerically* in which a large number of iterations is carried out of possible values of the variables and the equation solved repetitively.
(iv) Testing the model and the solution.
(v) Establishing controls over the solution, i.e. indicating changes in the values of the uncontrolled variables or the relationships between variables that would render the solution invalid.
(vi) Implementation, i.e. translating the tested solution into a set of operating procedures capable of being understood and applied by those who will be responsible for their use.

Table 12.2 Applications of OR

Aspect of OR	Typical supplies applications
(a) *Linear programming.* A mathematical technique for determining the optimum allocation of resources such as capital, raw materials or labour, or plan to obtain a desired objective such as minimum cost of operations or maximum profit when there are alternative uses of the resource in question. LP can also help to analyse alternative objectives such as the economics of alternative resources.	(i) Analysis of quotations from several suppliers who, because of limited resources, can accept only certain combinations of the business offered. Linear programming can indicate the combination of quotations that will minimise purchasing expenditure. (ii) Determining the relative advantages of a low price and a high probability of late delivery against a higher price with a better chance of delivery on time.
(b) *Queuing theory.* Mathematical analysis and solution of problems in which items requiring or providing service stand idle and in which is required to optimise either the arrival rate or service rate or both.	(i) Sequencing and scheduling arrivals of parts or components to achieve minimum costs. (ii) The most economical staffing of stores to provide the minimum waiting time.
(c) *Games theory.* A mathematical technique of decision-making in a competitive situation in which the outcome depends not only on the actions of a manager but also on those of his competitors. The aim of the game is to devise a strategy which maximises returns and minimises losses.	*Negotiation.* Decisions are based on the assumption that the rival is shrewd and will always play to minimise his opponent's gain.
(d) *Decision trees.* A decision tree is a type of flowchart or visual aid which summarises the various alternatives and options available in a complex decision process. Decision trees consist of three parts: (i) the initial decision point, (ii) the branches representing various outcomes, (iii) the paths, which may consist of several branches, representing the various probabilities and events of a particular outcome. The whole tree represents the decision problem. The object of decision trees is not to find optimum solutions but to represent visually a wide range of alternatives which can apply to specific policies and procedures.	Virtually any supplies problem that can be reduced to: (i) a set of mutually exclusive decisions (ii) for each decision, a set of possible outcomes, together with an assessment of the likelihood of each outcome occurring (iii) revenues or costs for each outcome.
(e) *Forecasting.* The process of estimating future quantities required normally using past experience as a basis. OR methods of forecasting include: *(i)* exponential smoothing *(ii)* moving averages *(iii)* trend analysis *(iv)* multiple regression analysis *(v)* curve fitting.	Any supplies problem involving the prediction of future requirements, e.g. stock levels, purchasing expenditure, stores space, purchase of sensitive commodities in various market conditions.
(f) *Probability theory.* An aspect of forecasting based on mathematical techniques for establishing the likelihood of particular events taking place. The probability of an event ranges from 0 to 1. (0 = event will certainly not occur; 1 = event is certain.)	(i) The application of statistical techniques, e.g. sampling, as a means of controlling quality. (ii) Determining the life expectancy of materials and components. (iii) Predicting the probability of stockouts at given levels of inventory.

(c) OR and supplies. Some reference to applications of OR techniques have already been made in this book, namely:

- Elementary inventory control (see 8:**9,10**)
- Network analysis (see 12 :**14**)
- Materials requirements planning (see 8:**14**)
- Replacement theory and capital expenditure evaluation (see 10:**5**) .

Many supplies problems can be solved by the application of techniques from such OR fields as linear programming, queuing theory and probability theory. The application of OR to supplies work has been assisted by computerisation which can deal easily with a large number of variables, e.g. many different items of stores in inventory control. In fact, with the increasing use of computers and availability of specialist software, many OR studies can now be performed by purchasing staff without the need for specialist assistance. In addition to the approaches referred to above some other applications of OR are given in Table 12.2.

(d) The limitations of OR. Decision-making is the process or activity of selecting a future course of action from a number of possible alternatives. Decisions can be classified into different categories such as strategic, operational and administrative and into those that are programmable and non-programmable. Programmable decisions can be worked out by computer since all the variables are quantifiable and the decision rules or constraints clearly defined. Non-programmable decisions cannot be quantified and require the exercise of human judgement. It is important therefore to recognise that OR is limited in its effectiveness to the analysis and comparison of relationships between controllable and uncontrollable variables that can be expressed in terms of a mathematical model.

There are times when the subjective judgement of the decision-maker must act contrary to the OR recommendation. OR, for example, can indicate the EOQs and most economic inventory levels in respect of raw materials and components but these recommendations may be disregarded by the purchasing function if it is known that a threatened strike will seriously disrupt production unless sufficient supplies can be obtained to ensure continuity of output at least in the short term.

References

[1] Central Unit on Procurement. *CUP Guidance Note 45. Debriefing.* p 1.
[2] GATT Agreement on Government Procurement Article 6. Paragraph 5.
[3] Central Unit on Procurement. *CUP Guidance Note 45. Debriefing.* pp 2–3.
[4] Central Unit on Procurement. *CUP Guidance No 1. Post Tender Negotiation.* p 3.
[5] Barfield J T, Raiborn CA and Kinney MR. *Cost Accounting,* West Publishing, 1994. Chap 26, pp 858–883.
[6] Chartered Institute of Management Accountants. *Management Accounting. Official Terminology* (Rev 1991) p 44.

[7] H M Treasury, BCPU, *Guidance Note 35, Life Cycle Costing*, pp 7–8.

[8] Chartered Institute of Management Accountants. *Management Accounting. Official Terminology* (Rev 1991) p 49.

[9] Yoshikawa T, Innes J and Falcolner M. *Cost management through functional analysis* in *Emerging Practices in Cost Management*. Ed. Brinker B, Warrent Gorham Lamont, Boston 1990, p 243.

[10] Chartered Institute of Management Accountants. *Management Accounting. Official Terminology* (Rev 1991) p 26.

[11] Chartered Institute of Management Accountants. *Management Accounting. Official Terminology* (Rev 1991) p 30.

[12] Lapsley J, Llewellyn S and Falconer M. *Cost Management in the Public Sector*. Longman, 1994, Ch 6, p 90.

[13] Burch J, *Cost and Management Accounting*, West Publishing, USA, 1994. Chap 10, p 458.

[14] Barker J. *How to Achieve More Effective Purchasing through Activity Based Costing*. Paper submitted to Second PSERG Conference, University of Bath 1993.

[15] Ness JA and Cucuzza TG. *Tapping the full potential of ABC. Harvard Business Review*. July/Aug 1995, pp 130–138.

[16] Chartered Institute of Management Accountants. *Management Accounting. Official Terminology* (Rev 1991) p 38.

[17] Chartered Institute of Management Accountants. *Management Accounting. Official Terminology* (Rev 1991) p 58.

[18] Krajewski LJ and Ritzman LP. *Operations Management*. Addison Wesley, 1990, Ch 6, p 208.

[19] French D and Saward H. *Dictionary of Management*, Pan Books, 1975, p 333.

[20] Lock D, *Project Management*, Gower Publishing, 1994, (Cover definition).

[21] Lock D, *Project Management*, Gower Publishing, 1994, (Cover definition). Ch 1, pp 3–4.

[22] Lock D, *Project Management*, Gower Publishing, 1994, (Cover definition). Ch 12, p 401.

[23] Owen F and Jones R, *Modern Analytical Techniques*, Polytech Publishers (1984), Ch 17, p 296.

[24] Lock D, *Project Management*, Gower Publishing, 1994, (Cover definition). Ch 7, p 203.

[25] Lock D, *Project Management*, Gower Publishing, 1994, (Cover definition). Ch 7, p 204.

Progress test 12

1. What are the principal types of tender?

2. What are the main disadvantages of tendering?

3. What are the pros and cons of Post-Tender Negotiation?

4. Give examples of quantitative and qualitative forecasting techniques.

5. Define life cycle costing and describe its aims.

6. What are the principal characteristics of target costing?

7. Name some of the ways in which production overhead costs can be absorbed.

8. How does Activity Based differ from Absorption Costing?

9. State some of the applications of ABC to purchasing.

10. What are the main causes of material price variances?

11. Distinguish between budgets and budgetary control.

12. What are some purchasing applications of learning curves?

13. What are some contributions of purchasing to project management?

14. What information is given by a Gantt chart?

15. Distinguish between CPM and PERT.

16. State some supplies applications of Operational Research.

17. (a) Forecasting is an important pre-requisite to strategic planning. Identify and explain three major forecasting methods.
    (b) How would you reduce initial errors often found in forecasting.
    (CIPS. *Purchasing and Supply Management. Planning Policy and Organisation* (1992))

18. Discuss the principal applications of the following techniques, highlighting their benefits, problems and relationship with each other.
    (a) Network analysis; (b) Bar charts.
    (CIPS. *Projects and Contracts Management* (1993))

19. Outline the necessary conditions for the successful implementation of the competitive bidding technique and explain why it is that, even where the conditions for competitive bidding are present, it may not achieve the lowest cost of supply. Discuss the alternative methods available to the buyer by which the lowest cost of supply may be achieved.
    (CIPS. *Purchasing and Supply Management II – Provisioning* (1994))

20. Explain the application of Critical Path Analysis in logistics and illustrate your answer by means of a simple example network.
    (CIPS. *Purchasing and Supply Management III. Logistics* (1994))

21. (a) What do you understand by a Target Cost contract? Describe how such a contract works.

(b) When would you, as a purchaser, consider using such a form of contract and for what reasons?

(CIPS. *Project and Contracts Management* (1994))

22. (a) Describe the two most widely used methods of project planning and illustrate your answers with simple diagrams using not more than seven activities for each method.
    (b) State the circumstances under which the use of one method rather than the other is to be preferred.

(CIPS. *Project and Contract Management* (1994))

23. Outline the requirements for the successful implementation of the competitive tendering method of supplier selection. To what extent do you consider that the method may be in conflict with the objectives of total quality, lowest cost of supply and control of the supplies base?

(CIPS. *Purchasing and Supply Management II. Provisioning* (1995))

24. Describe and explain the planning technique known as Critical Path Analysis (CPA) illustrating your answer by means of a worked example of the technique's application in a logistics context of your own choice.

(CIPS. *Purchasing and Supply Management III. Logistics* (1995))

13

NEGOTIATION

1. INTRODUCTION

Negotiation has been described [1] as 'perhaps the finest opportunity for the buyer to improve his (or her) company's profits and obtain recognition'.

2. DEFINITIONS

There are numerous definitions of negotiation. Three typical examples are quoted below:

(a) *The process whereby two or more parties decide what each will give and take in an exchange between them* [2].

This definition of negotiation highlights (1) its interpersonal nature, (2) the dependency of the parties, and (3) its allocation of resources.

(b) A formal negotiation is *an occasion where one or more representatives of two or more parties interact in an explicit attempt to reach a jointly acceptable position on one or more divisive issues about which they would like to agree* [3].

This definition highlights that negotiation is

(1) *Formal* – negotiation restricts the occasion to those in which –
(2) *representatives of the parties*, e.g. purchaser and supplier –
(3) *explicitly*, i.e. genuinely and deliberately, attempt to reach an agreement on –
(4) *divisive issues* about which they would like to agree.

(c) Negotiation is *any form of verbal communication in which the participants seek to exploit their relative competitive advantages and needs to achieve explicit or implicit objectives within the overall purpose of seeking to resolve problems which are barriers to agreement* [4].

This definition stresses three elements in negotiation:

(1) Negotiation involves communication, i.e. the exchange of information.

(2) Negotiation takes place in a context in which the participants use their comparative competitive advantages and perceived needs of the other party to influence the outcome of the negotiation process.

(3) Each participant has implicit as well as explicit objectives which determine

their negotiating strategies, e.g. a supplier will explicitly wish to obtain the best price but implicitly will be seeking a contribution to fixed overheads and endeavouring to keep the plant and work force employed.

3. APPROACHES TO NEGOTIATION

These may be classified as adversarial and partnership.

(a) Adversarial negotiation, also referred to as distributive or win-lose negotiation, is an approach in which the focus is on 'positions' staked out by the participants in which the assumption is that every time one party wins the other loses. As a result the other party is regarded as an adversary.

(b) Partnership negotiation, also referred to as integrative or win-win negotiation, is an approach in which the focus is on the merits of the issues identified by the participants on which the assumption is that through creative problem solving one or both parties can gain without the other having to lose. Since the other party is regarded as a partner rather than an adversary the participants may be more willing to share concerns, ideas and expectations.

(c) The characteristics of adversarial and partnership negotiation. These can be summarised as in Table 13.1.

(d) An evaluation of adversarial and partnership strategies

(i) *Adversarial strategies* may, on occasion, be appropriate where
- No on-going relationship or the potential for one exists or is desired, i.e. the deal is a 'one-off'.
- A quick simple solution to a disagreement is required.

(ii) *Partnership strategies* while more time consuming and difficult to achieve have the advantages of
- being more stable and lead to long-term relationships and creative solutions to mutual problems
- they may also be the only way of obtaining agreements when both parties to a negotiation have high aspirations and resist making concessions on these issues.

(e) Transforming adversarial attitudes. Fischer and Ury [5] suggest five tactics designed to transform an adversarial into a partnership approach:

(i) *Ascertain superordinate goals,* i.e. direct the attention of both parties to goals and objectives that supersede the short-term problems that they may be encountering, e.g. a long-term partnership purchasing agreement is more important than securing the lowest possible price.
(ii) *Separate the people from the problem.* To see the other party as a partner rather than an adversary is critical to developing the trust needed to achieve integrative agreement.

377

Table 13.1

Adversarial negotiation	Partnership negotiation
(i) The emphasis is on competing goals to be attained at the adversaries' expense.	The emphasis is on ascertaining goals held in common with the other party.
(ii) Strategy is based on secrecy, retention of information and low trust in the perceived adversary.	Strategy is based on openness, sharing of information and high trust in the perceived partner.
(iii) The desired outcomes of the negotiation are often misrepresented so that the adversary does not know what the opponent really requires to be the outcome of the negotiation. There is little concern for or empathy with the other party.	The desired outcomes of the negotiation are made known so that there are no 'hidden agendas' and issues are clearly understood. Each party is concerned for and has empathy with the other.
(iv) Strategies are unpredictable, based on various negotiating 'ploys' designed to out-manoeuvre or 'throw' the other.	Strategies are predictable. While flexible, such strategies are aimed at reaching an agreement acceptable to the other party.
(v) Parties use threats, bluffs and ultimatums with the aim of keeping the adversary on the defensive.	Parties refrain from threats, etc. which are seen as counter-productive to the rational solution of perceived problems.
(vi) There is an inflexible adherence to a fixed position which may be defended both by rational and irrational arguments. The approach is basically destructive.	The need for flexibility in the positions taken is assumed. The emphasis is on the use of imaginative, creative, logical ideas and approaches to a constructive resolution of differences.
(vii) The approach is basically hostile and aggressive, i.e. 'us against them'. This antagonism may be enhanced in team negotiations where members of the team may seek to outdo their colleagues in displaying macho attitudes.	The approach is basically friendly and non-aggressive 'we are in this together'. This involves downplaying hostility and giving credit to constructive contributions made by either party to the negotiations.
(viii) The unhealthy extreme of an adversarial approach is reached when it is assumed that movement towards one's own goal is facilitated by blocking measures that prevent the other party from attaining the goal.	The healthy extreme of the partnership approach is reached when it is assumed that whatever is good for the other party to the negotiation is necessarily good for both.
(ix) The key attitude is that of 'we win, you lose'.	The key attitude is how can the respective goals of each party be achieved so that both win.
(x) If an impasse occurs the negotiation may be broken off.	If an impasse occurs this is regarded as a further problem to be solved possibly through the intervention of higher management or an internal or external mediator or arbitrator.

(iii) Focus on interests not on positions. Positions are demands the negotiator makes. Interests are what underline demands or positions. See definition **2c** above.

(iv) Invent options for mutual gain. This means going beyond obvious issues and looking for broader solutions. In the search for mutual gain the task is to get the other side to agree to the decision you require. This means making it easy for them to agree. To achieve this aim is necessary to empathise with their perspective, search for precedents and develop proposals to which they can respond with the single word 'yes'.

(v) Use objective criteria. When interests appear incompatible re-focus on what is fair. This is more likely to be productive than seeking to win. Deciding what is fair requires both parties to determine criteria for judging fairness and to be fair and reasonable.

4. THE CONTENT OF NEGOTIATION

In any negotiation two goals or objectives should receive consideration. These may be referred to as *substance goals* and *relationship goals.*

(a) Substance goals. These are concerned with the 'content issues' of the negotiation. The possible content issues are legion and depend on the requirements relating to a specific situation. Most negotiations will take place in respect of high-value-usage items, i.e. the 15-20 per cent that constitute the major portion of inventory investment. Negotiation usually relates to non-standard items although a large user will seek, if possible, to negotiate preferential terms for standard supplies. Most negotiation topics affect price either directly or indirectly. Some of the most commonplace items are listed below.

- Amendments to the quoted or existing price.
- Type of pricing agreement.
- Quantity, cash and trade discounts.
- Terms of payment, e.g. extended credit.
- Basis on which price increases are to be determined.
- Carriage charges.
- Time of delivery.
- Method of delivery, e.g. road v. rail.
- Delivery to prescribed sites.
- Amendments to specifications.
- Amendments to quantities.
- Amendments to delivery dates.
- Packaging requirements, e.g. palletisation.
- Supply and ownership of jigs, moulds, patterns and special tooling.
- Allowances to scrap.
- Trade-in allowances.
- Supply of samples.
- Methods and place of inspection.
- Acceptable quality levels.

Methods of determining labour, materials and overhead elements in cost-type contracts.
- Charges for use of patents owned by the supplier.
- Sharing of savings due to improved design or production factors.
- Compensation for cancelled orders.
- Buyer's remedies in respect of rejected goods or later delivery.
- Conditions and warranties applicable to the contract.
- Passing of property in the goods.

(b) Relationship goals. These are concerned with outcomes relating to how well those involved in the negotiation are able to work together once the process is concluded and how well their respective organisations or 'constituencies' may work together. Some areas for relationship goals include:

- Partnership sourcing
- Preferred supplier status
- Supplier involvement in design and development and value analysis
- Sharing of technology.

5. WHAT IS AN EFFECTIVE NEGOTIATION?

Effective negotiation may be said to take place when:

(*i*) Substance issues are satisfactorily resolved *and*
(*ii*) Working relationships are preserved or even enhanced.

Fisher and Ury [6] identify three criteria for effective negotiation:

(*i*) The negotiation produces a *'wise' agreement*, i.e. one that is satisfactory to both sides
(*ii*) The negotiation is *'efficient'*, i.e. it is no more time consuming or costly than necessary
(*iii*) The negotiation is *'harmonious'*, i.e. it fosters rather than inhibits good interpersonal relationships.

6. FACTORS IN NEGOTIATION

Three important factors in a negotiation are the negotiators, the negotiating situation and time.

(a) The negotiators. In negotiations purchasers and suppliers are individuals usually acting as representatives of their respective organisations. Their behaviour in negotiations will be influenced partly by their personalities and partly by the role as representatives.

(1) *Personality.* This may be defined as the relatively enduring and stable patterns of behaving, thinking and feeling which characterise an individual [7]. It should be recognised, however, that there is no universal agreement about the meaning

of personality because behavioural scientists define the term from different perspectives. In the present context it can be loosely considered to mean 'how people affect others and how they understand and view themselves'. How people affect others depends primarily on:

- their external appearance (height, facial features, colour and other physical aspects)
- their behaviour (vulgar, aggressive, friendly, courteous, etc.).

Studies have shown that personality variables such as authoritarianism, anxiety, dogmatism, risk avoidance, self esteem and suspiciousness affect the degree of co-operation or competitiveness present in a negotiating situation. The implementation of negotiating strategies may be affected by personality factors and the mix of personality characteristics of the participants may determine the outcome of negotiations.

Transactional analysis, developed by Eric Berne in the 1950s, has considerable relevance to the understanding of negotiating behaviour. A *'transaction'* is the unit of social interaction: 'If two or more people encounter each other ... sooner or later one of them will speak, or give some other indication of acknowledging the presence of the others'. This is called the *transactional stimulus.* Another person will then say or do something which is in some way related to the stimulus and that is called the *transactional response.* Transactions tend to proceed in chains, so that each response is in turn a stimulus. Transactional analysis is based on the concept that persons respond to each other in terms of three ego states, namely Parent, Adult, and Child, or frames of mind which lead to certain types of behaviour. It is impractical to fully describe transactional analysis in this book. Readers should refer to Eric Berne's book *Games People Play* or the later account by T Harris, *I'm OK – You're OK.*

(2) *Negotiators as representatives.* In negotiations it is important for participants to know the extent of their authority to commit the organisations they are representing since such authority prescribes their options and responsibility for the outcome of the negotiations.

The degree of authority may range from that of an emissary commissioned to present, without variation, a position determined by his superiors to that of a free agent.

There is evidence that the fewer the constraints imposed on a negotiator the greater will be the scope for his or her personal characteristics such as knowledge, experience and personality to influence the negotiation process. Five sets of conditions prevent negotiators from responding spontaneously to their opposite numbers:

(i) When they have little latitude in determining either their positions or posture.
(ii) When they are held responsible for their performance.
(iii) When a negotiator has sole responsibility for the outcome of negotiations.
(iv) When negotiators are responsible to a constituency that is present in the negotiations.
(v) When they are appointed rather than elected.

In the above situations the behaviour of negotiators will be constrained by their obligations. The more complex and open-ended the negotiations the greater should be the status of the negotiators.

(b) The negotiating situation. This relates to the strengths and weakness of the participants in the negotiation. The factors identified by Porter as affecting the relative strengths of supplier and buyer groups are outlined in 2:5(4,5). The negotiating strengths of buyers and suppliers are:

(1) *The buyer's negotiating position.* The buyer will be in a strong position where:

- Demand is not urgent and can be postponed
- Suppliers are anxious to obtain the business
- There are many potential suppliers
- The buyer is in a monopsonistic or semi-monopsonistic position, i.e. the only or one of few firms requiring a particular item
- Demand can be met by alternatives or substitutes
- 'Make' as well as 'buy' alternatives are available
- The buyer has a reputation for fair dealing and prompt payment
- The buyer is well briefed regarding the supplier's order book, financial situation, manufacturing processes and other relevant intelligence.

(2) *The supplier's negotiating position.* The supplier will be in a strong position where:

- Demand is urgent
- Suppliers are indifferent about accepting the business
- The supplier is in a monopolistic or semi-monopolistic position
- Buyers wish to deal with the supplier due to his reputation for quality, reliability, etc.
- The supplier owns the necessary jigs, tools or specialised machinery
- The supplier is well briefed regarding the buyer's negotiating position.

(c) Time. Time affects negotiations in two ways:

(1) Senior management, design, production and stores staff should understand that 'necessity never made a good buyer'. They should therefore notify their requirements well in advance to ensure that the purchasing function has adequate procurement and lead time to obviate having to negotiate under the constraint of urgency.

(2) Negotiations may have a past and certainly have a future in addition to a present. The past is important to negotiations since:

(i) Past experience governs expectations and perceptions. It is the expectation of the most likely reaction by the other side on a particular issue which determines whether the bargaining situation is perceived as predominantly integrative or distributive.

(ii) A second way in which the past influences negotiations is that previous encounters usually produce precedents, conventions, custom and practice, which become identified with a particular relationship and influence the behaviour of the negotiating parties. Where there is no previous history of negotiation, as in new buy situations, the past will have no direct influence.

7. THE PROCESS OF NEGOTIATION

Negotiation falls into three distinct phases: pre-negotiation, the actual negotiation and post-negotiation. Each phase will be discussed in turn.

8. PRE-NEGOTIATION

'Cases are won in chambers' is the guiding principle in pre-negotiation, i.e. legal victories are often the outcome of the preceding research and planning of strategy on the part of counsel. Buyers can learn much by studying the strategies and tactics of legal, diplomatic and industrial relations and applying them to the purchasing field. The matters to be determined at the pre-negotiation stage are as follows:

(a) Who is to negotiate?

(1) *Individual approach.* When negotiations are to be between two individuals both should normally have sufficient status to settle unconditionally without reference back to higher authority. The majority of rebuy and modified rebuy negotiations are conducted on an interpersonal basis.

(2) *Team approach.* For important negotiations, especially where complex technical, legal, financial, etc. issues are involved or for 'new buy' or capital purchases, a team approach such as that adopted by Marks and Spencer (see Chapter 10) is usual since an individual buyer is rarely qualified to act as sole negotiator. In team negotiations it is important to:

- *Allocate roles.* Typical 'players' include:
  (i) The *spokesperson* who actually presents the case and acts as captain of the team in deciding how to respond to the situations arising within the course of the negotiation.
  (ii) The *recorder* who takes notes of the negotiation.
  (iii) The *experts*, e.g. management accountants, engineers or other technical design or production staff, legal advisers who provide 'back up' to the spokesperson. It is not essential that every member of the team should speak in order to make a useful contribution to the negotiation.
- *Avoid disagreement.* There should be no outward disagreement between team members while negotiations are in progress; any differences between members should be resolved in private sessions. The desirability of devising a code of signals enabling team members to communicate imperceptibly during negotiations should be considered.

There are, however, drawbacks to team negotiation: These include:

- *The tendency to 'group-think'*, i.e. for team members to hold illusions of group invulnerability, stereotyped perceptions of perceived opponents and unquestioning beliefs in group morality.
- *The emphasis on win-win* is, unless modified by the spokesperson, greater in team negotiations since team members may wish to demonstrate their 'toughness', inflexibility and ability to demolish rather than consider the merits of proposals made by the other side. The role of the spokesperson on each side in settling the 'tone' of the negotiations cannot be over emphasised.
- *Interpersonal negotiations tend to be concluded more swiftly and amicably* possibly because there is less stress on the negotiators who display a greater readiness to consider opposing viewpoints.

(b) The venue. The buyer should normally expect the vendor to come to him unless there are good reasons to the contrary, e.g. the buyer is seeking concessions or it is desirable to inspect the vendor's facilities. There are advantages in negotiating on home ground. Not only are surroundings familiar but access to files and expert advice is facilitated. The buyer is also under no obligation in respect of hospitality provided by the vendor.

(c) Gathering intelligence. This normally involves:

(i) ascertaining the strengths and weaknesses of the respective negotiating positions
(ii) assembling relevant data relating to costs, production, sales, etc.
(iii) preparing data which it is intended to present at the negotiation in the form of graphs, charts, tables, etc, so that it can be quickly assimilated.

(d) Determining objectives. Buyers should be clear as to what the negotiations are expected to achieve. A model of bargaining in an industrial relations context (see Fig 13.1) can be applied to purchasing.

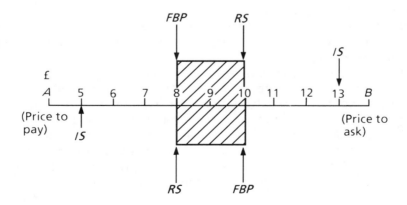

Fig 13.1 A model of bargaining in an industrial relations context

Assuming that the matter under negotiation is price:

(i) A-B represents the positions that the negotiators may take.

(ii) IS below A-B represents the buyer's 'ideal settlement', i.e. the most favourable price that can, with realism, be achieved in negotiation, i.e. £5.

(iii) IS above A-B represents the vendor's ideal settlement, i.e. £13.

Note: In most cases IS will represent the starting position of each of the negotiators subject, of course, to the point that if there is to be negotiation at all the initial demands must not be too far apart to preclude bargaining.

(iv) RS below A-B is the buyer's realistic settlement, i.e. £8, or that point of settlement fully justified by bargaining power which would be reached with reasonable skill in negotiation and no adverse, unforeseen circumstances.

(v) RS above the line is the vendor's realistic settlement, i.e. £10.

(vi) FBP below A-B is the buyer's fall-back position, i.e. £10, or the price beyond which he will not go. After this point he will break off negotiations or seek alternative means of meeting his requirements.

(vii) FBP above A-B is the vendor's fall-back position, i.e. £8.

(viii) The shaded portion represents the area of settlement. This model is based on the convention that each side will normally be prepared to move from the original position. The negotiated price will be between £8 and £10 depending on the skill of the negotiators and assuming that the bargaining positions are approximately equal.

Before commencing negotiations the buyer should have a clear mandate from his superiors to settle at any point not exceeding an agreed fall-back position. It is important to stress the importance of determining in advance what is a *good* agreement. Too often negotiators consider that their goal is to arrive at *an* agreement or even *any* agreement. They therefore should determine what is their own and what is likely to be the other side's BATNA. A BATNA is the Best Alternative To a Negotiated Agreement. While BATNAs and fall-back or reservation positions are similar in many respects they are different, e.g. if you are trying to outsource your catering function the BATNA may be to continue to provide this facility 'in-house'.

(e) Tactics and strategy. A tactic is a position, manoeuvre or attitude to be taken or adopted at an appropriate point in the negotiation process. Strategy comprises the overall tactics designed to achieve, as nearly as possible, the objectives of the negotiation. Among the tactics to be decided are:

(i) the order in which the issues to be negotiated shall be dealt with

(ii) whether to speak first or allow the opponent to open the negotiations

(iii) whether to build in recesses for discussion

(iv) what concessions to make should the need arise

(v) the timing of concessions

(vi) what issues can be linked, i.e. price and improved quality

(vii) what will be the opponent's reaction to each tactic

(viii) what tactics the opponent is likely to adopt and how these can be countered.

(f) The 'dummy run'. Before an important negotiation it is advisable to subject all arguments, tactics and overall strategies to a critical scrutiny.

9. THE ACTUAL NEGOTIATION

(a) Stages. Even with a philosophy of partnership negotiation the activities of the participants will change at each stage of the negotiation process. These activities alternate between competition and co-operation. It is useful for a negotiator to recognise this pattern of interaction and to recognise the stage that has been reached in a particular negotiation. The stages of a negotiation are indicated in Fig 13.2.

(b) Techniques. Specialised books of negotiation usually list a number of techniques available to negotiators. It is not possible to detail these in this book but some general findings include the following:

> *(i)* In framing an agenda the more difficult issues should appear later, thus enabling some agreement on less controversial matters to be reached early in the negotiation.
> *(ii)* Questions are a means both of eliciting information and keeping pressure on an opponent. Questions can also be used to control the pattern and progress of the negotiation.
> *(iii)* Concessions are a means of securing movement when negotiations are deadlocked. Research findings show that losers tend to make the first concession and that each concession tends to raise the aspirational level of the opponent. Buyers should avoid a 'pattern of concession' in which, through inadequate preparation, they are forced to concede more and more. The convention is that concession should be reciprocated. While flexibility is essential, there is no compulsion to make a counter-concession and the aim should be to concede less than has been obtained. The outcome tends to be more favourable when the concessions made are small rather than large. An experienced negotiator will often 'throw a sprat to catch a mackerel'.
> *(iv)* Negotiation is between people. It is essential to be able to weigh up the personalities of one's opponents and the drives that motivate them, e.g. achievement, fear, etc.

(c) Negotiating behaviour

(1) All negotiations involve interpersonal skills. The negotiating styles applicable vary according to the specific situation. Training in negotiation should, therefore, include training in behaviour analysis which should lead to an understanding of the responses likely to be evoked by particular behaviour, e.g. shouting usually causes the other person to shout back; humour may diffuse a situation. Lee and Lawrence *(Organisational Behaviour)* [8] have identified seven categories of behaviour, all of which may be encountered in negotiations (Table 13.2).

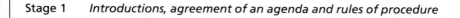

Stage 1   *Introductions, agreement of an agenda and rules of procedure*

Stage 2   *Ascertainment of the 'negotiating range'*
i.e. the issues which the negotiation will attempt to resolve.
With *adversarial* negotiations this may be a lengthy stage since
the participants often overstate their opening positions.
With *partnership* negotiations 'openness saves time'.

Stage 3   *Agreement of common goals which must be met if the negotiation
is to reach a successful outcome.*
This will usually require some movement on both sides from the
original negotiating range but the movement will be less or
unnecessary in partnership negotiations.

Stage 4   *Identification of and, when possible, removal of barriers that
prevent the attainment of agreed common goals. At this stage
there will be:*

(i) problem solving
(ii) consideration of solutions put forward by each
(iii) discertainment of what concessions can be made.

It may also be useful to:

(i) review what has been agreed
(ii) allow a recess for each side to reconsider its position and make
proposals or concessions which may enable further progress to be
made.

If no progress can be made it may be decided to:

• refer the issues back to higher management
• change the negotiators
• abandon the negotiations with the least possible damage to
relationships

Stage 5   *Agreement and closure*
Drafting of a statement setting out as clearly as possible the
agreement(s) reached and circulating it to all parties for comment
and signature.

Fig 13.2   The negotiating process

Table 13.2

Type of behaviour	Likely response
Proposing behaviour: e.g. suggesting actions. 'Shall we look at subcontracting?'.	Usually elicits either development behaviour in the form of support or reasoned negative behaviour in the form of difficulty-stating.
Development behaviour: e.g. building on or supporting proposals made by others. 'Having decided to subcontract, whom shall we approach?'	Usually leads to further development behaviour or perhaps a question asking for further explanation.
Reasoned negative behaviour: e.g. disagreeing with others in a reasoned way, stating difficulties with their ideas. 'Price is likely to be a difficulty because their material costs don't attract our quantity discounts.'	Tends to evoke similar negative behaviour in response, leading to a downward spiral in terms of communications and emotions. This spiral can be avoided by stating difficulties and identifying differences as reasonably as possible, perhaps by further questions.
Emotional negative behaviour: e.g. attacking others; being critical; defending against attacks in the same way. 'Rubbish!'	In general, attack begets either attack or defence. It can make resumption of constructive negotiation difficult.
Clarifying behaviour: e.g. checking whether people understand; summarising previous discussion. 'As I see it, this is what we have agreed.'	Tends to lead to supportive development behaviour, although there can be disagreement.
Seeking information behaviour: e.g. seeking facts, opinions, ideas. 'How much discount if we doubled the quantity?'	This almost always results in information giving. The certainty of response makes this a powerful shaping behaviour.
Giving information behaviour: e.g. giving facts, opinions, ideas. 'We need to reach a decision today.'	This is usually a response to other behaviour, especially seeking information. It is uncertain in its effect, since this depends largely on the content of the statement.

(2) The main fact that the negotiator can learn from these generalisations is that our outward behaviour must be arranged to have the desired effect on those with whom we are negotiating. The desired effect depends on the negotiator's goals. Thus, development behaviour is more likely than emotional disagreement to persuade the other party to accept our viewpoint. Proposing and giving information is indispensable to influencing a group. Sometimes it is better to begin a negotiation by asking questions rather than giving information about the subject matter. We should be aware of the different methods of dealing with disagreement.

(3) *Ploys.* A ploy is a manoeuvre in a negotiation aimed at achieving a particular

result. Most of the ploys mentioned below are appropriate to adversarial rather than partnership negotiating. Such ploys are of doubtful utility partly because they are easily recognised and countered by experienced negotiators and partly because they are detrimental to long-term relationships. Some ploys identified by Rowntree [9] include:

- *The 'Time's getting on' ploy* – Suggesting that a quick settlement is essential.
- *The 'Yes, but .....' ploy* – Acceptance of one part of the opponent's proposal, but in terms that may be unacceptable.
- *The 'Believe it or not' ploy* – Straight bluff ('I've already had three lower prices') should be called. ('Why don't you accept one of them'.)
- *The 'Or else' ploy* – A straight threat ('I'll take the business elsewhere'.) Never to be used unless meant.
- *The 'Hand on the door' ploy* – Another straight threat ('That is my final offer, if not accepted immediately, I shall leave.') Again. never to be used unless meant.
- *The 'Divide and rule' ploy* – Endeavouring to get agreement on issues one by one rather than deferring final agreement on one of the issues at stake until all others have been settled.
- *The 'Think of your reputation' ploy* – Suggesting loss of an opponent's credibility unless your proposals are agreed.
- *The 'Trust me' ploy* – Accept my proposals now and I'll try to get a better deal later.
- *The 'Beyond my remit' ploy* – Suggesting that a settlement cannot be reached until you have had advice from others not represented at the negotiation.

10. POST-NEGOTIATION

This involves:

(i) Drafting a statement detailing as clearly as possibly the agreements reached and circulating it to all parties for comment and signature.

(ii) Selling the agreement to the constituents of both parties, i.e. what has been agreed, why it is the best possible agreement, what benefits will accrue.

(iii) Implementing the agreements, e.g. placing contracts, setting up joint implementation teams, etc.

(iv) Establishing procedures for monitoring the implementation of the agreements and dealing with any problems that may arise.

11. GLOBAL NEGOTIATION

The growth of global purchasing has highlighted the importance of global negotiating skills. These include:

(i) A knowledge of the language of the country in which the other party to the negotiation is located.

(ii) A recognition of cultural influences on the negotiation process. Shenkar and Ronen [10], for example, point out that Japanese negotiations are characterised by politeness, a non-revealing manner, a non-confrontational approach and persistence. In contrast negotiators in the USA and Canada appeal to reason, adduce objective facts to counter subjective statement, take a moderate initial position and place great emphasis on the meeting of deadlines [11].

References

[1] Aljian GW. *Purchasing Handbook*, 4th edition. McGraw Hill, 1982. Section 11, p11.5.

[2] Rubin JZ and Brown BR. *The Social Psychology of Bargaining and Negotiation.* Academic Press, 1975.

[3] Gottschal RAW. *The background to the negotiating process* in Torrington D *Code of Personnel Management.* Gower Press, 1973.

[4] Lysons CK. Modified definition of that in *Purchasing*, 3rd edition, Pitman, 1993.

[5] Fischer R and Ury W. *Getting to YES.* Houghton-Mifflin, 1981.

[6] Fischer R and Ury W. *Getting to YES.* Houghton-Mifflin, 1981. Chap 1 pp 4-7.

[7] Cooper CL and Makin P. *Psychology for Managers*, British Psychological Society in Association with MacMillan, 1988. Ch 4, p 58.

[8] Lee R and Lawrence P. *Organisational Behaviour, Politics at Work,* Hutchinson, 1988. Ch 9, p 182.

[9] Rowntree D. *The Manager's Book of Checklists.* Gower Press, 1989. pp 207-8.

[10] Shenkar O and Ronen S. *The cultural context of negotiations: the implications of Chinese interpersonal norms. Journal of Applied Behavioural Science,* Vol 23, 1987. pp 263-275.

[11] Glenn ES. Witmeyer D and Stevenson KA. *Cultural styles of persuasion. International Journal of Intercultural Relations.* Vol 1, Pergamon, 1984.

Progress test 13

1. Define the term 'negotiation'.

2. What are the main differences between adversarial and partnership approaches to negotiation?

3. Indicate some ways of transforming adversarial attitudes.

4. Distinguish between 'substance' and 'relationship' negotiating goals.

5. Give examples of typical 'substance' issues that can be the subject matter of purchasing negotiations.

6. What are the elements of an effective negotiation?

7. What effects may the personalities of the participants have on a negotiation?

8. What factors influence the relative negotiating strengths of purchasers and suppliers?

9. What activities may be involved in 'pre-negotiation'?

10. What, if any, are the disadvantages of team negotiation?

11. Prepare a diagram showing a typical model of the negotiations process.

12. What is a BATNA?

13. Outline the stages of a typical negotiation.

14. Give examples of typical negotiating behaviour.

15. What is a 'ploy'?

16. What activities take place at the post-negotiation stage?

17. 'We must move away from the old adversarial approach we've had with major suppliers and develop more of a partnership.' Describe the various ways in which this objective might be achieved and the particular contribution of Purchasing and Supply.
   (CIPS. *Purchasing and Supply Management I – Planning, Policy and Organisation* (1992))

18. Distinguish between *Win/Win* and *Win/Lose* negotiation styles giving examples of when you would wish to use each. Detail the information you would require in order to formulate your negotiating strategy and tactics for a contract for 12 months supply of an important production component.
   (CIPS. *Purchasing and Supply Management II – Provisioning* (1992))

19. 'All negotiations can be analysed in terms of four phases' (Gavin Kennedy 1992). This is one possible approach. Identify and discuss the characteristics of the phases of negotiation and discuss how this knowledge can be used by the buyer to improve negotiating performance and achieve the desired outcome.
   (CIPS. *Purchasing and Supply Management II – Provisioning* (1994))

20. Price and Cost Analysis are important tools for the buyer in the preparation stage of negotiation. Discuss the information you would gather and how the techniques could be applied to an important assembly with a high labour content and high tooling costs, which would be supplied over a three year period. How would this information be integrated into your negotiating strategy?
   (CIPS. *Purchasing and Supply Management II – Provisioning* (1994))

21. One view is that successful negotiators not only spend a lot of time gathering information prior to important negotiations but also take considerable time in the integration of this information into the structure of their negotiating strategy.

  Discuss this view and illustrate its application in a typical negotiating situation with which you are familiar.

  (CIPS. *Purchasing and Supply Management II – Provisioning* (1995))

14

PURCHASING RESEARCH, PERFORMANCE AND ETHICS

1. PURCHASING RESEARCH

(a) Definition. Purchasing research is a formalised means of obtaining information to be used in making purchasing decisions. The importance of purchasing research has been enhanced by the following:

(i) Rapid changes in technology and economic circumstances are increasing the complexity of purchasing.
(ii) Much purchasing is undertaken in conditions of uncertainty so that strategic decisions have to be made involving individuals, organisations and events outside the direct control of the purchasing undertaking.
(iii) Electronic data processing provides the facility to store and process vast quantities of data which, when processed, can improve decision-making.

(b) Areas of research In selecting topics for research, it should be remembered that the greater the area of expenditure the greater is the potential for significant cost savings. Among the most important areas of research are the following:

(i) Materials and commodities
- trends in respect of the requirements of the undertaking for specific materials
- price analysis
- substitute materials or items
- specifications and standardisation
- value analysis
- usage analysis
- use of learning curves.

(ii) Purchasing policies and procedures

- What policies are in need of revision?
- Might it be more economical to make in rather than buy out or vice versa?
- What opportunities exist for the consolidation of purchasing requirements?
- Purchasing contributions to competitive advantage.
- Forms design, distribution and elimination.

- The application of Activity Based Costing to the purchasing function.
- How can the information made available by EDP be used more effectively?
- Can purchasing organisation for materials be improved by regrouping the purchasing, stores and other related subsystems, e.g. materials or logistics management approaches?
- To what extent can operational research methods be applied to purchasing?
- Internal and external customer satisfaction with the purchasing function.

(iii) Suppliers
- supplier appraisal
- supplier performance
- the possibilities for supplier development
- supplier reviews, i.e. how often suppliers are changed and how new suppliers are found
- global sourcing.

(iv) Staff
- staff responsibilities
- staff turnover, absenteeism, morale
- what overtime, if any, is worked
- staff succession
- staff training and development
- staff remuneration, facilities and incentives.

(v) Miscellaneous
- transportation of bought-out items
- securing supplies in conditions of uncertainty
- disposal of scrap and obsolete stores and equipment
- terms and conditions of purchase
- the measurement of purchasing performance
- purchasing ethics.

(c) Organisation for research. Some research is undertaken by all purchasing departments even though this may be only rudimentary, such as consulting directories to locate possible suppliers of an item not previously bought. Some willingness to initiate research is essential to the development of the status of purchasing. Unless such initiative is taken by purchasing the research role will be assumed by other functions such as design, marketing and production. Purchasing research may be formal or informal.

(1) *Small business units.* These may be unable to allocate resources such as personnel and finance to establish a formal purchasing research section. Staff should nevertheless be encouraged to keep up to date by meeting representatives, attending trade exhibitions, attending appropriate short course, having access to and opportunities for studying journals and other relevant literature, and networking with other purchasing staff at meetings of professional bodies such as the CIPS.

(2) *Research sections.* Systematic research requires time and freedom from other distractions. These conditions can best be provided by establishing a special purchasing research section as a centralised staff activity to provide assistance to line members of the purchasing function. Experience has shown that undertakings with formal purchasing research arrangements:

(*i*) engage in more research projects
(*ii*) do so at a greater depth
(*iii*) receive a significant contribution to profitability.

(3) *Other approaches.* When a specialised research section is not feasible, formalised purchasing research may be undertaken by:

(*i*) Project teams concerned with a specific problem or range of problems. These teams will probably include staff from outside the purchasing functions, e.g. design, production, finance, marketing, etc.
(*ii*) Use of specialised outside research facilities, e.g. the Commodities Research Unit.
(*iii*) Membership of a research consortium.
(*iv*) Use of outside consultants to investigate a specific matter.
(*v*) Use of research facilities of suppliers.

2. PURCHASING PERFORMANCE AND CONTROL

(a) Definition. The quantitative or qualitative assessment of the degree to which the purchasing function and those employed therein achieve the general or specific objectives assigned to them.

(b) Assessment may be *quantitative or qualitative.*

(1) *Quantitative assessments* are objective and measurable.
Qualitative assessments are subjective and intuitive.
Arjan Van Weele [1] states that the measures used to evaluate purchasing differ significantly according to whether the status of purchasing within an organisation is that of a clerical or commercial activity or a strategic business function.

(2) *Quantitative assessment* using such measures as number of orders placed, reduction in lead times, price savings, reduction of administrative costs, etc., will tend to be used where purchasing is regarded as a clerical or commercial activity. From this perspective the focus will be on *efficiency* defined by Van Weele as 'the relationship between planned and actual sacrifices made in order to be able to realise a goal previously agreed upon'. Purchasing performance is therefore 'the extent to which the purchasing function is able to realise its predetermined goals at the sacrifice of a minimum of the company's resources'.

(3) *Qualitative assessment* using judgmental impressions regarding the contribution of purchasing to supplier goodwill, partnership sourcing, value analysis, and internal customer satisfaction is applicable when procurement is regarded as a strategic business function. From this perspective the focus will be on

effectiveness, defined by Van Weele as 'the extent to which, by choosing a certain course of action, a previously established goal or standard can be met'. Purchasing performance is therefore the extent to which a goal is reached or not.

(c) General or specific. Assessment may relate to

(*i*) The overall performance of the purchasing function.
(*ii*) Special areas or activities within the function.
(*iii*) The contributions of individual staff members.

Specific objectives may be corporately prescribed normally in consultation with the head of the purchasing function or set by the latter in consultation with his or her staff.

(d) External or internal. *External* assessment may be by the executive to whom the head of the purchasing function reports, a group of senior managers, a related function, e.g. finance in respect of budgets, internal audit, outside consultants or by benchmarking. *Internal* assessments can be by the head of the purchasing function or senior staff.

(e) Individual or functional. Staff appraisal is referred to in Chapter 6. Such appraisals should refer to the assessment of individual performance over a specified period of time and is an essential senior management responsibility.

Functional appraisals, especially those based on quantitative criteria, relate to the results wholly or in part of the activity. In the ultimate, however, all performance measurement has an individual element in that the head of the function is accountable for achieving the required results.

3. THE AIMS OF PERFORMANCE MEASUREMENT

(*i*) To ensure a consensus between individual, functional and corporate aims and objectives.
(*ii*) To compare actual results with planned performance.
(*iii*) To ascertain preventable and non-preventable reasons for sub-standard performance and provide a basis, where required, for improvement.
(*iv*) To improve decision making.
(*v*) To identify and make visible the contribution of the purchasing function to organisational competitive advantage.
(*vi*) To provide feedback to staff which can improve motivation, encourage the search for improvement and the more efficient and effective discharge of purchasing responsibilities.

4. THE PREVALENCE OF PURCHASING PERFORMANCE MEASUREMENT

Measurement of purchasing performance is more usual in:

- Large enterprises.

- Public purchasing. A Guide to *Measuring Performance in Purchasing* (No 14) has been published by the Public Competition and Purchasing Unit of HM Treasury.
- Enterprises which recognise the strategic importance of the purchasing function. In 1978 Stevens [2] reported that 'the higher purchasing reports in the organisation the more heavily it uses a spread of evaluators. Where the percentage material cost/total cost ratio lies between 40 and 60 per cent the more likely purchasing is to use a spread of evaluators and at a fairly high incidence rate'.

5. PRINCIPLES OF PERFORMANCE MEASUREMENT

The method or methods used should be chosen after consideration of the following principles:

(i) Acceptability. The method of measuring performance should be discussed with and accepted by all the purchasing staff concerned.

(ii) Achievability. The method must use realistic standards of performance otherwise staff will not be motivated to attain them.

(iii) Appropriateness. The methods and factors must be relevant to the work of the staff and the department.

(iv) Flexibility. Methods of measurement must be capable of adaptation to meet changing circumstances.

(v) Continuity. The methods used should be retained over a reasonable period to facilitate comparison between past and present performance.

(vi) Comprehension. The methods adopted should be uncomplicated so that they can be easily understood by those whose performance is being measured.

(vii) Communication. The results of the performance measurement should be communicated to the staff and, where appropriate, the department.

6. METHODS OF EVALUATING PURCHASING PERFORMANCE

Because the size, organisation and importance of the purchasing function differs widely it is not feasible to devise a universally applicable measure of purchasing performance. In practice approaches to purchasing evaluation may be grouped under four main headings.

(a) *Accounting approaches,* namely

(i) Profit centres.
(ii) Activity based costing.
(iii) Standard costing and budgetary control.
(iv) Financial audits.

(b) *Comparative approaches*

(i) Benchmarking.

(ii) Ratios.

(c) *The purchasing management audit approach.*

(d) *Management by objectives.*

7. ACCOUNTING APPROACHES

(a) The profit centre approach. This regards the purchasing function as a part of the undertaking that controls assets and is responsible not only for expenditure but also for income. The aim of this approach is to demonstrate that the purchasing function is a profit rather than a cost centre. The approach involves establishing a centralised purchasing organisation that controls assets. The profitability of the centralised purchasing function is generated by an internal accounting transfer of items and services procured by purchasing to other functions at a price above their actual direct cost. In effect purchasing sells to other functions at what is termed a transfer price. The executive in charge of purchasing is therefore expected to base his/her decisions, where applicable, on profit criteria, and performance is measured by the profits generated by the function.

Example

Value of assets controlled by the supplies manager:

		£
Inventory		1,500,000
Purchasing function floorspace and equipment		250,000
Stores floorspace and equipment		750,000
		2,500,000
Annual rate of return required by the undertaking on assets employed	15%	375,000
Estimated annual operating expenses		
Purchasing	150,000	
Stores	475,000	625,000
Total expenses and return (a)		1,000,000
Total purchases for year (b)		20,000,000
(a) + (b)	5%	
Transfer cost of supplies to user functions (i.e. internal customers) will therefore be 5% + notional supplies profit (say 1%)	106	
Therefore profit on turnover of £20,000,000		200,000

$$\text{Return on assets controlled by supplies} = \frac{£200,000 \times 100}{£2,500,000} = 8\%$$

To reach the expected return of 15 per cent other than by increasing the notional profit the supplies function will either have to reduce the investment in inventory or operating expenses.

This approach is theoretical rather than practical, although it is advocated on the grounds that it:

(i) Provides a measure of the efficiency of the supplies function.
(ii) Allows supplier managers to control their budgets and spend to save money.
(iii) Enhances the status of the supplies function by providing measurable objectives.

The profit centre approach, however, has the following weaknesses:

(i) It is difficult to determine equitable transfer prices.
(ii) Decentralisation of control increases administrative costs.
(iii) Transfer charges may lead to inter-functional conflicts.

(b) Activity based costing. ABC costing, the basics of which have been described in 12:**10**, contributes to performance measurement by:

(1) *Distinguishing between value adding and non-adding activities.* ABC management stresses that the non-value adding activities must be reduced or eliminated and replaced with those that add value. Just-in-time, while different from ABC management, has similar aims in that both approaches seek to eliminate all wasteful activity by such means as using fewer suppliers, high reliability, minimal paperwork, reduced inventory, etc.

(2) *Analysis of cost drivers.* A cost driver is an activity which creates a cost. ABC highlights the fact that complex products require enhanced negotiation expenses, more suppliers and purchase orders, increased administrative costs and similar cost drivers. The following measures indicate the opportunities for cost savings through simplifying supplier driven activities.

(i) Number of suppliers per product $= \dfrac{\text{Number of suppliers}}{\text{Number of products}}$

Assuming 200 suppliers and 10 products this will be

$$\frac{200}{10} = 20 \text{ suppliers per product}$$

(ii) Number of orders per product $= \dfrac{\text{Purchase orders}}{\text{Number of products}}$

Assuming 1000 purchase orders and 10 products this will be

$$\frac{1000}{10} = 100 \text{ purchase orders per product}$$

Cost savings can be made by:

- Reducing the complexities of bought-out items, i.e. by standardisation.
- Reducing the amount of negotiation and number of suppliers by the introduction of single sourcing or an approved supplier list.
- Improved design using standard, simplified or fewer parts.
- Elimination of unprofitable products.

(3) *Allocation of overheads to products.* If an ABC analysis shows that product X requires the purchase of items from 12 suppliers while product Y only involves purchasing from two suppliers it is clear that product X will incur a considerably higher proportion of purchasing cost than product Y. This should be reflected in the allocation of purchasing function costs to products which takes place with ABC but not traditional costing.

(c) Standard costing and budgetary control. These are described in 12:**11, 12**.

(1) *Standard costing* can monitor performance by variance analysis.

(2) *Budgetary control* assists performance measurement by

- Defining the results to be achieved by functions and their staffs for the purpose of realising overall objectives.
- Indicating the extent by which actual results have exceeded or fallen below those budgeted.
- Establishing the extent and causes of budget variations.
- Appraising budgets to correct adverse trends or take advantage of favourable conditions.
- Exercising centralised control in circumstances of decentralised activity.
- Providing a basis for future policies and, where necessary, the revision of current policies.

(d) Financial audits. These are considered later under the heading of Purchasing and Fraud.

8. COMPARATIVE APPROACHES

(a) Benchmarking

(1) *Definition.* A benchmark is a fixed point of reference against which measurements and comparisons can be made. In the management context benchmarking has been defined [3] as:

> *'Measuring your performance against that of best-in-class companies, determining how the best-in-class achieve these performance levels and using the information as a basis for your own company's targets, strategies and implementation'.*

(2) *Types of benchmarking.* Harrison [4] identifies three types of benchmarking, each of which has its advantages and disadvantages and specific applications:

- *Internal benchmarking* is applicable in enterprises with a number of functions, departments or locations carrying out comparable activities. The aim is to ascertain and learn from the best internal role models.
- *Competitive benchmarking.* The systematic comparison of a business against that of key competitors. Technically this includes 'reverse engineering', i.e. the technique of buying and dismantling competitors products to ascertain their particular features and how they are made.

- *Best practice benchmarking.* Comparison against world class enterprises on a function by function or activity by activity basis.

(3) *The advantages of benchmarking.* These include:

- It provides information on what standards must be surpassed in order to achieve a competitive advantage.
- Benchmarking is motivating since it indicates standards and targets that have been achieved by others.
- Resistance to change may be lessened if ideas for improvement come from other enterprises or competitors.
- Benchmarking is broadening in that it prevents insularity, introspection and self-satisfaction.

(4) *What to benchmark.* There is virtually no aspect of purchasing that cannot be the subject of a benchmarking exercise. Benchmarking can apply to prices, delivery, quality, inventory and also to such matters as procurement staffing, training, pay and productivity, use of EDI, administrative procedures and all aspects of purchasing performance.

(5) *How to benchmark.* The application of the benchmarking concept to purchasing involves the steps indicated in Table 14.1.

(6) *Further aspects of benchmarking*

- Benchmarking is *not* industrial spying but is undertaken openly with the full co-operation of the company against which benchmarking is undertaken.
- Information which may be regarded as confidential or proprietary in content should not be asked for.
- Benchmarking is more than copying the practices of other organisations. All factors must be considered that made the activity successful, e.g. staff training and improvement.
- Benchmarks are not static. The aim should be 'continual improvement'. The Japanese word 'dantotsu' which means striving to be the 'best-of-the-best' is the essence of benchmarking.
- Benchmarking is closely related to Activity Based Management and Total Quality Management.

(b) Ratios. These show the relationship between two magnitudes or variables and can be used to indicate trends, set standards, control costs and as measures of efficiency. Ratios used to measure purchasing performance include:

(i) $\dfrac{\text{Operating cost of purchasing dept}}{\text{Total value of purchases}} \times 100 =$ Ratio of operating to procurement costs

(ii) $\dfrac{\text{Operating cost of purchasing dept}}{\text{Number of orders placed in period}} \times 100 =$ Average cost of orders placed

(iii) $\dfrac{\text{Total value of purchases}}{\text{Total value of sales}} \times 100 =$ Percentage of value of purchases to value of sales for a given period

Table 14.1 The benchmarking process

Stage 1 Decide what aspects of purchasing/logistics to benchmark
e.g.areas in which it is considered that
- There are significant 'gaps' between current purchasing policies/procedures/ performance and those of competitors.
- The contribution of purchasing to competitive advantage might be improved.
- Costs are significant.
- Further information on good practice is required.

Stage 2 Plan the benchmarking project
- Appoint a team leader to supervise the project.
- Select a team with appropriate skills.
- Ascertain what information on the selected topics is already available or can be obtained through personal contacts, library research, trade associations etc.

Stage 3 Create a base-line for benchmarking comparisons
The purpose of this stage is to identify accurately 'where we are now' so that effective comparisons can be made with best-in-class performances. This involves:
- Identifying the factors that influence performance in the chosen area.
- Determining what factors are important and those that are less important.
- Preparing a statement supported where appropriate by quantitative data of current performance.

Stage 4 Decide whom to benchmark against
The DTI [5] suggests the following important considerations in choosing companies against whom to benchmark:
- Do they know us? (There should already be a good relationship with customers/suppliers)
- Is their experience really relevant?
- Are they still good at the activity we want to measure?
- Are we legally able to exchange this kind of information?To the above one might add – are they competitors? Competitors are likely to be less willing to share information.

Stage 5 How will we collect the required information?
- Secure co-operation with 'best-in-class' performers often through high level contacts.
- Decide what questions to ask.
- Arrange visits and other means of exchanging information.

Stage 6 Analyse the information obtained
The DTI advises [6] that once it has been identified that other companies have a higher level of performance in a particular activity the team should
- Quantify the information as closely as possible.
- Ensure they are comparing like with like.
- Decide 'how much of this is applicable to us?'

Stage 7 Use the findings
At this stage the team:
- Prepares a report on the findings.
- Discusses the findings with senior management and other related functions.
- Sets new performance standards.
- Makes someone in authority responsible for devising an action plan to implement the new standards.
- Monitors progress to ensure that the plan is put into effect.

(iv) $\dfrac{\text{Value of purchase orders placed in period}}{\text{Number of buyers}} \times 100 =$ Average value of orders placed by buyers

(v) $\dfrac{\text{Value of purchase orders placed in period}}{\text{Number of purchase orders placed in period}} \times 100 =$ Average value of purchase orders

(vi) $\dfrac{\text{Value of purchase savings reported}}{\text{Value of purchase orders placed in period}} \times 100 =$ Percentage of purchase savings reported of total purchases (This can also be regarded as a measure of profitability.)

The above ratios are easily derived and are useful particularly when used as a basis of comparison over a number of years. They have the following disadvantages:

(i) In the case of (ii), (iv) and (v) the ratios show average values which may be distorted, e.g. by one abnormally large order.

(ii) With (i) and (ii) the ratio can be improved by increasing the numerator but the aim should be to reduce the total value of purchases and number of orders placed. A fall in the number of orders placed may not be due to purchasing.

(iii) With (vi) the value of savings reported by the purchasing department may not be wholly attributable to purchasing. The tendency is often to emphasise favourable elements in purchasing performance and minimise or cover up mistakes and losses. A study by the American Management Association [7] noted six areas in which reportable savings can be credited to purchasing:

(1) More economical sources of supply developed by the buyer

(2) Specification changes at the buyer's suggestion (to obtain lower price, longer life or to reduce inventory or installation costs)

(3) Improved order practice resulting in obtaining a lower price, e.g. combining orders

(4) Negotiation of lower price by the buyer

(5) Reduction of costs other than material price, e.g. handling or storage costs

(6) Increased return from sale of damaged, obsolete or surplus material and scrap.

(iv) The ratios give no indication of sound purchasing judgement.

9. THE PURCHASING MANAGEMENT AUDIT APPROACH

(a) Definitions. An audit may be defined, inter alia, as a check or examination. The term purchasing management audit has been defined by Scheuing [8] as:

A comprehensive, systematic, independent and periodic examination of a company's purchasing environment, objectives, strategies and tactics to identify problems and opportunities and facilitate the development of appropriate action plans.

Scheuing states that the operative words in this definition are:

(i) Comprehensive – the audit should cover every aspect of purchasing
(ii) Systematic – a standard set of questions should be developed and used repetitively
(iii) Independent – purchasing personnel should not evaluate themselves
(iv) Periodic – audits yield the greatest value if they are performed periodically, i.e. annually, thus facilitating comparisons, checks and balances and the evaluation of progress.

(b) The purpose of purchasing management audits. A review of some standard purchasing texts by Evans and Dale [9] indicated that purchasing audits serve four main purposes:

(i) They police the extent to which the purchasing policies laid down by senior management are adhered to
(ii) They help to ensure that the organisation is using techniques, procedures and methods which conform to best working practice
(iii) They monitor and measure the extent to which resources are used effectively
(iv) They assist in the prevention and detection of fraud and malpractice.

(c) Who should carry out the purchasing management audit? Such audits may be carried out by:

(i) External auditors
(ii) Internal auditors
(iii) A central purchasing function
(iv) A purchasing research function
(v) External management consultants.

Two principles are suggested as governing who should carry out the audit:

(i) The auditors should be external to the function or department which is the subject of the audit.
(ii) The auditors should have an in-depth knowledge of the purchasing function which will enable them not only to monitor adherence to policies and procedures but also be understand purchasing perspectives and problems and make recommendations as to how policies, procedures and practice can be improved. External consultants with specialist knowledge and experience are likely to carry greater authority and provide greater objectivity in relation to purchasing audits.

(d) The content of purchasing audits. Suggested headings and typical items for a management as distinct from a financial audit of the purchasing function are as follows:

(1) *Purchasing perspectives, problems and opportunities*

- What are the perceptions of a sample of purchasing staff of

- Their status in the organisation?
- Their involvement in strategic decision making?
- Their contribution to profitability and competitive advantage?
- What are the job satisfactions and job dissatisfactions identified by the purchasing staff interviewed?
- What are the main problems encountered by purchasing staff in doing their job? To what extent are these problems related to:
  - Management
  - Colleagues
  - Internal customers
  - Suppliers
  - Information
  - Resources
  - Other internal or external factors.
- What is the level of morale in the purchasing function?

(2) *Purchasing organisation*

- To whom does the person in charge of the purchasing function report?
- What aspects of purchasing are centralised/decentralised?
- Would any centralised aspects of purchasing benefit from decentralisation or vice-versa?
- With what other functional activities does purchasing inter-relate?
- What are the formal mechanisms for co-ordination of purchasing activities with other functions?
- What is the assessment of purchasing function performance by its internal customers?
- On what inter-functional/departmental committees is the purchasing function represented or could be represented?
- How might the internal organisation of the purchasing function be improved?
- How might the integration of purchasing with other related functions be improved?

The information will be obtained from organisation charts and formal/informal interviews.

(3) *Purchasing personnel*

- What staff are employed in the purchasing function?
- What are their grades, qualifications and respective lengths of service?
- Has every member of the purchasing function an appropriate job description?
- How do actual duties carried out relate to the job descriptions?
- What staff are over/under deployed?
- Is an attempt made to 'empower' purchasing staff?
- What training and development opportunities are provided for purchasing staff?
- How do salaries and remuneration packages compare with those in similar enterprises/industries?

This information will be obtained from job descriptions/specifications, training documents, human resource plans and formal/informal interviews.

(4) *Purchasing policies*

- What written/unwritten policies apply to the purchasing function?
- Is there a purchasing manual? How and how frequently is this updated?
- What guidance is provided to purchasing staff in respect of:
  - Value to which an individual at a particular grade can commit the enterprise?
  - Supplier relationships, e.g. disputes, prompt payment?
  - Conflicts of interest, e.g. gifts and entertainment?
  - Buying from abroad?
  - Environmental policies?
  - Reciprocal, local and intra company purchasing?
- What machinery exists for the investigation and enforcement of reported departures from policy compliance?

This information will be obtained largely from relevant documents, manuals, memoranda, instructions, etc.

(5) *Purchasing procedures*

- From what sources are requests to purchase obtained?
- How quickly are such requests processed?
- What procedures are laid down for such operational activities as requesting and evaluating quotations, issuing purchase order, receipt of goods and payment of suppliers?
- Are all appropriate procedures computerised?
- To what extent does the purchasing function make use of EDI?
- How are small orders processed?
- What procedures/activities (1) add value, (2) do not add value?
- How might purchasing documentation be improved, simplified or eliminated?
- How much time do purchasing staff spend on seeing supplier representatives?
- What are the procedures for capital purchases?

Much of this information will be obtained from trailing a sample of purchase orders through from the receipt of the requisition to receipt of the goods and payment of the suppliers and from formal and informal interviews.

(6) *Purchasing reports*

- What reports are prepared by the purchasing function?
- By whom is each report requested?
- By whom is each report prepared?
- At what intervals is each report prepared?
- What is the cost of preparing each report?
- To whom is each report sent?
- What use is made of each report by the receiver?

- Is the report really necessary?

Much of this information will be obtained by 'trailing' reports through from their inception to storage or disposal.

(7) *Purchases, suppliers and prices*

- What is the purchase budget in quantities and value for the period under review?
- What are the principal purchases?
- Who are the principal suppliers?
- What attempts have been made to achieve single and partnership sourcing?
- How and by what criteria are suppliers appraised?
- Are the results of appraisals communicated to suppliers?
- How do prices paid for a sample of purchases compare with what is obtainable in the market?
- In what ways does the purchasing function seek to obtain value for money?
- How and by whom are specifications prepared? Is there any purchasing involvement?
- What savings have been achieved in the period under review and how have these been achieved?

Much of this information will be obtained from the examination of a sample of orders and other purchase documentation and formal and informal interviews.

(8) *Inventory*

- Does the undertaking practice ABC analysis?
- How much inventory is carried: (1) strategic items; (2) bottleneck items; (3) leverage items; (4) non-critical items?
- What is the rate of turnover of a sample of items under each category?
- What items of inventory have been in stock for more than one year?
- What procedures are in place for the identification of obsolescent, slow moving or damaged inventory and for the prevention of pilferage?
- What procedures are in place for the disposal of surplus stock, obsolete or scrap supplies or discarded capital items?
- What stock-outs have been experienced in the period and why?
- What attempts has the purchasing/supplies function made to reduce inventory investment.

Much of this information will be obtained from an investigation of stores records, physical inspection of inventory and stores procedures and formal and informal interviews. From the above it can be seen that the main 'tools' used in a purchasing performance audit include:

(i) Formal/informal interviews
(ii) Sampling
(iii) Trailing a procedure or document through from its inception to its end or storage or disposal
(iv) Observation.

These 'tools' can be supported by such approaches as benchmarking and ratio analysis.

(e) Purchasing management audit reports. On completing the findings, the audit should be presented to senior management in the form of a suitable report with summarised recommendations with supporting reasons. In preparing such reports auditors should:

- Highlight policies, procedures and personnel where efficiency and effectiveness can be improved.
- Commend good practice and performance.
- Think beyond simple quantitative measures of performance and consider the full consequences, side effects and reactions likely to occur from their recommendations.
- Support constructive proposals made by purchasing staff which may receive greater attention if made by an outside source.

10. MANAGEMENT BY OBJECTIVES (MBO)

MBO aims to identify the objectives that a manager or function should be expected to achieve within a given time at the end of which the actual performance will be compared with the desired results. The objectives will be compared with the desired results. The objectives will be agreed by the head of the function in consultation with his/her superior. One approach to MBO known as *key results analysis* requires functional heads to identify their key tasks, performance standards and control information with a view to suggesting how their individual performance and the performance of their function can be improved. This analysis forms the basis of discussions both with their immediate superiors and subordinates. The discussions with superiors are to agree functional objectives. When these have been agreed discussions with subordinates are held to determine what objectives each must achieve if the functional/departmental objectives are to be attained. In this manner overall objectives are cascaded down through the organisation as shown:

Overall Objectives
↓ ↑
Functional Departmental Objectives
↓ ↑
Individual Objectives

Since, however, functions and individuals participate in the setting of their objectives, MBO also works from 'bottom up' as well as from 'top down'.

Three main types of objectives can be identified:

(1) *Improvement objectives* seek to improve performance in specific ways in respect of specified factors, e.g. 'To reduce by the next review period the prices paid for all costings used in the assembly of conveyor rollers by 5 per cent.' Such a

reduction may be achieved by negotiation with existing suppliers regarding ways of reducing the price, e.g. substituting aluminium for zinc, value analysis, or by finding new sources from which to purchase.

(2) *Personal development objectives* appertain to personal growth objectives or the acquisition of expanded job knowledge, skills and experience, e.g. 'To commence by the next review an approved course of study leading to the examinations of the Chartered Institute of Purchasing and Supply'.

(3) *Maintenance objectives*, which formally express intentions to maintain performance at its current level, e.g. 'To maintain the present zero defects level of component X purchased from supplier Y'.

The elements of MBO are therefore objectives and feedback.

(i) Objectives should be:

- specific and capable of being expressed precisely in writing
- measurable
- time constrained
- attainable with existing resources or resources to be made available
- linked vertically and horizontally and with organisational strategies
- limited in number
- where possible ranked in order of priority
- There is evidence that hard or difficult objectives produce stronger motivation and a higher level of individual performance than easy objectives.

(ii) Feedback should:

- be fair
- distinguish between controllable and uncontrollable reasons for failing to meet objectives
- when constructive lead to higher performance
- Successful achievement of objectives is reinforced by performance-based rewards.

11. PURCHASING AND FRAUD

(a) Purchasing is a function that is particularly vulnerable to fraud. Evans [10] states that 'fraud is not necessarily restricted to those with the title purchasing officer but may involve anyone in direct contact with suppliers', including engineers, works managers, sales and computer staff. Evans also points out that 'what appear to be fraud may, on occasion, be no more than incompetence.'

(b) Examples of supplies-related fraud

(i) Buyer/supplier collusion leading to approval for payment of fictitious charges.

(ii) Presentation of false invoices – typically the offender will set up a fictitious company with impressive stationery and invoice the purchaser for goods not supplied.

(iii) Re-presentation of genuine invoices that have not been cancelled at the time the cheque was signed for second payment.

(iv) Abstraction of tenders or arranging for the lowest tender to come from a desired source.

(v) Omission of credit notes for goods returned to the supplier.

(vi) Premature scrapping of assets in return for a 'kickback' from a scrap dealer.

(vii) Computer-based frauds which take advantages of inadequate controls or limited understanding of computers on the part of senior management.

(c) The prevention of fraud in relation to supplies depends on sound internal control, internal and external auditing and the detection of 'give away' signs.

(1) *Internal controls.* These refer to the whole system of controls, financial or otherwise, established by the management in order to carry on the enterprise in an orderly fashion, safeguard its assets including money and stock and secure as far as possible the accuracy and reliability of the records. Such controls include:

(i) Ensuring a separation between recording and custodian duties.

(ii) Only specified employees should have the power to requisition goods and then only up to an authorised limit which increases with the level of authority. The existence of a separate purchasing department or function considerably strengthens internal control by ensuring that user departments are prevented from ordering items without the order first being independently 'vetted'.

(iii) Conversely, the requisitioning department can act as a check on the purchasing since every order placed should be traceable to a requisition.

(iv) Goods inward should be received in specially designated areas. Control is best established at the gate or entrance. The receipt of all goods should be recorded. Goods Received Notes (GRNs) where used should be serially numbered to reduce the danger of introducing false documents and copies sent to the purchasing and finance departments.

(v) While it may be unrealistic to check all invoices presented for payment a sample should be examined on a random basis. A reduction in the supplier base reduces the procedures necessary to prevent fraud.

(vi) The main internal controls in respect of computers can be classified as (i) systems development and control, (ii) organisational controls and (iii) procedural controls. *Systems development controls* are those which ensure that the computer system operates as originally specified and all the relevant documentation has been properly prepared and maintained. *Organisational controls* seek to ensure that an acceptable standard of discipline and efficiency is maintained over the day to day running of the computer department. *Procedural controls* are those exercised over each computer application, e.g. purchasing and the payment of suppliers. The purpose is to ensure that the whole of the original data relevant to any application are accurately processed from

the point of origin to the final output and that master files used in the application are completely and accurately processed, amended and maintained. The head of the purchasing function should discuss the computerised purchasing system with the chief accountant and obtain confirmation that all the above controls appear to be adequate. External auditors should also be asked to pay special attention to computerised purchasing procedures.

(vii) One aim of internal controls is to increase the difficulties of a person who plans to perpetuate a fraud. These difficulties are increased when, not having all the relevant matters under their control, fraudsters have to seek the collusion of others. Persons who may be prepared to undertake fraud themselves are generally unwilling to accept the increased risk of betrayal or detection which exists where there is collusion. Fraud involving collusion is not, however, infrequent.

(2) *External auditing.* Controls such as the above are complemented by external audits which, in respect of companies (but not single traders or partnerships) are a statutory requirement under the Companies Acts. Auditors of companies must hold a Practising Certificate from a professional accountancy body approved by the Department of Trade and Industry. Contrary to popular belief it is not an auditor's primary function to prevent fraud but to make an independent examination of the books, accounts and vouchers of a business for the purpose of reporting whether the balance sheet and profit and loss account are properly prepared so as to show a 'true and fair view' of the affairs and profit (or loss) of the business according to the best of the information and explanations obtained. An audit may include a physical verification of assets such as inventory and the auditors may also make recommendations which can make the company less susceptible to fraud by its customers, suppliers and employees. Where a fraud is discovered the auditor is under a duty to prove that fraud to its full extent regardless of the amount in question.

(3)*'Give away' signs.* These include:

(i) Unfolded invoices that have not come through the post.

(ii) Too many orders to one supplier other than those where single sourcing arrangements apply.

(iii) Loss of supporting documentation.

(iv) Sudden unexplained affluence.

(v) Unwillingness of employees to take holidays or accept transfer or promotion to other work.

Evans and Maguire [11] state that the most common source through which fraud is discovered is outside information. These include the reporting of fraudulent practices by colleagues and disgruntled mistresses!

12. PURCHASING ETHICS

(a) Definition. Ethics is concerned with the moral principles and values which govern our beliefs, actions and decisions [12].

(b) The importance of ethics. Ethics is important in purchasing since:

(i) Purchasing staff are the representatives of their organisation in its dealing with suppliers.

(ii) Sound ethical conduct in dealing with suppliers is essential to the creation of long-term relationships and the establishment of supplier goodwill.

(iii) Purchasing staff are probably more exposed to the temptation to act unethically than most other employees.

(iv) It is impossible to claim 'professional' status for purchasing without reference to a consideration of its ethical aspects.

(c) The scope of ethics. Ethics is discussed in most textbooks on purchasing from a very narrow perspective as being primarily concerned with such issues as bribes and confidentiality. As the definition in **(a)** states, however, ethics is also concerned with *values*. A value has been defined as 'an enduring belief that a specific mode of conduct or end state of existence is personally and socially preferable to alternative modes of conduct or end states of existence' [13]. Values are concerned with questions relating to what is 'right', 'good' and 'just' and the basis on which we make ethical decisions. Thus individual behaviour will differ according to whether we base our ethical decisions on

(i) the *utilitarian* view – conduct is ethical which secures the greatest good of the greatest number

(ii) the *individualistic* view – conduct is good which promotes *my* personal interests or *my* organisation irrespective of how this affects the interests of other people or organisations

(iii) the *human-rights* view – conduct is good which respects fundamental human rights shared by all human beings

(iv) the *'justice'* view. Justice is standard for judging legal and moral questions. Conduct is just which is impartial, equal and fair.

(d) Ethical codes. In 1:5 it was stated that one of the essentials of a profession is 'integrity maintained by adherence to a code of conduct'. Professions as diverse as medicine, law, accountancy and architecture have issued codes of conduct. The codes of conduct issued by the Chartered Institute of Purchasing and Supply in the UK and the National Association of Purchasing Management in the USA are reproduced in Appendices 1 and 2 respectively.

As membership of a professional institute is not essential for employment as a buyer, such ethical codes do not have the same enforcement sanctions as those appertaining to law or medicine, where to be 'struck off' for unprofessional conduct means the revocation of the right to practice. Statements of purchasing ethics are not without value, however, since:

(i) They remind purchasing staff of aspects of their work where they may experience conflicts of interest between their 'self interest' and duties to their employers

(ii) They highlight practices which may compromise the professional objectivity and integrity of purchasing staff *(iii)* They provide standards for the buyer to attain.

Such ethical statement are, however, open to the objections that:

(i) They only relate to individual ethics. Individual ethics are, however, influenced by corporate ethics

(ii) They are only general statements. Every word and sentence of such statements requires considerable analysis and commentary as to how it shall be interpreted and applied.

(e) Corporate ethics and purchasing. Corporate ethics are statements issued by companies and other organisations describing their general value systems and providing guidelines for decision making consistent with those principles. Such corporate statements may relate to (1) the social responsibilities of the organisation and (2) the responsibilities of individual members.

(f) Social responsibility and purchasing. Clutterbuck, Dearlove and Snow [14] identify seven key stakeholders or 'communities' who demand attention from socially concerned companies, namely (1) customers; (2) employees; (3) suppliers; (4) shareholders; (5) the political arena; (6) the broader community and (7) the environment. In this book the ways in which purchasing relates to social responsibilities to suppliers and the environment may be briefly considered.

(g) Social responsibilities to suppliers. Clutterbuck, Dearlove and Snow [15] instance the following:

(1) *Provision of practical help and advice.* This can be provided by

- Helping suppliers to purchase more efficiently and economically.
- Assistance with finding other non-competitive customers to prevent too great a reliance on a single big company.
- Providing feedback on unsuccessful bids.
- Providing advice and assistance with design and production.
- Provision of advice and help with regard to training and HRM.

(2) *Purchasing policy*

- Placing a proportion of orders with local suppliers thus assisting the prosperity of the communities in which the company is located.
- Supplier development.
- Measurement of supplier performance and the provision of constructive feedback.

(3) *Monitoring supplier practices*

- Dealing only with suppliers that have high ethical standards.
- Ensuring that suppliers have an environmental or 'green' policy where this is appropriate.
- Encouraging suppliers to adopt a responsible attitude to various community groups, e.g. disabled personnel, ex-offenders, youth programmes.

(4) *Prompt payment.* Helping suppliers with cash flow problems by

- Paying invoices on time.
- Ensuring that both finance and purchasing departments are aware of the policy and adhere to it.
- Dealing with complaints as expeditiously as possible so that payments are not needlessly deferred.

(5) *Partnership sourcing.* This is dealt with in 9:**11**.

(h) Social responsibility to the environment. The Department of the Environment has stated [16] that

> 'The procurement of supplies and equipment is a potent instrument of environmental policy. Careful purchasing of it gives full weight to environmental considerations in the selection of products and can help improve environmental standards by reducing pollution and waste. It can also, through the natural operation of the market, influence purchasers and suppliers in their pricing policies and product ranges.'

The DTI suggests that key measures designed to give practical effect to the above objectives include:

(i) The preparation of an environmental policy statement and ensuring that everyone responsible for purchasing is familiar with it.

(ii) Ensuring that factors such as the scope for waste minimisation and the potential for recycling opportunities are taken into consideration in purchasing decisions.

(iii) Preparing purchasing guidelines which set out clear performance requirements for the procurement of all goods and services (including catering suppliers; furniture and fittings and contracted-out services such as publications).

(iv) Incorporating environmental performance requirements into purchasing specifications especially in relation to

- maximum energy efficiency
- minimum dependence on production and use of ozone depleting substances, toxic chemicals and other pollutants, e.g. lead, formaldehyde
- minimum dependence on non-renewable natural resources such as non-sustainably produced hardwoods
- maximum recyclability
- maximum use of products based on recycled materials and minimum use of unnecessary packaging and other superfluous material.

(v) Ensuring that these guidelines are incorporated into all standard contract conditions for the purchasing of goods and services.

(vi) Requiring providers of contract services, e.g. cleaning, catering and transportation, to carry out their operations to high standards of environmental performance.

(vii) Keeping under constant scrutiny purchasing procedures such as stock and inventory control arrangements to discourage unnecessary procurement of supplies and excessive stockholdings.

(viii) Ensuring that purchasing staff and the users of purchased products are aware of the availability of new products and services which achieve high environmental standards and meet their operational needs.

(i) Corporate guidelines in respect of individual purchasing ethics. As shown by the 'guidance' appended to the *Ethical Code of the CIPS* these apply to:

- Declaration of interest
- Confidentiality of information
- Fair competition
- Business gifts
- Hospitality.

The NAPM *Principles and Standards of Purchasing Practice* expand the above to include:

- Receptivity to competent counsel from colleagues.
- Consistent striving for knowledge of materials and processes of manufacture and practical administrative measures.
- According a prompt and courteous reception, so far as conditions will permit, to all who call on a legitimate business mission.

Most of the above are reasonably self-explanatory but business gifts, hospitality and reception of representatives may be briefly considered.

(j) Business gifts and hospitality. Policies with regard to the receipt by purchasing staff of gifts from suppliers especially at Christmas and hospitality at other times vary widely. The three most common policies are:

(i) Purchasing staff are forbidden to accept gifts of any kind and those received must be returned.
(ii) Purchasing staff may retain gifts that are clearly of an advertising nature, e.g. calendars, diaries, pencils, etc.
(iii) Purchasing staff are allowed to decide for themselves whether a proffered gift of hospitality is an appreciation of cordial business relationships or an attempt at commercial bribery.

The writer's considered view is that the third of the above policies is the best since it regards staff as responsible individuals capable of distinguishing a gift or hospitality from a bribe. There is also the fact that the first two policies encourage subterfuge, e.g. having gifts sent to the buyer's home address. There is, however, the danger that younger less experienced and lower paid staff are likely to be flattered to receive gifts, the implications of which are not always recognised. For this reason all purchasing staff should have some training in ethics as applied to purchasing. This aspect is referred to in **(m)** below.

(k) The reception of representatives. There is evidence that sales representatives have often a poor opinion of buyers. This is likely to be enhanced where sales representatives are kept waiting unnecessarily. It should be appreciated by purchasing staff that allowing for travelling time and discussion a sales representative has a relatively short working day in which to fit in calls. Unsolicited sales calls tend to be unwelcome before 9.30am and 1.30pm and after 12.15 and 4.30pm. If kept waiting, the salesperson's whole programme of visits in a particular area may be disrupted. Other factors in the reception of sales representatives should include:

(i) A suitable room for interviews.
(ii) Information regarding the times between which representatives will be seen.
(iii) The provision of honest information.

While purchasing staff should be open to information about new products and suppliers they should be frank but courteous in informing a representative if there is no possibility of business to avoid future calls. Above all a buyer should never be patronising, rude or supercilious. Such behaviour demeans both the representative *and* the buyer and is clearly not conducive to establishing supplier goodwill. While there must clearly be an exchange of pleasantries it should be remembered that 'time is money' both for the purchaser and supplier.

(l) The promotion of ethical standards. While professional associations issue codes of ethics and companies statements of corporate ethical policy it is a fact that as Dubinsky and Gwin [17] suggest business people tend to employ two sets of ethical standards – a personal set and a business set and may well have more strict personal than business ethical standards.

How an individual will react with regard to a particular ethical dilemma depends on many factors including:

- Family and cultural influences
- Religious or humanistic values
- The behaviour of superiors
- The behaviour of peers
- The prevailing norms and values of society
- The fear of the consequences of discovery of unethical behaviour.

The findings of an American study in which businessmen were asked to rank the influences which they considered contributed most to ethical or unethical behaviour are shown in Table 14.2.

From the table it is clear that an important determinant of both ethical and unethical conduct is the behaviour of an individual's superiors. This highlights the need for purchasing staff at all levels to receive ethical training and for the provision of machinery for ethical policies to be enforced.

(m) Ethical training. Ethical training sessions for purchasing staff can provide a number of benefits. They reinforce the organisation's ethical codes and policies, they remind staff that top management expects participants to consider ethical issues in making purchasing decisions. They clarify what is and what is not acceptable. Such training can include:

(i) The field of ethics.

Table 14.2 Determinants of ethical behaviour

Factors determining ethical decisions		Factors determining unethical decisions	
Factor	Av. rank	Factor	Av. rank
The individual's personal code of behaviour	1.5	The behaviour of a person's superiors in the company	1.9
The behaviour of a person's superiors in the company	2.8	Ethical climate in the industry	2.6
Formal company policy	3.8	The behaviour of a person's equals in the company	3.1
The behaviour of person's equals in the company	4.0	Lack of company policy	3.3
		Personal financial needs	4.1

(ii) The feasibility of ethics in business.

(iii) How people may rationalise their unethical behaviour

- 'I was only doing what I was told'.
- 'It's not really illegal'.
- 'It's in everyone's interest'.
- 'Everybody does it'.
- 'No one will ever know'.
- 'The company owes me this because it doesn't pay me enough'.

(iv) Factors to be considered when receiving a gift or the offer of hospitality including:

- the motive of the donor, i.e. whether the gift is a token of appreciation or a bribe
- the value of the gift or the hospitality – when does it exceed what is permissible
- the type of gift or the nature of the hospitality
- the manner in which the offer is made, i.e. openly or surreptitiously
- what strings, if any, are attached
- what impression the gift or hospitality will make on superiors, colleagues, subordinates, bearing in mind the human propensity to think the worst
- what would be the employer's reaction if the matter was brought to his attention
- whether the buyer can honestly be satisfied that the gift will not influence his/her objectivity in dealing with suppliers.

(If the buyer has doubts about any of the above the gift or hospitality should be refused.)

(v) Double standards, i.e. some companies offer gifts to the buyers of customers but refuse permission to their own staff to receive gifts.

(vi) What should a member of the purchasing staff do if he discovers his superior, colleagues or subordinates acting contrary to the company's ethical code?

(vii) What are the possible penalties for unethical behaviour?

(viii) Fostering ethical standards.

- Dealing with ethical suppliers.
- Management support for ethical behaviour.

Mini case studies. Here are some short purchasing dilemmas for students to consider.

(1) A representative telephones you to say that he has left the employment of a supplier from whom you are currently buying large quantities of a component. He knows the price you are paying and states that his new company can undercut your present price by 20%. You have been dealing satisfactorily with your present supplier for a number of years.

(2) You are negotiating on a one-to-one basis with a small machine shop to carry out operations on 100,000 items to relieve capacity on your own production department. You inadvertently mention that you are very pleased with the price and that subject to discussion with your own production manager the subcontractor is likely to receive the order. He then asks – why not let me increase the price by another £1 – 50p for me and 50p for you?

(3) You can buy cheaper from an overseas supplier but you know he pays starvation wages and the loss of the order will cause unemployment locally.

(4) You have negotiated and signed a contract with a supplier. When you arrive home you find that an expensive piece of jewellery has been sent anonymously to your wife.

(5) You mention to the representative of a steel stockist that you are proposing to build an extension to your house. He says 'Why not let us supply you with the steelwork at cost price'.

(6) On two occasions a supplier has delivered substandard components which can nevertheless be used. You telephone the supplier's production manager to complain. He says 'Don't write about it because it might affect a promotion I'm expecting. Let's keep it to ourselves and I will put it right'.

(7) You inform a potential supplier that on average your company buys 100,000 units of a certain item each year and therefore obtain a substantial quality discount. You know that the average usage is only 50,000 units.

(8) A supplier asks you, in confidence, to give details of competitive quotes saying that he will beat any price offered and 'that must be good for you'.

(9) A supplier offers you a bribe saying 'We do exactly the same for your boss and he has no worries'.

(10) One of your subordinates tells you that last night he took his family to a football match and had the use of the hospitality box (including dinner) provided by a company which you know is seeking a share of your business.

What would you do if you were absolutely sure of not being found out?

(n) The Prevention of Corruption Acts 1906 and 1916. All buyers should be aware of the provisions of these Acts. The 1906 Act states:

(1) If any agent corruptly accept or obtains, or agrees to accept or attempts to obtain, from any person, for himself or for any other person, any gift or consideration as an inducement or reward for doing or forbearing to do, or for having after the passing of this Act done or forborne to do, any act in relation to his principals' affairs or business, or for showing or forbearing to show favour of disfavour to any person in relation to his principals' affairs or business; or

If any person knowingly gives to any agent, or if any agent knowingly uses with intent to deceive his principal, any receipt, account, or other document in respect of which the principal is interested, and which contains any statement which is false or erroneous or defective in any material particular and which to his knowledge is intended to mislead the principal: he shall be guilty of a misdemeanour, and shall be liable on conviction on indictment to imprisonment, with or without hard labour, for a term not exceeding two years, or to a fine not exceeding five hundred pounds or to both ...

(2) For the purpose of this Act the expression 'consideration' includes valuable consideration of any kind, the expression 'agent' includes any person employed by or acting for another; and the expression 'principal' includes an employer.

Note: (1) The 1916 Act increased the penalties for persons convicted of corrupt practices who are employed by public bodies.
(2) The test of corruption in the majority of cases is secrecy; the defence against a charge of bribery or corruption is openness. It is wise, therefore, for an employee to make a disclosure of gifts offered or received to his employer who then has the responsibility of deciding whether the gift can be accepted or returned and what action, if any, should be taken against the individual or undertaking proffering the gift.

References

[1] Van Weele AJ. *Purchasing performance measurement and evaluation. Journal of Purchasing and Materials Management.*
[2] Stevens J. *Measuring Purchasing Performance.* Business Books, 1978. Appendix p 212.
[3] Pryor LS. *Benchmarking: a self-improvement strategy. Journal of Business Strategy.* Nov/Dec 1989. pp 28–32.
[4] Harrison J. *The role and practice of benchmarking* in *Knight Wendling Newsletter No 12.* 1994 p9.
[5] DTI. *Best Practice Benchmarking.* DTI. 1992. p 7.
[6] DTI. *Best Practice Benchmarking.* DTI. 1992. p 9.
[7] American Management Association. *Evaluating Purchasing Performance.* 1963.
[8] Scheuing EE. *Purchasing Management.* Prentice Hall, 1989. Ch 6, p 137.
[9] Evans EF and Dale BG. *The use of audits in purchasing. International Journal of Physical Distribution and Materials Management.* Vol 18, No 7. 1988, pp 17–23.
[10] Evans E. *Fraud and incompetence in purchasing. Internal Auditing.* May 1987, pp 132–134.
[11] Evans E and Maguire R. *Purchasing fraud – a growing phenomenon. Purchasing and Supply Management.* May 1993. pp 24–26.

[12] Sims D, Fineman S and Gabriel Y. *Organising and Organisations.* Sage Publications, 1993. Thesaurus p 247.

[13] Rokeach M. *The Nature of Human Values.* Free Press 1973. p159.

[14] Clutterbuck D, Dearlove D and Snow D. *Actions Speak Louder – A Management Guide to Corporate Social Responsibility.* Kogan Page in Association with Kingfisher. 1992. Introduction.

[15] Clutterbuck D, Dearlove D and Snow D. *Actions speak louder – A Management Guide to Corporate Social Responsibility.* Kogan Page in Association with Kingfisher. 1992. Chap 4, pp 105-121.

[16] Department of the Environment. *Environmental Action Guide for Building and Purchasing Managers.* HMSO. 1991, p6.

[17] Dubinsky AJ and Gwin JH. *Business ethics: buyers and sellers. Journal of Purchasing and Materials Management.* Winter 1981. pp 9-16.

Progress test 14

1. State five areas of purchasing research and indicate some examples of matters that can be investigated under each heading.

2. What are the aims of measuring purchasing performance?

3. State three methods of measuring purchasing performance.

4. Describe the profit centre approach to the measurement of purchasing performance.

5. How may activity based costing contribute to the management of purchasing performance?

6. What is benchmarking?

7. What are the principal stages of benchmarking?

8. State four ratios that can be used in the measurement of purchasing performance.

9. Describe what is meant by a purchasing management audit.

10. State some headings that can be used in the auditing of purchasing.

11. What factors must be remembered when framing objectives for use with MBO?

12. Give examples of ways in which fraud may take place in relation to purchasing.

13. Suggest some internal controls that may be used to prevent fraud in relation to purchasing.

14. Why is ethics an important aspect of purchasing?

15. What are some social responsibilities of management in respect of suppliers?

16. Give some examples of ways in which the purchasing function may have responsibilities in respect of environmental issues.

17. What policies may an undertaking lay down in respect of the receipt of gifts and hospitality by purchasing staff?

18. Outline what you would include in a short course of ethical training designed for purchasing staff.

19. What are the provisions of the Prevention of Corruption Acts 1906-1916?

20. In measuring the performance of Purchasing, it is essential to measure the *true cost of supply* effectively. Explain the meaning of this statement and how you would attempt to measure the true cost of supply.
(CIPS. *Purchasing and Supply Management I, Planning, Policy and Organisation* (1992))

21. Examine the reasons why a professional buyer may need to consider environmental or 'green' issues when selecting a source of supply for his company's requirements.
(CIPS. *Introduction to Purchasing and Supply Management* ((1992))

22. Discuss methods typically used for measuring purchasing performance showing, in each case, the validity as a means of assessment.
(CIPS. *Introduction to Purchasing and Supply Management* ((1993))

23. Evaluate the way in which a Purchasing Research Activity is likely to assist an organisation in its strategy.
(CIPS. *Purchasing and Supply Management I, Planning, Policy and Organisation* ((1992))

24. You have recently been appointed Purchasing and Supplies Manager in an organisation which has not previously measured functional performance. Policy changes now require all departmental heads to measure operational and strategic performance in their various functional areas. Explain how you would achieve this objective and with whom you would consult.
(CIPS. *Purchasing and Supply Management I, Planning, Policy and Organisation* (1993))

25. A pre-requisite for improvement of any activity is appraisal of current performance. Discuss how you would undertake a performance appraisal at both the individual and departmental level of the purchasing function in a large organisation.

(CIPS. *Purchasing and Supply Management I, Planning, Policy and Organisation* (1994))

26. The need for effective purchasing research increases as the purchasing activity becomes more strategically involved within an organisation. Explain the role and contribution such purchasing research could make to an organisation in formulating strategy.

(CIPS. *Purchasing and Supply Management I, Planning, Policy and Organisation* (1995))

APPENDIX 1

The Ethical Code of the Chartered Institute of Purchasing and Supply

Introduction

1. In applying to join the Institute, members undertake to abide by "The Constitution, Memorandum and Articles of Association, Rules and By-Laws of the Institute". The Code set out below was approved by the Institute's Council on 26 February 1977 and is binding on members.
2. The cases of members reported to have breached the Code shall be investigated by a Disciplinary Committe appointed by the Council; where a case is proven, a member may, depending on the circumstances and the gravity of the charge, be admonished, reprimanded, suspended from membership or removed from the list of members. Details of cases in which members are found in breach of the Code will be notified in the publications of the Institute.

Precepts

3. Members shall never use their authority or office for personal gain and shall seek to uphold and enhance the standing of the Purchasing and Supply profession and the Institute by:

   (a) maintaining an unimpeachable standard of integrity in all their business relationships both inside and outside the organisations in which they are employed;

   (b) fostering the highest possible standards of professional competence against those for whom they are responsible;

   (c) optimising the use of resources for which they are responsible to provide the maximum benefit to their employing organisation;

   (d) complying both with the letter and the spirit of:

   (i) the law of the country in which they practise;

   (ii) such guidance on professional practice as may be issued by the Institute from time to time;

   (iii) contractual obligations;

   (e) rejecting any business practice which might reasonably be deemed improper.

Guidance

In applying these precepts, members should follow the guidance set out below:

   (a) *Declaration of interest* – Any personal interest which may impinge or might reasonably be deemed by others to impinge on a member's impartiality in any matter relevant to his or her duties should be declared.

(b) *Confidentiality and accuracy of information* – The confidentiality of information received in the course of duty should be respected and should never be used for personal gain; information given in the course of duty should be true and fair and never designed to mislead.

(c) *Competition* – While bearing in mind the advantages to the member's employing organisation of maintaining a continuing relationship with a supplier, any arrangment which might, in the long term, prevent the effective operation of fair competition, should be avoided.

(d) *Business gifts* – Business gifts, other than items of very small intrinsic value such as business diaries or calendars should not be accepted.

(e) *Hospitality* – Modest hospitality is an accepted courtesy of a business relationship. However, the recipient should not allow him or herself to reach a position whereby he or she might be deemed by others to have been influenced in making a business decision as a consequence of accepting such hospitality; the frequency and scale of hospitality accepted should not be significantly greater than the recipient's employer would be likely to provide in return.

(f) When it is not easy to decide between what is and is not acceptable in terms of gifts or hospitality, the offer should be declined or advice sought from the member's superior.

5. Advice on any aspect of the precepts and guidance set out above may be obtained on written request to the Institute.

APPENDIX 2

Principles and standards of purchasing practice (NAPA)

The following principles are advocated by the National Association of Purchasing Agents of America:

LOYALTY TO HIS COMPANY
JUSTICE TO THOSE WITH WHOM HE DEALS
FAITH IN HIS PROFESSION

From these principles are derived the NAPA standards of purchasing practice.

(1) To consider, first, the interests of his company in all transactions and to carry out and believe in its established policies.

(2) To be receptive to competent counsel from his colleagues and to be guided by such counsel without impairing the dignity and responsibility of his office.

(3) To buy without prejudice, seeking to obtain the maximum ultimate value for each dollar expenditure.

(4) To strive consistently for knowledge of the materials and processes of manufacture, and to establish practical methods for the conduct of his office.

(5) To subscribe to and work for honesty and truth in buying and selling, and to denounce all forms or manifestations of commercial bribery.

(6) To accord a prompt and courteous reception, so far as conditions will permit, to all who call on a legitimate business mission.

(7) To respect his obligations and to require that obligations to him and to his concern be respected, consistent with good business practice.

(8) To avoid sharp practice.

(9) To counsel and assist fellow purchasing agents in the performance of their duties, whenever occasion permits.

(10) To cooperate with all organisations and individuals engaged in activities designed to enhance the development and standing of purchasing.

INDEX